F   A   E CINEMA

28.

fantasy AND THE *cinema*

Edited by **JAMES DONALD**

BFI PUBLISHING

First published in 1989 by the
British Film Institute
21 Stephen Street, London W1P 1PL

© British Film Institute 1989
Introductions and editorial matter © James Donald 1989
All previously published material © original source
Previously unpublished material © author 1989

Cover stills: (front) *Dracula* (Tod Browning, 1931)
(back) *The Psychopath* (Freddie Francis, 1966)
Part title stills:
(I) *The Night of the Living Dead* (George A. Romero, 1968)
(II) *Vertigo* (Alfred Hitchcock, 1958)
(III) *Punch and Judy* (Jan Švankmajer, 1966)
Designed by Robert Carter
Set in Berkeley Oldstyle Book by
Fakenham Photosetting Limited,
Fakenham, Norfolk
and printed in Great Britain by
Anchor Press Ltd, Tiptree, Essex

British Library Cataloguing in Publication Data

Fantasy and the cinema: a reader.
   1. Cinema films: Fantasy films
   I. Donald, James, *1948–*
   791'.43'09'0915

   ISBN 0–85170–228–7
   ISBN 0–85170–229–5 pbk

CONTENTS

PREFACE

This is primarily a reader to teach with. As I argue in the Introduction, fantasy offers film studies one way forward which retains the impetus and critical edge of work done in the 1970s while avoiding some of the more sterile debates and routines the subject got bogged down in as it became academically more respectable. The reader is divided into three sections. The first explores 'the fantastic' as a genre or mode. The second deploys a psychoanalytic notion of 'fantasy' as 'the *mise en scène* of desire' to examine ideas about spectatorship, difference and so forth in ways that reflect critically on earlier explanations. And the third section tackles questions about aesthetics and politics, and about the social function of cinema, which often used to be discussed in terms of avant-garde film practices. Although the articles in this section do champion particular film styles and film-makers, however, they also turn to other ideas and traditions of thought – psychoanalysis, feminism, cultural difference, postmodernism, Bakhtin – to suggest alternatives to the old polarities of avant-garde vs. entertainment, realism vs. anti-realism, or popular vs. art cinema. The framework the reader offers for teaching about film and cinema is not, therefore, an objective survey of the field; nor do the different perspectives and approaches of the various articles make up a single 'position' or 'line'. The book represents a mildly polemical attempt to stimulate a critical and, I hope, invigorating dialogue between film studies and contemporary cultural theory. I also hope it might provoke you to look more closely at different, often overlooked, films, and to look at all films a bit differently.

The reader had its origins in courses on 'Fantasy and the cinema' that I taught for the University of London Extra-mural Department/British Film Institute certificate and diploma in film studies in 1984/5 and 1986/7. I would like to thank the students on those courses for allowing me to try out ideas on them, and for their valuable comments, contributions and counter-arguments – particularly Julia Britton, Morgan Evans, George Knapp, Joanna Ramsey and Ulli Sieglohr. The second of these courses I taught with Irene Kotlarz, and this book was first thought of very much as a collaborative venture between us. It was Irene who originally suggested to me that fantasy might offer an alternative to the limiting rubric of 'realism and anti-realism', and we agreed the initial structure and selection of articles together. Unfortunately, her commitments as director of the Bristol Animation Festival meant that she was unable to take part in the final selection and the writing of the introductory material. If the responsibility for those must therefore be mine alone, I would still like to dedicate the book to her.

The other main influence on my thinking about fantasy was the work I did with Victor Burgin and Cora Kaplan in editing *Formations of Fantasy* (London: Methuen, 1986); I hope this volume provides a useful companion to that one. Here, as there, the normal practice has been to use the spelling *fantasy*, rather than to use *phantasy* to designate unconscious fantasies. (Where authors have used the latter, however, it has not been changed.) The rationale for this is given by Laplanche and Pontalis in a note to their essay 'Fantasy and the origins of sexuality' (*Formations of Fantasy*, p. 32):

> Whether or not this distinction is in fact justified, it seems undesirable to use it in translations of Freud's work. It betrays little respect for the text to render words such as *Phantasie* or *Phantasieren*, which Freud invariably employed, by different terms according to the context. Our opposition to this terminological and conceptual innovation rests on three grounds: (i) the distinction should not be introduced into translations of Freud's work, even if this interpretation of his thought were correct; (ii) this interpretation of Freud's thought is incorrect; (iii) this distinction contributes less to the study of the problem than Freud's concept.

The selection of articles is by no means comprehensive. Some key texts have not been available for republication. Some are already widely available in other places. Others may have slipped by me altogether. Still, I hope those that have been included, along with others listed in the bibliography, provide a reasonably wide-ranging introduction to the topic.

The publishers and I would like to thank the following for their permission to reprint copyright material: the author and *Wide Angle* for Thomas Elsaesser, 'Social Mobility and the Fantastic: German Silent Cinema'; *Nouvelle Revue de Psychanalyse* for Roger Dadoun, 'Fetishism in the Horror Film'; the author and *Screen* for Barbara Creed, 'Horror and the Monstrous-Feminine: An Imaginary Abjection'; the author and the Regents of the University of California for Carol J. Clover, 'Her Body, Himself: Gender in the Slasher Film'; the author and *Camera Obscura* for Elisabeth Lyon, 'The Cinema of Lol V. Stein'; the author and *Screen* for Donald Greig, 'The Sexual Differentiation of the Hitchcock Text'; the author and *Camera Obscura* for Constance Penley, 'Time Travel, Primal Scene and the Critical Dystopia'; the author and *Framework* for Patricia Mellencamp, 'Uncanny Feminism: The Exquisite Corpses of Cecelia Condit'.

Stills are courtesy of Cecelia Condit, Decla-Bioscop, Hammer, Image Ten, Paramount, Prana, RKO, Santa Fe Productions, Twentieth Century-Fox, Universal, Vortex and Warner.

Finally, my thanks to Robert Carter for the elegance of his design, to Simon Field, Tim Highstead, Deborah Phillips and Donna Sotto-Morettini at the Institute of Contemporary Arts in London for their collaboration on events accompanying the publication of the book, and to Roma Gibson and Geoffrey Nowell-Smith at BFI Publishing for their unflappability and support.

London, November 1988   *James Donald*

General Introduction

There is nothing new about using fantasy as a key to understanding the fascination of cinema. Hollywood has been known as 'the dream factory' – a cultural industry, a dynamic of desire – at least since the 1940s, when the anthropologist Hortense Powdermaker used the term as the title of her influential book. For her, *fantasy* was not necessarily a derogatory term. She saw nothing inherently wrong in escapism.

> One can escape into a world of imagination and come from it refreshed and with new understanding. One can expand limited experiences into broad ones. One can escape into saccharine sentimentality or into fantasies which exaggerate existing fears. Hollywood provides ready-made fantasies or day-dreams; the problem is whether these are productive or nonproductive, whether the audience is psychologically enriched or impoverished.[1]

This liberal view of fantasy as wish-fulfilment contrasted with a traditional Marxist denunciation of Hollywood dreams as delusion and false consciousness – 'an ideological force to dope the workers', as the British Communist film-maker Ralph Bond put it in the 1930s.[2] More recent radical work has continued to be concerned with the fantasy elements of popular cinema, but without dismissing them as the new opium of the people. In the 1970s, the Marxist literary and cultural critic Fredric Jameson resisted the temptation to see them as purely delusory or repressive. Maybe they do manipulate their audience to some extent, he suggests, but they can only do so if they offer something in return. And that is a particular form of wish fulfilment: the projection of an optical illusion of social harmony.

> . . . all contemporary works of art – whether those of high culture and modernism or of mass culture and commercial culture – have as their underlying impulse – albeit in what is often distorted and repressed, unconscious form – our deepest fantasies about the nature of social life, both as we live it now, and as we feel in our bones it ought to be lived.[3]

Similarly, in the most influential statement of feminist film theory in the 70s, Laura Mulvey argued that Hollywood 'seems to have evolved a particular illusion of reality in which [the] contradiction between libido and ego has found a beautifully complementary phantasy world', and attempted to show how 'the determining male gaze projects its phantasy on to the female figure which is styled accordingly'.[4]

This, then, seems to be the dominant view of fantasy and cinema: films as mass-produced daydreams, as vehicles of either a coercive or a potentially liberating wish-fulfilment. Alternatively, in another commonsense usage, fantasy can denote a particular genre – the 'fantasy films' of science fiction, horror or swords-and-sorcery which generate their own prolific sub-culture of fandom and buffery. The articles in this book, however, try to get behind these notions to explore a number of quite fundamental questions about cinema which they both imply and often avoid. Why do film images and narratives take the form they do? What is the nature of audiences' investment in them? What is the social function of these products of the dream factory? Is wish-fulfilment all there is to fantasy and the fantastic?

If these questions seem strangely familiar, that is no doubt because they overlap with the interest in cinema as an ideological force explored in the debates about 'realism' which dominated – and in the end constricted – anglophone film studies in the 1970s and 80s. The polemic here is that these questions remain legitimate and important, but that new points of entry and new perspectives are needed. What this book attempts is, implicitly at least, both a development of, and a reaction against, those ideas. It is therefore worth taking another brief – and partial – canter through 70s film theory to suggest why this reformulation is worthwhile.

THE REALISM DEBATES

Very broadly, it is possible to identify two strands in what now is conventionally referred to as the *Screen* project of the 1970s. One was the exposé of the mechanisms, and thereby the ideological complicity, of 'classic realist' (or mainstream entertainment) films. This activist criticism was presented as part of a Brechtian 'politics of interruption' which might undermine the cultural power of the institution cinema – Godard's Hollywood-Mosfilm.

The other strand was the attempt to identify and promote politically 'progressive' films. This led in various directions. Some people claimed that appropriate models for a radical film-making practice could be found in, say, Godard, Brecht or the Soviet cinema of the 1920s. Some insisted on the need for a 'negative aesthetics' of textual avant-gardism – Peter Gidal has been an eloquent advocate of this position through his films and polemics.[5] Others argued that it is necessary to work 'within' existing popular forms, because that is the (film) language the people who need persuading understand: this was the case for 'progressive realism', most clearly articulated in the debate about the *Days of Hope* films for BBC television.[6] And yet others argued that what is needed is not just different films, but different ways of reading existing films which would reveal the tensions and fissures within them ('It is said that analysing pleasure, or beauty, destroys it,' declared Laura Mulvey in a memorable provocation. 'That is the intention of this article.'[7]) This strand developed out of the influential work by two editors of *Cahiers du Cinéma*, Jean-Louis Comolli and Jean Narboni. In their taxonomy of the ideological implications of cinematic forms, their Category E provided a let-out clause for those who wanted to have their cake (by disapproving of films politically) and eat it too (by continuing to enjoy them). This category consisted of 'films which seem at first sight to belong firmly within the ideology and to be completely under its sway, but which turn out to be so only in an ambiguous manner.'[8] Such films therefore invited a symptomatic reading that could reveal the ideological cracks which riddled their apparent formal coherence. This was the rubric under which an interest developed in film-makers like Sirk and Rossellini, and in genres like melodrama.

This was an invigorating and eye-opening debate but, especially perhaps as it was translated into the form of educational courses, it increasingly tended to be reduced to the binary formula of 'realism versus anti-realism'. Lost as 'realism' was set in place as a normative pole in this way was an often neglected aspect of *Screen*'s approach – the detailed concern with the production of different 'realisms', their political aspirations, and the institutions that sustained them in, for example, the Soviet Union of the 1920s, Italian neo-realism, and British cinema of the 1930s and 40s. Any film-making practice which did not conform to the ideal type of the 'classic realist text' was defined as simply different from, or (if you were lucky) opposed to, that realism. Thus a remarkably diverse collection of film-making practices and styles were lumped together as if they were all somehow the same thing ('anti-realism'). The contexts and traditions of the various avant-gardes and modernisms from which they emerged were repressed.

The primarily formal or textual criteria for distinguishing between realism and anti-realism were given a political edge by the principle that to challenge the forms of language is to challenge the official law (Kristeva), and by an Althusserian reading of ideology as 'a process producing subjects'. The outcome was *Screen*'s triple alliance: a semiotic argument about the positioning of the spectator in relation to the film text, the Althusserian version of ideology, and a Lacanian theory of the construction of the subject. By the end of the 70s, this strategy was becoming difficult to sustain. This may have been in part because the alternative or oppositional films that it encouraged were actually producing not revolutionary cadres, but fairly traditional avant-garde coteries (though by now people seemed less worried by this). But the loss of confidence also reflected the critique – or implosion – of the Althusserian conceptions that formed the cornerstone of the strategy. The contradictions inherent in the idea that ideology is both an effect and a support not only of the timeless unconscious but also of the historically specific requirements of the social relations of production became increasingly apparent. It also became increasingly difficult to take it for granted that, in the end, the science of Marxism (in epistemological terms) and the demands of reproduction (in historical terms) mean that the operation of the ideological apparatus and the articulation of its elements are always predictable.

At the same time, it transpired that the feminist reading of Lacan on which *Screen* theory drew did not simply complement the Althusserian view of subjectivity or plug the gaps in the account of how films interpellate spectators. On the contrary, it undermined the premise that ideology really can allot people the perceptions, *savoir faire* and sense of identity appropriate to their position in the division of labour and the division of genders. In contrast to this assumption that the internalisation of norms more or less works, the starting point of psychoanalysis is that it does not. 'The unconscious constantly reveals the "failure" of identity,' observed Jacqueline Rose. Nor is this a personal problem to be overcome. 'Instead "failure" is something endlessly repeated and relived moment by moment in our individual histories. It appears not only in the symptom, but also in dreams, in slips of the tongue and in forms of sexual pleasure which are pushed to the sidelines of the norm.' Psychoanalysis recognises 'a resistance to identity which lies at the very heart of psychic life'.[9]

What emerged, then, was an uncertainty which Robert Lapsley and Michael Westlake identify in the oscillation between two positions on the avant-garde in film theory.

> At one pole was the Althusserian and Brechtian position, characterised by a confidence that theoretical issues relating beyond art to the social formation were in principle settled, with the outstanding question therefore being how art can best serve the cause of revolutionary change. At the other, there was the Lacanian and post-structuralist position, in which the question of progressive art was settled – it should displace subjectivity – but in which there was far less confidence in relation to the social formation, both in terms of what it was and of the desirability of revolution.[10]

THE TURN TO FANTASY

So the question becomes, how to get out of this impasse without falling into either a naive, pre-structuralist 'cultural politics' or a sophisticated but quiescent post-structuralism? What seems to be called for is a new account of the formation of subjectivity which does not see it as *either* a manifestation of unconscious drives *or* as an effect of the demands of the social and the symbolic. Rather, in the failure of, or resistance to, identity it would recognise a complex interaction marked by the dynamics of both the psychic and the social. It is in this context that the psychoanalytic concept of *fantasy* has become increasingly important; or, more specifically, Jean Laplanche and J.-B. Pontalis's definition of fantasy as 'the *mise en scène* of desire'. The great advantage of this approach is that it is responsive both to the fragmentation and mobility of identities, and also to their historical and cultural specificity. It makes it possible to focus on the translation of the social into a psychic reality, the articulation of history and the unconscious, without reducing either to the other or assuming that either term provides a sufficient explanation of the forms taken by the other.

At the same time, there has been a revival of interest in fantasy and the fantastic as a literary and cinematic genre or mode – in a number of essays by Harold Bloom, for example, in Rosemary Jackson's book *Fantasy: the literature of subversion* (1981), and in Christine Brooke-Rose's *A Rhetoric of the Unreal* (1981). Much of this work was inspired by Tzvetan Todorov's *The Fantastic*, which soon established itself as a classic of structuralist criticism in the 1970s. Perhaps because of the focus on the question of realism at that time, the book had only a marginal impact on film studies – the notable exception being Mark Nash's article on *Vampyr*. There are, of course, a variety of explanations for the current switch of interest from the aesthetic rationality of realism to popular genres like science fiction, horror, weepies and melodrama. One which may have some weight is that it indicates a new theoretical scepticism, a greater wariness of pat formulae about the relationship between aesthetics and politics, and a renewed sensitivity to both the tackiness and the sublimity of cinema.

The question of fantasy, then, involves not so much a different cinematic canon, nor just a symptomatology of repression and wish-fulfilment. Rather, it indicates a different way of thinking about our fantasmatic investment as spectators in filmic representations and in the institution cinema. It helps to explain the fascination, and so the power, of cinema.

NOTES

1 Hortense Powdermaker, *Hollywood the Dream Factory: an anthropologist looks at the movie makers* (London: Secker & Warburg, 1950), pp. 12–13.

2 Ralph Bond, *Plebs*, August 1931, cited in Don Macpherson (ed.), *Traditions of Independence* (London: BFI, 1980), p. 114.

3 Fredric Jameson, 'Reification and utopia in mass culture', *Social Text*, no. 1, Winter 1979, p. 147.

4 Laura Mulvey, 'Visual pleasure and narrative cinema', *Screen*, vol. 16, no. 3, Autumn 1976, p. 11.

5 See, for example, Peter Gidal (ed.), *Structural Film Anthology* (London: BFI, 1978).

6 The main contributions to the debate are collected together in Tony Bennett, Susan Boyd-Bowman, Colin Mercer and Janet Woollacott (eds.), *Popular Television and Film* (London: BFI, 1981).

7 Mulvey, 'Visual pleasure', p. 8.

8 Jean-Louis Comolli and Jean Narboni, 'Cinema/ideology/criticism', in *Screen Reader 1* (London: Society for Education in Film and Television, 1977), p. 7.

9 Jacqueline Rose, 'Femininity and its discontents', in *Sexuality in the Field of Vision* (London: Verso, 1986), pp. 90–1.

10 Robert Lapsley and Michael Westlake, *Film Theory: an introduction* (Manchester: Manchester University Press, 1988), p. 201.

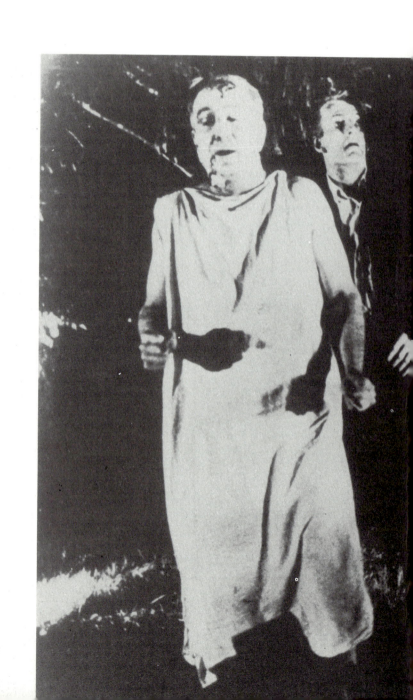

I

THE CINEFANTASTIC

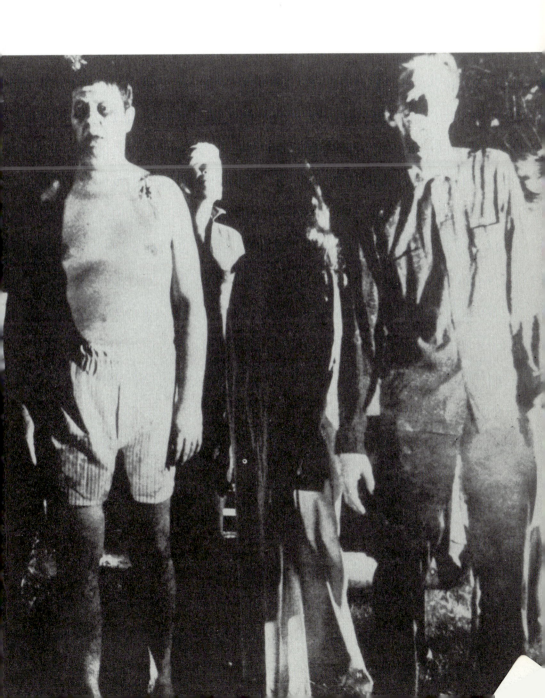

Introduction

In a common-sense way, we can all recognise a fantasy film when we see one. Science fiction films like *It Came from Outer Space* and *Star Wars* or horror films like *Dracula* and *I Walked with a Zombie* might be the sort of thing that comes immediately to mind: films which show worlds, whether ours or not, that depart from the rules of everyday reality, often using cinema's spectacular capacity for illusion and trickery to conjure up before our eyes weird creatures and strange happenings in impossible narratives. Does this sort of recognition offer an adequate basis for defining a genre of fantasy within the cinema? My examples already suggest that the fantastic can surface in a number of genres. And apart from science fiction and horror, wouldn't we have to say that melodramas and weepies, westerns and musicals are also in some sense fantasies? Indeed, would it be possible to exclude *any* forms of entertainment cinema from the description?

Broadened to that degree, the category of fantasy becomes virtually useless as a means of distinguishing between different types of film. So is it useful to attempt a definition of a cinematic genre of the fantastic in film at all?

If it is, the place to begin is probably with Christian Metz's image of the cinema as an apparatus or machine.

> The cinematic institution is not just the cinema industry (which works to fill cinemas, not to empty them), it is also the mental machinery – another industry – which spectators 'accustomed to the cinema' have internalised historically and which has adapted them to the consumption of films.[1]

From this point of view, genre can be seen as a gearing mechanism within the cinematic machine. Stephen Neale, for example, sees genres as 'a means of regulating memory and expectation, a means of containing the possibilities of reading.'[2] They involve not just the obvious iconographic and narrative conventions I have mentioned, but also 'systems of orientations, expectations and conventions that circulate between industry, text and subject'. What distinguishes one genre from another, Neale suggests, are not so much particular formal elements as the way such elements – which may be common to a number of genres – are combined so as to produce particular narrative structures and modes of address.

Without doubt, the most influential attempt to identify a (literary) genre of 'the fantastic' in recent years has been Tzvetan Todorov's structuralist study, *The Fantastic*, first published in French in 1970 and in English in 1973.[3] This broke new ground by insisting that the genre cannot logically be defined either in terms of a fantasy/reality opposition or in terms of the texts' supposed psychological effects on the reader – terror, horror, shock, or whatever. Instead, Todorov defines the fantastic in terms of textual operations and modes of reading. The key to the fantastic, he argues, is *hesitation*. Confronted by an event which cannot be explained by reason alone, a person has to opt for one of two solutions: 'either he is the victim of an illusion of the senses, of a product of the imagination – and laws of the world then remain what they are; or else the event has taken place, it is an integral part of reality – but then this reality is controlled by laws unknown to us' (p. 25). It is the moment of uncertainty between these two possibilities that constitutes the fantastic. To opt for either possible answer is to slip from the fantastic into a neighbouring genre – the *uncanny* if the incredible, extraordinary or disquieting phenomenon can be accommodated somehow within the laws of rationality; the *marvellous* if it is truly supernatural.

Who is it that experiences this hesitation between the rational and the supernatural? At one level it is clearly a character within the narration – Alphonse van Worden in Jan Potocki's novel *The Saragossa Manuscript* is one of Todorov's examples. But if a story is to achieve its fantastic effect, then the reader too has to be at least temporarily in the dark – it does not work if we are told beforehand that a character is mad or suffers from delusions. 'The fantastic therefore implies an integration of the reader into the world of the characters; that world is defined by the reader's own ambiguous perception of the events narrated' (p. 31). This also means that the reader – the implied reader, that is – has to read the fantastic narrative in a particular way. Narratives containing supernatural or extraordinary events will not be fantastic if they are interpreted allegorically (animals speaking or acting anthropomorphically in a fable being understood as vehicles for conveying a moral, for example) or poetically, in which case the truth status of events is not an issue. Both are inimical to the fantastic because they remove the element of cognitive uncertainty.

For Todorov, then, a work belongs to the genre of the fantastic only if it meets three conditions.

> First, the text must oblige the reader to consider the world of characters as a world of living persons and to hesitate between a natural and a supernatural explanation of the events described. Second, this hesitation may also be experienced by a character; thus the reader's role is so to speak entrusted to a character, and at the same time the hesitation is represented, it becomes one of the themes of the work – in the case of naive reading, the actual reader identifies himself with the character. Third, the reader must adopt a certain attitude with regard to the text: he will reject allegorical as well as 'poetic' interpretations. (p. 33)

According to Todorov, the first and third of these characteristics define the genre; the second is less essential.

Todorov's is a rigorously exclusive definition of the genre. In practice, it applies only to some Gothic novels of the late eighteenth and early nineteenth centuries and a few works that appeared in their wake. This transience he explains in terms of the historical availability of forms of discourse through which certain taboos may be addressed. Here he touches on the social function of the fantastic. The supernatural and the fantastic, he suggests, offered ways of transgressing the modes of censorship and repression then in operation. They allowed the representation of certain 'themes of the other' – incest, homosexuality, promiscuity, necrophilia, sensual excesses – and also such themes of the self as psychosis, madness and drug-induced hallucination. 'It is as if we were reading a list of forbidden themes, established by some censor,' comments Todorov (p. 158). What rendered this literary strategy largely redundant, in his view, was the incorporation of such themes into a scientific discourse – psychoanalysis – in the latter part of the nineteenth century.

Todorov's definition of genre is also more narrowly formal than Neale's. But it was his ideas about the relation of reader to text, rather than his comments on the ideological and historical significance of 'the fantastic', that were taken up in relation to film.

VAMPYR

Probably the most ambitious attempt to apply Todorov's approach to cinema is Mark Nash's article on Carl-Th. Dreyer's *Vampyr* (1931).[4] The film is based on two tales by the nineteenth-century writer Sheridan Le Fanu. It tells the story of a young man, David Gray, who visits a village troubled by a vampire – not a dashing Dracula figure in this instance, but an old woman. The owner of the local château has two daughters, one of whom is already infected by vampirism. After the father is killed by one of the vampire's assistants, Gray helps to destroy the vampire – although not before he has had a nightmarish vision of seeing himself screwed down into a coffin. Eventually, he and the younger daughter Gisèle drift away in a boat and escape through a wood into misty sunshine. The fascination of the film lies less in this narrative, however, than in the narration of the film which produces a dreamlike – and perhaps fantastic – atmosphere.

Nash's argument is that the film produces the fantastic's required hesitation in the spectator through the manipulation of what, by analogy with the conventions of literary narration, he calls its 'pronoun functions'. These refer to the various ways that a story can be told – in the first person by a character within the story; by an omniscient narrator who addresses her/his reportage and authorial commentary to the narratee; or 'objectively', with events being related with no external commentary on the significance of events or on characters' feelings and motivation. First person narration, Nash observes,

... is particularly suited to the fantastic because it facilitates the identification of the reader with the character of the narrator in the diegesis,
whose discourse can then be used by the author to lie, creating uncertainty as to the reality of the events described. When the problem of
belief is not at issue, as in the neighbouring genre of the marvellous
(where it is a condition of the genre that we accept everything we are
told), the impersonal mode of narration is more often used. (p. 30)

In short, first-person narration allows a partial, possibly deluded perspective
on events – was this happening? was I dreaming? was I mad?

The hesitation between natural and supernatural explanations of
events in *Vampyr*, Nash suggests, is initially motivated by the assertion in an
inter-title that David Gray, the hero, is one of those people whose 'imagination
is so developed that their vision reaches beyond that of most men' – this
relates to Todorov's second characteristic of the fantastic, the unreliability or
instability of characters' perceptions within the tale. But it also contributes to
the reader/spectator's uncertainty, which is thereafter achieved by the film's
play on the 'reality status' of what we as spectators see. This may or may not be
what Gray is seeing. If it is what he sees, it may really be happening, it may be
a figment of his imagination, or he may be dreaming. The reason we can never
be quite sure is that, in addition to the conventional interplay between point-
of-view and 'impersonal' shots, there is in *Vampyr* a third, disconcerting
perspective. This consists of shots or series of shots which are coded as
subjective, but which turn out not to represent the point of view of any of the
characters within the diegesis. In other words, the camera sometimes seems to
wander off in an arbitrary way and to act as an independent observer.

Every narrative film consists of a series of looks of the camera (a
continuous mode), which may, through the conventions of subjective
camera and reverse field (the point-of-view shot) be doubled with the
look of a character in the diegesis. The coding of such conventions by
what I call pronoun functions may, however, be displaced by marking
the shots as if they pertained to a character in the diegesis and then
revealing (by the articulation of surrounding shots) the absence of any
such character, that is, by creating 'false' pronouns ('false' only in the
sense that they refer to no character in the diegesis – their reference to
the organising subject of the discourse constitutes them, as we have
seen, as linguistically 'true' pronouns). By means of these 'false' pronouns the presence of the camera, unmediated by character, and by
implication the organising subject, are (re-)inscribed into the text.
(p. 38)

Although, as Nash himself soon acknowledged, this approach tended to stop
short 'at a somewhat formalist level of analysis',[5] it did allow him to display
how the effect of the fantastic is created by a narrative strategy that constantly
undermines any certainty about what is going on. One example that he looks
at in detail is the sequence near the beginning of the film when the chatelain,

the father of the two sisters threatened by the vampire, visits David Gray as he sleeps in the inn.

> *Scene.* Gray lies in bed, the key turns of its own accord in the lock and the person we later learn to be the father enters, leaving the parcel inscribed with the words 'To be opened after my death'. Gray asks with staring eyes 'Who are you?' being met with the reply, 'Quiet ... She must not die. Do you hear, she must not die.'
>
> The uncertainty of the diegetic reality of this segment is marked in a number of ways. They key's turning and the lighting round the door which changes before the father enters and is then restored when he leaves are both cues suggesting the supernatural, since the preceding inter-title has stated that Gray remains awake. While the organisation of the alternating shots of Gray and the father could have suggested spatio-temporal continuity, a continuation of the coding of the supernatural, this is systematically undermined by the displacement of these looks by *discours* [i.e. the filmic equivalent of first-person or interventionist authorial narration], also present in the close-ups of the key in the door and the parcel. While the father is the object of both Gray's and our looks, the return of his gaze is, as it were, reappropriated by *discours*: the shots of Gray which might, because of the system Gray/non-Gray, be from the father's position are strongly marked by *discours*, the insistence of the place of the camera. This interaction is placed outside that convention of alternating looks which would enable the events to be read as 'real'. The articulation of successive shots in this segment creates uncertainty – is it part of the text that ghosts are real, or is this perhaps a dream? (pp. 49/50)

Nash also provides a breakdown of, and commentary on, the famous sequence of Gray's 'dream' near the end of the film. In this, Gray's image splits after a fall. One shadow then finds a coffin containing his own corpse and he also sees, through a glass panel, Gisèle, one of the daughters, tied to a bed. The screwing down of the coffin lid is seen from the point of view of the corpse. This perspective continues as the coffin is carried through a churchyard into the Park, where the little procession passes the bench on which the 'original' Gray is still seated. Here the merging of the two images of Gray perhaps codes the sequence as 'dream'. On the other hand, the conscious Gray subsequently finds Gisèle exactly as he saw her in the dream.

David Bordwell also comments on this sequence in his chapter on *Vampyr* in his book on Dreyer.[6] He notes the way that, here as elsewhere in the film, the camera is used to create 'contradictory spaces'.

> [T]he corpse's eye view in this sequence bares the device not only of Gray's point of view but also of the film's very act of constructing space. Through the window of the coffin we (and Gray) see the soldier glancing down at us, then a tool fastening the coffin lid down, and then – abruptly – the face of Marguerite Chopin [the vampire] appears and peers down at us. Just as throughout the film we have not been able to

Vampyr (Carl Dreyer, 1931)

determine confidently who is present outside the frame, we have had no idea that Chopin was even in the room. The small window of the coffin, the frame for Gray's vision, decisively demonstrates the limitations of Bazin's 'window on the world'. One can see in this sequence a negation of classical representation itself ... [T]he seeing but dead subject is the contradictory limit of that representational system which stabilises space around the pivot point of the observer. (pp. 107/8)

Apart from this construction of contradictory spaces, Bordwell also attributes the spectator's constant puzzlement to the way that the film's plot is unfolded, with only very partial narrative information being provided. He illustrates this by the segment that follows the father's nocturnal visit to Gray.

David Gray, seeing the shadow of a gravedigger, is led to explore a decrepit building. He watches the shadow of the peg-legged soldier move on its own. Glimpsing an old woman walking down a corridor, he flees. He watches the shadow return to the soldier's body. He hears the old woman ask the soldier, 'Where is he?' Shadows dance jauntily on the wall; we glimpse the old woman again. Gray discovers a coffin beside a discarded doctor's shingle. He passes through a consulting room. Meeting a gnomish man who looks like a cross between Albert Schweitzer and Mark Twain, Gray asks if there are any children here. The old man says no. 'But,' says Gray, 'there are dogs.' The old man responds, 'There are no children and no dogs. Good night.' And he shows Gray out. (p. 93)

What is happening here in terms of the story is quite simple: the vampire Marguerite Chopin has arrived looking for her assistant, the doctor. The spectator cannot be certain of this, though. As Bordwell observes, 'the plot (the set of events as narrated) does not clearly present the story (that hypothetical concept of the "actual" events which we construct as implicit background to the plot). Indeed, much of *Vampyr* is built so as to make the following of story events exceptionally difficult'. In this sequence, the disturbance is achieved not by reordering events, but through the oblique perspective and the fragmentary way that narrative information is given out.

[B]y introducing the old woman, the doctor, and his assistant before we can posit a *causal* relation between them and the old chatelain seen in the previous scene; by presenting the major characters at one remove (as shadows, voices, distant figures); by crosscutting; by inserting retarding devices (the dancing shadows, the coffin, the empty examination room, the 'children and dogs' dialogue); and finally, by presenting the entire building's contents through Gray's exploration of it – in such ways, the film carefully obfuscates the story by means of the plot. Form has been made difficult. (pp. 93/4)

Bordwell emphasises the systematic uncoupling of cause-effect motivation in the narrative – he calls it narrative retardation – but argues that the film *is* comprehensible because it counterbalances these with structures of intelligibility. They constitute the film's narrative recoil, 'its effort to organize its own

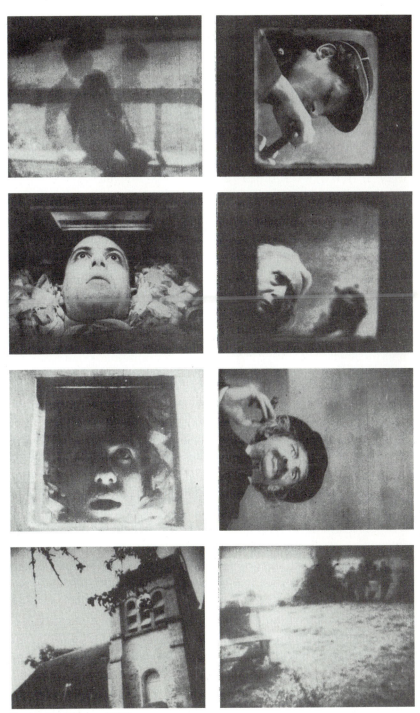

Vampyr (Carl Dreyer, 1931)

17

disruptions'. For example, in the first section of the film, the intertitles provide an explanatory commentary on the film. In the second part, it is the book about vampires that the father gives to Gray which enables us (and the characters) to see what is going on. And in the third section of the film, argues Bordwell, 'we find neither titles nor texts, but instead embedded dreams, which play a role similar to that of the other inserted materials'. (pp. 109, 110)

Bordwell's conclusion that 'the film insistently challenges our perception, forcing us to struggle to grasp its spaces, its time, its logic' (p. 116) seems to place it within Todorov's conception of the fantastic. Nevertheless, Bordwell feels that *Vampyr* is 'somewhat unassimilable even to the fantastic genre' (p. 95). He suggests that Todorov's emphasis on the instability of the hesitation that characterises the genre means that tales must in the end plump either for the natural explanation of the uncanny or for the supernatural explanation of the marvellous. And whereas Mark Nash suggests a certain stability in *Vampyr*'s final sequence, 'accepting more conventionalised rules of editing, closing the work with an impression of "smoothness", spatio-temporal continuity', Bordwell argues that the ending is as unstable as what goes before. It is 'far from a model of spatio-temporal continuity'; the logic of events continues to be troubling. 'What makes the dead chatelain's face reappear to haunt the doctor and Justin? What shuts the door of the mill-cage to trap the doctor? What forces make the gears grind to a halt in the very last shot?' (p. 95) In short, Bordwell seems to be suggesting that, if anything, the film is *too* fantastic.

It is worth underlining that Todorov's concern in his book was to define the fantastic as a *theoretical* genre rather more than as an historical one. Although he does also argue from historical examples, it does not in principle matter whether any existing work actually measures up to his ideal criteria. A pure work of the fantastic would indeed retain the hesitation and uncertainty until the last moment and even 'beyond the narrative' – Todorov cites only two that do, James's *The Turn of the Screw* and Mérimée's 'La Vénus d'Ille' (*The Fantastic*, p. 43) – even though most tales containing elements of the fantastic return to the reassurance of the *uncanny* or the *marvellous*. Bordwell's comments may therefore, paradoxically, underline the remarkable affinity between Todorov's theory and Dreyer's film. On the other hand, this affinity is also a reminder of the limits of Todorov's approach: there are simply very few films – even ones that are evidently dealing with fantastic themes – that aspire to *Vampyr*'s level of formal hesitation and uncertainty. This limited range of empirical applicability may be one reason why other critics have opened out his exclusive definition of the fantastic as a genre and approached it instead as a *mode* (Harold Bloom, Rosemary Jackson) or as an *element* in writing within a variety of genres (Christine Brooke-Rose, Kathryn Hume).[7] Such critics have also rejected his searching but narrowly focused structuralist concentration on questions of form to consider messier cultural questions about 'history' and 'ideology'.

HISTORY AND IDEOLOGY

To historicise the concept of genre means looking at the different organisation of narrative strategies and spectator expectations within cinema institutions at particular times and in particular places. It means switching the focus of study away from postulating the theoretical criteria of a pure genre against which actual texts might be measured to cycles of films and schools of film-makers. In his article 'Social Mobility and the Fantastic: German silent cinema', for example, Thomas Elsaesser tries to investigate the social and political meaning of films produced in Germany in the second and third decades of this century, while at the same time respecting 'the autonomy of the textual level'. This distinguishes his essay from many others which deal historically with ideological aspects of the fantastic and horror – Franco Moretti's 'Dialectic of fear', a study of the Frankenstein and Dracula myths, and Robin Wood's 'An introduction to the American horror film', a study of post-*Psycho* Hollywood horror, are among the most interesting of these.[8] Whereas they see history as a background to be *symbolised* or *metaphorised* in literary or cinematic fictions, Elsaesser tries critically but sympathetically to reconceptualise the approach to the relationship between German history and the German silent cinema that he inherits from critics like Siegfried Kracauer and Lotte Eisner.[9] He sees history as *worked* in texts, inscribed in the very imbalances, excesses, and intensities to be found in films like *Student of Prague, The Golem, The Cabinet of Dr Caligari* and *Nosferatu*. Their vampires, golems, doubles, monsters, and Faust-figures should be seen as:

> ... a displacement, an abstraction and reification of social and political moments. This displacement, however – being an unequal substitution, a 'failed' transformation – has left its own traces which manifest themselves in the intensity, the uncanniness with which the displaced and repressed elements irrupt into idyllic worlds and relationships.

Elsaesser's argument is that 'history' was encoded in German silent cinema through a process or act of repression, and returns in the form of the uncanny and the fantastic – the *form*, note. To this extent, Elsaesser's emphasis on the *enunciation* of the fantastic and the uncanny, rather than the representation of social and psychic fears, recalls Todorov. But he is less of a structuralist and more of a cultural historian than Todorov, and he therefore brings into play a less formal, more social and psychoanalytic conception of the *uncanny*. (S.S. Prawer, incidentally, cites *Vampyr* as 'one of the most powerful projections of the uncanny in the history of the cinema.'[10])

Like Elsaesser, writers like Moretti and Wood draw on psychoanalysis. Often, though, they use it to offer a sociologised and rather over-literal version of the 'return of the repressed' as an explanation of films of terror and the fantastic. They also tend to assume that psychoanalysis offers a fairly straightforward account of the mechanisms of ideology – that is, they use it to provide an explanation not only of why and how social and psychic fears are represented in horror fictions, but also of how these act on their audiences. Although Roger Dadoun ends on a not dissimilar note, suggesting that horror films both feed the spectator's capacity for perversion and alienation and, at the same time, offer a degree of compensation and catharsis, he also stresses the difficulty of making direct links between the social and the psychic. Indeed, he criticises Freud for failing to say what 'transformational mechanisms' would make it possible to link together the various notions of fetishism – as individual perversion, as collective religious ritual, as a mode of perceiving commodities under capitalism. He therefore hypothesises a 'fetish function', and attempts to elucidate its operation within horror films – especially Dracula films.

In her study of the 'monstrous-feminine', primarily in *Alien*, Barbara Creed draws on Dadoun's article, which was written in the high noon of 'structuralist' psychoanalysis in France (it first appeared in 1970). But she is more indebted to Julia Kristeva's ideas about *abjection* in *Powers of Horror*[11], which represent a significant reworking of Lacanianism. In this context, the interest of abjection is that, like Dadoun's fetish function, it provides a way of thinking the transactions between the psychic and the socio-cultural without disavowing the difficulty (some would say impossibility) of the process. Kristeva is particularly interested in the 'abjection' of the non-human as a key aspect of the structuration of subjectivity in terms of the limit or boundary drawn symbolically between the human and the non-human. This offers a rather different, and certainly less functionalist, approach to subject-formation than Althusser's ideas about ideology and interpellation – and one that recalls some of Todorov's ideas about the fantastic themes of the self. 'Abjection,' declares Kristeva, 'preserves what existed in the archaism of pre-objectal relationship.'[12] This leads her to lay great stress on the archaic mother and the monstrous feminine as forms of the abject – figures which are also central to the arguments of Dadoun and Moretti. Carol J. Clover also develops a psychoanalytically informed argument about what a particular cycle or sub-genre of fantasy-horror films, the slasher movies of the 1970s and 80s, might reveal about processes of subject-formation. Her account turns less on ideas about abjection and the archaic than on questions of identification and sexual difference. These have been at the heart of feminist debates in film theory over the past decade or so, and they are taken up again in Part II.

In their different ways, the articles in this section all imply the need for a theory of genre that gets beyond the mechanical imagery of apparatus and machine while retaining Metz's attempt to hold together the social, institutional, textual and psychic aspects of cinema and its pleasures. One concept that may contribute to this rethinking, it has been argued, is fantasy as the *mise en scène* of desire – the theme of Part II.[13] Meanwhile, what the articles here begin to explain is the scandalous and resilient appeal of a cinema of fantasy and terror.

NOTES

1 Christian Metz, *Psychoanalysis and Cinema: the imaginary signifier* (London: Macmillan, 1982), p. 7.

2 Stephen Neale, *Genre* (London: BFI, 1980), p. 55.

3 Tzvetan Todorov, *The Fantastic: a structural approach to a literary genre*, trans. Richard Howard (Ithaca: Cornell University Press, 1973). Page references are given in the text.

4 Mark Nash, '*Vampyr* and the fantastic', *Screen*, vol. 17, no. 3, Autumn 1976. Page references are given in the text.

5 Mark Nash, *Dreyer* (London: BFI, 1977), p. 56.

6 David Bordwell, *The Films of Carl-Theodor Dreyer* (Berkeley: University of California Press, 1981). Page references are given in the text.

7 Harold Bloom, '*Clinamen*: towards a theory of fantasy', in *Agon* (Oxford: Oxford University Press, 1982); Rosemary Jackson, *Fantasy: the literature of subversion* (London: Methuen, 1981); Christine Brooke-Rose, *A Rhetoric of the Unreal: studies in narrative and structure, especially of the fantastic* (Cambridge: Cambridge University Press, 1981); Kathryn Hume, *Fantasy and Mimesis: responses to reality in Western literature* (London: Methuen, 1984).

8 Franco Moretti, 'Dialectic of fear', in *Signs Taken for Wonders* (London: Verso, 1983). Robin Wood's 'An introduction to the American horror film' is a bricolage of texts written for *Film Comment*. It first appeared as a single article in a publication accompanying a horror retrospective at the 1979 Toronto Film Festival, and is anthologised in Bill Nichols (ed.), *Movies and Methods*, vol. II (Berkeley: University of California Press, 1985). It forms part of chapters 5 and 9 of Wood's *Hollywood from Vietnam to Reagan* (New York: Columbia University Press, 1986).

9 Siegfried Kracauer, *From Caligari to Hitler: a psychological history of the German film* (Princeton: Princeton University Pres, 1947); Lotte Eisner, *Haunted Screen* (London: Secker and Warburg, 1973; first published Paris 1952, revised and reissued 1965). For another interesting article which draws critically on the Kracauer tradition, see Andreas Huyssen, 'The vamp and the machine: Fritz Lang's *Metropolis*', *New German Critique*, nos. 24/5, 1981–2, reprinted in Huyssen, *After the Great Divide: modernism, mass culture, postmodernism* (Bloomington: Indiana University Press, 1986).

10 S. S. Prawer, *Caligari's Children: the film as tale as terror* (Oxford: Oxford University Press, 1980), p. 139.

11 Julia Kristeva, *Powers of Horror: an essay on abjection* (New York: Columbia University Press, 1982).

12 Ibid., p. 10.

13 Constance Penley, 'Feminism, film theory and the bachelor machines', *m/f*, no. 10, 1985. For another excellent critique of 'apparatus theory', see Joan Copjec, 'The delirium of clinical perfection', *Oxford Literary Review*, vol. 8, nos. 1–2, 1986.

Nosferatu (F. W. Murnau, 1921)

Social Mobility and the Fantastic
German Silent Cinema
THOMAS ELSAESSER

Almost all attempts to define the German cinema of the silent era start with the observation that it is a cinema of the 'fantastic', having given rise to such notable figures as Dr Caligari, The Student of Prague, Nosferatu the Vampire, the Golem, or the female robot in *Metropolis*. The dark, daemonic, haunted amd somehow profoundly irrational character of this tradition has been argued in two well-known books – Siegfried Kracauer's *From Caligari to Hitler* and Lotte Eisner's *The Haunted Screen*. Kracauer's is an extended speculation about the social and political meaning that can be attached to such a pronounced trend, and as a methodology, his thesis has served ever since to supply the model whereby to correlate fantasy in popular film and current political events. But I want to take my cue from Lotte Eisner's assertion: 'It is reasonable to argue that the German cinema is a development of German Romanticism, and that modern technique (i.e. cinematography) merely lends a visible form to Romantic fancies.'[1]

This assertion begs two questions: what precisely is the historical reality – or indeed is there a precise historical reality – to which Romantic figurations and motifs answer, and if so, why should the motifs return with such force in an apparently quite different historical context? And secondly, can we actually assume that a different technology does not affect the meaning and function of themes that the new medium appropriates in the form of an extended quotation?

What one finds when studying the relations between the emergence of the Gothic novel and contemporary history, between stories of Romantic agony, horror, the supernatural and say, urbanisation, the industrial revolution or new forms of political or social control, is invariably a pattern whereby the fantastic both represents conflicts and disguises them, where it raises the question of agency and at the same time attributes it to supernatural forces. Relevance and contemporaneity translate themselves into the violence and urgency of the irruption whose occurrence, however, is set, more often than not, in another – more distant – age: Medieval courts, Renaissance principalities, or the struggles of the Reformation and counter-reformation provide the scenery for depicting class-relations, sexuality and its destructive power, for giving vent to hostile feelings towards clergy and other father/authority figures.

It is therefore perfectly possible to find parallels between the 1830s and 1840s in Europe, and the Germany of the 1910s and early 20s. For while the unification of the German Reich under Bismarck had finally done away with the small feudal courts and petty aristocratic principalities which had blocked Germany's industrial development and its emergence as a bourgeois nation-state, it had left intact a powerful caste system, and a culture as well as an educational system which was deeply saturated and at the same time made contradictory with an elitist, feudal heritage. The presence of an Imperial court, a bureaucratic-military administration – even after the defeat in 1918 – and a strongly politicised working class, gave the struggle of the various sections of the bourgeoisie for power and hegemony quite distinctive features in Germany, which might account for the Romantic and fantastic motifs by the time-lag that separated Germany from its European neighbours, especially Britain and France.

However, it has been suggested that Germany experiences a revival of romantic art and fantastic literature after every revolution that failed – notably, 1798, 1848, 1918, 1968 – and that the prevalence of fantasy is the reaction, usually of a cultural and/or geographic minority, to their exclusion from the sweep of historical events, and as such, it is the expression of a frustrated desire for change, rather than a resistance to change. In this manner, a cyclical movement unites Goethe's Faust/Prometheus figures, E.T.A. Hoffmann's doubles and artist-magicians, the Golems of the Prague School with the Aguirres of Werner Herzog, and Syberberg's Hitler.

This is suggestive, but perhaps too general. And not only that – it might altogether be the wrong model for seeing the shaping influence of history on literary or filmic texts in which fantastic motifs predominate. The German silent cinema, however influential it has been on certain aspects of Hollywood film-making (film noir, for instance, and the horror film), nonetheless consti-tutes a body of films whose textual construction did not impose itself on the commercial cinema, and it has thus remained an 'alternative cinema', so different, in fact, that it has almost become incomprehensible, in much the same way as certain Romantic narrative genres became obsolete once the novel – whether Dickens', Balzac's or lesser novelists' view of it – had appropriated the codes of representation and conflict in which a society recognises its moral or psychological reality. In other words, the whole body of techniques whereby critics talk about the ways a work of literature reflects its society, and by extension, the way film reflect social forces and trends, seems misapplied, and nowhere more spectacularly than in Kracauer's reading of the German cinema. What is not permissible, if we are to understand the manner in which history has entered into these films, is the double reductions which Kracauer operates on his material. In order to establish the homology between German cinema and German history on which his thesis rests, he first of all has to 'narrativise' German history in a particular fashion, by which I do not primarily mean the inevitability he posits, where all events are seen to lead up to Hitler and Fascism; what is problematic is the process and selection of the forces and determinants he deems as pertinent to our understanding of this history. That he has to narrativise, even personalise these forces is evident if we look at the protagonist he creates: the 'German soul', the national character, who becomes the plaything of instinct, sex, fate, destiny, tyrants and demons. The history he thus constructs is itself an expressionist drama, and while he makes it clear that the categories he employs are those that the films themselves suggest, the tautologous nature of the reasoning seems inescapable: the films reflect German history, because this history has been narrated in terms and categories derived from the films.

Even more problematic, however, is the way in which Kracauer 'narrativises' the films in his plot/content analysis. For it is only with considerable violence that the visual and narrative organization of the films he discusses can be made to submit to his reading which is actually derived from an altogether different paradigm: that of the classical narrative film as it established itself in the late 1920s and early 30s, under the increasing dominance of Hollywood. What this means is that the specific formal features of the fantastic films, and which alone can give us a clue about the mode of historical inscription, are ignored, in favour of ransacking them for their most obvious motifs, which turn out to be those elements borrowed and quoted from Romantic literature and painting.

II How can one break this hermeneutic circle which seems to vitiate both Eisner's and Kracauer's construction of the aesthetic or historical specificity of the fantastic in the German cinema? I think ultimately only by looking at concrete examples. My starting point is a specific motif, a social one: economic success and social mobility. What interests me is *how* it gets encoded in fantastic forms, and *why* – given that it is a theme not only common to a lot of quite dissimilar films in Germany, but one that the cinema of other countries has made use of, especially in America, yet more often in a combination of realistic and fantastic form, notably in the 30s (for example in the films of Preston Sturges or Frank Capra). In general terms, the possibility of improving one's fortunes is a subject that appeals to a wide spectrum of possible audiences – from working class to petit-bourgeois, from intellectuals to white-collar workers, and only excludes those that never go to the cinema anyway: the rich, the super-rich, and aristocrats. It is heavily couched in fantasy, but the fantasy has to stand in some relation to what is actually possible and feasible in a given society, with regards to social mobility. As a thesis we might say that the more the 'rags-to-riches' theme is treated realistically, the more we may assume that the society in question does allow its members a degree of social mobility (and this is certainly true about the American cinema). But in the European cinema, the motif comprises two elements which stand in a certain tension to each other, if not in an outright contradiction. On the one hand, it is the direct expression of the ambition and desire of that class who seeks refuge in the cinema because their real prospects are so limited. On the other hand, being chosen by fate and chance for social success is itself a distorted version of a class-struggle, insofar as a personal, individual solution is offered by the film, while the question of the whole class or group is blocked off and suppressed. Social rise is thus a version of the class-struggle that denies the existence of this struggle.

The point is now that in popular literature – as well as in American films – the theme crops up most consistently as a fairy-tale motif: as a Cinderella story, or any tale that involves an orphan and a prince charming. In this guise, it has a predominantly female protagonist. But already in Dickens we find a slightly different constellation. Oliver Twist, forced to participate in a robbery, and consumed by a desire to escape into a better world, copes with his fear and anxiety by falling unconscious.

He wakes up, and the setting he wakes into, is indeed the cosy world of the middle class, the world of wish-fulfilment. This moment of falling unconscious, under the conflicting pressure of anxiety and desire becomes, I think, constitutive also for the German silent cinema, and the introduction of the fantastic, as opposed to the fairy-tale. We find it, for instance, in Murnau's *Phantom* (1922). A poor clerk, his mind full of fantasies and day-dreams, is knocked unconscious by a white horse-and-carriage, as he crosses the street with an armful of books. A young lady, also in white, steps out of the carriage, bends over him to make sure he is unharmed, and then rides on. But for the young man, the incident sparks off a vision, and a passion which pursues him all his life: it becomes the phantom of the title. Turned away by the girl's parents he becomes a criminal, even attempts murder, only so as not to be refused again.

What in *Phantom* is, emblematically, the combination of unconsciousness, white horse and woman in white, at the margins of which are criminality and violent death, was, in *The Student of Prague* (1913) the lady on horseback, whom Baldwin, the student of the title, rescues from the lake, after her horse has bolted. From there on, his goal is to possess this woman, which, as it turns out, necessitates eliminating the lady's cousin and fiancée. The film ends with the hero committing suicide.

But on the surface of both films the question of social rise is altogether a peripheral issue. For instance, as is well-known, *The Student of Prague* is actually about Baldwin selling his shadow to the mysterious Scapinelli, who in turn promises him riches and happiness. The social rise, to which Baldwin accedes with ease once he has the money, belongs altogether to the realm of magic and the fantastic, as if the dream of happiness had to be tabooed and repressed so completely that only a fantastic guise could represent it. The film generously borrows from the Faust legend as well as E.T.A. Hoffmann and Poe's *William Wilson*: what is different is precisely the sociological emphasis. The protagonist effectively barred from social status, and who has to pay for his ambitions with his death, is the petit-bourgeois intellectual – the 'student'. In Germany throughout the nineteenth century he was made to feel socially inferior to the nobility, while educationally and intellectually having every right to feel superior to the members of a petty and decaying aristocracy. The subject was treated in a brutally realistic manner by a dramatist of Goethe's generation. In Reinhold Lenz's 'The Tutor' (1774) just such a student-intellectual literally goes mad and castrates himself.

Thus, in *The Student of Prague*, the choice of setting and character already contains a covert social dimension, which alludes to German history and its vicissitudes. But also present is another subtext, which the film both points to and then disavows. One of the most popular genres of the German commercial cinema from its earliest days right up to the 1950s were comedies and musicals, set in the carefree milieu of wining and dining, wenching and duelling students,

The Student of Prague (Stellan Rye, 1913)

in short, what everyone associates with Heidelberg and *The Student Prince*. A film like *The Student of Prague* sets up expectations of this kind, but does not fulfil them. It works with popular assumptions, but reshapes them in an apparently completely different genre. As Bert Brecht noted, the form of humour that sees in student life nothing but carousing and caressing is already the expression of a massive displacement of social reality. German students, especially since the opening up of higher education early this century, were particularly abject creatures, acquiring hard-earned knowledge difficult to sell, from professors who vampyrise their students' best energies and ideas. Cast out into an uncertain society, they become the very prototype of the anal-aggressive male, depicted in the novels of Heinrich Mann, and analysed as the proto-fascist of *The Authoritarian Personality*.

Now, it is precisely this knowledge of what students' life was really like that *The Student of Prague* makes its starting point: Baldwin is sick of the student scene, which is going on in the background of the opening shot. With a dismissive gesture he sits down at a table apart from the others. He is broke, worried about this future and in such a morose and depressed state than even his girl-friend cannot cheer him up. But instead of investigating the causes, or what brought him to this state, the film blocks and breaks off the subject at this point to introduce Scapinelli, the mysterious figure in hat and black overcoat. The visual composition with which it does so is significant: throughout this scene, Baldwin sits with his back to his girl-friend dancing lasciviously on the tables behind to attract his eye. He looks straight into the camera, so that he is doubly separated from what goes on: spatially, and in terms of his field of vision. By contrast, we, the spectators are made to identify with two distinct points of view: we participate as spectator-voyeurs in the girl's self-display (and are thus part of the 'student scene') but we also identify with Baldwin's refusal to participate: as spectators we are already split well before Baldwin's double appears. While a classical narrative ('realistic film') would develop its narrative out of the need to reconcile and mediate between these two levels, after having set up such a division or contradiction, *The Student of Prague* does indeed introduce a media-tor, in the figure of Scapinelli, who enters not from the background or from the direction of Baldwin's gaze, but sideways, from off-screen, and his black carriage completely blocks out the background of the girl and fellow-students. If Scapinelli provides the means whereby the contradiction is resolved, he does so in an excessive, monstrous, tabooed way: he enters the frame of the fiction in much the same way as Nosferatu's ghost-ship enters the Bremen harbour to bring the plague. The basic strategy of *The Student of Prague* is thus to allude to a 'real' problem, with which the audience can identify, interrupt its development, disguise its direct investigation and reinforce it on another level by introducing a magic and demonic chain of causality, via mystery-figures and chance. These are internalised, they force a split upon the protagonist, and so act as repressive and inhibitive agents rather than simply as fairy-tale donors or helpers in the Proppian sense.

Thus, what is being repressed is the initial situation, in its social and historical dimension. The fact that it is repressed, rather than elided or passed over, is what characterises the film as belonging to the genre of the fantastic, as opposed to say, social comedy in the style of Chaplin or Capra. The repressed dimension returns to the hero in a horribly altered (disfigured) form, as the nightmare of the split self, as a crisis of identity and a compulsion towards self-destruction and self-annihilation. In Hoffmann, Poe or Dostoevski's *The Double*, the uncanny is the result of trying to defend against a ubiquitous pressure and violence upon the self, but the hero is able to do so only by personalising this violence and at the same time, turning it against the self. It is the structure of repression itself, more than what is being repressed or what materialises in its stead which produces the effect of the fantastic. For if one looks at the literary antecedents, one finds that the motif of the Double is quite closely allied in German and English romantic literature with a detection plot, whose solution, as in Poe's *William Wilson*, is the establishment of an identity between criminal and investigator, in other words, an explicitly Oedipal plot, which cannot but end in suicide or self-mutilation. In *The Student of Prague* this 'pure' storyline is complicated by all manner of other motifs (as I indicated, mostly of a sociological nature) until it resurfaces at the end when Baldwin aims at his double but actually kills himself. What seems to happen is that between hero and world, an alien power interposes itself, and the films of the fantastic operate quite a decisive break between cause and effect, by letting substitute motivation and an irrational causality fill the gap – a process which the opening scene of *The Student of Prague* visualises in concrete and literal terms.

With this, the fantastic film embodies the central characteristic of the German silent cinema, namely the virtual absence of narratives based on action suspense, the preference of composition over montage, the frequent time-ellipses and the generally static impression which the films convey. This is true even of films without a supernatural or fantastic element, such as *The Last Laugh* or other Carl Mayer *Kammerspiel* films (*Sylvester, Shattered, Backstairs*). The manifest lack of unambiguous causal links between sequences becomes the very hall-mark of the German cinema – which is what invites symbolic interpretations of the kind that Kracauer gives. But ironically, it is only by eliminating this characteristic hesitation, the hovering effect of the narratives, and by smoothing out, levelling off, filling in the gaps, fissures and ellipses of the films he discusses that Kracauer is able to bend their narratives into the shape that his thesis requires, and thereby submit them to the causality and inevitability that their textual construction so consistently eschews and renders opaque.

III If one therefore wants to avoid making analysis a self-fulfilling prophecy, any reasoning about the social or political meaning of films of the fantastic has to respect both the autonomy of the historical dimension and the autonomy of the textual level, and seek structures – not where they overlap or mirror each other, but at the points of contact, where there is evidence that the text has seized, worked over, displaced or objectified elements of the historical or the social sphere, in order to bring them to representation within the text's own formal or generic constraints. The model sketched here, therefore, aims not to discover homologies, but to valorise imbalances, excesses, intensities – that is to say, the very figures of fantastic discourse. Obviously, it is not possible to undertake an extensive demonstration at this point. But after isolating a specifically social moment – that of class-mobility and social rise – and tracing its transformation into a textual effect, let me now reverse the process and start with a recurrent textual effect, to see what it might tell us about its social or material basis. One of the most typical figures of the fantastic in the German cinema is that of the sorcerer's apprentice, that is, the creation and use of magic forces which outstrip their creator and over whom he loses control. This primarily romantic motif – Faustian, Promethean, Franken-steinian – returns with particular vehemence in what we might call the industrial machine age, whether as *The Golem*, or in *Metropolis*, or the slightly earlier, very popular *Homunculus* serial. The fact that it is a figure often connected with technology should not lead us to interpret it wholly in such a context: in *The Golem*, for instance, it is associated with forces of a quite different kind, where Rabbi Loew creates the Golem, to defend himself against the arbitrary and financially as well as sexually predatory rule of an absolutist

The Golem (Paul Wegener, 1920)

aristocracy. In this respect, it is an anti-feudal parable, typical for the bourgeoisie in its revolutionary militant phase. Likewise, it would be a rationalisation and a simplification if one saw the Frankenstein myth principally as a 'reaction' to industrialisation. What is at issue is first of all a lack, an absence, an imbalance of forces, which is being compensated by means that themselves turn out to be excessive, irrepressible, destructive. As such, it is a formal principle – an attempt at finding a system of equivalence or substitution (which fails). Within the context of nineteenth-century society, this lack or failure has a definite political character; we find the motif of such an imbalance in conservative and liberal writers when discussing conditions which are recognised as in need of change, but where the cure is suspected to be worse than the ill. It thus becomes the favourite metaphor of the radical turned conservative – a stance as topical for the German Romantics of the 1820s as for German Expressionists disappointed with the socialist revolution of 1919, for the model is that of the 'excesses' of the French Revolution (see, for instance, Carlyle's *History*).

However, looked at from a slightly different angle, the same motif might yield a quite different historical perspective. If we see the Double, for instance, not as a duplication of the self or a mirror, but as an indication that a part of the self, or a partial drive has emancipated itself and formed a new – monstrous – entity, then the motif of the Double is indeed quite close structurally to the motif of the creature, emancipating itself from the creator and turning against him. This is important in view of the much-repeated interpretation of the double, of shadows, etc. in the German cinema as the expression of the 'soul', as the symbolic representation of internal irrational forces of the self. For it is equally possible – if we take several motifs of the 'fantastic' together – to view them as objectifications and representations of parts or aspects of the self, formed under pressure from external events. As I argued with respect to *The Student of Prague*, the internalisation and psychologisation of these forces constitutes a consequence, not an origin, and thus can be seen as a displacement, an abstraction and reification of social and political moments. This displacement, however, has left its own trace – it being an unequal substitution, a 'failed' transformation – which manifests itself in the intensity, the uncanniness, with which the displaced and repressed elements irrupt into idyllic worlds and relationships.

One way of recovering the historical dimension of the uncanny motif, therefore, is to point not so much to the emergence of the machine, but to the changing relations of production during the Romantic period, especially as they affect artists and intellectuals, increasingly thrown upon the market with their products, and finding there that they no longer control the modes of reproduction and distribution of their works. To some of Hoffmann's tales, notably the *Sandman* or *Mlle de Scuderi*, and to Balzac's early stories, applies what Marx (as early as 1830) wrote about alienation and reification, namely that in the capitalist production process, the product confronts the producer as something alien, and his own person comes to seem to him uncanny.

It is this process that we find represented in so many of the films and their dominant motifs – the Double, the Faustian overreaching, the creator half-possessed by his creature, etc. And it reappears as a *dominant* configuration at precisely the point in history, when the conditions of production for artists and intellectuals undergo a further significant change, not least through the cinema, which by the early 20s was very much perceived as a dangerously powerful rival to theatre and serious fiction. The role of the writer as the representative of his time – as someone in whom the times reflect themselves and find their ideal (artistic) expression – dramatically declines, and another power – that of technological reproduction, the emergent mass-media – interposes itself, as both a lure and a threat.

To construct these films of the German cinema as objectifications of the concrete historical situation of their makers – the scriptwriters and directors – would, I think, not be permissible, if it were not for the fact that we are actually dealing with a counter-cinema, that is, one conceived in conscious opposition not only to Hollywood films (or more accurately, the swamping of the European market prior to World War One by French films), but also in opposition to the burgeoning mass-commercial film production in Germany itself. Paul Wegener, Hans Heinz Ewers, Robert Wiene, Murnau and Lang saw themselves very much as part of an offensive to make the cinema respectable for bourgeois audiences, and to give it the status of art. We therefore ought to talk of the German Expressionist cinema as an art-cinema, and it is here that the forms of the fantastic are developed, in the context of a self-conscious attempt to make 'art' in the cinema, and to appeal to a specific, self-selected part of the audience.

The latter, of course, applies with especial force to a film like *The Cabinet of Dr Caligari*, conceived and marketed very deliberately as a high-brow product, and by no stretch of credulity can the film be regarded as an unself-conscious bodying forth of the 'German soul' brooding expressionistically about Fate and Destiny. Thus, a few words about *Dr Caligari*, once again inverting my perspective by talking about it as an objectification and fantasmatisation of another kind of alienation – that of the spectators, rather than the producer. (It has often been pointed out that *The Cabinet of Dr Caligari* is in fact an allegory of the film-maker, but to concretise this idea would require more space than I can permit myself at present).

In *Dr Caligari*, too, the initial situation contains a social aspect involving class/status differences. Caligari, asking deferentially for a permit to put up his tent-show, is treated by the town clerk and his subordinates in a brusque, humiliating and insulting manner. There can be little doubt that this scene transmits to the spectator an identifiable experience of the arbitrary and haughty behaviour that a militarist bureaucracy (which is what the civil service was, even during the Weimar Republic) displayed towards civilians. What we all at some stage have murmured under our breath: 'I could have killed him' – Caligari acts out. He takes revenge on the hated town-clerk by way of his medium Cesare, thus setting off the chain of events which make up the narrative. But here too, any analysis of the origins and causes of such an all-powerful but at the same time petty bureaucracy is blocked and displaced. Instead, we find a commensurate magic omnipotence – one which in effect overcompensates. Thus, in Caligari's medium Cesare, as in *The Golem*, a force is set free which at least in part, escapes its creator's control. Cesare is Caligari's double and the embodiment or condensation of rebellious, anti-authoritarian drives which stand in direct contradiction to his own authoritarianism. What makes the film significant is less its striking decor as such, but the degree to which the decor permits a particularly complex and contradictory narrative to articulate itself within the space of a single fiction. There has been much debate about the meaning of the framing device, but it seems to me that it is only one – albeit an important one – of the many strategies in the film for sustaining a multi-perspectival narrative. Perhaps the easiest way to locate these strategies is to ask some simple questions, such as, why does Francis – the narrator in the frame, and Caligari's chief antagonist in the story – 'go mad'? Or: What is the relation between the murder of the town-clerk and the murder of Allan, Francis' friend? These rather naive questions, which doubtless would be asked by every spectator if the film were a 'realistic' film, somehow seem irrelevant. And this is so, I think, because questions of motivation and causality have, in the process of editing the film into such static, self-contained tableaux, become almost illeg-ible. It would lead too far to enter into the full history of the tableau-scene as a form of 'negative' dramaturgy – one finds its theory in Diderot – but as part of a

The Cabinet of Dr Caligari (Robert Wiene, 1919)

rhetoric of muteness and self-repression, it is the most direct link between bourgeois drama/melodrama of the stage, and silent German cinema. This illegibility of both the temporal and causal sequence in the film, the opaqueness of the emotional relationship between, say, Francis, Jane, Allen, and the breaking off or fading out of several scenes, so to speak, in mid-gesture, on a note of suspension, is in fact evidence of the dynamic interplay of forces between reality and filmic form, the work of resistances without which there would be no narrative and no narrator. The act of narration *per se* establishes itself in *Dr Caligari*, and subsequently in countless films of the classic German cinema (with their frame-tales, their narrator-figures, their nested narratives) as a field of force, as a struggle for control over the intensities of the discourse itself.

    The static quality of this, as of other films, therefore, should not be mistaken for clumsiness of *mise en scène*, or the primitive state of film-form, but rather as the containment of an agitation, which, banished from articulating itself in a linear fashion, such as we are used to from classical narrative, creates a different kind of economy of the filmic signifier. *Dr Caligari* displaces not only its social themes, by making them into enigmas whose resolutions lead elsewhere (thereby creating the conditions for narration, for there being 'texts' that need deciphering), it also displaces an already constituted cinematic narrative: the subtext in *Dr Caligari* is the genre of the detective serial – those featuring Joe Deeb or Stuart Webb, for example – which was extremely popular in Germany in the early 20s.

The particular, and perhaps unique, economy of *Dr Caligari*, shows itself, if one tries to answer the question of what motivates the characters, by putting it in slightly different terms, namely: who narrates the story, whose story is it, and to whom is it narrated? If one follows accounts like Kracauer's, it is the story of Caligari, the mad doctor, the premonitory materialisation of a long line of tyrants, the faithful image of German military dictatorship and its demonic, mesmerising hold over others. But can we construct for Caligari's behaviour a certain motivational logic, a certain coherence *within* the story? The doctor, researching in his archives, finds the secret of somnambulism and brings a patient under his control. Disguising himself as a fairground operator, he uses his power to avenge himself on his enemies (the town-clerk) and subsequently, to lure a young woman into his tent. He beckons Jane inside, showing her the upright box, flings it open with a leer to reveal the rigid figure of Cesare, who, as she gets closer, opens his eyes, whereupon she stands transfixed in fascination, until she breaks away with a terrified, distraught expression on her face. The sexual connotations of the scene are unmistakable, and here Caligari's powers compensate a kind of impotence, his behaviour towards Jane is the very epitome of the 'dirty old man' exposing himself: showing Cesare is literally an 'exhibition'. Cesare's abduction of the girl strengthens this particular interpretation: the medium becomes, as it were, the detachable part of Caligari, not so much his double as his tool. Caligari's story would be centred on a disturbed relationship to sexuality and political power, in which impotence is being overcompensated by exhibition ('I'll show you'), but where showing involves an alternation of hiding and revealing, that is, flashing, blinking.

It is interesting that Cesare, unlike *The Golem* and other 'creatures' does not turn against his master. Instead, when pursued by Francis, he drops the girl, becomes weak, withers or fades away, or as the intertitle puts it, he dies of exhaustion. In this respect, he is rather similar to Nosferatu, fading with daylight (like over-exposed film-stock). When Cesare does return to his creator, the very sight of him and the necessity to recognise him as part of himself, drives Caligari mad.

IV But is it possible to see the film centred on Caligari? The story is initiated by Francis, and in this sense it is his story, too, about how he came to be at the place from which he tells it, as the recollection of a series of events whose memory is activated by the sight of a figure in white passing by, who subsequently turns out to be Jane. What, then, is Francis' story, and why does he go mad? It is, essentially, the tale of a suitor who is ignored or turned down: the narrative comes full circle when Francis pleads with Jane to marry him, and she replies that 'we queens may never choose as our hearts dictate'. In the story itself, the choice is between Francis and Allen. After the visit to the fair-ground, where Allen is told by Cesare that he has only until dawn to live, the friends part with the remark: 'We must let her choose. But whatever her choice, we shall always remain friends.' In this situation of rivalry, the main beneficiary of Allen's death seems to be Francis, a benefit which his horrified reaction both suppresses and expresses.

This moment of recognition (in the script it appears as 'a look of comprehension') is itself turned into an enigma (that is, disavowed); 'I shall not rest until I get to the bottom of these events', and it opens up the detection-narrative, with its false trail-false suspect strategy, in which substitution plays a major part. In this respect, Cesare is Francis' double: he kills the rival and abducts the bride, thus acting out Francis' secret desires. The fact that throughout the rape/abduction scene both Francis and Caligari sit stupidly in front of Cesare's dummy, not only accentuates the gesture of disavowal, it also establishes a parallelism of desire between Francis and Caligari, underlined later by the repetition of an identical composition and shot: first Caligari is put in a straight-jacket and locked into a cell, and then, Francis is shown in the same position. The investigation of the series of crimes thus culminates in the visual statement that the criminal is the alter ego of the detective, the story of Oedipus, in other words, but itself held in suspense by the reversibility which the framing of the tale imposes on any attempt at decipherment.

Yet it is equally possible to read *The Cabinet of Dr Caligari* as Jane's story, in which case, her doctor-father and Dr Caligari feature as doubles of each other, and Cesare as the disavowed phallus–fetish of a curiosity which the scene in Caligari's tent marks as explicitly sexual. One recalls that she is motivated to visit Caligari by 'her father's long absence', and that in the face of Francis' protestations that it could not have been Cesare who abducted her, Jane insists vehemently on being right, as if to defend *her* version against the rival claims of Francis.

What implications can one draw from this? It would appear that in *The Cabinet of Dr Caligari* a visual form and a mode of narration has been found where several different 'versions' or narrative perspectives converge or superimpose themselves on the same fictional space: its economy is that of condensation, itself the outcome of a series of displacements which de-centre the narrative, while at the same time creating entry-points for a number of distinct and different spectator-fantasies, centred on male and female oedipal scenarios.

Technically, this is accomplished by a dis-articulation of action-time in favour of narrated time, and (supported by the decor, but by no means confined to it) the projection of a purely interior space organised to bring to the fore visually the repetition and parallels which the narrative elides and mutes. What we have is a lacunary, elliptical text, in which the figures of the fantastic can be seen as a particular textual economy of narrative perspectivism and spectator-projection: paradoxically, this economy (which has the force of repression) here works both towards opening up the text and at the same time condensing its elements into a tight Oedipal logic. *Dr Caligari* thus posits a very strong internal system of relations between the different characters, where they act as substitutes for each other, either as doubles or (fetishised) part-objects. The narrative effects these forms of containment by a repression of desire, so that in the language of such an (oedipalised) fantasy a specifically bourgeois renunciation of desire legitimates itself. The 'political' nature of the psychic repression is named, shown, hinted at, only to become in turn the object of further repression. It is as if the social motifs have been substituted by sexual motifs, but these are themselves distorted by the force of narration itself, so that the film offers 'solutions' which leave everything open, or rather, produce radically equivocal textual ensembles. It would therefore be inaccurate to say that in the German silent cinema all social conflicts become internalised, 'psychologised' – unless one added that this interiorisation is of such a virulent kind that it tends to threaten and disturb the very process of psychological containment or resolution.

This can also be argued by reference to another film – Murnau's *Nosferatu*. The hero's initial situation has, once again, economic overtones: Jonathan Harper undertakes his journey to Transylvania in order to make money and improve his prospects for advancement in his firm. This entails ignoring the entreaties of his bride, from whose domesticity (flowers, cats) he seems positively anxious to escape. The journey thereby has the signs of a detour: if the economic motif splits the couple, Nosferatu unites them, in the characteristic structure of a lack, an absence, being overcompensated, by the insertion of another force, and of a different degree of intensity. Again, all the characters are closely interwoven: Renfield, the estate agent, manipulates Jonathan, but he is himself the tool of Nosferatu, who in turn comes under the power and influence of Nina, who thereby closes the gap of not being able to exert influence on Jonathan. The protagonists are important to the narrative only insofar as they can enter into such substitute relationships, but more explicitly than in virtually any other film of the German fantastic, *Nosferatu* is the enactment of a deal, a bargain, an exchange, where there is a strict incommensurability of the entities being exchanged. A crucial scene makes this explicit: as the Count is about to sign the papers, Jonathan accidentally (?) displays/exhibits the medallion which bears the image of Nina. Nosferatu grasps it, and it is this image which is being exchanged between the men: it substitutes itself for the money that would otherwise seal the deal. In a business based on real-estate (like the film industry), Nosferatu acquires a view (of Nina: the house serves him as nothing but an observation post) and Jonathan gains social status (for having a Count as his client). If Nosferatu is Jonathan's double, insofar as Nina acquires the lover that Jonathan seems so reluctant to be, the 'undeadness' of desire is shown to have social consequences – Nosferatu brings with him the plague, itself seen as the reverse-side of trade (Nosferatu is both captain and cargo, producer and product).

V   The films of the German fantastic cinema thus seem to encode in their encounter with the social reality of the Weimar Republic not the street-battles, inflation, unemployment, but something else, though no less historical. A double perspective opens the texts of the fantastic towards society: on the one hand, that of the artist-intellectual whose changing relations to the modes of cultural production, such as the cinema, are condensed into the neo-romantic motifs of the sorcerer's apprentice and that of the producer confronting the product of his labour/desire as an alienated self-image. To return to the quotation from Lotte Eisner: one can now argue that the Romantic project – the transformation of history into inwardness, and inwardness into phenomenological and sensuous immediacy of contemplation – has been accomplished by the cinema, but with a vengeance. For it shows this transformation to have been an act of repression, and history returns in the form of the uncanny and fantastic. Romanticism wedded to technology has produced a wholly fetishised, reified form of immediacy.

On the other hand, the films open up a perspective towards a class of spectators whose precarious *social* position – 'students', clerks, young men with frustrated ambitions and vague resentments – make them members of the petit-bourgeoisie, whose engagement with the class-struggles takes the form of avoiding class-struggle, by imagining themselves above it and outside. Which is to say, a class who compensates for its fear of proletarianisation by dreaming of the by-pass or detour around social conflict in the shape of personal fantasies of success. The logic of the films consists in accommodating this situation and this desire but translating it into transactions of unequal exchange, which the narrative 'integrates' by its heavily metaphoric economy. Telling is selling, and the cinema offers the spectator a narrative position in exchange for a desire: we arrive at what Roland Barthes has called 'contract-narratives' – which is to say, narratives where the strategies of narration (framing, nesting, etc.) are 'determined not by a desire to narrate, but by a desire to exchange: [narrative] is a *medium of exchange*, an agent, a currency, a gold standard'.[2]

The cinema enters the social arena not by a mimesis of class-conflicts or the movements of a collective unconscious, but as that form of social relation in which the consumption of narratives and images intervenes to block or displace the contradictions of history into effects of disavowal and substitution. Films are not versions of (bourgeois) historiography; rather, they act upon another history – that of commodity-relations and the modes of production and consumption. It is this physical reality which the cinema, in Kracauer's phrase, attempts (in vain) to redeem, by inserting itself as a quasi-magical power, a fetish-object, into the reified and abstracted relationships which characterise our society.

Revised 1986

NOTES

1   Lotte Eisner, *The Haunted Screen* (London: Secker and Warburg, 1969), p. 113.
2   Roland Barthes, *S/Z* (London: Jonathan Cape, 1975), p. 90.

Fetishism in the Horror Film
ROGER DADOUN

Freud's short article on 'Fetishism'[1] (1927) provides the initial hypothesis for our analysis of certain fundamental aspects of the horror film. It puts forward some strong, simple statements: 'the fetish is a substitute for the penis',[2] and more precisely 'the fetish is a substitute for the woman's (the mother's) penis which the little boy once believed in and [. . .] does not want to give up';[3] the need to have recourse to a fetish is closely linked to castration: 'the horror of castration has set up a memorial to itself in the creation of this substitute'.[4] Freud does not greatly elaborate on these assertions, but a few apparently marginal points are relevant to our topic. At the end of his article Freud shifts unexpectedly from depth psychology to ethnography; he evokes what he calls a 'variant' of fetishism 'in the Chinese custom of mutilating the female foot and then revering it like a fetish after it has been mutilated'.[5] What Freud is here presenting as an obvious parallel in fact poses serious problems: between the individual sexual practice of the fetishist, coloured by anxiety and perceived as perversion, and a collective usage, inscribed in a certain kind of historical causality, there is all the distance separating two organisational models each with its own features, its own originality. Freud does not say what *transformational mechanisms* would allow us to pass from one level to the other or to link two separate modes of organisation to the same psychological nucleus. His comparison is nevertheless extremely suggestive, indicating to what extent fetishism in its essence, or rather, *by virtue of its structure*, cannot just be dealt with as the form taken by a traumatised or perverse subjectivity – to what extent it operates in the socio-cultural field. The horror film, precisely, seems to me to illustrate the work of what might be called the *fetish function*: a function well situated by language, which designates by the same term 'fetishism' a libidinal organisation described by psychoanalysis, elementary religious forms or practices defined more or less clearly in anthropology and the orthodox Marxist insistence on the fact that, in certain societies, things are not seen as the product of work and of socio-economic relations.

Freud's article is characterised by a certain stylistic tension. The fetishistic phenomenon is described with clarity and rigour, in that unified, 'objective' style which is one of the great qualities of Freud's writing. At the same time, scattered in the text, a few very strong terms, indicating extreme emotional states, open suddenly on to dark, vertiginous chasms, or, to put it another way,

First published as 'Le Fétichisme dans le film d'horreur' in
NOUVELLE REVUE DE PSYCHANALYSE, Paris, Autumn 1970

clothe the neutral, realistic writing in an 'atmosphere' which comes close to the fantastic. Freud evokes 'the horror of castration', 'the fright of castration' (the word 'fright' is used twice), and he vividly describes the 'panic' of the 'grown man [. . .] when the cry goes up that Throne and Altar are in danger'. If the overall tone invites comparison with the atmosphere of the horror film, a 'realistic' detail is almost a technical instruction to the film producer: 'the inquisitive boy peered at the woman's genitals *from below*'[6], a remark that deserves to be linked to the low-angle shot thanks to which important objects (the castle) or characters (Dracula) are seen *from below*. A recent rerun of Hitchcock's film *Psycho* makes me think of the house where the psychotic son keeps the mummified corpse of the mother to identify with: the building is at the top of a hill, and the mother's room is always seen from the bottom of the stairs, up until the final sequence where the perspective (the procedure) is reversed in preparation for the *dénouement*.

II I shall not attempt an overview of psychoanalytical observations relating to fetishism, but it might be useful to recall the very brief résumé offered by the psychoanalyst Masud R. Khan in his study of foreskin fetishism in a male homosexual. In the aetiology of fetishism, as he emphasises, more and more elements come to be included:

– the primary pre-Oedipal relationship to the mother (to the breast);
– internal objects and first stages in the development of the ego;
– the transitional object and primitive aspects of mental functioning;
– the anxiety of separation and terror of abandonment;
– disturbances in the development of the image of one's own body as a separate whole, and the threat of disintegration arising from problems in the mother-child relationship;
– primary bisexual identification with the mother and the desire to bear a child;
– the terror-panic of incest;
– the defence against archaic anxiety affects which threaten the relationship to the mother and are accompanied by the fear of sinking into psychotic states.

These elements constitute so many axes along which the objects, forms, symbols and movements which characterise the horror film can easily be distributed. Indeed, they illuminate the very structure of the horror story. The fear of separation and abandonment, for example, is constantly being played out in horror films. The friend, husband or guardian always manages to leave the heroine alone in her room, in the vaults or in the forest – and her loneliness, as well as making the spectator experience the anxiety of sep aration, calls for the intervention of an evil being, a werewolf, vampire or monster, and allows the drama to unfold.

In Masud Khan's account of fetishism, two essential characteristics emerge and might usefully be underlined: the *archaic* aspects of the various kinds of identification and the almost exclusively *sado-defensive* function of sexuality. Archaic identification comes long before the appearance of the father-figure. It is the figure of the pre-Oedipal mother that predominates, even though at this stage it is hardly possible to speak of a 'figure'. The mother as a spatio-temporal form is dissolved. She is no longer there, no longer present or clearly delineated. She simply marks a time *before*, a previous state which is never named; and she is that in which everything becomes engulfed, the oceanic thing (Lovecraft) that calls for fusion – thereby putting the subject in touch with his own terror of fusion and formlessness. If it is true that the fetishistic act culminates in this trance-like moment, this hallucinatory state in which everything vacillates and is confused, in which the subject himself becomes the fetish-object, one cannot but be struck by the analogy with an important moment in the horror film. This is the moment of transubstantiation, when the vampire absorbs his (or her) victim by kissing him (or her), when both become one and the same – a kind of communal thing, outside time (eternal) and space (ubiquitous), which the cinema helps us sense by cutting or fading to an insistent, emphatic, black. The network of anxieties in which the subject is caught – castration, abandonment, fusion, disintegration – allows his sexuality no other function than that of defence. A 'memorial' is 'set up'; as Freud would say, which saves the subject from collapse; we ought perhaps to say that it is 'put together' [*bricolé*],[7] if we wish to take into account Masud Khan's judicious observation according to which the fetish is a kind of collage. Against disintegration, a totality; against primitive identification with the mother, a phallus; against the anxiety of psychotic collapse, sexuality; against spatio-temporal disorganisation, a ritual – and that completes the construction, on the positive side of fetishism, as it were, of a sexualised phallic object, all the more rigid and impressive for being fragile and threatened. In this object, one may perhaps have the pleasure of recognising a familiar figure of the horror film, Count Dracula.

III 'He has retained that belief, but he has also given it up',[8] writes Freud, explaining the fate of the mother's phallus in the child's psyche. This statement, at once 'stupefying' (in its logical structure) and 'banal' (in its everyday applications), is analysed most perceptively by Octave Mannoni in terms of the more general formula, 'I know very well, but all the same' – which is also the title of the article placed at the beginning of his latest book.[9] His analysis throws some light on what I was saying at the beginning about the shift in Freud's article from fetishism as a perversion to 'the Chinese custom'. As Mannoni emphasises, the point is less to 'elucidate the fetishist perversion' than to investigate a problematic of belief, centring on the mechanism of Freud's *Verleugnung* or disavowal,[10] which Mannoni calls the 'repudiation of reality'. Mannoni also brings ethnography in to support his argument. He quotes the passage in Don Talayesva's book *Sun Chief*[11] where the Hopi Indian child discovers that the Katcina – terrifying figures who seek out children in order to eat them – are not gods, but masks hiding familiar adults, and especially the child's own father. But belief in the Katcina, far from being weakened by the evidence of their non-existence, is thereby as it were consolidated and assured. Demystification, it could be said, actually contributes to the myth: 'this ceremony of demystification, and the denial inflicted on belief in the Katcina, will become the institutional basis for the new belief in the Katcina that constitutes the essential part of the Hopi religion'.

This is one way into the psychology and the sociology of belief, which seems to be extraordinarily fertile ground; and the notion of disavowal can be applied most effectively to the spectacle. We know very well that 'it's only a play' or 'it's only a film', but all the same – this 'but all the same' being experienced by the spectator in the form of his own presence at, or 'participation' in the spectacle. The horror film, considered from this angle, is characterised by the fact that it moves away from reality, from 'I know very well', to a considerable extent (in general one tends to forget . . .) so as to allow various fantasies (castration, disintegration, etc.) to be represented more intensely; in other words to bring 'but all the same' into sharper focus, to let the spectator experience it more directly. It therefore meets with various kinds of resistance to a much greater extent than other genres. People refuse to watch horror films or make fun of them; they follow the herd, relegating the horror film to a marginal or semi-clandestine status. On the other hand, acceptance often amounts to abandoning the cinema. The spectator will tend – and will be led by the institution itself – to reject the institutional components of the spectacle, preferring to adopt a form of (imaginary) behaviour allied to a fetishist ritual. (Thus Masud Khan quotes P. Greenacre: 'In certain cases, it's not the possession of the object so much as the ritual use made of it that is essential.')

Like any other formula, Mannoni's 'I know very well, but all the same . . .' contains, in a condensed or even elliptical form, a logical development which it might be useful to spell out. The underlying principle seems to be this: an extreme tension between *being* and *having* imposes a reversal that could well lead in the very direction of fetishism. What is included in the knowledge of 'I know very well' is transformed by 'but all the same', which functions as a logical operator. This transformed knowledge is made up of two layers in violent conflict with each other, yet welded together. In an archaic layer, the mother is seen as a totality, as *the one who is*, more so than anyone; a more recent, more 'realistic' layer includes the discovery that she does not have a phallus, the recognition of a fundamental (and doubtless founding) lack, of *what she does not have*, of what is more lacking in her than in anyone. To avoid the cataclysm inscribed in a composite entity which brings together the fullness of being and essential lack, absolute being and absolute non-having, and because he is unable to work out any compromises on the level of knowledge itself, the subject has no other option than to reverse the formula. The antagonistic components are, as it were, brought down to the same level (repression, denial), and the line that separated them, phallic and totalising, is, as Freud would say, set up as a memorial:

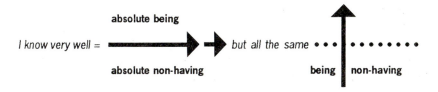

A more concrete diagram will bring us closer to the fantasies and figures of the horror film:

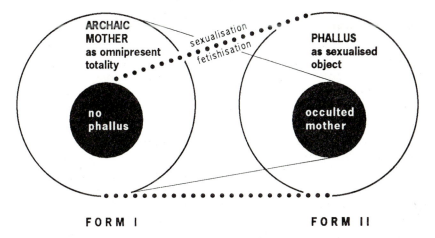

We recognise that the total being of the mother does not have a phallus, but this recognition is disavowed or 'repudiated' as the phallus is erected into a sexualised total object. At the same time, the omnipresent mother is occulted or concealed, transformed into absence. But just as the mother's omnipresence and all-powerfulness vanish into thin air, into the gaping hole [*béance*][12] opened up by the recognition that she lacks, does not have, a phallus, so the fetish-*memorial* is built on nothing, since the phallus as a total object is not supplied with libidinal energy of a living, creative sort, but with emptiness, irreality, non-being. It is a lure [*leurre*]. In the horror film Form 1 describes the fantasmatic background (reign of the archaic mother, anxieties of castration, fusion, etc.) against which Form II stands out as the plastic and symbolic form, the composite figure, the patchwork structure, in which we recognise our old friend Count Dracula.

IV   No life-blood ever really circulates in Count Dracula's veins. Even the meagre flow that might come from cultural recognition is denied him. Because he is the place of unconscious fantasy, he is excluded from the circuit. The genre of the horror film has been short-circuited – it has no duration, no depth, no points of contact. As an object of analysis, if you set aside a few coteries which fetishise it in their own way, it meets with an ignorant smile from people who don't really know why they are smiling and should perhaps begin to do a bit of thinking. It is surely enough, in the present context, to recall that Freud himself encourages us to consider the horror film, and to consider it as important. When he wrote, in a letter to Wilhelm Fliess dated 24 January 1897, 'the story of the devil, the vocabulary of popular swear-words, the songs and habits of the nursery – all these are now gaining significance for me',[13] he was defining an open programme which his disciples have done little to renew. With its 'diabolical' themes addressed to a 'popular' audience, the horror film fits squarely into the field of psychoanalytical investigation. That it should have been kept out points to the affinity or complicity that exists between psychoanalysis – its official schools, at least – and the hegemonic culture of our society. This culture is forever cultivating the 'high' genres. It has immense powers – political, administrative, academic, editorial, etc. – and, in its commitment to order, hierarchy, equilibrium and security, it will repress anything that smacks of threat, of disorder, of fantasy, of the archaic. Like the 'mentally ill' relegated to the sidelines of communities, societies and consciences, the horror film leads a marginal existence in a kind of half-light which has the advantage of leaving the hegemonic culture with the monopoly of the light and encouraging a socio-economic response which brings us back to fetishism, in another register.

V   A cinematic fantasy in the broad sense, *King Kong* (1933) shows how it is possible in the spectacle for fetishistic elements pertaining to normally separate domains to converge – a phenomenon which is at its most obvious in the horror film. The opening sequence conjures up the economic situation in the United States immediately after the Depression. Hungry people queue for soup; a young woman, the heroine, steals a piece of fruit from a stall. It is a shot of extraordinary eloquence. Around the barely visible piece of fruit, three people (the stall-holder, the young woman and a passer-by who turns out to be a film director and hires the young woman), have a discussion, an argument; they try to reach a compromise. Human relationships and their outcome gravitate around a tiny stolen apple, a radiating, fetishistic centre. That's the end result of a socio-economic system in which Marxism sees the fetishism of goods, money and capital taken to an extreme, to the point of caricature. Although this opening sequence was for a long time banned, and is often still omitted, it is indispensable to a critical understanding of the film. The second part only acquires its full meaning if the concept of fetishism is brought into play. On the boat taking the film crew to a faraway island, the director takes the young woman through her part, treats her like an object, a commodity. The fear that he is trying to get her to express is treated in the same way, for that is what he is going to sell; fetishism invades everything, people and feelings included. A new commodity – emotions, affects, fantasies – is drawn into the economic circuit, confirming and exacerbating the process of reification so forcefully portrayed by Lukács.

This line of interpretation is pursued in the third part of the film. Here we are dealing with fetishisation in the traditional sense, which has to do with the history of religion (which was where Marx found the term). A tribe of

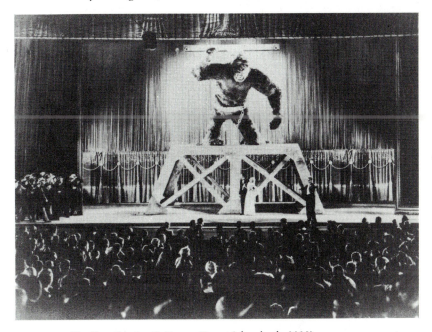

King Kong (Merian C. Cooper/Ernest Schoedsack, 1933)

primitive 'blacks' worships a monstrous beast, King Kong, their idol, and periodically sacrifice a young girl to him. By a stroke of genius, Ernest B. Schoedsack, who co-produced *King Kong* with Merian C. Cooper, makes use of this primitive religious fetishism to illustrate the restoration of fetishist values in capitalist society; captured and transported to New York, King Kong becomes a superb commodity, capable of lining the hero's pocket with millions of dollars. The sequence where King Kong is exhibited in the theatre before a rich, smiling, bourgeois audience in a bright, luxurious and carefree atmosphere, counterbalances the darkness and misery of the opening sequence and shows the surprising efficiency of the socio-cultural industry.

The makers of *King Kong* thus manage to maintain a dialectical and anti-fetishising attitude to the phenomenon, as their framing of the film by two vigorous critical sequences attests. (I have already described the opening sequence.) The final sequence proclaims that the Beast, fear and fantasy cannot with impunity be treated as things. King Kong, breaking loose from his chains, ravages the city-prison, the temple of fetishism. He releases his hold on the Empire State Building, the 'erected memorial', only under machine gun fire from the air, a sinister omen. Nevertheless, it is also true that in general the cinema has fulfilled the *fetish function* to a remarkable degree. It is significant that the great period of the horror film in the United States comes immediately after the crash of 1929 (*Dracula* dates from 1930, *Frankenstein* from 1931; 1932 especially sees the production of *Island of Lost Souls, The Mummy, Freaks, The Most Dangerous Game, The Living Dead*, etc., and *King Kong* dates from 1933). It is as if, in the process of fetishisation, the socio-cultural industry, in this case the cinema, takes over from the faltering economic system. To do this, it must not only place itself squarely within the system (that goes without saying), but also and above all submit itself, its agents (the actors or the directors) and its themes to a fetishising treatment. While being subjected more completely than anything else to the constraints, the rules and the ideals of the economic system, the cinema projects the delusion of being an autonomous world, above reality, concerned only with the higher pursuit of image-making. The public at large never gets to know about the creative work involved, except in terms of 'inspiration'. The actors acquire star status and inhabit an ethereal world of their own; themes tend to follow a rigid and high ritualised pattern.

Because of its deep affinities with the economic crisis – the terms most commonly used to describe the impact of the Depression on the American people were 'panic', 'turmoil', 'fear', 'amazement', etc. – and above all because it works intensively, electively, on the level of the fantasy and what might be called the fundamental affects (anxieties of abandonment, disintegration, castration, dissolution), thereby encouraging a more demanding and more critical self-consciousness on the part of the subject, the horror film was no doubt destined, more than any other kind of film, to undergo the effects of fetishisation. Hence the creation of fantasy figures, beings whose specific role is to keep anxiety in its place, to deny human torments, the constraints of space, time and history, fictional types which are clearly in Freud's 'memorial' category: *Frankenstein, Dracula, King Kong, The Mummy*, etc. The work of those who have made the film is 'scotomised':[14] while in the case of love or adventure films, and all those with a so-called 'psychological' component, the names of the actors and directors are generally well known, people tend strangely not to know the actors and directors of horror films. The characters assume such gigantic proportions that, like primitive fetishes or capitalist gold, they absorb the human agents. Even the secret of how certain things are done is lost, if it is true that we still don't properly understand the trick effects worked out by Willis O. Brien for *King Kong*. Later on, as a result of critical re-appraisal, certain actor figures become detached from the legendary characters – Bela

Lugosi from Dracula, Boris Karloff from Frankenstein's monster – but how could you possibly, even now, separate Max Schreck from Nosferatu's mask and corpse-like body? The 'devaluation' of cinematographic fetishes tends nowadays to revalorise the actor's work, and it's often Christopher Lee or Barbara Steele or Peter Cushing one is looking at in the figures they represent.

VI Through a remarkable parallel, what goes on at the level of individual or team work in the present-day production of films also operates in structures elaborated collectively down the centuries. One might well refer again to *King Kong* – now attempting, however, to get beyond its ethnographical reference to a primitive religion, as primary as the process of the same name, hence of course its interest – to point out that certain dominant forms of the horror film, like the Werewolf or the Vampire, are themselves the survivals, the remains, of a long religious process. These are reconstituted more or less randomly – hence the analogy with 'bricolage'. Dozens of features borrowed from various cultural strata are pieced together, mounted in a kind of mythological patchwork. These result in unified forms which are organised more or less coherently (on the level of the fantasy, the narrative, the spectacle, or whatever). There is nevertheless something to be gained from relating them to the religious traditions from which they developed. If in what follows I focus on the figure of the vampire, or to be more precise, the Dracula form, this is of course because – leaving aside the formidable question of personal preferences – the Dracula films, from *Nosferatu* to *Kiss of the Vampire*, offer us such a variety and abundance of fetishist fantasies and symbols; but also because of certain historico-religious aspects which happen to have been well described in a recent book.

Under the title *From Zalmoxis to Genghis-Khan*[15] Mircea Eliade offers a series of 'comparative studies on the religions and folklore of Dacia and Eastern Europe'. Finding the figure of the wolf in the roots of many names and in rites – everyone knows that Romulus and Remus were the foster sons of the she-wolf – Eliade establishes the existence of a ritual lycanthropy, closely associated with secret warrior clans. The initiate wears a wolf's skin or a wolf mask, identifies with the wolf and imitates its behaviour, eats human flesh and drinks blood. This elementary form of religious life seems to be extremely ancient, since statuettes representing wolf-hounds and figurines showing what are probably dancers in wolf masks have been found in the Neolithic civilisation of Vinča. Although it features in a number of Indo-European cultures, the 'magico-religious complex of the wolf' – to which the belief in lycanthropy and werewolves belongs – was especially flourishing in the Carpathian mountains and in Transylvania, the very region where Bram Stoker situated the story of *Dracula*.[16]

Seasonal ceremonies during which young people wear wolf masks [...] are still popular in the Balkans, in Romania, especially in the twelve days between Christmas Eve and Epiphany. Originally these were ceremonies connected with the periodical return of the dead and they involved all kinds of animal masks: horse, wolf, goat, bear, etc.

It is interesting to note that similar beliefs underlie the initiatory rites of the Kwakiutl Indians. In the hut set aside for the initiation ceremony, the young *hamatsa* – members of the cannibal society – would transform themselves into wolves; 'as they devoured the corpses, they were possessed by a kind of furious madness, they would bite those next to them and swallow pieces of raw flesh'.[17]

These rituals may have corresponded to some vital function in hunting societies and systems of the totemic type. As a result of transformations we know very little about, and also no doubt of pressures brought to bear by hostile cultures – we shall see how Christianity is a factor operating against vampire rituals and lycanthropy – these elements moved into the realm of folklore, to survive only as isolated fragments, as 'superstitions' or picturesque curiosities. Finally they were taken up and exploited by literature (tales of fantasy of all kinds, Bram Stoker) and the cinema – but only, in my view, in so far as they found an echo in the unconscious, echoed in our unconscious fantasies. They are not difficult to find in the horror film. You have the return of the dead, the theme of the undead and the devouring of corpses – especially clear in *Night of the Living Dead*. The eating of human flesh becomes the more refined drinking of human blood and ends up as vampirism. The theme of the periodical return of the dead becomes the vampire's disappearance by day and reappearance at night, whether for reasons to do with the plot or because of the link with the rhythms of dreams and fantasy. Secret brotherhoods and groups of initiates reappear in the communities of vampires and followers of Satan – as depicted for instance by Roman Polanski in *Dance of the Vampires* and *Rosemary's Baby*. The ritual wearing of masks, which implies a mystical identification with the (totemic) animal, is interpreted literally (this being one of the main mechanisms, one of the ruses of the unconscious), so that characters acquire the ability to change their form, really to become animals. The handsome hero becomes a werewolf, Dracula becomes a dog or a vampire (a bat-like creature): the atmosphere of certain horror films is already defined in Iranian texts which speak of 'brigands' or 'prowlers' who live off corpses and terrorise the poor villagers.

The original figure of Zalmoxis, an immortal divinity of the Geto-Dacians, takes us into a more familiar, more traditional, religious universe, which is still alive in the horror story. The universal theme of the descent, down innumerable stairs, into the subterranean dwelling (grotto, cave, etc.) where gods, demons and the souls of the dead come to rest and where there are hidden riches, treasures and secrets, leads directly into Dracula's vault, a terrifying place where vampires and their secrets lie buried. In the opposite direction, in the upper regions, there is an obvious similarity between the flight of the vampires and a rite which features in the cult of Zalmoxis, namely the messenger projected into the air and pierced by lances, which could be related to the theme of Abaris flying on an arrow. Two points about Zalmoxis himself are also worth noting. He is known as King, as Master of Men; and the root of his name in Thracian, *zamol*, means Earth, power of the earth. Dracula, as we know, is Prince of Darkness and closely linked to the powers of the earth, if not even to their source.

All these beliefs are linked, furthermore, to shamanistic rites. The reference to shamanism invokes a network of fantasies relating to the body –

Dracula (Tod Browning, 1931)

the body dismembered or divided into pieces, the renewal of organs or viscera, the transformation and alteration of internal objects, death and resurrection given concrete expression – which finds a strong echo in horror films. This echo is generally deformed, however. A psychological split somehow imposed by the Manichean ideology of good and evil, which also fits in with the needs of a stereotyped narrative, gathers all the *negative* things together in Dracula's body: an empty body, a bottomless pit (insatiable mother), the illusory form, the delusion, impasse or failure of shamanistic magic. The *positive* things are organised around the figure of a research scientist, doctor or professor, the possessor of traditional and esoteric knowledge, who will succeed in defeating the vampire. But, in a sense, the struggle is conducted entirely in the arena of fetishism. The fetishes which together make up the Dracula form (as in a collage), and which are archaic in terms of the fantasies and the socio-cultural/religious strata they evoke, are contrasted with forms that are more recent but no less fetishised: the Cross and the Scientist, whose psychological and ideological virtue is to give expression, consistency and brilliance to the fetishistic values of the hegemonic culture.

VII It follows from everything I have said so far that one cannot proceed to a simple and linear analysis of fetishism in the horror film. Too many elements, factors and functions come into play, all of them different by virtue of their origins and the systems to which they pertain. Moreover, these elements, factors and functions have been constructed differently, and handled in ways that are often contradictory. A variety of approaches and combinations would seem to be called for. And yet, you only have to accept a degree of schematisation and ambiguity in this concept of fetishism for it to emerge as a framework and interpretative tool which can really help to organise and illuminate some of the most significant images and structures of the horror film, and especially those centred on Dracula and the theme of the Vampire. Freud's outline interpretation of fetishism, broken down into its component parts – the archaic mother and the mother's phallus, the sexualised phallic object, the missing phallus, the anxiety of castration, the specific defence mechanisms, etc. – will allow us to find our way in the gloomy labyrinths of Dracula's world.

VIII The *imago* of the archaic mother permeates the atmosphere of the horror film and underpins its development. We are dealing with a figure more complex and many-sided than might be thought. An essential aspect, as specified in Freud's analysis of fetishism, is the way she appears as a phallic woman, a woman with a penis, a murderous, all-devouring or castrating mother. She evokes the anxiety of castration in its primordial, founding intensity – more so than the father, with whom the son can struggle on equal terms as it were, even benefiting from maternal complicity and ever-increasing strength. This aspect is treated in such an obvious, detailed and realistic way in certain films that you reach the point where the realism and accurate observation create more of a clinical dimension than a specifically horrific atmosphere. Hitchcock's *Psycho*, with its strictly deliberate title, is a good example. The figure of the bad mother appears in this film as separate (since she doesn't completely invade the son's psyche until the very end), precise and obvious. The most horrific moment of the film, the scene that is the fantasmatic and emotional pivot of the whole story, is the one where the mother is everywhere, occupying the whole screen from one edge of the frame to the other. On one side, sitting in an armchair, is the mummified corpse of the mother, a grimacing skeleton, the real mother but the dead mother. On the other side, alive, bounding with energy, but 'unreal' and fantastic, a pathetic mask somehow combined with a dressing gown and a female wig, is the mother played by the son, the *imago* made concrete, along with the sign that advertises her function – the knife. The organisation of space gives concrete expression to the dramatic structure. There are three places which become progressively less intense and morbid: the house on the hill, the place of anxiety and terror from which the mother reigns over what is below, a forbidden monument dedicated to her destructive powers; the motel, the place where people come and go, and where the son's two personalities are also in transit, a place more and more empty or emptied of the son's presence as he becomes vampirically absorbed in the mother's house; and an outside world, an elsewhere, a multiform and dynamic reality to which the son no longer has access, a world content to send emissaries, to emit the signals which allow the psychosis to express itself and to be understood, a world that finally triumphs in the prolixity of the psychiatrist.

In *The Psychopath* by Freddie Francis, the great creator of horror films, the *imago* of the bad mother is treated in a more everyday and more rational context which allows the horror film and the thriller to be cleverly combined. The mother, supposedly paralysed and confined to a wheelchair, takes her revenge on those who harmed the father. She kills them one after the other, but not before giving the victim a warning in the form of a doll representing him. The mother reigns over a world of dolls and effigies – of fantasies. And the dominant, dominating fantasy is that of the son-doll, son-effigy, son-fetish. Just as the psychotic son in *Psycho* plays the criminal mother, the mother in *The Psychopath* – or so it would seem – plays out as a cripple the destiny she dreams of and brings into being for her son. The latter is the victim of an accident which, thanks to a bit of cunning detective work, can easily be traced back to her. She then proceeds to 'get him ready'. He is placed in an armchair, isolated in a cell, touched up and transformed into a doll – he is the mother's fetish in every way. Here again, as in *Psycho*, filmic space is organised according to the imaginary structure. On one side of the frame, in a high cell, confined to an armchair, sits the son-fetish, the mother's phallus in disguise, detached, erect, made flesh. From the other edge, the mother, now a threatening figure, appears all of a sudden with a knife. The mother is now agile and alive – alive by virtue of the son's symbolic death – getting ready to kill the young woman who might remove him from her control.

The reason why I have said so much about these two films is to bring out the contrast with horror films of the Dracula type where the mother figure is strikingly absent. In Tod Browning's classic *Dracula*, Dracula's three daughters make their appearance, but there is never any question of a mother. In Don Sharp's *Kiss of the Vampire* (1962), Count Ravno has a son and a daughter, but again there is no reference to a mother. I can, in fact, think of one film in the genre in which the son-vampire is kept locked away in a castle by his mother. When he is set free by a scatterbrained young girl, he proceeds to stalk his mother, an old lady of harmless demeanour. The emphasis on the fantastic and the picturesque in this variant only serves to underline the fact that the absent mother is a structural necessity. For the mother is not absent in the everyday, realistic sense. Her absence, or rather her non-presence, must be understood as a very archaic mode of presence, or again, as the massive, diffuse, irrefutable action or pressure of a very archaic maternal *imago* (= Form I in my diagram). This is perhaps the only way in which these things can be expressed. The concealment of the archaic mother cannot of course be given a concrete form, but it can be read in a series of enclosures and expulsions, in a movement whereby spaces, one inside the other, become progressively smaller and more confining, leading us finally to the purest, most original sign of archaic motherhood, a *pinch of earth*. The archaic mother can be expressed in this way – through a series of enclosures ever more rigorous, confining and distressing – because she is characterised in the first instance by her uterine, enveloping quality.

The fact that the opening sequences of the vampire films are virtually identical from a structural point of view clearly demonstrates that we are dealing, over and beyond the simple repetition of a narrative structure, with a basic, psychological meaning. Some vague call leads the hero (alone in *Dracula*, often accompanied by his dear wife in other films) to leave his familiar world (ruled by the reality principle). He embarks on a difficult journey across an unknown land characterised by desolate, threatening landscapes and steep, narrow, rocky roads which always seem to *close* behind him. This uncomfortable and perilous journey might already be described as a highly abridged, simplistic version of the great mythological quest. The traveller has passed the first test when he arrives in a little village, *closed in on itself* and on its fear, whose few inhabitants treat him with hostility, as an outsider. This hostile reaction, the warnings and threats he receives, are a kind of second test – which he sails through. The third test, and third enclosure, is a dark, dense, lonely forest, one that is *closed* with no other exit than the road, the umbilical cord that leads to the castle. This is the place for an accident, a *broken axle*, which leaves the hero alone, bereft, as it were lost and enveloped in the dark vegetation. Dracula's castle is a new and striking enclosure, the central precinct, the pivotal point where horizontal progression is transformed into vertical descent, it is the place in the middle where complex and contradictory determinations meet, clash and are explained; a place where meetings, dialogues, discoveries and confrontations take place – too full, too highly charged not to give rise to the conflagration that often marks the end of the story.

Envelopment and anxiety are taken a stage further when the hero, with a courage or rather a *naïvety*, a *lack of awareness* that makes us shudder, goes down a twisting staircase lined with *cobwebs* and through one *creaking* door after the other to the vault. This is an arched, dark, enveloping space, as *uterine* as you could possibly imagine. Here he finds himself *shut in*, no longer symbolically but physically. The process whereby space shrinks and symbolic forms become condensed or concentrated leads us – along with the hero – to a new envelope, a new receptacle: the coffin. And tradition dictates – as does the very meaning, logic and direction of the fantasy – that the *bottom* of the coffin should contain a little of the *native earth*, the maternal soil, that the vampire always carries with him. This latter sign may be omitted – there may be no earth or no mention of earth at the end of this process whereby spaces and forms are made to fit into each other – but it is nevertheless the point which the hero is always moving towards, the culmination of his quest.

The crossing of the different spaces amounts at each stage to a *transgression* which becomes ever more acute as the spatial or plastic form (castle, coffin, etc.) becomes smaller, more precise, more enveloping. This recurrent alternation between *prohibition* and *transgression* is related to another, similar alternation whose usefulness is obvious at the level of the narrative. Its most remarkable advantage, however, is that it allows us to sense the non-presence, the occultation of the mother on the fantasmatic level: the discovery of something – of something horrific, which is in fact the horrific thing itself, namely the phallus-fetish which carries the mother's absence in its very core, as an essential attribute – is generally preceded by something else that makes us aware of emptiness and lack. The territory which the hero explores at the beginning is deserted. The village appears at first sight to be abandoned. The hero finds himself alone in the big forest and the camera often lingers complacently over this threatening absence of living beings – until the carriage-hearse, sent or driven by the vampire, suddenly appears. The castle too seems deserted; they take a long time to open the door. Sometimes the door opens on its own; there is no one behind it, no one in the great hall, ancient or baroque, which the hero examines with obvious interest – until Dracula himself suddenly appears at the top of the stairs or from a secret door. There are long moments of emptiness in the basement or the crypt, and the coffin itself is often empty – until a presence suddenly emerges, bludgeoned into consciousness. As we might expect this horrific emptiness isn't simply negative. It is an emptiness full of fantasmatic activity and meaning, a silence full of muffled echoes. We have seen how it announces, contains, Dracula's subsequent appearances. It is also furnished more or less rhetorically with easily readable signs: great, forbidding doors or hidden ones; creaking sounds, rusty metal, chains; steep or rickety stairs, huge stone slabs; dust, rubbish, etc. All these elements relate back to the *imago* of the bad archaic mother. Bad for the hero, without any doubt, yet good for the vampire for whom she is a source of shelter, security and energy. This ambivalence, together with the basic concealment or occultation to which I have referred, suggests the notion of a still more archaic mother, a mother-thing situated beyond good and evil, beyond all organised forms and all events. This is a totalising and oceanic mother, a 'shadowy and deep unity',[18] evoking in the subject the anxiety of fusion and dissolution; a mother who comes before the discovery of the essential *béance*, that of the phallus. This mother is nothing but a fantasy inasmuch as she is only ever established as an omnipresent and all-powerful totality, an absolute being, by the very intuition – she has no phallus – that deposes her; also inasmuch as she is only made available to perception in the very act of her concealment (as the diagram shows – the big 'omnipresent mother' circle in Form I moves towards and disappears into the small 'occulted mother' circle in Form II); and finally – an essential point in this context – inasmuch as the story will only admit her as something that comes *before*, and this before is never perceived or named.

IX What, on the contrary, *is* perceived and named, what is present and actual, the fullest form, or so it would seem, larger than life, better than anything else, more insistent, more intense, always ready to occupy (with a flourish) the empty spaces and blank frames reserved for him (the big posters, the hoardings, the cinema displays are also, of course, all devoted to him), always there making his presence felt is Dracula – so much so that, thanks to the intervention of a demon-god and Freddie Francis, he becomes the target of a monk's courageous resolve; the form occupying a throne, towering above the castle, the village, the land, the whole universe; the fetish form. As a '*substitute for the mother's penis*', according to Freud's definition, he is a phallic form. This form is not directed towards creative erotic development or genital fulfilment, but *stands in for something else*. It depends on the mother figure, whose absence it incorporates as an essential characteristic, and it sets up as a memorial the very thing it should defend itself against. Sexual energy has served to transform the mother form (Form I) into a complicated, stable, reified product. The Dracula fetish may therefore be called a sexualised total object.

And this is exactly how he appears – not to see Dracula as a relatively full erotic form is one of the commonest mistakes. The vampire's phallic exhibitionism confirms his fetishistic nature. (A remark attributed to a fetishist in Freud's article is relevant here. His 'fetish was an athletic support-belt which could also be worn as bathing drawers'.[19] It hid the genitals, says Freud, and the difference between them, and made castration a present reality; but it might be added that the belt also enclosed, immobilised and showed off the genitals.) Dracula carries his body like an erect phallus: you only have to think of his usual stiff posture, his long black cape, his sudden appearances like a bolt from the blue. As if to emphasise this phallic value, the camera often marks a pause – while Dracula poses. In a film like *Nosferatu*, a prototype of the horror film, the human vampire, as it appears to us almost constantly, is nothing other than this erection, a walking phallus or 'phallambulist', as one might say in French.[20] His rigidity is at the same time, obviously, that of the corpse, but the signs of an aggressive sexuality are abundant and spectacular enough for us to be able to say that the phallic dimension predominates. Nosferatu might be called the Pointed One, bearing in mind all the simple and basic symbolism attached to pointedness. His face is pointed, so are his ears, his shoulders, his knees, his back and of course his nails and fangs. According to a primitive mental operation which prefers not to distinguish the structure of the parts from that of the whole, Nosferatu is an agglomeration of points.

The vampire as a walking phallus can only parade in front of us – out there on the catwalk. But the fantasy also needs its anchorage points, just as the story needs action. The (phallic) structure of the global form (Dracula) has to find an echo in other forms. It has to be embodied or reproduced in miniature. It requires precise details and markers around which psychic crystallisation can take place. It is here that the main clichéd images of the horror film come in. The internal form of the *castle* points towards the archaic mother, but its external form (a huge turreted building surrounded by jagged rocks), announces and demands the presence of the vampire's erect body. The famous *fangs*, the organs which express an aggressive sexuality, are not only the vampire's favourite sexual tool; they are also unique in that they can emerge from a woman's mouth – transforming her, via a striking return of the repressed, into the very thing that gave birth to the vampire form, the phallic woman, the bad mother. Fangs play a spectacular role in modern horror series, notably Terence Fisher's films; tightly clenched, claw-like *hands* are a feature of Tod Browning's *Dracula* and long pointed *nails* of Murnau's *Nosferatu*. The metaphor of the 'penetrating look' or 'piercing eyes' is taken literally – an effective way of displacing the phallic sign. Browning's Dracula has a look that radiates outwards, a laser beam, and the victim is mesmerised and overcome; in *Dracula has Risen from the Grave*, Freddie Francis takes the image of 'blood-shot eyes' to the extreme. Dracula's eyes are just this, and since an erection is produced by a rush of blood, the blood rushing into Dracula's eyes is an erection. The whole body and the various organs (eyes, hands, etc.) participate in the crucial act of the kiss-bite when the fangs, as they are sunk into the woman's neck (sometimes passionately) or the man's (aggressively rather), make two little slits, two little holes with the merest trace of blood around them – a remarkably condensed expression of the fetishistic link between sexuality and castration.[21]

X The Dracula form, the phallus-fetish, stands out against the background of the archaic mother and is part of that background. But the substitute for the missing penis, the absent phallus, can only be, in the last resort, an illusion, a delusion. According to the pattern of belief outlined earlier, the mother's penis is there – that's what we set out to demonstrate, and that's what the more spectacular aspects of the horror film insistently proclaim – and it isn't there. The originality of the horror film is that it manages to make us aware of the conjunction: it's there – it isn't there. Dracula makes his entry, he is there, he is seen by spectators and characters alike. And yet, as far as the logic of the fantasy is concerned, *he shouldn't be there*. This is where that remarkable device of the mirror comes in: Dracula is present in the room and he isn't present on the other side of the room, in the other half of reality caught in the mirror. This division, this splitting of reality into two sides which 'deny' each other – which finds its perfect model in the absence of the reflection in the mirror – takes various forms. Dracula has no shadow and makes no noise. We think he is dead and buried, but he isn't. He is all-powerful, he has a whole country under his control, he rules over a huge community, he's a kind of Superman, capable of the most staggering physical exploits. At the same time he is surprisingly weak, so much so that he depends on the services of a sick and deformed servant. By night he is everything, by day nothing. Dracula's fangs, a sharp, intense expression of his energy, are counterbalanced by what they produce, the two little holes where this energy, although it passes into a new recruit, is also lost, since the vampire circuit is never-ending. And even this typical action of the fangs is an illusion. You only have to pass a flame over the fresh wounds for healing to take place immediately: the vampire doesn't really bite, nothing has happened. Another split. Externally Dracula is lord and master, a formidable 'master of men' like Zalmoxis. But the religious form has been emptied, and inside there is nothing. Dracula's body does not bleed. And even that prestigious outer envelope, that impressive silhouette draped in black, is misleading. A stake driven into the heart is all it takes for it to crumble into dust and be blown away on the wind (*Horror of Dracula*).[22]

XI The anxiety of castration and the fantasies woven around the mother's phallus produce horror forms which, however all-consuming, have no exclusive monopoly over the cinema screen. There are other factors at work. Ideological pressures, economic and production constraints, and narrative structures complicate things – or make them simpler – and above all valorise certain kinds of defence. Already within the Dracula system, efficient mechanisms come into play; fetishisation is also an axis along which sexuality develops; and the creation of the fetish introduces a stable reference point, a certain order (too much, in many ways) to which the narrative ritual of the horror film partly corresponds (the linking of sequences, crucial moments, binary rhythms, etc.). Vampirism certainly operates in the direction of the two chasms in our diagram – no phallus and occulted mother. That's where all the energy disappears. But there remains the link between one vampire and the next. This establishes a bridge between two voids, thanks to which a newly established community or fraternity (the *Männerbunde* cited by

Mircea Eliade) can sweep away all distinctions (sexual, social, etc.) and obey only the law of desire. Around the cradle of the child born of the intercourse between Satan and Rosemary – a cradle in the negative, draped in black, with an inverted crucifix – the diabolists in *Rosemary's Baby* lyrically proclaim their solidarity. In a sense, the homosexual foreskin fetishist described by Masud Khan is doing the same thing in changing partners all the time – he is setting up a kind of community with himself as the centre.

It is clear, however, since the threat comes from the mother's absent phallus, that the principal defence is sex. The vampire, marked and fascinated by the mother's missing penis and identifying with the archaic mother, doesn't have a phallus but becomes one instead. He moves from what he does not *have* to what he can *be*, if only in illusion. Although so vulnerable to cowardly attacks in his coffin during the day, he performs a *tour de force* – according to Masud Khan's French expression – and turns his essential impotence and inertia into a paranoid aggression which at least opens up a huge field of action for him and preserves him from catatonic collapse, decomposition and disso-lution. Just as the vampire, by virtue of always turning towards other people, watching them, waiting for them, desiring them, ends up – not only because he sucks their blood – becoming a little like them, and finding a little consist-ency for his empty form, so the others, when confronted with the vampire, reveal the process of fetishisation which is at work in them. Struggling against the vampire's evil spells, the Scientist (in *Kiss of the Vampire*, *The Devil Rides Out*, etc.) looks in the book-fetish, in some Lovecraftian Necronomikon, for set recipes, little packages of knowledge – so many cabbalistic formulae to accom-pany the ritual handling of fetishistic objects. The delusions of the main protagonists are hardly more impressive than this reification of knowledge. How lightly the four English tourists in *Dracula – Prince of Darkness* make their way into the vampire's jaws! Is it possible to get rid of one's fantasms so easily, to leave one's anxieties behind, to ignore all threats, to go to Dracula's castle and be waited on hand and foot, as in some up-market holiday camp? In the end we're not surprised when the chubbiest of the four gracefully offers himself up to the sacrificial knife in the underground chamber, and a Dracula in powder form is regenerated by his rich, red blood.

Two privileged sexual instruments neutralise the vampire: the stake and the cross. Embedded in the vampire's heart, the stake destroys him completely – provided always that Dracula is immobilised and impotent in his coffin. It is usually the Scientist, the one supposed to know, who performs the operation. This is a decisive moment when reality triumphs over appearances; the true phallus (the vertical penis-stake) triumphs over the false one (Dracula lying horizontal and inert in the coffin, the maternal receptacle). From the fact that the vampire's whole being resided in his heart, we now gather that all the rest, his whole body, was only a disguise, a mask. A little blood spurts out of the heart as the stake is driven into it, but it then turns out to be hollow, a gaping wound. This is castration made flesh and blood and absence –

although in a flash of intuition and for a moment only, since straightaway its 'basis' disintegrates. The hero or scientist, as he stands in front of the little pile of ash indistinguishable from the native earth in the coffin henceforth forever closed, is left only with the feeling of terror overcome, of a nightmare dispelled.

The stake can only act, of course, on a Dracula already dead. The cross, on the contrary, is engaged in a permanent and highly active struggle with the vampire. It makes him flee, it burns him if it touches him, it pins him down. At the end of *Dracula has Risen from the Grave*, the cross becomes the stake, and the vampire is destroyed as he is impaled on it. This antagonism

Dracula has Risen from the Grave (Freddie Francis, 1968)

between the cross and the vampire could easily be seen as the survival of a conflict between primitive religions attached to the figure of the mother, which maintain magic and mystical relations with the animal world, and Christianity as the religion of the Father and especially the Son, inasmuch as the Son fully assumes the Father's power – the Father's sexual power. But in its struggle with Dracula as the fetishistic phallic form, the cross reveals and exaggerates its own phallic symbolism. It tends to escape from the religious and social system in which it is inscribed and to become a fetish, underlining the profoundly fetishistic character of the system as a whole. The cross, in the horror film, is not so much a symbol of Christianity as something that brings about a regression to a magic stage. It takes its place alongside all the paraphernalia of fetishism: the stake, garlic, amulets of all kinds. It is effective in its fight against the vampire only in so far as it shares his basic character. The magic transformation of the cross is very well described in *Curse of the Werewolf*. The hero is unable to struggle against the sinister fate of becoming a werewolf. Although love succeeds for a while in postponing the evil moment – in *Nosferatu* also only love can triumph over the vampire – his criminal instincts carry the day, and he embarks on a killing spree. The kindness of a priest and his adoptive father's affectionate concern have no effect on him: the only way to stop the senseless carnage is to strike him with a silver bullet made from the metal of a crucifix. The crucifix very clearly loses, abandons, its religious form to become quite simply a magic projectile – one which has a phallic value because it is the colour of semen and has ejaculatory properties. And it is the father who administers the *coup de grâce*, presenting us with the spectacle of an inverted Christianity. Instead of the Son made God, crucified only to rise again from the dead, the son turned beast is struck down at the top of the church and totally annihilated.

Running parallel to fetishism or within its system, other aspects of the horror film might have been mentioned. Certainly, there is a great deal to say about the treatment of death; and I have not spoken of a fantasy which runs very deep and is hard to pin down: that of the missing breast, linked to the desire of the male to bear a child. Certain things that Dracula does would support this suggestion. When he kisses/bites his victim, he cradles him as if to feed him; he carries him in his arms down to the vault, like a baby or like a bride. Are not his devouring powers (his fangs), his insatiable thirst (vampirism is a bottomless pit, the mythological vessel full of holes) the other side (this side, for the spectator) of a primeval desire to provide food and drink, to be the inexhaustible mother?

'*But all the same*' ... this is cinema. In other words, individual motivations, fantasies and interests come into play, are recognised and handled within aesthetic, social, ideological and economic systems which do not fail to impose their laws. While responsibility for the fetishistic perversion is assumed by the fetishist alone, in his agonising uniqueness, in the cinema the spectator's potential for perversion is managed by the institution. This potential is summoned by the institution which 'deals with it' so that the anxieties and fantasies themselves feed the process of alienation. But by way of compensation, as it were, society also provides *catharsis*. What this means, when all is said and done, is that the distribution of fetishistic values over various systems – from the fantasmatic to the economic, from the narrative to the religious or folkloric – gives the subject room for play; it introduces slippage and mobility. The interplay of fantasy, form and ideology thus also lends itself to political analysis.

Translated by Annwyl Williams

This article appeared, in a different translation, in *Enclitic*, vol. 1 no. 2, 1977.

NOTES

Translator's notes are given in square brackets.

1 J. Strachey (ed.) and trans., *The Standard Edition of the Complete Psychological Works of Sigmund Freud* [*SE*] (London: Hogarth Press, 1953–66), vol. XXI, pp. 149–57.

2 [*SE*, vol. XXI, p. 152.]

3 [*SE*, vol. XXI, pp. 152–3.]

4 [*SE*, vol. XXI, p. 154.]

5 [*SE*, vol. XXI, p. 157.]

6 [*SE*, vol. XXI, p. 155.]

7 [There is no satisfactory English equivalent for the French intellectual use of the term 'bricolage' which is associated with the work of Claude Lévi-Strauss. *Collins-Robert* gives 'tinkering about', 'do-it-yourself' and 'odd jobs'. The emphasis is on putting something together (or repairing something) using the materials to hand.]

8 [*SE*, vol. XXI, p. 154.]

9 Octave Mannoni, *Clefs pour l'imaginaire, ou, l'Autre scène* (Paris: Editions du Seuil, 1969).

10 [This is the English translation given by J. Laplanche and J.-B. Pontalis in *Vocabulaire de la Psychanalyse* (Paris: Presses Universitaires de France, 1968), p. 115.]

11 D. C. Talayesva, *Sun Chief. The Autobiography of a Hopi Indian*, ed. Leo W. Simmons (New Haven and London: Yale University Press, 1963 [copyright 1942]).

12 [*Béance* is a Lacanian term difficult to translate into English. 'Gaping hole' is a close equivalent but only very marginally acceptable, if at all, as a translation. I also render the term by 'absence', or leave the word in French.]

13 [*SE*, vol. I, p. 243.]

14 [This is a term used by Freud in his article on *Fetishism*. It refers to the complete obliteration of a perception 'so that the result is the same as when a visual impression falls on a blind spot in the retina' (*SE*, vol. XXI, pp. 153–4). But 'scotomiser' in French is also a more ordinary word than 'scotomise' in English.]

15 *De Zalmoxis à Gengis-Khan* (Payot, 1970).

16 Bram Stoker, *Dracula* (London: Constable and Co., 1897). *The Annotated Dracula*, exact reproduction of the text from the first edition of Bram Stoker's *Dracula*, ed. Leonard Wolf (London: New English Library, 1975).

17 Robert Eisler's work, *Man into Wolf. An Anthropological Interpretation of Sadism, Masochism and Lycanthropy* (London: Routledge and Kegan Paul, 1951/New York: Philosophical Library, 1952) provides a huge amount of documentary material on these themes. Working in an anthropological/evolutionary perspective, Eisler considers sadism and lycanthropy to be the archetypal imprints on the human psyche of the disturbing transition from a frugivorous, vegetarian, pacificist state to a carnivorous and predatory one. He supports this thesis with an amazing range of references – mythological, ethnographic, historical, literary, psychological, etc.

18 ['Une ténébreuse et profonde unité'. This is a quotation from Baudelaire's poem 'Correspondances' (*Les Fleurs du Mal*, ed. A. Adam, Paris: Garnier, 1961, p. 13, line 6)].

19 [*SE*, vol. XXI, p. 156.]

20 [By analogy with 'somnambule' = sleepwalker.]

21 Erections of the fangs, the eyes and even the skin, associated with magnetism and snake-taming, come into their own in John Gilling's *The Reptile* (1966). The reptile woman, who bites her victims and infects them with 'the black death', is nothing but a *montage*: the head is made out of huge, bulging eyes, enormous fangs and scaly skin; it is 'mounted' on a female body which doesn't really exist, is only a pretence. This snake is tamed and 'set up' by an exotic character representing a secret and primitiive sect, the Sect of the Snake, which wields its power in a strictly magnetic way: infantile omnipotence of thought! The overdetermination of symbols and archaic references is further enriched by a cosmic dimension: the woman-reptile simulacrum can only be kept in a basement which houses a boiling spring, a true image of the beginning of the world, a primal chaos. Gilling's film is further characterised by a remarkable confrontation between spaces invested with a different value (the castle, the cottage, the inn); it would seem that at a certain level of regression, the characters, who probably depend too much on cultural systems of perception, lose their ability to signify, and spatial figures, closely linked to elementary tactile and motor values, take over.

22 [The American title of the 1958 remake of *Dracula*, directed by Terence Fisher.]

Horror and the Monstrous-Feminine
An Imaginary Abjection
BARBARA CREED

Mother ... isn't quite herself today   *Norman Bates,* PSYCHO

I
All human societies have a conception of the monstrous-feminine, of what it is about woman that is shocking, terrifying, horrific, abject. 'Probably no male human being is spared the terrifying shock of threatened castration at the sight of the female genitals,' Freud wrote in his paper, 'Fetishism' in 1927.[1] Joseph Campbell, in his book, *Primitive Mythology*, noted that:

> ... there is a motif occurring in certain primitive mythologies, as well as in modern surrealist painting and neurotic dream, which is known to folklore as 'the toothed vagina' – the vagina that castrates. And a counterpart, the other way, is the so-called 'phallic mother,' a motif perfectly illustrated in the long fingers and nose of the witch.[2]

Classical mythology also was populated with gendered monsters, many of which were female. The Medusa, with her 'evil eye', head of writhing serpents and lolling tongue, was queen of the pantheon of female monsters; men unfortunate enough to look at her were turned immediately to stone.

It is not by accident that Freud linked the sight of the Medusa to the equally horrifying sight of the mother's genitals, for the concept of the monstrous-feminine, as constructed within/by patriarchal and phallocentric ideology, is related intimately to the problem of sexual difference and castration. In 1922 he argued that the 'Medusa's head takes the place of a representation of the female genitals';[3] if we accept Freud's interpretation, we can see that the Perseus myth is mediated by a narrative about the *difference* of female sexuality as a difference which is grounded in monstrousness and which invokes castration anxiety in the male spectator. 'The sight of the Medusa's head makes the spectator stiff with terror, turns him to stone.'[4] The irony of this was not lost on Freud, who pointed out that becoming stiff also means having an erection. 'Thus in the original situation it offers consolation to the spectator: he is still in possession of a penis, and the stiffening reassures him of the fact.'[5] One wonders if the experience of horror – of viewing the horror film – causes similar alterations in the body of the male spectator. And what of other phrases that apply to both male and female viewers – phrases such as: 'It scared the shit out of me'; 'It made me feel sick'; 'It gave me the creeps'? What is the relationship between physical states, bodily wastes (even if metaphoric ones) and the horrific – in particular, the monstrous-feminine?

II Julia Kristeva's *Powers of Horror*[6] provides us with a preliminary hypothesis for an analysis of these questions. Although this study is concerned with literature, it nevertheless suggests a way of situating the monstrous-feminine in the horror film in relation to the maternal figure and what Kristeva terms 'abjection', that which does not 'respect borders, positions, rules' ... that which 'disturbs identity, system, order' (p. 4). In general terms, Kristeva is attempting to explore the different ways in which abjection, as a source of horror, works within patriarchal societies, as a means of separating the human from the non-human and the fully constituted subject from the partially formed subject. Ritual becomes a means by which societies both renew their initial contact with the abject element and then exclude that element.

Through ritual, the demarcation lines between human and non-human are drawn up anew and presumably made all the stronger for that process. One of the key figures of abjection is the mother who becomes an abject at that moment when the child rejects her for the father who represents the symbolic order. The problem with Kristeva's theory, particularly for feminists, is that she never makes clear her position on the oppression of women. Her theory moves uneasily between explanation of, and justification for, the formation of human societies based on the subordination of women.

Kristeva grounds her theory of the maternal in the abject, tracing its changing definitions from the period of the pagan or mother-goddess religions through to the time of Judaic monotheism and to its culmination in Christianity. She deals with abjection in the following forms: as a rite of defilement in paganism; as a biblical abomination, a taboo, in Judaism; and as self-defilement, an interiorisation, in Christianity. Kristeva, however, does not situate abjection solely within a ritual or religious context. She argues that it is 'rooted historically (in the history of religions) and subjectively (in the structuration of the subject's identity), in the cathexis of maternal function – mother, woman, reproduction' (p. 91). Kristeva's central interest, however, lies with the structuring of subjectivity within and by the processes of abjectivity in which the subject is spoken by the abject through both religious and cultural discourses, that is, through the subject's position within the practices of the rite as well as within language.

> But the question for the analyst-semiologist is to know how far one can analyze ritual impurity. The historian of religion stops soon: the critically impure is that which is based on a natural 'loathing'. The anthropologist goes further: there is nothing 'loathsome' in itself; the loathsome is that which disobeys classification rules peculiar to the given symbolic system. But as far as I am concerned, I keep asking questions. . . . Are there no subjective structurations that, within the organization of each speaking being, correspond to this or that symbolic-social system and represent, if not stages, at least *types* of subjectivity and society? Types that would be defined, in the last analysis, according to the subject's position in language . . .? (p. 92)

A full examination of this theory is outside the scope of this article; I propose to draw mainly on Kristeva's discussion of abjection in its construction in the human subject in relation to her notions of (a) the 'border' and (b) the mother-child relationship. At crucial points, I shall also refer to her writing on the abject in relation to religious discourses. This area cannot be ignored, for what becomes apparent in reading her work is that definitions of the monstrous as constructed in the modern horror text are grounded in ancient religious and historical notions of abjection – particularly in relation to the following religious 'abominations': sexual immorality and perversion; corporeal alteration, decay and death; human sacrifice; murder; the corpse; bodily wastes; the feminine body and incest.

The place of the abject is 'the place where meaning collapses' (p. 2), the place where 'I' am not. The abject threatens life; it must be 'radically excluded' (p. 2) from the place of the living subject, propelled away from the body and deposited on the other side of an imaginary border which separates the self from that which threatens the self. Kristeva quotes Bataille:

> Abjection (. . .) is merely the inability to assume with sufficient strength the imperative act of excluding abject things (and that act establishes the foundations of collective existence). (p. 56)

Although the subject must exclude the abject, it must, nevertheless, be tolerated, for that which threatens to destroy life also helps to define life. Further, the activity of exclusion is necessary to guarantee that the subject take up his/her proper place in relation to the symbolic.

> To each ego its object, to each superego its abject. It is not the white expanse or slack boredom of repression, not the translations and transformations of desire that wrench bodies, nights and discourse; rather it is a brutish suffering that 'I' puts up with, sublime and devastated, for 'I' deposits it to the father's account (*verse au père* – *père-version*): I endure it, for I imagine such is the desire of the other. . . . On the edge of non-existence and hallucination, of a reality that, if I acknowledge it, annihilates me. There, abject and abjection are my safeguards. The primers of my culture. (p. 2)

The abject can be experienced in various ways – one of which relates to biological bodily functions, the other of which has been inscribed in a symbolic (religious) economy. For instance, Kristeva claims that food loathing is 'perhaps the most elementary and archaic form of abjection' (p. 2). Food, however, only becomes abject if it signifies a border 'between two distinct entities or territories' (p. 75). Kristeva describes how, for her, the skin on the top of milk, which is offered to her by her father and mother, is a 'sign of their desire', a sign separating her world from their world, a sign which she does not want. 'But since the food is not an "other" for "me", who am only in their desire, I expel *myself*, I spit *myself* out, I abject *myself* within the same motion through which "I" claim to establish *myself*' (p. 3). Dietary prohibitions are, of course, central to Judaism. Kristeva argues that these are directly related to the prohibition of incest; she argues this not just because this position is supported by psychoanalytic discourse and structural anthropology but also because 'the biblical text, as it proceeds, comes back, at the intensive moments of its demonstration and expansion, to that mytheme of the archaic relation to the mother' (p. 106).

The ultimate in abjection is the corpse. The body protects itself from bodily wastes such as shit, blood, urine and pus by ejecting these substances just as it expels food that, for whatever reason, the subject finds loathsome. The body extricates itself from them and from the place where they fall, so that it might continue to live.

> Such wastes drop so that I might live, until, from loss to loss, nothing remains in me and my entire body falls beyond the limit – *cadere*, cadaver. If dung signifies the other side of the border, the place where I am not and which permits me to be, the corpse, the most sickening of wastes, is a border that has encroached upon everything. It is no longer I who expel. 'I' is expelled. (pp. 3–4)

Within the biblical context, the corpse is also utterly abject. It signifies one of the most basic forms of pollution – the body without a soul. As a form of waste it represents the opposite of the spiritual, the religious symbolic.

> Corpse fanciers, unconscious worshippers of a soulless body, are thus preeminent representatives of inimical religions, identified by their murderous cults. The priceless debt to great mother nature, from which the prohibitions of Yahwistic speech separates us, is concealed in such pagan cults. (p. 109)

In relation to the horror film, it is relevant to note that several of the most popular horrific figures are 'bodies without souls' (the vampire), the 'living corpse' (the zombie) and corpse-eater (the ghoul). Here, the horror film constructs and confronts us with the fascinating, seductive aspect of abjection. What is also interesting is that such ancient figures of abjection as the vampire, the ghoul, the zombie and the witch (one of whose many crimes was that she used corpses for her rites of magic) continue to provide some of the most compelling images of horror in the modern cinema. The werewolf, whose body signifies a collapse of the boundaries between human and animal, also belongs to this category.

Abjection also occurs where the individual fails to respect the law and where the individual is a hypocrite, a liar, a traitor.

> Any crime, because it draws attention to the fragility of the law, is abject, but premeditated crime, cunning murder, hypocritical revenge are even more so because they heighten the display of such fragility. He who denies morality is not abject; there can be grandeur in amorality.... Abjection, on the other hand, is immoral, sinister, scheming, and shady.... (p. 4)

Thus, abject things are those which highlight the 'fragility of the law' and which exist on the other side of the border which separates out the living subject from that which threatens its extinction. But abjection is not something of which the subject can ever feel free – it is always there, beckoning the self to take up its place, the place where meaning collapses. The subject, constructed in/through language, through a desire for meaning, is also spoken by the abject, the place of meaninglessness – thus, the subject is constantly beset by abjection which fascinates desire but which must be repelled for fear of self-annihilation. The crucial point is that abjection is always ambiguous. Like Bataille, Kristeva emphasises the attraction, as well as the horror, of the undifferentiated.

> We may call it a border; abjection is above all ambiguity. Because, while releasing a hold, it does not radically cut off the subject from what threatens it – on the contrary, abjection acknowledges it to be in perpetual danger. But also because abjection itself is a composite of judgement and affect, of condemnation and yearning, of signs and drives. Abjection preserves what existed in the archaism of pre-objectal relationship. . . . (pp. 9–10)

To the extent that abjection works on the socio-cultural arena, the horror film would appear to be, in at least three ways, an illustration of the work of abjection. Firstly, the horror film abounds in images of abjection, foremost of which is the corpse, whole and mutilated, followed by an array of bodily wastes such as blood, vomit, saliva, sweat, tears and putrifying flesh. In terms of Kristeva's notion of the border, when we say such-and-such a horror film 'made me sick' or 'scared the shit out of me' we are actually foregrounding that specific horror film as a 'work of abjection' or 'abjection at work' – in both a literal and metaphoric sense. Viewing the horror film signifies a desire not only for perverse pleasure (confronting sickening, horrific images, being filled with terror/desire for the undifferentiated) but also a desire, having taken pleasure in perversity, to throw up, throw out, eject the abject (from the safety of the spectator's seat).

Secondly, there is, of course, a sense in which the concept of a border is central to the construction of the monstrous in the horror film; that which crosses or threatens to cross the 'border' is abject. Although the specific nature of the border changes from film to film, the function of the monstrous remains the same – to bring about an encounter between the symbolic order and that which threatens its stability. In some horror films the monstrous is produced at the border between human and inhuman, man and beast (*Dr Jekyll and Mr Hyde*, *Creature from the Black Lagoon*, *King Kong*); in others the border is between the normal and the supernatural, good and evil (*Carrie*, *The Exorcist*, *The Omen*, *Rosemary's Baby*); or the monstrous is produced at the border which separates those who take up their proper gender roles from those who do not (*Psycho*, *Dressed to Kill*, *Reflection of Fear*); or the border is between normal and abnormal sexual desire (*Cruising*, *The Hunger*, *Cat People*).

In relation to the construction of the abject within religious discourses, it is interesting to note that various sub-genres of the horror film seem to correspond to religious categories of abjection. For instance, blood as a religious abomination becomes a form of abjection in the 'splatter' movie (*Texas Chainsaw Massacre*); cannibalism, another religious abomination, is central to the 'meat' movie (*Night of the Living Dead*, *The Hills Have Eyes*); the corpse as abomination becomes the abject of ghoul and zombie movies (*The Evil Dead*; *Zombie Flesheaters*); blood as a taboo object within religion is central to the vampire film (*The Hunger*) as well as the horror film in general (*Bloodsucking Freaks*); human sacrifice as a religious abomination is constructed as the abject of virtually all horror films; and bodily disfigurement as a religious abomination is also central to the slasher movie, particularly those in which woman is slashed, the mark a sign of her 'difference', her impurity (*Dressed to Kill*, *Psycho*).

III The third way in which the horror film illustrates the work of abjection refers to the construction of the maternal figure as abject. Kristeva argues that all individuals experience abjection at the time of their earliest attempts to break away from the mother. She sees the mother-child relation as one marked by conflict: the child struggles to break free but the mother is reluctant to release it. Because of the 'instability of the symbolic function' in relation to this most crucial area – 'the prohibition placed on the maternal body (as a defense against autoeroticism and incest taboo)' (p. 14) – Kristeva argues that the maternal body becomes a site of conflicting desires. 'Here, drives hold sway and constitute a strange space that I shall name, after Plato (*Times*, 48–53), a *chora*, a receptacle' (p. 14). The position of the child is rendered even more unstable because, while the mother retains a close hold over the child, it can serve to authenticate her existence – an existence which needs validation because of her problematic relation to the symbolic realm.

> It is a violent, clumsy breaking away, with the constant risk of falling back under the sway of a power as securing as it is stifling. The difficulty the mother has in acknowledging (or being acknowledged by) the symbolic realm – in other words, the problem she has with the phallus that her father or husband stands for – is not such as to help the future subject leave the natural mansion. (p. 13)

In the child's attempts to break away, the mother becomes an abject; thus, in this context, where the child struggles to become a separate subject, abjection becomes '*a precondition of narcissism*' (p. 13). Once again we can see abjection at work in the horror text where the child struggles to break away from the mother, representative of the archaic maternal figure, in a context in which the father is invariably absent (*Psycho*, *Carrie*, *The Birds*). In these films, the maternal figure is constructed as the monstrous-feminine. By refusing to relinquish her hold on her child, she prevents it from taking up its proper place in relation to the Symbolic. Partly consumed by the desire to remain locked in a blissful relationship with the mother and partly terrified of separation, the child finds it easy to succumb to the comforting pleasure of the dyadic relationship. Kristeva argues that a whole area of religion has assumed the function of tackling this danger:

> This is precisely where we encounter the rituals of defilement and their derivatives, which, based on the feeling of abjection and all converging on the maternal, attempt to symbolize the other threat to the subject: that of being swamped by the dual relationship, thereby risking the loss not of a part (castration) but of the totality of his living being. The function of these religious rituals is to ward off the subject's fear of his very own identity sinking irretrievably into the mother. (p. 64)

How, then, are prohibitions against contact with the mother enacted and enforced? In answering this question, Kristeva links the universal practices of rituals of defilement to the mother. She argues that within the practices of all rituals of defilement, polluting objects fall into two categories: excremental, which threatens identity from the outside, and menstrual, which threatens from within.

> Excrement and its equivalents (decay, infection, disease, corpse, etc.) stand for the danger to identity that comes from without: the ego threatened by the non-ego, society threatened by its outside, life by death. Menstrual blood, on the contrary, stands for the danger issuing from within identity (social or sexual); it threatens the relationship between the sexes within a social aggregate and, through internaliza-tion, the identity of each sex in the face of sexual difference. (p. 71)

Both categories of polluting objects relate to the mother; the relation of men-strual blood is self-evident, the association of excremental objects with the maternal figure is brought about because of the mother's role in sphincteral training. Here, Kristeva argues that the subject's first contact with 'authority' is with the maternal authority when the child learns, through interaction with the mother, about its body: the shape of the body, the clean and unclean, the proper and improper areas of the body. Kristeva refers to this process as a 'primal mapping of the body' which she calls 'semiotic'. She distinguishes between maternal 'authority' and 'paternal laws':

> Maternal authority is the trustee of that mapping of the self's clean and proper body; it is distinguished from paternal laws within which, with the phallic phase and acquisition of language, the destiny of man will take shape. (p. 72)

In her discussion of rituals of defilement in relation to the Indian caste system, Kristeva draws a distinction between the maternal authority and paternal law. She argues that the period of the 'mapping of the self's clean and proper body' is characterised by the exercise of 'authority without guilt', a time when there is a 'fusion between mother and nature'. However, the symbolic ushers in a 'totally different universe of socially signifying performances where embarrass-ment, shame, guilt, desire etc. come into play – the order of the phallus'. In the

Indian context, these two worlds exist harmoniously side by side because of the working of defilement rites. Here, Kristeva is referring to the practice of public defecation in India. She quotes V. S. Naipaul who says that no one ever mentions 'in speech or in books, those squatting figures, because, quite simply, no one sees them'. Kristeva argues that this split between the world of the mother (a universe without shame) and the world of the father (a universe of shame), would in other social contexts produce psychosis; in India, it finds a 'perfect socialization':

> This may be because the setting up of the rite of defilement takes on the function of the hyphen, the virgule, allowing the two universes of *filth* and *prohibition* to brush lightly against each other without necessarily being identified as such, as *object* and as *law*. (p. 74)

Images of blood, vomit, pus, shit, etc., are central to our culturally/socially constructed notions of the horrific. They signify a split between two orders: the maternal authority and the law of the father. On the one hand, these images of bodily wastes threaten a subject that is already constituted, in relation to the symbolic, as 'whole and proper'. Consequently, they fill the subject – both the protagonist in the text and the spectator in the cinema – with disgust and loathing. On the other hand, they also point back to a time when a 'fusion between mother and nature' existed; when bodily wastes, while set apart from the body, were not seen as objects of embarrassment and shame. Their presence in the horror film may invoke a response of disgust from the audience situated as it is within the symbolic but at a more archaic level the representation of bodily wastes may invoke pleasure in breaking the taboo on filth – sometimes described as a pleasure in perversity – and a pleasure in returning to that time when the mother-child relationship was marked by an untrammelled pleasure in 'playing' with the body and its wastes.

The modern horror film often 'plays' with its audience, saturating it with scenes of blood and gore, deliberately pointing to the fragility of the symbolic order in the domain of the body which never ceases to signal the repressed world of the mother. This is particularly evident in *The Exorcist*, where the world of the symbolic, represented by the priest-as-father, and the world of the pre-symbolic, represented by woman aligned with the devil, clashes head-on in scenes where the foulness of woman is signified by her putrid, filthy body covered in blood, urine, excrement and bile. Significantly, a pubescent girl about to menstruate played the woman who is possessed – in one scene blood from her wounded genitals mingles with menstrual blood to provide one of the film's key images of horror. In *Carrie*, the film's most monstrous act occurs when the couple are drenched in pig's blood which symbolises menstrual blood – women are referred to in the film as 'pigs', women 'bleed like pigs', and the pig's blood runs down Carrie's body at a moment of intense pleasure, just as her own menstrual blood runs down her legs during a similar pleasurable moment when she enjoys her body in the shower. Here, women's blood and pig's blood flow together, signifying horror, shame and humiliation. In this film, however, the mother speaks for the symbolic, identifying with an order which has defined women's sexuality as the source of all evil and menstruation as the sign of sin. The horror film's obsession with blood, particularly the bleeding body of woman, where her body is transformed into the 'gaping wound', suggests that castration anxiety is a central concern of the horror film – particularly the slasher sub-genre. Woman's body is slashed and mutilated, not only to signify her own castrated state, but also the possibility of castration for the male. In the guise of a 'madman' he enacts on her body the one act he most fears for himself, transforming her entire body into a bleeding wound.

Kristeva's semiotic posits a pre-verbal dimension of language which relates to sounds and tone and to direct expression of the drives and physical contact with the maternal figure; 'it is dependent upon meaning, but in a way that is not that of *linguistic* signs nor of the *symbolic* order they found' (p. 72). With the subject's entry into the symbolic, which separates the child from the mother, the maternal figure and the authority she signifies are repressed. Kristeva argues that it is the function of defilement rites, particularly those relating to menstrual and excremental objects, to point to the 'boundary' between the maternal semiotic authority and the paternal symbolic law.

> Through language and within highly hierarchical religious institutions, man hallucinates partial 'objects' – witnesses to an archaic differentia-tion of the body on its way toward ego identity, which is also sexual identity. The *defilement* from which ritual protects us is neither sign nor matter. Within the rite that extracts it from repression and depraved desire, defilement is the translinguistic spoor of the most archaic boun-daries of the self's clean and proper body. In that sense, if it is a jettisoned object, it is so from the mother. . . . By means of the symbolic institution of ritual, that is to say, by means of a system of ritual exclusions, the partial-object consequently becomes *scription* – an inscription of limits, an emphasis placed not on the (paternal) Law but on (maternal) Authority through the very signifying order. (p. 73)

Kristeva argues that, historically, it has been the function of religion to purify the abject but with the disintegration of these 'historical forms' of religion, the work of purification now rests solely with 'that catharsis par excellence called art'. (p. 17)

> In a world in which the Other has collapsed, the aesthetic task – a descent into the foundations of the symbolic construct – amounts to retracing the fragile limits of the speaking being, closest to its dawn, to the bottomless 'primacy' constituted by primal repression. Through that experience, which is nevertheless managed by the Other, 'subject' and 'object' push each other away, confront each other, collapse, and start again – inseparable, contaminated, condemned, at the boundary of what is assimilable, thinkable: abject. (p. 18)

This, I would argue, is also the central ideological project of the popular horror film – purification of the abject through a 'descent into the foundations of the symbolic construct'. In this way, the horror film brings about a confrontation with the abject (the corpse, bodily wastes, the monstrous-feminine) in order, finally, to eject the abject and re-draw the boundaries between the human and non-human. As a form of modern defilement rite, the horror film works to separate out the symbolic order from all that threatens its stability, particularly the mother and all that her universe signifies. In Kristeva's terms, this means separating out the maternal authority from paternal law.

As I mentioned earlier, the central problem with Kristeva's theory is that it can be read in a prescriptive rather than a descriptive sense. This problem is rendered more acute by the fact that, although Kristeva distinguishes between the maternal and paternal figures, when she speaks of the subject who is being constituted, she never distinguishes between the child as male or female. Obviously, the female child's experience of the semiotic chora must be different from that of the male's experience in relation to the way it is spoken to, handled, etc. For the mother is already constituted as a gendered subject living within a patriarchal order and thus aware of the differences between the 'masculine' and the 'feminine' in relation to questions of desire. Thus, the mother might relate to a male child with a more acute sense of pride and pleasure. It is also possible that the child, depending on its gender, might find it more or less difficult to reject the mother for the father. Kristeva does not consider any of these issues. Nor does she distinguish between the relation of the adult male and female subject to rituals of defilement – for instance, menstruation taboos, where one imagines notions of the gendered subject would be of crucial importance. How, for instance, do women relate to rites of defilement, such as menstruation rites which reflect so negatively on them? How do women within a specific cultural group see themselves in relation to taboos which construct their procreative functions as abject? Is it possible to intervene in the social construction of woman as abject? Or is the subject's relationship to the processes of abjection, as they are constructed within subjectivity and language, completely unchangeable? Is the abjection of women a precondition for the continuation of sociality? Kristeva never asks questions of this order. Consequently her theory of abjection could be interpreted as an apology for the establishment of sociality at the cost of women's equality. If, however, we read it as descriptive, as one which is attempting to explain the origins of patriarchal culture, then it provides us with an extremely useful hypothesis for an investigation of the representation of women in the horror film.[7]

IV The science-fiction horror film *Alien* is a complex representation of the monstrous-feminine in terms of the maternal figure as perceived within a patriarchal ideology. She is there in the text's scenarios of the primal scene, of birth and death; she is there in her many guises as the treacherous mother, the oral sadistic mother, the mother as primordial abyss; and she is there in the film's images of blood, of the all-devouring vagina, the toothed vagina, the vagina as Pandora's box; and finally she is there in the chameleon figure of the alien, the monster as fetish-object of and for the mother. But it is the archaic mother, the reproductive/generative mother, who haunts the *mise en scène* of the film's first section, with its emphasis on different representations of the primal scene.

According to Freud, every child either watches its parents in the act of sexual intercourse or has phantasies about that act – phantasies which relate to the problem of origins. Freud left open the question of the cause of the phantasy but suggested that it may initially be aroused by 'an observation of the sexual intercourse of animals'.[8] In his study of 'the Wolf Man', Freud argued that the child did not initially observe his parents in the act of sexual intercourse but that he witnessed the copulation of animals whose behaviour he then displaced onto his parents. In situations where the child actually witnesses sexual intercourse between its parents, Freud argued that all children arrive at the same conclusion: 'They adopt what may be called a *sadistic view of coition*'.[9] If the child perceives the primal scene as a monstrous act – whether in reality or phantasy – it may phantasise animals or mythical creatures as taking part in the scenario. Possibly the many mythological stories in which humans copulate with animals and other creatures (Europa and Zeus, Leda and the Swan) are reworkings of the primal scene narrative. The Sphinx, with her lion's body and woman's face, is an interesting figure in this context. Freud suggested that the Riddle of the Sphinx was probably a distorted version of the great riddle that faces all children – Where do babies come from? An extreme form of the primal phantasy is that of 'observing parental intercourse while one is still an unborn baby in the womb'.[10]

One of the major concerns of the sci-fi horror film (*Alien, The Thing, Invasion of the Body Snatchers, Altered States*) is the reworking of the primal scene in relation to the representation of other forms of copulation and pro-creation. *Alien* presents various representations of the primal scene. Behind each of these lurks the figure of the archaic mother, that is, the image of the mother in her generative function – the mother as the origin of all life. This archaic figure is somewhat different from the mother of the semiotic chora, posed by Kristeva, in that the latter is the pre-Oedipal mother who exists in relation to the family and the symbolic order. The concept of the parthenogenic, archaic mother adds another dimension to the maternal figure and presents us with a new way of understanding how patriarchal ideology works to deny the 'difference' of woman in her cinematic representation.

The first birth scene occurs in *Alien* at the beginning, where the camera/spectator explores the inner space of the mother-ship whose life support system is a computer aptly named – 'Mother'. This exploratory sequence of the inner body of the 'Mother' culminates with a long tracking shot down one of the corridors which leads to a womb-like chamber where the crew of seven are woken up from their protracted sleep by Mother's voice monitoring a call for help from a nearby planet. The seven astronauts emerge slowly from their sleep pods in what amounts to a re-birthing scene which is marked by a fresh, antiseptic atmosphere. In outer space, birth is a well controlled, clean, painless affair. There is no blood, trauma or terror. This scene could be interpreted as a primal fantasy in which the human subject is born fully developed – even copulation is redundant.

The second representation of the primal scene takes place when three of the crew enter the body of the unknown space-ship through a 'vaginal' opening: the ship is shaped like a horseshoe, its curved sides like two long legs spread apart at the entrance. They travel along a corridor which seems to be made of a combination of inorganic and organic material – as if the inner space of this ship were alive. Compared to the atmosphere of the Nostromo, however, this ship is dark, dank and mysterious. A ghostly light glimmers and the sounds of their movements echo throughout the caverns. In the first chamber, the three explorers find a huge alien life form which appears to have been dead for a long time. Its bones are bent outward as if exploded from the inside. One of the trio, Kane, is lowered down a shaft into the gigantic womb-like chamber in which rows of eggs are hatching. Kane approaches one of the eggs; as he touches it with his gloved hand it opens out, revealing a mass of pulsating flesh. Suddenly, the monstrous thing inside leaps up and attaches itself to Kane's helmet, its tail penetrating Kane's mouth in order to fertilise itself inside his stomach. Despite the warnings of Ripley, Kane is taken back on board the Nostromo where the alien rapidly completes its gestation processes inside Kane.

This representation of the primal scene recalls Freud's reference to an extreme primal scene fantasy where the subject imagines travelling back inside the womb to watch her/his parents having sexual intercourse, perhaps to watch her/himself being conceived. Here, three astronauts explore the gigantic, cavernous, malevolent womb of the mother. Two members of the group watch the enactment of the primal scene in which Kane is violated in an act of phallic penetration – by the father or phallic mother? Kane himself is guilty of the strongest transgression; he actually peers into the egg/womb in order to investigate its mysteries. In so doing, he becomes a 'part' of the primal scene, taking up the place of the mother, the one who is penetrated, the one who bears the offspring of the union. The primal scene is represented as violent, monstrous (the union is between human and alien), and is mediated by the question of incestuous desire. All re-stagings of the primal scene raise the question of incest, as the beloved parent (usually the mother) is with a rival. The first birth scene, where the astronauts emerge from their sleep pods, could be viewed as a representation of incestuous desire *par excellence*: the father is completely absent; here, the mother is sole parent and sole life-support.

From this forbidden union, the monstrous creature is born. But man, not woman, is the 'mother' and Kane dies in agony as the alien gnaws its way through his stomach. The birth of the alien from Kane's stomach plays on what Freud described as a common misunderstanding that many children have about birth, that is, that the mother is somehow impregnated through the mouth – she may eat a special food – and the baby grows in her stomach from which it is also born. Here, we have a third version of the primal scene.

A further version of the primal scene – almost a convention[11] of the science fiction film – occurs when smaller crafts or bodies are ejected from the mother-ship into outer space; although sometimes the ejected body remains attached to the mother-ship by a long life-line or umbilical chord. This scene is

Alien (Ridley Scott, 1979)

presented in two separate ways: one when Kane's body, wrapped in a white shroud, is ejected from the mother-ship; and the second, when the small space capsule, in which Ripley is trying to escape from the alien, is expelled from the underbelly of the mother-ship. In the former, the 'mother's' body has become hostile; it contains the alien whose one purpose is to kill and devour all of Mother's children. In the latter birth scene the living infant is ejected from the malevolent body of the 'mother' to avoid destruction; in this scenario, the 'mother's' body explodes at the moment of giving birth.

Although the 'mother' as a figure does not appear in these sequences – nor indeed in the entire film – her presence forms a vast backdrop for the enactment of all the events. She is there in the images of birth, the representations of the primal scene, the womb-like imagery, the long winding tunnels leading to inner chambers, the rows of hatching eggs, the body of the mother-ship, the voice of the life-support system, and the birth of the alien. She is the generative mother, the pre-phallic mother, the being who exists prior to knowledge of the phallus.

 V In explaining the difficulty he had in uncovering the role of the mother in the early development of infants, Freud complained of the almost 'prehistoric' remoteness of this 'Minoan-Mycenaean' stage:

> Everything in the sphere of this first attachment to the mother seemed to me so difficult to grasp in analysis – so grey with age and shadowy and almost impossible to revivify – that it was as if it had succumbed to an especially inexorable repression.[12]

Just as the Oedipus complex tends to hide the pre-Oedipal phase in Freudian theory, the figure of the father, in the Lacanian re-writing of Freud, obscures the mother-child relationship of the imaginary. In contrast to the maternal figure of the Lacanian imaginary, Kristeva posits another dimension to the mother – she is associated with the pre-verbal or the semiotic and as such tends to disrupt the symbolic order.[13]

I think it is possible to open up the mother-question still further and posit an even more archaic maternal figure, to go back to mythological narratives of the generative, parthenogenetic mother – that ancient archaic figure who gives birth to all living things. She exists in the mythology of all human cultures as the Mother-Goddess who alone created the heavens and earth. In China she was known as Nu Kwa, in Mexico as Coatlicue, in Greece as Gaia (literally meaning 'earth') and in Sumer as Nammu. In 'Moses and Monotheism', Freud attempted to account for the historical existence of the great mother-goddesses.

> It is likely that the mother-goddesses originated at the time of the curtailment of the matriarchy, as a compensation for the slight upon the mothers. The male deities appear first as sons beside the great mothers and only later clearly assume the features of father-figures. These male gods of polytheism reflect the conditions during the patriarchal age.[14]

Freud proposed that human society developed through stages from patriarchy to matriarchy and finally back to patriarchy. During the first, primitive people lived in small hordes, each one dominated by a jealous, powerful father who possessed all the females of the group. One day the sons, who had been banished to the outskirts of the group, overthrew the father – whose body they devoured – in order to secure his power and to take his women for themselves. Overcome by guilt, they later attempted to revoke the deed by setting up a totem as a substitute for the father and by renouncing the women whom they had liberated. The sons were forced to give up the women, whom they all wanted to possess, in order to preserve the group which otherwise would have been destroyed as the sons fought amongst themselves. In 'Totem and Taboo', Freud suggests that here 'the germ of the institution of matriarchy'[15] may have originated. Eventually, however, this new form of social organisation, constructed upon the taboo against murder and incest, was replaced by the reestablishment of a patriarchal order. He pointed out that the sons had:

> ... thus created out of their filial sense of guilt the two fundamental taboos of totemism, which for that very reason inevitably corresponded to the two repressed wishes of the Oedipus complex.[16]

Freud's account of the origins of patriarchal civilisation is generally regarded as mythical. Lévi-Strauss points out that it is 'a fair account not of the beginnings of civilisation, but of its present state' in that it expresses 'in symbolical form an inveterate fantasy' – the desire to murder the father and possess the mother.[17] In her discussion of 'Totem and Taboo', Kristeva argues that a 'strange slippage' (p. 56) has taken place in that although Freud points out that morality is founded on the taboos of murder and incest his argument concentrates on the first to the virtual exclusion of the latter. Yet, Kristeva argues, the 'woman – or mother – image haunts a large part of that book and keeps shaping its background', (p. 57). She poses the question:

> Could the sacred be, whatever its variants, a two-sided formation? One aspect founded by murder and the social bond made up of a murderer's guilt-ridden atonement, with all the projective mechanisms and obsessive rituals that accompany it; and another aspect, like a living, more secret and invisible, non-representable, oriented toward those uncertain spaces of unstable identity, toward the fragility – both threatening and fusional – of the archaic dyad, toward the non-separation of subject/object, on which language has no hold but one woven of fright and repulsion? (pp. 57–8)

From the above, it is clear that the figure of the mother in both the history of human sociality and in the history of the individual subject poses immense problems. Freud attempts to account for the existence of the mother-goddess figure by posing a matriarchal period in historical times while admitting that everything to do with the 'first attachment to the mother' is deeply repressed – 'grey with age and shadowy and almost impossible to revivify'. Nowhere does he attempt to specify the nature of this 'matriarchal period' and the implications of this for his own psychoanalytical theory, specifically his theory of the Oedipus complex which, as Lacan points out, 'can only appear in a patriarchal form in the institution of the family'.[18] Kristeva criticises Freud for failing to deal adequately with incest and the mother-question while using the same mystifying language to refer to the mother; the other aspect of the sacred is 'like a lining', 'secret and invisible', 'non-representable'. In his re-reading of Freud, Lacan mystifies the figure of women even further: '... the woman is not-all, there is always something with her which eludes discourse'.[19] Further, all three writers conflate the archaic mother with the mother of the dyadic and triadic relationship. They refer to her as a 'shadowy' figure (Freud); as 'non-representable' (Kristeva); as the 'abyss of the female organ from which all life comes forth' (Lacan[20]), then make no clear attempt to distinguish this aspect of the maternal imago from the protective/suffocating mother of the pre-Oedipal or the mother as object of sexual jealousy and desire as she is represented in the Oedipal configuration.

The maternal figure constructed within/by the writings of Freud, Lacan and Kristeva is inevitably the mother of the dyadic or triadic relationship – although the latter figure is more prominent. Even when she is represented as the mother of the imaginary, of the dyadic relationship, she is still constructed as the *pre-Oedipal* mother, that is, as a figure about to 'take up a place' in the symbolic – as a figure always in relation to the father, the representative of the phallus. Without her 'lack', he cannot signify its opposite – lack of a lack or presence. But if we posit a more archaic dimension to the mother – the mother as originating womb – we can at least begin to talk about the maternal figure as *outside* the patriarchal family constellation. In this context, the mother-goddess narratives can be read as primal-scene narratives in which the mother is the sole parent. She is also the subject, not the object, of narrativity.

For instance in the 'Spider Woman' myth of the North American Indians, there was only the Spider Woman, who spun the universe into existence and then created two daughters from whom all life flowed. She is also the Thought Woman or Wise Woman who knows the secrets of the universe. Within the Oedipus narrative, however, she becomes the Sphinx, who also knows the answers to the secret of life but here her situation has been changed. She is no longer the subject of the narrative; she has become the object of the narrative of the male hero. After he has solved her riddle, she will destroy herself. The Sphinx is an ambiguous figure; she knows the secret of life and is thereby linked to the mother-goddess but her name, which is derived from 'sphincter', suggests she is the mother of toilet training, the pre-Oedipal mother who must be repudiated by the son so that he can take up his proper place in the symbolic. It is interesting that Oedipus has always been seen to have committed two horrific crimes: patricide and incest. But his encounter with the Sphinx, which leads to her death, suggests he is also responsible for another horrific crime – that of matricide. For the Sphinx, like the Medusa, is a mother-goddess figure; they are both variants of the same mythological mother who gave birth to all life. Lévi-Strauss has argued that a major issue in the Oedipus myth is the problem of whether or not man is born from woman. This myth is also central to *Alien*:

> Although the problem obviously cannot be solved, the Oedipus myth provides a kind of logical tool which relates the original problem – born from one or born from two? – to the derivative problem: born from different or born from same?[21]

The Medusa, whose head, according to Freud, signifies the female genitals in their terrifying aspect, also represents the procreative function of woman. The blood which flows from her severed head gives birth to Pegasus and Chrysaor. Although Neptune is supposed to be the father, the nature of the birth once again suggests the parthenogenetic mother. In *Alice Doesn't,*Teresa de Lauretis argues that:

> ... to say that narrative is the production of Oedipus is to say that each reader – male or female – is constrained and defined within the two positions of a sexual difference thus conceived: male-hero-human, on the side of the subject; and female-obstacle-boundary-space, on the other.[22]

If we apply for definition to narratives which deal specifically with the archaic mother – such as the Oedipus and Perseus myths – we can see that the 'obstacle' relates specifically to the question of origins and is an attempt to repudiate the idea of woman as the source of life, woman as sole parent, woman as archaic mother.

In his article, 'Fetishism in the Horror Film', Roger Dadoun also refers to this archaic maternal figure. He describes her as:

> ... a mother-thing situated beyond good and evil, beyond all organised forms and all events. This is a totalising and oceanic mother, a 'sha- dowy and deep unity', evoking in the subject the anxiety of fusion and dissolution; a mother who comes before the discovery of the essential *beánce*, that of the phallus. This mother is nothing but a fantasy inas- much as she is only ever established as an omnipresent and all-power- ful totality, an absolute being, by the very intuition – she has no phallus – that deposes her ... (p. 54 of this volume).[23]

Dadoun places emphasis on her 'totalizing, oceanic' presence. I would stress her archaism in relation to her generative powers – the mother who gives birth all by herself, the original parent, the godhead of all fertility and the origin of procreation. What is most interesting about the mythological figure of woman as the source of all life (a role taken over by the male god of monotheistic religions) is that, within patriarchal signifying practices, particularly the horror film, she is reconstructed and represented as a *negative* figure, one associated with the dread of the generative mother seen only as the abyss, the monstrous vagina, the origin of all life threatening to re-absorb what it once birthed. Kristeva also represents her in this negative light:

> Fear of the uncontrollable generative mother repels me from the body; I give up cannibalism because abjection (of the mother) leads me toward respect for the body of the other, my fellow man, my brother. (pp. 78–9)

In this context it is interesting to note that Freud linked the womb to the *unheimlich*, the uncanny:

> It often happens that neurotic men declare that they feel that there is something uncanny about the female genital organs. This *unheimlich*

place, however, is the entrance to the former *Heim* [home] of all human beings, to the place where each one of us lived once upon a time and in the beginning. There is a joke saying that 'Love is home-sickness'; and whenever a man dreams of a place or a country and says to himself, while he is still dreaming: 'this place is familiar to me, I've been here before', we may interpret the place as being his mother's genitals or her body.[24]

Freud also supported, and elaborated upon, Schelling's definition of the uncanny as 'something which ought to have remained hidden but has come to light.'[25] In horror films such as *Alien*, we are given a representation of the female genitals and the womb as uncanny – horrific objects of dread and fascination. Unlike the mythological mother-narratives, here the archaic mother, like the Sphinx and the Medusa, is seen only in a negative light. But the central characteristic of the archaic mother is her total dedication to the generative, procreative principle. She is outside morality and the law. Ash's eulogy to the alien is a description of this mother:

> I admire its purity; a survivor unclouded by conscience, remorse or delusions of morality.

Clearly, it is difficult to separate out completely the figure of the archaic mother, as defined above, from other aspects of the maternal figure – the maternal authority of Kristeva's semiotic, the mother of Lacan's imaginary, the phallic woman, the castrated woman. While the different figures signify quite separate things about the monstrous-feminine, as constructed in the horror film, each one is also only part of the whole – a different aspect of the maternal figure. At times the horrific nature of the monstrous-feminine is totally dependent on the merging together of all aspects of the maternal figure into one – the horrifying image of woman as archaic mother, phallic woman and castrated body represented as a single figure within the horror film. However, the archaic mother is clearly present in two distinct ways in the horror film.

1) The archaic mother – constructed as a negative force – is represented in her phantasmagoric aspects in many horror texts, particularly the sci-fi horror film. We see her as the gaping, cannibalistic bird's mouth in *The Giant Claw*; the terrifying spider of *The Incredible Shrinking Man*; the toothed vagina/womb of *Jaws*; and the fleshy, pulsating, womb of *The Thing* and *Poltergeist*. What is common to all of these images of horror is the voracious maw, the mysterious black hole which signifies female genitalia as a monstrous sign which threatens to give birth to equally horrific offspring as well as threatening to incorporate everything in its path. This is the generative archaic mother, constructed within patriarchal ideology as the primeval 'black hole'. This, of course, is also the hole which is opened up by the absence of the penis; the horrifying sight of the mother's genitals – proof that castration can occur.

However, in the texts cited above, the emphasis is not on castration; rather it is the gestating, all-devouring womb of the archaic mother which generates the horror. Nor are these images of the womb constructed in relation to the penis of the father. Unlike the female genitalia, the womb cannot be constructed as a 'lack' in relation to the penis. The womb is not the site of castration anxiety. Rather, the womb signifies 'fullness' or 'emptiness' but always it is its *own point of reference*. This is why we need to posit a more archaic dimension to the mother. For the concept of the archaic mother allows for a notion of the feminine which does not depend for its definition on a concept of the masculine. The term 'archaic mother' signifies woman as sexual difference. In contrast the maternal figure of the pre-Oedipal is always represented in relation to the penis – the phallic mother who later becomes the castrated mother. Significantly, there is an attempt in *Alien* to appropriate the procreative function of the mother, to represent a man giving birth, to deny the mother as signifier of sexual difference – but here birth can exist only as the other face of death.

2) The archaic mother is present in all horror films as the blackness of extinction – death. The desires and fears invoked by the image of the archaic mother, as a force that threatens to re-incorporate what it once gave birth to, are always there in the horror text – all pervasive, all encompassing – because of the constant presence of death. The desire to return to the original oneness of things, to return to the mother/womb, is primarily a desire for non-differentiation. If, as Georges Bataille[26] argues, life signifies discontinuity and separateness, and death signifies continuity and non-differentiation, then the desire for and attraction of death suggests also a desire to return to the state of original oneness with the mother. As this desire to merge occurs after differentiation, that is after the subject has developed as separate, autonomous self, then it is experienced as a form of psychic death. In this sense, the confrontation with death as represented in the horror film, gives rise to a terror of self-disintegration, of losing one's self or ego – often represented cinematically by a screen which becomes black, signifying the obliteration of self, the self of the protagonist in the film and the spectator in the cinema. This has important consequences for the positioning of the spectator in the cinema.

One of the most interesting structures operating in the screen–spectator relationship relates to the sight/site of the monstrous within the horror text. In contrast to the conventional viewing structures working within other variants of the classic text, the horror film does not constantly work to suture the spectator into the viewing processes. Instead, an unusual phenomenon arises whereby the suturing processes are momentarily undone while the horrific image on the screen challenges the viewer to run the risk of continuing to look. Here, I refer to those moments in the horror film when the spectator, unable to stand the images of horror unfolding before his/her eyes, is forced to look away, to not-look, to look anywhere but at the screen. Strategies of identification are temporarily broken, as the spectator is constructed in the place of horror, the place where the sight/site can no longer be endured, the place where pleasure in looking is transformed into pain and the spectator is punished for his/her voyeuristic desires. Perhaps, this should be referred to as a *fifth* look operating alongside the other 'looks' which have been theorised in relation to the screen–spectator relationship.[27]

Confronted by the sight of the monstrous, the viewing subject is put into crisis – boundaries, designed to keep the abject at bay, threaten to disintegrate, collapse. According to Lacan, the self is constituted in a process which he called the 'mirror phase', in which the child perceives its own body as a unified whole in an image it receives from outside itself. Thus, the concept of identity is a structure which depends on identification with another. Identity is an imaginary construct, formed in a state of alienation, grounded in mis-recognition. Because the self is constructed on an illusion, Lacan argues that it is always in danger of regressing:

> Here we see the ego, in its essential resistance to the elusive process of Becoming, to the variations of Desire. This illusion of unity, in which a human being is always looking forward to self-mastery, entails a constant danger of sliding back again into the chaos from which he started; it hangs over the abyss of a dizzy Assent in which one can perhaps see the very essence of Anxiety.[28]

The horror film puts the viewing subject's sense of a unified self into crisis, specifically in those moments when the image on the screen becomes too threatening or horrific to watch, when the abject threatens to draw the viewing subject to the place 'where meaning collapses', the place of death. By not-looking, the spectator is able momentarily to withdraw identification from the image on the screen in order to reconstruct the boundary between self and screen and reconstitute the 'self' which is threatened with disintegration. This process of reconstitution of the self is reaffirmed by the conventional ending of the horror narrative in which the monster is usually 'named' and destroyed.[29]

Fear of losing oneself and one's boundaries is made more acute in a society which values boundaries over continuity and separateness over sameness. Given that death is represented in the horror film as a threat to the self's boundaries, symbolised by the threat of the monster, death images are most likely to cause the spectator to look away, to not-look. Because the archaic mother is closely associated with death in its negative aspects, her presence is marked negatively within the project of the horror film. Both signify a monstrous obliteration of the self and both are linked to the demonic. Again, Kristeva presents a negative image of the maternal figure in her relationship to death:

> What is the demoniacal – an inescapable, repulsive, and yet nurtured abomination? The fantasy of an archaic force, on the near side of separation, unconscious, tempting us to the point of losing our differences, our speech, our life; to the point of aphasia, decay, opprobrium, and death? (p. 107)

Alien collapses the image of the threatening archaic mother, signifying woman as 'difference', into the more recognised figure of the pre-Oedipal mother;[30]

this occurs in relation to two images of the monstrous-feminine: the oral-sadistic mother and the phallic mother. Kane's transgressive disturbance of the egg/womb initiates a transformation of its latent aggressivity into an active, phallic enemy. The horror then played out can be read in relation to Kristeva's concept of the semiotic chora. As discussed earlier, Kristeva argues that the maternal body becomes the site of conflicting desires (the semiotic chora). These desires are constantly staged and re-staged in the workings of the horror narrative where the subject is left alone, usually in a strange hostile place, and forced to confront an unnameable terror, the monster. The monster represents both the subject's fears of being alone, of being separate from the mother, and the threat of annihilation – often through re-incorporation. As oral-sadistic mother, the monster threatens to re-absorb the child she once nurtured. Thus, the monster, like the abject, is ambiguous; it both repels and attracts.

In *Alien*, each of the crew members comes face to face with the alien in a scene whose *mise en scène* is coded to suggest a monstrous, malevolent maternal figure. They watch with fascinated horror as the baby alien gnaws its way through Kane's stomach; Dallas, the captain, encounters the alien after he has crawled along the ship's enclosed, womb-like air ducts; and the other three members are cannibalised in a frenzy of blood in scenes which emphasise the alien's huge razor-sharp teeth, signifying the monstrous oral-sadistic mother. Apart from the scene of Kane's death, all the death sequences occur in dimly-lit, enclosed, threatening spaces reminiscent of the giant hatchery where Kane first encounters the pulsating egg. In these death sequences the terror of being abandoned is matched only by the fear of re-incorporation. This scenario, which enacts the conflicting desires at play in the semiotic chora, is staged within the body of the mother-ship, the vessel which the space-travellers initially trust, until 'Mother' herself is revealed as a treacherous figure programmed to sacrifice the lives of the crew in the interests of the Company.

The other face of the monstrous-feminine in *Alien* is the phallic mother. Freud argued that the male child could either accept the threat of castration, thus ending the Oedipus complex, or disavow it. The latter response requires the (male) child to mitigate his horror at the sight of the mother's genitals – proof that castration can occur – with a fetish object which substitutes for her missing penis. For him, she is still the phallic mother, the penis-woman. In 'Medusa's Head' Freud argued that the head with its hair of writhing snakes represented the terrifying genitals of the mother, but that this head also functioned as a fetish object.

> The hair upon the Medusa's head is frequently represented in works of art in the form of snakes, and these once again are derived from the castration complex. It is a remarkable fact that, however frightening they may be in themselves, they nevertheless serve actually as a mitigation of horror, for they replace the penis, the absence of which is the cause of horror.[31]

Freud noted that a display of the female genitals makes a woman 'unapproachable and repels all sexual desires'. He refers to the section in Rabelais which relates 'how the Devil took flight when the woman showed him her vulva'.[32] Perseus' solution is to look only at a reflection, a mirror-image of her genitals. As with patriarchal ideology, his shield reflects an 'altered' representation, a vision robbed of its threatening aspects. The full difference of the mother is denied; she is constructed as other, displayed before the gaze of the conquering male hero, then destroyed.[33] The price paid is the destruction of sexual heterogeneity and repression of the maternal signifier. The fetishisation of the mother's genitals could occur in those texts where the maternal figure is represented in her phantasmagoric aspects as the gaping, voracious vagina/womb. Do aspects of these images work to mitigate the horror by offering a substitute for the penis?

Roger Dadoun argues very convincingly that the Dracula variant of the vampire movie seems 'to illustrate the work of what might be called the *fetish function*':

> ... against primitive identification with the mother, a phallus; against the anxiety of psychotic collapse, sexuality; against spatio-temporal disorganisation, a ritual – and that completes the construction, on the positive side of fetishism, as it were, of a sexualised phallic object, all the more rigid and impressive for being fragile and threatened. In this object, one may perhaps have the pleasure of recognising a familiar figure of the horror film, Count Dracula. (p. 41 of this volume)

Dadoun argues that the archaic mother exists as a 'non-presence', and 'must be understood as a very archaic mode of presence' (p. 52). Signs of the archaic mother in the Dracula film are: the small, enclosed village; the pathway through the forest that leads like an umbilical cord to the castle; the central place of enclosure with its winding stairways, spider webs, dark vaults, worm-eaten staircases, dust and damp earth – 'elements which all relate back to the *imago* of the bad archaic mother' (p. 53). At the centre of this, Dracula himself materialises. With his black cape, pointed teeth, rigid body – carried 'like an erect phallus' – piercing eyes and 'penetrating look', he is the fetish form, 'a substitute for the mother's penis' (pp. 54; 55).

> It is clear, however, since the threat comes from the mother's absent phallus, that the principal defence is sex. The vampire, marked and fascinated by the mother's missing penis and identifying with the archaic mother, doesn't have a phallus but becomes one instead. He moves from what he does not *have* to what he can *be*, if only in illusion ... (p. 57 of this volume)

As he emerges in Dadoun's argument, the Dracula figure is very much acting on behalf of the mother – he desires to be the phallus for the mother. When he is finally penetrated by the stake, his heart 'turns out to be hollow, a gaping wound. This is castration made flesh and blood and absence ...' (p. 57). However, it is possible that we could theorise fetishism differently by asking:

Who is the fetish-object a fetish for? The male or female subject? In general, the fetishist is usually assumed to be male, although Freud did allow that female fetishism was a possibility.[34] The notion of female fetishism is much neglected although it is present in various patriarchal discourses.

In her article, 'Woman-Desire-Image', Mary Kelly argues that 'it would be a mistake to confine women to the realm of repression, excluding the possibility, for example, of female fetishism':

> When Freud describes castration fears for the woman, this imaginary scenario takes the form of losing her loved objects, especially her children; the child is going to grow up, leave her, reject her, perhaps die. In order to delay, disavow, that separation she has already in a way acknowledged, the woman tends to fetishise the child: by dressing him up, by continuing to feed him no matter how old he gets, or simply by having another 'little one'.[35]

In *The Interpretation of Dreams*, Freud discusses the way in which the doubling of a penis-symbol indicates an attempt to stave off castration anxieties. Juliet Mitchell refers to doubling as a sign of a female castration complex: 'We can see the significance of this for women, as dreams of repeated number of children – "little ones" – are given the same import.'[36] In this context, female fetishism represents an attempt by the female subject to continue to 'have' the phallus, to take up a 'positive' place in relation to the symbolic.

Female fetishism is clearly represented within many horror texts – as instances of patriarchal signifying practices – but only in relation to male fears and anxieties about women and the question: What do women want? (*The Birds, Cat People, Alien, The Thing*.) Women as yet do not speak their own 'fetishistic' desires within the popular cinema – if, indeed, women have such desires. The notion of female fetishism is represented in *Alien* in the figure of the monster. The creature is the mother's phallus, attributed to the maternal figure by a phallocentric ideology terrified at the thought that women might desire to have the phallus. The monster as fetish object is not there to meet the desires of the male fetishist, but rather to signify the monstrousness of woman's desire to have the phallus.

In *Alien*, the monstrous creature is constructed as the phallus of the negative mother. The image of the archaic mother – threatening because it signifies woman as difference rather than constructed as opposition – is, once again, collapsed into the figure of the pre-Oedipal mother. By re-locating the figure of woman within an Oedipal scenario, her image can be recuperated and controlled. The womb, even if represented negatively, is a greater threat than the mother's phallus. As phallic mother, woman is again represented as monstrous. What is horrific is the desire to cling to her offspring in order to continue to 'have the phallus'. Her monstrous desire is concretised in the figure of the alien; the creature whose deadly mission is represented as the same as that of the archaic mother – to reincorporate and destroy all life.

If we consider *Alien* in the light of a theory of female fetishism, then the chameleon nature of the alien begins to make sense. Its changing appearance represents a form of doubling or multiplication of the phallus, pointing to the mother's desire to stave off her castration. The alien is the mother's phallus, a fact which is made perfectly clear in the birth scene where the infant alien rises from Kane's stomach and holds itself erect, glaring angrily around the room, before screeching off into the depths of the ship. But the alien is more than a phallus; it is also coded as a toothed vagina, the monstrous-feminine as the cannibalistic mother. A large part of the ideological project of *Alien* is the representation of the maternal fetish object as an 'alien' or foreign shape. This is why the body of the heroine becomes so important at the end of the film.

Much has been written about the final scene, in which Ripley/ Sigourney Weaver undresses before the camera, on the grounds that its voyeurism undermines her role as successful heroine. A great deal has also been written about the cat. Why does she rescue the cat and thereby risk her life, and the lives of Parker and Lambert, when she has previously been so careful about quarantine regulations? Again, satisfactory answers to these questions are provided by a phallocentric concept of female fetishism. Compared to the horrific sight of the alien as fetish object of the monstrous feminine, Ripley's body is pleasurable and reassuring to look at. She signifies the 'acceptable' form and shape of woman. In a sense the monstrousness of woman, represented by Mother as betrayer (the computer/life support system), and Mother as the uncontrollable, generative, cannibalistic mother (the alien), is controlled through the display of woman as reassuring and pleasurable sign. The image of the cat functions in the same way; it signifies an acceptable, and in this context, a reassuring, fetish object for the 'normal' woman.[37] Thus, Ripley holds the cat to her, stroking it as if it were her 'baby', her 'little one'. Finally, Ripley enters her sleep pod, assuming a virginal repose. The nightmare is over and we are returned to the opening sequence of the film where birth was a pristine affair. The final sequence works, not only to dispose of the alien, but also to repress the nightmare image of the monstrous-feminine, constructed as a sign of abjection, within the text's patriarchal discourses.

Kristeva's theory of abjection, if viewed as decription rather than prescription, provides a productive hypothesis for an analysis of the monstrous-feminine in the horror film. If we posit a more archaic dimension to the mother, we can see how this figure, as well as Kristeva's maternal authority of the semiotic, are both constructed as figures of abjection within the signifying practices of the horror film. We can see its ideological project as an attempt to shore up the symbolic order by constructing the feminine as an imaginary 'other' which must be repressed and controlled in order to secure and protect the social order. Thus, the horror film stages and re-stages a constant repudiation of the maternal figure.

But the feminine is not *per se* a monstrous sign; rather, it is constructed as such within a patriarchal discourse which reveals a great deal about

Alien (Ridley Scott, 1979)

male desires and fears but tells us nothing about feminine desire in relation to the horrific. When Norman Bates remarked to Marion Crane in *Psycho* that: 'Mother . . . isn't quite herself today', he was dead right. Mother wasn't herself. She was someone else. Her son – Norman.

NOTES

1 Sigmund Freud, 'Fetishism', *On Sexuality* (Harmondsworth: Penguin, Pelican Freud Library), vol. 7, 1981, p. 354.

2 Joseph Campbell, *The Masks of God: Primitive Mythology* (New York: Penguin, 1969), p. 73.

3 Sigmund Freud, 'Medusa's Head', in James Strachey (ed.), *The Standard Edition of the Complete Psychological Works of Sigmund Freud*, vol. 18 (London: Hogarth Press, 1964), pp. 273–74.

4 Ibid., p. 273.

5 Ibid.

6 Julia Kristeva, *Powers of Horror: An Essay on Abjection* (New York: Columbia University Press, 1982). All page citations will be included in the text.

7 For a critique of *Powers of Horror* see Jennifer Stone, 'The Horrors of Power: A Critique of "Kristeva"', in F. Barker, P. Hulme, M. Iversen, D. Loxley (eds.), *The Politics of Theory* (Colchester, University of Essex, 1983), pp. 38–48.

8 Sigmund Freud, 'From the History of an Infantile Neurosis', *Case Histories II* (Harmondsworth: Penguin, Pelican Freud Library), vol. 9, 1981, p. 294.

9 Sigmund Freud, 'On the Sexual Theories of Children', *On Sexuality* (Harmondsworth: Penguin, Pelican Freud Library), vol. 7, 1981, p. 198.

10 Sigmund Freud, 'The Paths to the Formation of Symptoms', *Introductory Lectures on Psychoanalysis* (Harmondsworth: Penguin, Pelican Freud Library), vol. 1, 1981, p. 417.

11 Daniel Dervin argues that this structure does deserve the status of a convention. For a detailed discussion of the primal scene phantasy in various film genres, see his 'Primal Conditions and Conventions: The Genres of Comedy and Science Fiction', *Film/Psychology Review*, Winter-Spring 1980, pp. 115–47.

12 Sigmund Freud, 'Female Sexuality', *On Sexuality* (Harmondsworth: Penguin, Pelican Freud Library), vol. 7, 1981, p. 373.

13 For a discussion of the relation between 'the semiotic' and the Lacanian 'imaginary' see Jane Gallop, *Feminism and Psychoanalysis: The Daughter's Seduction* (London: Macmillan Press, 1983), pp. 124–5.

14 Sigmund Freud, 'Moses and Monotheism', in James Strachey (ed.), *The Standard Edition of the Complete Psychological Works of Sigmund Freud*, vol. 23, p. 83.

15 Sigmund Freud, 'Totem and Taboo', *The Origins of Religion* (Harmondsworth: Penguin, Pelican Freud Library), vol. 13, 1985, p. 206.

16 Ibid., p. 205.

17 Lévi-Strauss, quoted in George Bataille, *Death and Sensuality: A Study of Eroticism and the Taboo* (New York: Walker and Company, 1962), p. 200.

18 Jacques Lacan, *The Language of The Self* (ed.) Anthony Wilden (Baltimore: Johns Hopkins Press, 1970), p. 126.

19 Jacques Lacan, *Le Séminaire* XX, p. 34, translated in Stephen Heath, 'Difference', *Screen*, Autumn 1978, vol. 19 no. 3, p. 59.

20 Jacques Lacan, *Le Séminaire* II, p. 196, translated in Stephen Heath, 'Difference', p. 54.

21 Claude Lévi-Strauss, *Structural Anthropology* (trans. C. Jacobson and B. G. Schoepf) (New York: Doubleday, 1976), p. 212.

22 Teresa de Lauretis, *Alice Doesn't: Feminism, Semiotics, Cinema* (Indiana University Press, 1984), p. 121.

23 Roger Dadoun, 'Fetishism in the Horror Film'. Page citations are given in brackets in the text and refer to the article as reprinted in this volume.

24 Sigmund Freud, 'The Uncanny', in James Strachey (ed.), *The Standard Edition of the Complete Psychological Works of Sigmund Freud*, vol. 17, p. 245.

25 Ibid., p. 225.

26 Georges Bataille, *Death and Sensuality: A Study of Eroticism and the Taboo.*

27 For a discussion of cinema and the structures of the 'look' see Paul Willemen, 'Letter To John', *Screen*, Summer 1980, vol. 21 no. 2, pp. 53–66.

28 Jacques Lacan, 'Some Reflections on the Ego', *The International Journal of Psychoanalysis*, vol. 24, 1953, p. 15.

29 For a discussion of the relationship between the female spectator, structures of looking and the horror film see Linda Williams, 'When The Woman Looks', in Mary Anne Doane, Patricia Mellencamp and Linda Williams (eds.), *Re-Vision*, American Film Institute Monograph Series, vol. 3 (Frederick, MD: University Publications of America, 1984).

30 Dadoun refers to a similar process when he speaks of the displacement of the large 'omnipresent mother' into the small 'occulted mother' (p. 54).

31 Sigmund Freud, 'Medusa's Head', p. 105.

32 Ibid., p. 106.

33 For a fascinating discussion of the place of woman as monster in the Oedipal narrative see Teresa de Lauretis, *Alice Doesn't*, chapter 5.

34 Sigmund Freud, 'An Outline of Psychoanalysis', in James Strachey (ed.), *The Standard Edition of the Complete Psychoanalytic Works of Sigmund Freud*, vol. 23, p. 202: 'This abnormality, which may be counted as one of the perversions, is, as is well known, based on the patient (who is *almost always* male) not recognizing the fact that females have no penis . . .' (my emphasis).

35 Mary Kelly, 'Woman-Desire-Image', *Desire* (London: Institute of Contemporary Arts, 1984), p. 31.

36 Juliet Mitchell, *Psychoanalysis and Feminism* (Harmondsworth: Penguin, 1974), p. 84.

37 The double bird images of Hitchcock's *The Birds* function in the same way: the love birds signify an 'acceptable' fetish, the death birds a fetish of the monstrous woman.

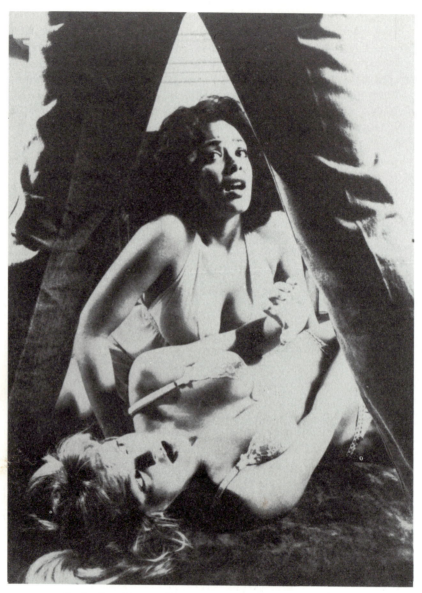

Slumber Party Massacre (Amy Jones, 1982)

Her Body, Himself
Gender in the Slasher Film
CAROL J. CLOVER

THE CINEFANTASTIC & VARIETIES OF HORROR

On the high side of horror lie the classics: F. W. Murnau's *Nosferatu*, *King Kong*, *Dracula*, *Frankenstein*, and various works by Alfred Hitchcock, Carl Theodor Dreyer, and a few others – films that by virtue of age, literary ancestry, or fame of director have achieved reputability within the context of disreputability.[1] Further down the scale fall the productions of Brian De Palma, some of the glossier satanic films (*Rosemary's Baby*, *The Omen*, *The Exorcist*), certain sci-fi hybrids (*Alien/Aliens*, *Blade Runner*), some vampire and werewolf films (*Wolfen*, *An American Werewolf in London*), and an assortment of other highly produced films, often with stars (*Whatever Happened to Baby Jane*, *The Shining*). At the very bottom, down in the cinematic underbrush, lies – horror of horrors – the slasher (or splatter or shocker) film: the immensely generative story of a psycho-killer who slashes to death a string of mostly female victims, one by one, until he is himself subdued or killed, usually by the one girl who has survived.

Drenched in taboo and encroaching vigorously on the pornographic, the slasher film lies by and large beyond the purview of the respectable (middle-aged, middle-class) audience. It has lain by and large beyond the purview of respectable criticism. Staples of drive-ins and exploitation houses, where they 'rub shoulders with sex pictures and macho action flicks', these are films that are 'never even written up'.[2] Books on horror film mostly concentrate on the classics, touch on the middle categories in passing, and either pass over the slasher in silence or bemoan it as a degenerate aberration.[3] The one full book on the category, William Schoell's *Stay Out of the Shower*, is immaculately unintelligent.[4] Film magazine articles on the genre rarely get past technique, special effects, and profits. The Sunday *San Francisco Examiner* relegates reviews of slashers to the syndicated 'Joe Bob Briggs, Drive-In Movie Critic of Grapevine, Texas', whose low-brow, campy tone ('We're talking two breasts, four quarts of blood, five dead bodies. . . . Joe Bob says check it out') establishes what the paper and others like it deem the necessary distance between their readership and that sort of film.[5] There are of course the exceptional cases: critics or social observers who have seen at least some of these films and tried to come to grips with their ethics or aesthetics or both. Just how troubled is their task can be seen from its divergent results. For one critic, *The Texas Chainsaw Massacre* is 'the *Gone With* the Wind of meat movies'.[6] For another it is a 'vile little piece of sick crap . . . nothing but a hysterically paced, slapdash, imbecile concoction of cannibalism, voodoo, astrology, sundry hippie-esque cults, and unrelenting sadistic violence as extreme and hideous as a complete lack of imagination can possibly make it'.[7] Writes a third: '[Director Tobe] Hooper's cinematic intelligence becomes more apparent in every viewing, as one gets over the initial traumatizing impact and learns to respect the pervasive felicities of camera placement and movement.'[8] The Museum of Modern Art bought the film in the same year that at least one country, Sweden, banned it.

Robin Wood's tack is less aesthetic than anthropological. 'However one may shrink from systematic exposure to them [slasher films], however one may deplore the social phenomena and ideological mutations they reflect, their popularity . . . suggests that even if they were uniformly execrable they shouldn't be ignored.'[9] We may go a step further and suggest that the qualities that locate the slasher film outside the usual aesthetic system – that indeed render it, along with pornography and low horror in general, the film category 'most likely to be betrayed by artistic treatment and lavish production values'[10] – are the very qualities that make it such a transparent source for (sub)cultural attitudes towards sex and gender in particular. Unmediated by otherworldly fantasy, cover plot, bestial transformations, or civilised routine, slasher films present us in startlingly direct terms with a world in which male and female are at desperate odds but in which, at the same time, masculinity and femininity are more states of mind than body. The premise of this essay, then, is that the slasher film, not despite but exactly because of its crudity and compulsive repetitiveness, gives us a clearer picture of current sexual attitudes, at least among the segment of the population that forms its erstwhile audience, than do the legitimate products of the better studios.

Before we turn to the generic particulars, however, let us review some of the critical and cinematic issues that attend the study of the sensation genres in general and horror in particular. We take as our point of departure not a slasher film but Brian De Palma's art-horror film Body Double (1984). The plot – a man witnesses and after much struggle solves the mysterious murder of a woman with whom he has become voyeuristically involved – concerns us less than the three career levels through which the hero, an actor named Jake, first ascends and then descends. He aspires initially to legitimate roles (Shakespeare), but it becomes clear during the course of a method-acting class that his range of emotional expression is impaired by an unresolved childhood fear. For the moment he has taken a job as vampire in a 'low-budget, independent horror film', but even that job is threatened when, during a scene in which he is to be closed in a coffin and buried, he suffers an attack of claustrophobia and must leave the set. A plot twist leads him to the underworld of pornography, where he takes on yet another role, this time in a skin flick. Here, in the realm of the flesh with a queen of porn, the sexual roots of Jake's paralysis – fear of the (female) cavern – are exposed and finally resolved. A new man, he returns to 'A Vampire's

Kiss' to master the burial scene, and we are to understand that Shakespeare is the next stop.

The three cinematic categories are thus ranked by degree of sublimation. On the civilized side of the continuum lie the legitimate genres; at the other end, hard on the unconscious, lie the sensation or 'body' genres, horror and pornography, in that order. For De Palma, the violence of horror reduces to and enacts archaic sexual feelings. Beneath Jake's emotional paralysis (which emerges in the 'high' genre) lies a death anxiety (which is exposed in the burying-alive of horror), and beneath *that* anxiety lies a primitive sexual response (which emerges, and is resolved, in pornography). The layers of Jake's experience accord strikingly, and perhaps not coincidentally, with Freud's archaeology of 'uncanny' feelings. 'To some people,' Freud wrote, 'the idea of being buried alive by mistake is the most uncanny thing of all. And yet psychoanalysis has taught us that this terrifying phantasy is only a transformation of another phantasy which originally had nothing terrifying about it at all, but was qualified by a certain lasciviousness – the phantasy, I mean, of intra-uterine existence [*der Phantasie vom Leben im Mutterleib*].'[11] Pornography thus engages directly (in pleasurable terms) what horror explores at one remove (in painful terms) and legitimate film at two or more. Beneath the 'legitimate' plot of *The Graduate* (in which Ben must give up his relationship with a *friend*'s mother in order to marry and take his proper social place) lies the plot of *Psycho* (in which Norman's unnatural attachment to his *own* mother drives him to murder women to whom he is attracted); and beneath *that* plot lies the plot of the porn film *Taboo*, in which the son simply has sex with his mother ('Mom, am I better than Dad?'). Pornography, in short, has to do with sex (the act) and horror with gender.

It is a rare Hollywood film that does not devote a passage or two – a car chase, a sex scene – to the emotional/physical excitement of the audience. But horror and pornography are the only two genres specifically devoted to the arousal of bodily sensation. They exist solely to horrify and stimulate, not always respectively, and their ability to do so is the sole measure of their success: they 'prove themselves upon our pulses'.[12] Thus in horror-film circles, 'good' means scary, specifically in a bodily way (ads promise shivers, chills, shudders, tingling of the spine; Lloyd's of London insured audiences of *Macabre* against death by fright),[13] and *Hustler's Erotic Film Guide* ranks pornographic films according to the degree of erection they produce (one film is ranked a 'pecker popper', another 'limp'). The target is in both cases the body, our witnessing body. But *what* we witness is also the body, another's body, in experience: the body in sex and the body in threat. The terms 'flesh film' ('skin flicks') and 'meat movies' are remarkably apt.

Cinema, it is claimed, owes its particular success in the sensation genres (witness the early and swift rise of vampire films) to its unprecedented ability to manipulate point of view. What written narrative must announce, film can accomplish silently and instantaneously through cutting. Within the space of seconds, the vampire's first-person perspective is displaced by third-person or documentary observation. To these simple shifts can be added the variables of distance (from the panorama of the battlefield to the closeup of an eyeball), angle, frame tilt, lighting effects, unsteadiness of image, and so on – again, all subject to sudden and unannounced manipulation.[14] A current horror-film favorite locates the I-camera with the killer in pursuit of a victim; the camera is hand-held, producing a jerky image, and the frame includes in-and-out-of-focus foreground objects (trees, bushes, window frames) behind which the killer (I-camera) is lurking – all accompanied by the sound of heartbeat and heavy breathing. 'The camera moves in on the screaming, pleading victim, "looks down" at the knife, and then plunges it into the chest, ear, or eyeball. Now that's sick.'[15]

Lagging behind practice is a theoretical understanding of effect. The processes by which a certain image (but not another) filmed in a certain way (but not another) causes one person's (but not another's) pulse to race finally remains a mystery – not only to critics and theorists but even, to judge from interviews and the trial-and-error (and baldly imitative) quality of the films themselves, by the people who make the product. The process of suture is sensed to be centrally important in effecting audience identification, though just how and why is unclear.[16] Nor is identification the straightforward notion some critics take it to be.[17] Where commentators by and large agree is in the importance of the 'play of pronoun function'.[18] If the fantastic depends for its effect on an uncertainty of vision, a profusion of perspectives and a confusion of subjective and objective, then cinema is preeminently suited to the fantastic. Indeed, to the extent that film can present 'unreal' combinations of objects and events as 'real' through the camera eye, the 'cinematic process itself might be called fantastic'.[19] The 'cinefantastic' in any case succeeds, far more efficiently and effectively and on a far greater scale than its ancestral media, in the production of sensation.

The fact that the cinematic conventions of horror are so easily and so often parodied would seem to suggest that, individual variation notwithstanding, its basic structures of apperception are fixed and fundamental. The same is true of the stories they tell. Students of folklore or early literature recognise in the slasher film the hallmarks of oral story: the free exchange of themes and motifs, the archetypal characters and situations, the accumulation of sequels, remakes, imitations. This is a field in which there is in some sense no original, no real or right text, but only variants; a world in which, therefore, the meaning of the individual example lies outside itself. The 'art' of the horror film, like the 'art' of pornography, is to a very large extent the art of rendition, and it is understood as such by the competent audience.[20] A particular example may have original features, but its quality as a horror film lies in the ways it delivers the cliché. James B. Twitchell rightly recommends an

> ethnological approach, in which the various stories are analyzed as if no one individual telling really mattered. . . . You search for what is stable and repeated; you neglect what is 'artistic' and 'original'. This is why, for me, auteur criticism is quite beside the point in explaining

horror.... The critic's first job in explaining the fascination of horror is not to fix the images at their every appearance but, instead, to trace their migrations to the audience and, only then, try to understand why they have been crucial enough to pass along.[21]

That auteur criticism is at least partly beside the point is clear from interviews with such figures as John Carpenter (*Halloween*, *The Fog*). These suggest that, like the purveyors of folklore, the makers of film operate more on instinct and formula than conscious understanding. So bewildered was Hitchcock by the unprecedented success of *Psycho* that he approached the Stanford Research Institute about doing a study of the phenomenon.[22]

What makes horror 'crucial enough to pass along' is, for critics since Freud, what has made ghost stories and fairy tales crucial enough to pass along: its engagement of repressed fear and desires and its reenactment of the residual conflict surrounding those feelings. Horror films thus respond to interpretation, as Robin Wood puts it, as 'at once the personal dreams of their makers and the collective dreams of their audiences – the fusion made possible by the shared structures of a common ideology'.[23] And just as attacker and attacked are expressions of the same self in nightmares, so they are expressions of the same viewer in horror film. Our primary and acknowledged identification may be with the victim, the adumbration of our infantile fears and desires, our memory sense of ourselves as tiny and vulnerable in the face of the enormous Other; but the Other is also finally another part of ourself, the projection of our repressed infantile rage and desire (our blind drive to annihilate those towards whom we feel anger, to force satisfaction from those who stimulate us, to wrench food for ourselves if only by actually devouring those who feed us) that we have had in the name of civilisation to repudiate. We are both Red Riding Hood *and* the Wolf; the force of the experience, the horror, comes from 'knowing' both sides of the story – from giving ourselves over to the cinematic play of pronoun functions. It is no surprise that the first film to which viewers were not admitted once the theatre darkened was *Psycho*. Whether Hitchcock actually meant with this measure to intensify the 'sleep' experience is unclear, but the effect both in the short run, in establishing *Psycho* as the ultimate thriller, and in the long run, in altering the cinema-going habits of the nation, is indisputable. In the current understanding, horror is the least interruptable of all film genres. That uninterruptability itself bears witness to the compulsive nature of the stories it tells.

Whatever else it may be, the slasher film is clearly 'crucial enough to pass along'. Profits and sequels tell much of the story. *Halloween* cost $320,000 to make and within six years had grossed over $75,000,000; even a highly produced film like *The Shining* has repaid itself tenfold.[24] *The Hills Have Eyes*, *The Texas Chainsaw Massacre*, and *Alien* (a sci-fi/slasher hybrid) are currently at Part Two. *Psycho* and *A Nightmare on Elm Street* are at Part Three. *Halloween* is at Part Four, and *Friday the Thirteenth* is at Part Six. These are better taken as remakes than sequels; although the later part purports to take up where the earlier part left off, it in most cases simply duplicates with only slight variation the plot and circumstances – the formula – of its predecessor. Nor do different titles indicate different plots; *Friday the Thirteenth* is set at summer camp and *Halloween* in town, but the story is much the same, compulsively repeated in those ten films and in dozens like them under different names. The audience for that story is by all accounts largely young and largely male – most conspicuously groups of boys who cheer the killer on as he assaults his victims, then reverse their sympathies to cheer the survivor on as she assaults the killer.[25] Our question, then, has to do with that particular audience's stake in that particular nightmare; with what in the story is 'crucial' enough to warrant the price of admission, and what the implications are for the current discussion of women and film.

THE SLASHER FILM

The immediate ancestor of the slasher film is Hitchcock's *Psycho* (1960). Its elements are familiar: the killer is the psychotic product of a sick family, but still recognisably human; the victim is a beautiful, sexually active woman; the location is not-home, at a Terrible Place; the weapon is something other than a gun; the attack is registered from the victim's point of view and comes with shocking suddenness. None of these features is original, but the unprecedented success of Hitchcock's particular formulation, above all the sexualization of both motive and action, prompted a flood of imitations and variations. In 1974, a film emerged that revised the *Psycho* template to a degree and in such a way as to mark a new phase: *The Texas Chainsaw Massacre* (Tobe Hooper). Together with *Halloween* (John Carpenter, 1978), it engendered a new spate of variations and imitations.

The plot of *Texas Chainsaw* is simple enough: five young people are driving through Texas in a van; they stop off at an abandoned house and are murdered one by one by the psychotic sons of a degenerate local family; the sole survivor is a woman. The horror, of course, lies in the elaboration. Early in the film the group picks up a hitchhiker, but when he starts a fire and slashes Franklin's arm (having already slit open his own hand), they kick him out. The abandoned house they subsequently visit, once the home of Sally's and Franklin's grandparents, turns out to be right next door to the house of the hitchhiker and his family: his brother Leatherface; their father; an aged and only marginally alive grandfather; and their dead grandmother and her dog, whose mummified corpses are ceremonially included in the family gatherings. Three generations of slaughterhouse workers, once proud of their craft but now displaced by machines, have taken up killing and cannibalism as a way of life. Their house is grotesquely decorated with human and animal remains – bones, feathers, hair, skins. The young people drift apart in their exploration of the abandoned house and grounds and are picked off one by one by Leatherface and Hitchhiker. Last is Sally. The others are attacked and killed with dispatch, but Sally must fight for her life, enduring all manner of horrors through the night. At dawn she manages to escape to the highway, where she is picked up by a passing trucker.

Likewise the nutshell plot of *Halloween*: a psychotic killer (Michael) stalks a small town on Halloween and kills a string of teenage friends, one by one; only Laurie survives. The twist here is that Michael has escaped from the asylum in which he has been incarcerated since the age of six, when he killed his sister minutes after she and her boyfriend parted following an illicit interlude in her parents' bed. That murder, in flashback, opens the film. It is related entirely in the killer's first person (I-camera) and only after the fact is the identity of the perpetrator revealed. Fifteen years later, Michael escapes his prison and returns to kill Laurie, whom he construes as another version of his sister (a sequel clarifies that she is in fact his *younger* sister, adopted by another family at the time of the earlier tragedy). But before Michael gets to Laurie, he picks off her high school friends: Annie, in a car on her way to her boyfriend's; Bob, going to the kitchen for a beer after sex with Lynda; Lynda, talking on the phone with Laurie and waiting for Bob to come back with the beer. At last only Laurie remains. When she hears Lynda squeal and then go silent on the phone, she leaves her own baby-sitting house to go to Lynda's. Here she discovers the three bodies and flees, the killer in pursuit. The remainder of the film is devoted to the back-and-forth struggle between Laurie and Michael. Again and again he bears down on her, and again and again she either eludes him (by running, hiding, breaking through windows to escape, locking herself in) or strikes back (once with a knitting needle, once with a hanger). In the end, Doctor Loomis (Michael's psychiatrist in the asylum) rushes in and shoots the killer (though not so fatally as to prevent his return in the sequels).

Before we turn to an inventory of generic components, let us add a third, more recent example: *The Texas Chainsaw Massacre II*, from 1986. The slaughter-house family (now named the Sawyers) is the same, though older and, owing to their unprecedented success in the sausage business, richer.[26] When Mr Sawyer begins to suspect from her broadcasts that a disk jockey named Stretch knows more than she should about one of their recent crimes, he dispatches his sons Leatherface and Chop Top (Hitchhiker in Part One) to the radio station late at night. There they seize the technician and corner Stretch. At the crucial moment, however, power fails Leatherface's chainsaw. As Stretch cowers before him, he presses the now still blade up along her thigh and against her crotch, where he holds it unsteadily as he jerks and shudders in what we understand to be orgasm. After that the sons leave. The intrepid Stretch, later joined by a Texas Ranger (Dennis Hopper), tracks them to their underground lair outside of town. Tumbling down the Texas equivalent of a rabbit hole, Stretch finds herself in the subterranean chambers of the Sawyer operation. Here, amidst all the slaughterhouse paraphernalia, the Sawyers live and work. The walls drip with blood. Like the decrepit mansion of Part One, the residential parts of the establishment are quaintly decorated with human and animal remains. After a long ordeal at the hands of the Sawyers, Stretch manages to scramble up through a culvert and beyond that up onto a nearby pinnacle, where she finds a chainsaw and wards off her final assailant. The Texas Ranger evidently perishes in a grenade explosion underground, leaving Stretch the sole survivor.

The spiritual debt of all the post-1974 slasher films to *Psycho* is clear, and it is a rare example that does not pay a visual tribute, however brief, to the ancestor – if not in a shower stabbing, then in a purling drain or the shadow of a knife-wielding hand. No less clear, however, is the fact that the post-1974 examples have, in the usual way of folklore, contemporized not only Hitchcock's terms but also, over time, their own. We have, in short, a cinematic formula with a twenty-six-year history, of which the first phase, from 1960 to 1974, is dominated by a film clearly rooted in the sensibility of the 1950s, while the second phase, bracketed by the two *Texas Chainsaw* films from 1974 and 1986, responds to the values of the late sixties and early seventies. That the formula in its most recent guise may be in decline is suggested by the campy, self-parodying quality of *Texas Chainsaw II*, as well as the emergence, in legitimate theatre, of the slasher satire *Buckets of Blood*. Between 1974 and 1986, however, the formula evolved and flourished in ways of some interest to observers of popular culture, above all those concerned with the representation of women in film. To apprehend in specific terms the nature of that mutation, let us, with *Psycho* as the benchmark, survey the genre by component category: killer, locale, weapons, victims, and shock effects.

KILLER

The psychiatrist at the end of *Psycho* explains what we had already guessed from the action: that Norman Bates had introjected his mother, in life a 'clinging, demanding woman', so completely that she constituted his other, controlling self. Not Norman but 'the mother half of his mind' killed Marion – *had* to kill Marion – when he (the Norman half) found himself aroused by her. The notion of a killer propelled by psychosexual fury, more particularly a male in gender distress, has proved a durable one, and the progeny of Norman Bates stalk the genre up to the present day. Just as Norman wears his mother's clothes during his acts of violence and is thought, by the screen characters and also, for a while, by the film's spectators, to *be* his mother, so the murderer in the *Psycho*-imitation *Dressed to Kill* (Brian De Palma, 1980), a transvestite psychiatrist, seems until his unveiling to be a woman; like Norman, he must kill women who arouse him sexually. Likewise, in muted form, Hitchhiker/Chop Top and Leatherface in the *Texas Chainsaw* films: neither brother shows overt signs of gender confusion, but their cathexis to the sick family – in which the mother is conspicuously absent but the preserved corpse of the grandmother (answering the treated body of Mrs Bates in *Psycho*) is conspicuously present – has palpably arrested their development. Both are in their twenties (thirties, in Part Two), but Hitchhiker/Chop Top seems a gangly kid and Leatherface jiggles in baby fat behind his butcher's apron. Like Norman Bates,

The Texas Chainsaw Massacre (Tobe Hooper, 1974)

whose bedroom still displays his childhood toys, Hitchhiker/Chop Top and Leatherface are permanently locked in childhood. Only when Leatherface 'discovers' sex in Part Two does he lose his appetite for murder. In *Motel Hell*, a sendup of modern horror with special reference to *Psycho* and *Texas Chainsaw II*, we are repeatedly confronted with a portrait of the dead mother, silently presiding over all manner of cannibalistic and incestuous doings on the part of her adult children.

No less in the grip of boyhood is the killer in *The Eyes of Laura Mars* (1978). The son of a hooker, a hysterical woman gone for days at a time, the killer has up to now put his boyish anger to good use in police work – the film makes much of the irony – but the sight of Laura's violent photographs causes it to be unleashed in full force. The killer in *Hell Night* is the sole member of his family to survive, as a child, a murderous rampage on the part of his father; the experience condemned him to an afterlife as a murderer himself. In *Halloween* the killer *is* a child, at least in the first instance: Michael, who at the age of six is so enraged at his sister (evidently for her sexual relations with her boyfriend) that he stabs her to death with a kitchen knife. The remainder of the film details his return rampage at the age of twenty-one, and Dr Loomis, who has overseen the case in the interim, explains that although Michael's body has attained maturity, his mind remains frozen in infantile fury. In *It's Alive*, the killer is literally an infant, evidently made monstrous through intrauterine apprehension of its parents' ambivalence (early in the pregnancy they considered an abortion).

Even the killers whose childhood is not immediately at issue and who display no overt gender confusion are often sexually disturbed. The murderer in *Nightmare on Elm Street* is an undead child molester. The killer in *Slumber Party Massacre* says to a young woman he is about to assault with a power drill: 'Pretty. All of you are very pretty. I love you. Takes a lot of love for a person to do this. You know you want it. You want it. Yes.' When she grasps the psychodynamics of the situation in the infamous crotch episode of *Texas Chainsaw II*, Stretch tries a desperate gambit: 'You're really good, you really are good,' she repeats; and indeed, immediately after ejaculation Leatherface becomes palpably less interested in his saw. The parodic *Motel Hell* spells it out. 'His pecker don't work; you'll see when he takes off his overalls – it's like a shrivelled prune,' Bruce says of his killer-brother Vincent when he learns of Terry's plans to marry him. Terry never does see, for on her wedding night he attempts (needless to say) not sex but murder. Actual rape is practically nonexistent in the slasher film, evidently on the premise – as the crotch episode suggests – that violence and sex are not concomitants but alternatives, the one as much a substitute for and a prelude to the other as the teenage horror film is a substitute for and a prelude to the 'adult' film (or the meat movie a substitute for and prelude to the skin flick).[27] When Sally under torture (*Texas Chainsaw I*) cries out 'I'll do anything you want', clearly with sexual intention, her assailants respond only by mimicking her in gross terms; she has profoundly misunderstood the psychology.

Female killers are few and their reasons for killing significantly different from men's. With the possible exception of the murderous mother in *Friday the Thirteenth I*, they show no gender confusion. Nor is their motive overtly psychosexual; their anger derives in most cases not from childhood experience but from specific moments in their adult lives in which they have been abandoned or cheated on by men (*Strait Jacket, Play Misty for Me, Attack of the 50-Foot Woman*). (Films like *Mother's Day, Ms. 45*, and *I Spit On Your Grave* belong to the rape-revenge category.) *Friday the Thirteenth I* is something of an anomaly. The killer is revealed as a middle-aged woman whose son, Jason, drowned years earlier as a consequence of negligence on the part of the camp counselors. The anomaly is not sustained in the sequels (Parts Two to Six), however. Here the killer is Jason himself, not dead after all but living in a forest hut. The pattern is a familiar one; his motive is vengeance for the death of his mother, his excessive attachment towards whom is manifested in his enshrining of her severed head. Like Stretch in the crotch episode of *Texas Chainsaw II*, the girl who does final combat with Jason in Part Two sees the shrine, grasps its significance (she's a psych major), and saves herself by repeating in a commanding tone, 'I am your mother, Jason; put down the knife.' Jason, for his part, begins to see his mother in the girl (I-camera) and obeys her.

In films of the *Psycho* type (*Dressed to Kill, Eyes of Laura Mars*), the killer is an insider, a man who functions normally in the action until, at the end, his other self is revealed. *Texas Chainsaw* and *Halloween* introduced another sort of killer: one whose only role is that of killer and one whose identity as such is clear from the outset. Norman may have a normal half, but these killers have none. They are emphatic misfits and emphatic outsiders. Michael is an escapee from a distant asylum; Jason subsists in the forest; the Sawyer sons live a bloody subterranean existence outside of town. Nor are they clearly seen. We catch sight of them only in glimpses – few and far between in the beginning, more frequent towards the end. They are usually large, sometimes overweight, and often masked. In short, they may be recognizably human, but only marginally so, just as they are only marginally visible – to their victims and to us, the spectators. In one key aspect, however, the killers are superhuman: their virtual indestructibility. Just as Michael (in *Halloween*) repeatedly rises from blows that would stop a lesser man, so Jason (in the *Friday the Thirteenth* films) survives assault after assault to return in sequel after sequel. Chop Top in *Texas Chainsaw II* is so called because of a metal plate implanted in his skull in repair of a head wound sustained in the truck accident in Part One. It is worth noting that the killers are normally the fixed elements and the victims the changeable ones in any given series.

TERRIBLE PLACE

The Terrible Place, most often a house or tunnel, in which the victims sooner or later find themselves is a venerable element of horror. The Bates mansion is just one in a long list of such places – a list that continues, in the modern

Psycho (Alfred Hitchcock, 1958)

slasher, with the decaying mansion of *Texas Chainsaw I*, the abandoned and haunted mansion of *Hell Night*, the house for sale but unsellable in *Halloween* (also a point of departure for such films as *Rosemary's Baby* and *Amityville Horror*), and so on. What makes these houses terrible is not just their Victorian decrepitude but the terrible families – murderous, incestuous, cannibalistic – that occupy them. So the Bates mansion enfolds the history of a mother and son locked in a sick attachment, and so the *Texas Chainsaw* mansion/labyrinth shelters a lawless brood presided over by the decaying corpse of the grandmother. Jason's forest hut (in the *Friday the Thirteenth* sequels) is no mansion, but it houses another mummified mother (or at least her head), with all the usual candles and dreadful paraphernalia. The terrors of the *Hell Night* mansion stem, we learn, from an early owner's massacre of his children. Into such houses unwitting victims wander in film after film, and it is the conventional task of the genre to register in close detail those victims' dawning understanding, as they survey the visible evidence, of the human crimes and perversions that have transpired there. That perception leads directly to the perception of their own immediate peril.

In *Texas Chainsaw Massacre II*, house and tunnel elide in a residential labyrinth underground, connected to the world above by channels and culverts. The family is intact, indeed thrives, but for reasons evidently having to do with the nature of their sausage business has moved residence and slaughterhouse underground. For Stretch, trying desperately to find a way out, it is a ghastly place: dark, full of blind alleys, walls wet with blood. Likewise the second basement of the haunted mansion in *Hell Night*: strewn with decaying bodies and skeletons, lighted with masses of candles. Other tunnels are less familial: the one in *Body Double* that prompts Jake's claustrophobic faint, and the horror-house tunnel in *He Knows You're Alone* in which the killer lurks. The morgue episode in the latter film, certain of the hospital scenes in *Halloween II*, and the bottom-cellar scenes from various films may be counted as Terrible Tunnels: dark, labyrinthine, exit-less, underground and palpably damp, and laced with heating ducts and plumbing pipes. In *Hell Night*, as in *Texas Chainsaw II*, Terrible House (the abandoned mansion) and Terrible Tunnel (the second basement) elide.

The house or tunnel may at first seem a safe haven, but the same walls that promise to keep the killer out quickly become, once the killer penetrates them, the walls that hold the victim in. A phenomenally popular moment in post-1974 slashers is the scene in which the victim locks herself in (a house, room, closet, car) and waits with pounding heart as the killer slashes, hacks, or drills his way in. The action is inevitably seen from the victim's point of view; we stare at the door (wall, car roof) and watch the surface break with first the tip and then the shaft of the weapon. In Hitchcock's *The Birds*, it is the birds' beaks we see penetrating the door. The penetration scene is commonly the film's pivotal moment; if the victim has up to now simply fled, she has at this point no choice but to fight back.

WEAPONS

In the hands of the killer, at least, guns have no place in slasher films. Victims sometimes avail themselves of firearms, but like telephones, fire alarms, elevators, doorbells, and car engines, guns fail in the squeeze. In some basic sense, the emotional terrain of the slasher film is pretechnological. The preferred weapons of the killer are knives, hammers, axes, icepicks, hypodermic needles, red hot pokers, pitchforks, and the like. Such implements serve well a plot predicated on stealth, the unawareness of later victims that the bodies of their friends are accumulating just yards away. But the use of noisy chainsaws and power drills and the nonuse of such relatively silent means as bow and arrow, spear, catapult, and even swords,[28] would seem to suggest that closeness and tactility are also at issue. The sense is clearer if we include marginal examples like *Jaws* and *The Birds*, as well as related werewolf and vampire genres. Knives and needles, like teeth, beaks, fangs, and claws, are personal, extensions of the body that bring attacker and attacked into primitive, animalistic embrace.[29] In *I Spit On Your Grave*, the heroine forces her rapist at gunpoint to drop his pants, evidently meaning to shoot him in his genitals. But she changes her mind, invites him home for what he all too readily supposes will be a voluntary follow-up of the earlier gang rape. Then, as they sit together in a bubble bath, she castrates him with a knife. If we wondered why she threw away the pistol, now we know: all phallic symbols are not equal, and a hands-on knifing answers a hands-on rape in a way that a shooting, even a shooting preceded by a humiliation, does not.[30]

Beyond that, the slasher evinces a fascination with flesh or meat itself as that which is hidden from view. When the hitchhiker in *Texas Chainsaw I* slits open his hand for the thrill, the onlookers recoil in horror – all but Franklin, who seems fascinated by the realisation that all that lies between the visible, knowable outside of the body and its secret insides is one thin membrane, protected only by a collective taboo against its violation. It is no surprise that the rise of the slasher film is concomitant with the development of special effects that let us see with our own eyes the 'opened' body.

VICTIMS

Where once there was one victim, Marion Crane, there are now many: five in *Texas Chainsaw I*, four in *Halloween*, fourteen in *Friday the Thirteenth III*, and so on. (As Schoell puts it, 'Other film-makers figured that the only thing better than one beautiful woman being gruesomely murdered was a whole series of beautiful women being gruesomely murdered.'[31]) Where once the victim was an adult, now she is typically in her teens (hence the term 'teenie-kill pic'). Where once she was female, now she is both girl and boy, though most often and most conspicuously girl. For all this, her essential quality remains the same. Marion is first and foremost a sexual transgressor. The first scenes show her in a hotel room dressing at the end of a lunch hour, asking her lover to marry her. It is, of course, her wish to be made an honest woman of that leads her to abscond with $40,000, an act that leads her to the Bates motel in Fairvale. Here, just as we watched her dress in the opening sequences, we now watch her undress. Moments later, nude in the shower, she dies. A classic publicity poster for *Psycho* shows Janet Leigh with a slightly uncomprehending look on her face sitting on the bed, dressed in a bra and half-slip, looking backward in such a way as to outline her breasts. If it is the task of promotional materials to state in one image the essence of a film, those breasts are what *Psycho* is all about.

In the slasher film, sexual transgressors of both sexes are scheduled for early destruction. The genre is studded with couples trying to find a place beyond purview of parents and employers where they can have sex, and immediately afterwards (or during) being killed. The theme enters the tradition with the Lynda-Bob subplot of *Halloween*. Finding themselves alone in a neighbourhood house, Lynda and Bob make hasty use of the master bedroom. Afterwards, Bob goes downstairs for a beer. In the kitchen he is silently dispatched by the killer, Michael, who then covers himself with a sheet (it's Halloween), dons Bob's glasses, and goes upstairs. Supposing the bespectacled ghost in the doorway to be Bob, Lynda jokes, bares her breasts provocatively, and finally, in irritation at 'Bob's' stony silence, dials Laurie on the phone. Now the killer advances, strangling her with the telephone cord, so that what Laurie hears on the other end are squeals she takes to be orgasmic. *Halloween II* takes the scene a step further. Here the victims are a nurse and orderly who have sneaked off for sex in the hospital therapy pool. The watching killer, Michael again, turns up the thermostat and, when the orderly goes to check it, kills him. Michael then approaches the nurse from behind (she thinks it's the orderly) and strokes her neck. Only when he moves his hand towards her bare breast and she turns around and sees him does he kill her.

Other directors are less fond than John Carpenter of the mistaken-identity twist. Denise, the English vamp in *Hell Night*, is simply stabbed to death in bed during Seth's postcoital trip to the bathroom. In *He Knows You're Alone*, the student having the affair with her professor is stabbed to death in bed while the professor is downstairs changing a fuse; the professor himself is stabbed when he returns and discovers the body. The postcoital death scene is a staple of the *Friday the Thirteenth* series. Part Three offers a particularly horrible variant. Invigorated by sex, the boy is struck by a gymnastic impulse and begins walking on his hands; the killer slices down on his crotch with a machete. Unaware of the fate of her boyfriend, the girl crawls into a hammock after her shower; the killer impales her from below.[32] Brian De Palma's *Dressed to Kill* presents the infamous example of the sexually desperate wife, first seen masturbating in her morning shower during the credit sequence, who lets herself be picked up later that day in a museum by a man with whom she has sex first in a taxi and later in his apartment. On leaving his place in the evening, she is suddenly attacked and killed in the elevator. The cause-and-effect relationship between (illicit) sex and death could hardly be more clearly drawn. *All* of the killings in *Cruising* occur during (homo)sexual encounters; the difference here is that the killer is one of the participants, not a third party.

Killing those who seek or engage in unauthorised sex amounts to a generic imperative of the slasher film. It is an imperative that crosses gender lines, affecting males as well as females. The numbers are not equal, and the scenes not equally charged; but the fact remains that in most slasher films after 1978 (following *Halloween*), men and boys who go after 'wrong' sex also die. This is not the only way males die; they also die incidentally, as girls do, when they get in the killer's way or try to stop him, or when they stray into proscribed territory. The victims of *Hell Night*, *Texas Chainsaw*, and the *Friday the Thirteenth* films are, respectively, those who trespass in Garth Manor, those who stumble in the environs of the slaughterhouse family, and those who become counselors at a cursed camp, all without regard to sex. Boys die, in short, not because they are boys but because they make mistakes.

Some girls die for the same mistakes. Others, however, and always the main one, die – plot after plot develops the motive – because they are female. Just as Norman Bates's Oedipal psychosis is such that only female victims will do, so Michael's sexual anger towards his sister (in the *Halloween* series) drives him to kill her – and after her a string of sister surrogates. In much the same way, the trans-sexual psychiatrist in *Dressed to Kill* is driven to murder only those women who arouse him and remind him of his hated malenesss. In *The Eyes of Laura Mars*, the killer's hatred of his mother drives him to prey on women specifically – and, significantly, one gay male. *He Knows You're Alone* features a killer who in consequence of an earlier jilting preys exclusively on brides-to-be.

But even in films in which males and females are killed in roughly even numbers, the lingering images are inevitably female. The death of a male is always swift; even if the victim grasps what is happening to him, he has no time to react or register terror. He is dispatched and the camera moves on. The death of a male is moreover more likely than the death of a female to be viewed from a distance, or viewed only dimly (because of darkness or fog, for example), or indeed to happen offscreen and not be viewed at all. The murders of women, on the other hand, are filmed at closer range, in more graphic detail, and at greater length. The pair of murders at the therapy pool in *Halloween II* illustrates the standard iconography. We see the orderly killed in two shots: the first at close range in the control room, just before the stabbing, and the second as he is being stabbed, through the vapors in a medium long shot; the orderly never even sees his assailant. The nurse's death, on the other hand, is shot entirely in medium closeup. The camera studies her face as it registers first her unwitting complicity (as the killer strokes her neck and shoulders from behind), then apprehension, and then, as she faces him, terror; we see the knife plunge into her repeatedly, hear her cries, and watch her blood fill the therapy pool. This cinematic standard has a venerable history, and it remains intact in the slasher film. Indeed, 'tits and a scream' are all that is required of actresses auditioning for the role of victim in 'Co-Ed Frenzy', the fictive slasher film whose making constitutes the frame story of *Blow-Out*. It is worth noting that none of the auditioners has both in the desired amount, and that the director must resort to the use of doubles: one for the tits, one for the screams.

FINAL GIRL

The image of the distressed female most likely to linger in memory is the image of the one who did not die: the survivor, or Final Girl. She is the one who encounters the mutilated bodies of her friends and perceives the full extent of the preceding horror and of her own peril; who is chased, cornered, wounded; whom we see scream, stagger, fall, rise, and scream again. She is abject terror personified. If her friends knew they were about to die only seconds before the event, the Final Girl lives with the knowledge for long minutes or hours. She alone looks death in the face; but she alone also finds the strength either to stay the killer long enough to be rescued (ending A) or to kill him herself (ending B). She is inevitably female. In Schoell's words: 'The vast majority of contemporary shockers, whether in the sexist mold or not, feature climaxes in which the women fight back against their attackers – the wandering, humorless psychos who populate these films. They often show more courage and level-headedness than their cringing male counterparts.'[33] Her scene occupies the last ten to twenty minutes (thirty in the case of *Texas Chainsaw I*) and constitutes the film's emphatic climax.

The sequence first appears in full-blown form (ending A) in *Texas Chainsaw I* with Sally's spirited self-defence and eventual rescue. Her brother and companions were dispatched suddenly and uncomprehendingly, one by one, but Sally survives the ninth round: long enough to see what has become of her fellows and is in store for her, long enough to meet and even dine with the whole slaughterhouse family, long enough to undergo all manner of torture (including the ancient grandfather's efforts to strike a fatal hammer blow on the temple as they bend her over a washtub), and long enough to bolt and rebolt, be caught and recaught, plead and replead for her life, and eventually escape to the highway. For nearly thirty minutes of screen time – a third of the film – we watch her shriek, run, flinch, jump through windows, sustain injury and mutilation. Her will to survive is astonishing; in the end, bloody and staggering, she finds the highway, Leatherface and Hitchhiker in pursuit. Just as they bear down on her, a truck comes by and crushes Hitchhiker. Minutes later a pickup driver plucks Sally up and saves her from Leatherface. The final shots show us Leatherface from her point of view (the bed of the pickup): standing on the highway, wounded (having gashed open his abdomen during the truck episode) but upright, waving the chainsaw crazily over his head.

Halloween's Final Girl is Laurie. Her desperate defense is shorter in duration than Sally's but no less fraught with horror. Limping from a knife wound in the leg, she flees to a garden room and breaks in through the window with a rake. Neighbors hear her screams for help but suspect a Halloween prank and shut the blinds. She gets into her own babysitting house – by throwing a potted plant at a second-storey window to rouse the children – just as the killer descends. Minutes later he comes through the window and they grapple; she manages to fell him with a knitting needle and grabs his butcher knife – but drops it when he seems dead. As she goes upstairs to the children, the killer rises, takes the knife, and goes after her. She takes refuge in a closet, lashing the two doorknobs together from the inside. As the killer slashes and stabs at the closet door – we see this from her inside perspective – she bends a hanger into a weapon and, when he breaks the door down, stabs him in the eye. Again thinking him vanquished, she sends the children to the police and sinks down in pain and exhaustion. The killer rises again, but just as he is about to stab her, Doctor Loomis, alerted by the children, rushes in and shoots the killer.

Given the drift in just the four years between *Texas Chainsaw* and *Halloween* – from passive to active defense – it is no surprise that the films following *Halloween* present Final Girls who not only fight back but do so with ferocity and even kill the killer on their own, without help from the outside.[34] Valerie in *Slumber Party Massacre* (a film directed by Amy Jones and scripted by Rita Mae Brown) takes a machete-like weapon to the killer, striking off the bit from his drill, severing his hand, and finally impaling him. Alice assaults and decapitates the killer of *Friday the Thirteenth*. Pursued by the killer in *Hell Night*, Marti pries the gate key from the stiff fingers of a corpse to let herself out of the mansion grounds to safety; when the car won't start, she repairs it on the

The Texas Chainsaw Massacre (Tobe Hooper, 1974)

spot; when the car gets stuck in the roadway, she inside and the killer on top, she releases it in such a way as to cast the killer on the gate's upper spikes. The grittiest of the Final Girls is Nancy of *Nightmare on Elm Street I*. Aware in advance that the killer will be paying her a visit, she plans an elaborate defense. When he enters the house, she dares him to come at her, then runs at him in direct attack. As they struggle, he springs the contraptions she has prepared; he is stunned by a swinging sledge hammer, jolted and half incinerated by an electrical charge, and so on. When he rises yet again, she chases him around the house, bashing him with a chair.[35] In *Texas Chainsaw II*, from 1986, the Final Girl sequence takes mythic measure. Trapped in the underground slaughterhouse, Stretch repeatedly flees, hides, is caught, tortured (at one point forced to don the flayed face of her murdered technician companion), and nearly killed. She escapes with her life chiefly because Leatherface, having developed an affection for her after the crotch episode, is reluctant to ply his chainsaw as the tyrannical Mr Sawyer commands. Finally Stretch finds her way out, leaving the Texas Ranger to face certain death below, and clambers up a nearby pinnacle, Chop Top in pursuit. At the summit she finds the mummified grandmother, ceremoniously enthroned in an open-air chamber, and next to her a functional chainsaw. She turns the saw on Chop Top, gashing his abdomen and tossing him off the precipice. The final scene shows her in extreme long shot, in brilliant sunshine, waving the buzzing chainsaw triumphantly overhead. (It is a scene we are invited to compare to the final scene of *Texas Chainsaw I*, in which the wounded Leatherface is shown in long shot at dawn, staggering after the pickup on the highway waving his chainsaw crazily over *his* head.) In Part One the Final Girl, for all her survivor pluck, is, like Red Riding Hood, saved through male agency. In Part Two, however, there is no male agency; the figure so designated, the Texas Ranger, proves so utterly ineffectual that he cannot save himself, much less the girl. The comic ineptitude and failure of would-be 'woodsmen' is a repeated theme in the late slasher films. In *Slumber Party Massacre*, the role is played by a woman – though a butch one (the girls' basketball coach). She comes to the slumber party's rescue only to fall victim to the drill herself. But to focus on just who brings the killer down, the Final Girl or a male rescuer, is – as the easy alternation between the two patterns would seem to suggest – to miss the point. The last moment of the Final Girl sequence is finally a footnote to what went before – to the quality of the Final Girl's fight, and more generally to the qualities of character that enable her, of all the characters, to survive what has come to seem unsurvivable.

The Final Girl sequence too is prefigured, if only rudimentarily, in *Psycho*'s final scenes, in which Lila (Marion's sister) is caught reconnoitering in the Bates mansion and nearly killed. Sam (Marion's boyfriend) detains Norman at the motel while Lila snoops about (taking note of Norman's toys). When she perceives Norman's approach, she flees to the basement. Here she encounters the treated corpse of Mrs Bates and begins screaming in horror. Norman bursts in and is about to strike when Sam enters and grabs him from behind. Like her generic sisters, then, Lila is the spunky inquirer into the Terrible Place: the one who first grasps, however dimly, the past and present danger, the one who looks death in the face, and the one who survives the murderer's last stab.

There the correspondences end, however. The *Psycho* scene turns, after all, on the revelation of Norman's psychotic identity, not on Lila as a character – she enters the film midway and is sketchily drawn – and still less on her self-defense. The Final Girl of the slasher film is presented from the outset as the main character. The practiced viewer distinguishes her from her friends minutes into the film. She is the girl scout, the bookworm, the mechanic. Unlike her girlfriends (and Marion Crane) she is not sexually active. Laurie (*Halloween*) is teased because of her fears about dating, and Marti (*Hell Night*) explains to the boy with whom she finds herself sharing a room that they will have separate beds. Although Stretch (*Texas Chainsaw II*) is hardly virginal, she is not available, either; early in the film she pointedly turns down a date, and we are given to understand that she is, for the present, unattached and even lonely. So too Stevie of Carpenter's *The Fog*, like Stretch a disk jockey; divorced mother and a newcomer in town, she is unattached and lonely but declines male attention. The Final Girl is also watchful to the point of paranoia; small signs of danger that her friends ignore she takes in and turns over. Above all she is intelligent and resourceful in extreme situations. Thus Laurie even at her most desperate, cornered in a closet, has the wit to grab a hanger from the rack and bend it into a weapon; Marti can hot-wire her getaway car, the killer in pursuit; and the psych major of *Friday the Thirteenth II*, on seeing the enshrined head of Mrs Voorhees, can stop Jason in his tracks by assuming a stridently maternal voice. Finally, although she is always smaller and weaker than the killer, she grapples with him energetically and convincingly.

The Final Girl is boyish, in a word. Just as the killer is not fully masculine, she is not fully feminine – not, in any case, feminine in the ways of her friends. Her smartness, gravity, competence in mechanical and other practical matters, and sexual reluctance set her apart from the other girls and ally her, ironically, with the very boys she fears or rejects, not to speak of the killer himself. Lest we miss the point, it is spelled out in her name: Stevie, Marti, Terry, Laurie, Stretch, Will. Not only the conception of the hero in *Alien* and *Aliens* but also her name, Ripley, owes a clear debt to slasher tradition.

With the introduction of the Final Girl, then, the *Psycho* formula is radically altered. It is not merely a question of enlarging the figure of Lila but of absorbing into her role, in varying degrees, the functions of Arbogast (investigator) and Sam (rescuer) and restructuring the narrative action from beginning to end around her progress in relation to the killer. In other words, *Psycho*'s detective plot, revolving around a revelation, yields in the modern slasher film to a hero plot, revolving around the main character's struggle with and eventual triumph over evil. But for the femaleness, however qualified, of that main character, the story is a standard one of tale and epic.

SHOCK

One reason that the shower sequence in *Psycho* has 'evoked more study, elicited more comment, and generated more shot-for-shot analysis from a technical viewpoint than any other in the history of cinema' is that it suggests so much but shows so little.[36] Of the forty-odd shots in as many seconds that figure the murder, only a single fleeting one actually shows the body being stabbed. The others present us with a rapid-fire concatenation of images of the knife-wielding hand, parts of Marion, parts of the shower, and finally the bloody water as it swirls down the drain. The horror resides less in the actual images than in their summary implication.

Although Hitchcock is hardly the first director to prefer the oblique rendition of physical violence, he may, to judge from current examples, be one of the last. For better or worse, the perfection of special effects has made it possible to show maiming and dismemberment in extraordinarily credible detail. The horror genres are the natural repositories of such effects; what can be done is done, and slashers, at the bottom of the category, do it most and worst. Thus we see a head being stepped on so that the eyes pop out, a face being flayed, a decapitation, a hypodermic needle penetrating an eyeball in closeup, and so on.

With this new explicitness also comes a new tone. If the horror of *Psycho* was taken seriously, the 'horror' of the slasher films is of a rather more complicated sort. Audiences express uproarious disgust ('gross!') as often as they express fear, and it is clear that the makers of slasher films pursue the combination. More particularly: spectators fall silent while the victim is being stalked, scream out at the first stab, and make loud noises of revulsion at the sight of the bloody stump. The rapid alternation between registers – between something like 'real' horror on one hand and a camp, self-parodying Horror on the other – is by now one of the most conspicuous characteristics of the tradition. In its cultivation of intentionally outrageous excess, the slasher film intersects with the cult film, a genre devoted to such effects. Just what this self-ironising relation to taboo signifies, beyond a remarkably competent audience, is unclear – it is yet another aspect of the phenomenon that has lain beyond criticism – but for the time being it stands as a defining characteristic of the lower genres of popular culture.

THE BODY

On the face of it, the relation between the sexes in slasher films could hardly be clearer. The killer is with few exceptions recognizably human and distinctly male; his fury is unmistakably sexual in both roots and expression; his victims are mostly women, often sexually freed and always young and beautiful. Just how essential this victim is to horror is suggested by her historical durability. If the killer has over time been variously figured as shark, fog, gorilla, birds, and slime, the victim is eternally and prototypically the damsel. Cinema hardly invented the pattern. It has simply given visual expression to the abiding proposition that, in Poe's famous formulation, the death of a beautiful woman is the 'most poetical topic in the world'.[37] As slasher director Dario Argento puts it, 'I like women, especially beautiful ones. If they have a good face and figure, I would much prefer to watch them being murdered than an ugly girl or a man.'[38] Brian De Palma elaborates: 'Women in peril work better in the suspense genre. It all goes back to the *Perils of Pauline*.... If you have a haunted house and you have a woman walking around with a candelabrum, you fear more for her than you would for a husky man.'[39] Or Hitchcock, during the filming of *The Birds*: 'I always believe in following the advice of the playwright Sardou. He said "Torture the women!" The trouble today is that we don't torture women enough.'[40] What the directors do not say, but show, is that 'Pauline' is at her very most.effective in a state of undress, borne down upon by a blatantly phallic murderer, even gurgling orgasmically as she dies. The case could be made that the slasher films available at a given neighborhood video rental outlet recommend themselves to censorship under the Dworkin-MacKinnon guidelines at least as readily as the hard-core films the next section over, at which that legislation is aimed; for if some victims are men, the argument goes, most are women, and the women are brutalised in ways that come too close to real life for comfort. But what this line of reasoning does not take into account is the figure of the Final Girl. Because slashers lie for all practical purposes beyond the purview of legitimate criticism, and to the extent that they have been reviewed at all have been reviewed on an individual basis, the phenomenon of the female victim-hero has scarcely been acknowledged.

It is, of course, 'on the face of it' that most of the public discussion of film takes place – from the Dworkin-MacKinnon legislation to Siskel's and Ebert's reviews to our own talks with friends on leaving the movie house. Underlying that discussion is the assumption that the sexes are what they seem; that screen males represent the Male and screen females the Female; that this identification along gender lines authorises impulses towards sexual violence in males and encourages impulses towards victimisation in females. In part because of the massive authority cinema by nature accords the image, even academic film criticism has been slow – slower than literary criticism – to get beyond appearances. Film may not appropriate the mind's eye, but it certainly encroaches on it; the gender characteristics of a screen figure at a visible and audible given for the duration of the film. To the extent that the possibility of cross-gender identification has been entertained, it has been in the direction female-with-male. Thus some critics have wondered whether the female viewer, faced with the screen image of a masochistic/narcissistic female, might not rather elect to 'betray her sex and identify with the masculine point of view'.[41] The reverse question – whether men might not also, on occasion, elect to betray their sex and identify with screen females – has scarcely been asked, presumably on the assumption that men's interests are well served by the traditional patterns of cinematic representation. Then too there is the matter of the 'male gaze'. As E. Ann Kaplan sums it up: 'Within the film text itself, men gaze at women, who become objects of the gaze; the spectator, in turn, is made to identify with this male gaze, and to objectify the women on the screen; and the camera's original "gaze" comes into play in the very act of filming.'[42] But if it is so that all of us, male and female alike, are by these processes 'made to' identify with men and 'against' women, how are we then to explain the appeal to a largely male audience of a film genre that features a female victim-hero? The slasher film brings us squarely up against a fundamental question of film analysis: where does the literal end and the figurative begin; how do the two levels interact and what is the significance of the particular interaction; and to which, in arriving at a political judgment (as we are inclined to do in the case of low horror and pornography), do we assign priority?

A figurative or functional analysis of the slasher begins with the processes of point of view and identification. The male viewer seeking a male character, even a vicious one, with whom to identify in a sustained way has little to hang on to in the standard example. On the good side, the only viable candidates are the schoolmates or friends of the girls. They are for the most part marginal, undeveloped characters; more to the point, they tend to die early in the film. If the traditional horror film gave the male spectator a last-minute hero with whom to identify, thereby 'indulging his vanity as protector of the helpless female',[43] the slasher eliminates or attenuates that role beyond any such function; indeed, would-be rescuers are not infrequently blown away for their efforts, leaving the girl to fight her own fight. Policemen, fathers, and sheriffs appear only long enough to demonstrate risible incomprehension and incompetence. On the bad side, there is the killer. The killer is often unseen, or barely glimpsed, during the first part of the film, and what we do see, when we finally get a good look, hardly invites immediate or conscious empathy. He is commonly masked, fat, deformed, or dressed as a woman. Or 'he' *is* a woman: woe to the viewer of *Friday the Thirteenth I* who identifies with the male killer only to discover, in the film's final sequences, that he was not a man at all but a middle-aged woman. In either case, the killer is himself eventually killed or otherwise evacuated from the narrative. No male character of any stature lives to tell the tale.

The one character of stature who does live to tell the tale is of course female. The Final Girl is introduced at the beginning and is the only character to be developed in any psychological detail. We understand immediately from the attention paid it that here is the main story line. She is intelligent, watchful, level-headed; the first character to sense something amiss and the only one to deduce from the accumulating evidence the patterns and extent of the threat; the only one, in other words, whose perspective approaches our own privileged understanding of the situation. We register her horror as she stumbles on the corpses of her friends; her paralysis in the face of death duplicates those moments of the universal nightmare experience on which horror frankly trades. When she downs the killer, we are triumphant. She is by any measure the slasher film's hero. This is not to say that our attachment to her is exclusive and unremitting, only that it adds up, and that in the closing sequence it is very close to absolute.

An analysis of the camerawork bears this out. Much is made of the use of the I-camera to represent the killer's point of view. In these passages – they are usually few and brief, but powerful – we see through his eyes and (on the sound track) hear his breathing and heartbeat. His and our vision is partly obscured by bushes or windowblinds in the foreground. By such means we are forced, the argument goes, to identify with the killer. In fact, however, the relation between camera point of view and the processes of viewer identification are poorly understood; the fact that Steven Spielberg can stage an attack in *Jaws* from the shark's point of view (underwater, rushing upward towards the swimmer's flailing legs) or Hitchcock an attack in *The Birds* from the birds-eye perspective (from the sky, as they gather to swoop down on the streets of Bodega Bay) would seem to suggest either that the viewer's identificatory powers are unbelievably elastic or that point-of-view shots can sometimes be pro forma.[44] But let us for the moment accept the equation point of view = identification. We are linked, in this way, with the killer in the early part of the film, usually before we have seen him directly and before we have come to know the Final Girl in any detail. Our closeness to him wanes as our closeness to the Final Girl waxes – a shift underwritten by story line as well as camera position. By the end, point of view is hers: we are in the closet with her, watching with her eyes the knife blade stab through the door; in the room with her as the killer breaks through the window and grabs at her; in the car with her as the killer stabs through the convertible top, and so on. With her, we become if not the killer of the killer then the agent of his expulsion from the narrative vision. If, during the film's course, we shifted our sympathies back and forth, and dealt them out to other characters along the way, we belong in the end to the Final Girl; there is no alternative. When Stretch eviscerates Chop Top at the end of *Texas Chainsaw II*, she is literally the only character left alive, on either side.

Audience response ratifies this design. Observers unanimously stress the readiness of the 'live' audience to switch sympathies in midstream, siding now with the killer and now, and finally, with the Final Girl. As Schoell, whose book on shocker films wrestles with its own monster, 'the feminists', puts it:

> Social critics make much of the fact that male audience members cheer on the misogynous misfits in these movies as they rape, plunder, and murder their screaming, writhing female victims. Since these same critics walk out of the moviehouse in disgust long before the movie is over, they don't realize that these same men cheer on (with renewed enthusiasm, in fact) the heroines, who are often as strong, sexy, and

independent as the [earlier] victims, as they blow away the killer with a shotgun or get him between the eyes with a machete. All of these men are said to be identifying with the maniac, but they enjoy *his* death throes the most of all, and applaud the heroine with admiration.[45]

What film-makers seem to know better than film critics is that gender is less a wall than a permeable membrane.[46]

No one who has read 'Red Riding Hood' to a small boy or participated in a viewing of, say, *Deliverance* (an all-male story that women find as gripping as men) or, more recently, *Alien* and *Aliens*, with whose space-age female Rambo, herself a Final Girl, male viewers seem to engage with ease, can doubt the phenomenon of cross-gender identification.[47] This fluidity of engaged perspective is in keeping with the universal claims of the psychoanalytic model: the threat function and the victim function coexist in the same unconscious, regardless of anatomical sex. But why, if viewers can identify across gender lines and if the root experience of horror is sex blind, are the screen sexes not interchangeable? Why not more and better female killers, and why (in light of the maleness of the majority audience) not Pauls as well as Paulines? The fact that horror film so stubbornly genders the killer male and the principal victim female would seem to suggest that representation itself is at issue – that the sensation of bodily fright derives not exclusively from repressed content, as Freud insisted, but also from the bodily manifestations of that content.

Nor is the gender of the principals as straightforward as it first seems. The killer's phallic purpose, as he thrust his drill or knife into the trembling bodies of young women, is unmistakable. At the same time, however, his masculinity is severely qualified: he ranges from the virginal or sexually inert to the transvestite or transsexual, is spiritually divided ('the mother half of his mind') or even equipped with vulva and vagina. Although the killer of *God Told Me To* is represented and taken as a male in the film text, he is revealed, by the doctor who delivered him, to have been sexually ambiguous from birth: 'I truly could not tell whether that child was male or female; it was as if the sexual gender had not been determined . . . as if it were being developed.'[48] In this respect, slasher killers have much in common with the monsters of classic horror – monsters who, in Linda Williams's formulation, represent not just 'an eruption of the normally repressed animal sexual energy of the civilised male' but also the 'power and potency of a *non-phallic* sexuality'. To the extent that the monster is constructed as feminine, the horror film thus expresses female desire only to show how monstrous it is.[49] The intention is manifest in *Aliens*, in which the Final Girl, Ripley, is pitted in the climactic scene against the most terrifying 'alien' of all: an egg-laying Mother.

Nor can we help noticing the 'intrauterine' quality of the Terrible Place, dark and often damp, in which the killer lives or lurks and whence he stages his most terrifying attacks. 'It often happens,' Freud wrote, 'that neurotic men declare that they feel there is something uncanny about the female genital organs. This *unheimlich* place, however, is an entrance to the former *Heim* [home] of all human beings, to the place where each one of us lived once upon a time and in the beginning.... In this case too then, the *unheimlich* is what once was *heimisch*, familiar; the prefix "*un*" ["un-"] is the token of repression.'[50] It is the exceptional film that does not mark as significant the moment that the killer leaps out of the dark recesses of a corridor or cavern at the trespassing victim, usually the Final Girl. Long after the other particulars have faded, the viewer will remember the images of Amy assaulted from the dark halls of a morgue (*He Knows You're Alone*), Sally or Stretch facing dismemberment in the ghastly dining room or underground labyrinth of the slaughterhouse family (*Texas Chainsaw I–II*), or Melanie trapped in the attic as the savage birds close in (*The Birds*). In such scenes of convergence the Other is at its bisexual mightiest, the victim at her tiniest, and the component of sadomasochism at its most blatant.

The gender of the Final Girl is likewise compromised from the outset by her masculine interests, her inevitable sexual reluctance (penetration, it seems, constructs the female), her apartness from other girls, sometimes her name. At the level of the cinematic apparatus, her unfemininity is signalled clearly by her exercise of the 'active investigating gaze' normally reserved for males and hideously punished in females when they assume it themselves; tentatively at first and then aggressively, the Final Girl looks *for* the killer, even tracking him to his forest hut or his underground labyrinth, and then *at* him, therewith bringing him, often for the first time, into our vision as well.[51] When, in the final scene, she stops screaming, looks at the killer, and reaches for the knife (sledge hammer, scalpel, gun, machete, hanger, knitting needle, chainsaw), she addresses the killer on his own terms. To the critics' objection that *Halloween* in effect punished female sexuality, director John Carpenter responded:

> They [the critics] completely missed the boat there, I think. Because if you turn it around, the one girl who is the most sexually uptight just keeps stabbing this guy with a long knife. She's the most sexually frustrated. She's the one that killed him. Not because she's a virgin, but because all that repressed energy starts coming out. She uses all those phallic symbols on the guy.... She and the killer have a certain link: sexual repression.[52]

For all its perversity, Carpenter's remark does underscore the sense of affinity, even recognition, that attends the final encounter. But the 'certain link' that puts killer and Final Girl on terms, at least briefly, is more than 'sexual repression'. It is also a shared masculinity, materialised in 'all those phallic symbols' – and it is also a shared femininity, materialised in what comes next (and what Carpenter, perhaps significantly, fails to mention): the castration, literal or symbolic, of the killer at her hands. His eyes may be put out, his hand severed, his body impaled or shot, his belly gashed, or his genitals sliced away or bitten off. The Final Girl has not just manned herself; she specifically unmans an oppressor whose masculinity was in question to begin with. By the time the drama has played itself out, darkness yields to light (often as day breaks) and the close quarters of the barn (closet, elevator, attic, basement) give way to the open expanse of the yard (field, road, lakescape, cliff). With the Final Girl's appropriation of 'all those phallic symbols' comes the quelling, the dispelling, of the 'uterine' threat as well. Consider again the paradigmatic ending of *Texas Chainsaw II*. From the underground labyrinth, murky and bloody, in which she faced saw, knife, and hammer, Stretch escapes through a culvert into the open air. She clambers up the jutting rock and with a chainsaw takes her stand. When her last assailant comes at her, she slashes open his lower abdomen – the sexual symbolism is all too clear – and flings him off the cliff. Again, the final scene shows her in extremely long shot, standing on the pinnacle, drenched in sunlight, buzzing chainsaw held overhead.

The tale would indeed seem to be one of sex and parents. The patently erotic threat is easily seen as the materialised projection of the dreamer's (viewer's) own incestuous fears and desires. It is this disabling cathexis to one's parents that must be killed and rekilled in the service of sexual autonomy. When the Final Girl stands at last in the light of day with the knife in her hand, she has delivered herself into the adult world. Carpenter's equation of the Final Girl with the killer has more than a grain of truth. The killers of *Psycho*, *The Eyes of Laura Mars*, *Friday the Thirteenth II–VI*, and *Cruising*, among others, are explicitly figured as sons in the psychosexual grip of their mothers (or fathers, in the case of *Cruising*). The difference is between past and present and between failure and success. The Final Girl enacts in the present, and successfully, the parenticidal struggle that the killer himself enacted unsuccessfully in his own past – a past that constitutes the film's backstory. She is what the killer once was; he is what she could become should she fail in her battle for sexual selfhood. 'You got a choice, boy,' says the tyrannical father of Leatherface in *Texas Chainsaw II*, 'sex or the saw; you never know about sex, but the saw – the saw is the family.'

But the tale is no less one of maleness. If the early experience of the Oedipal drama can be – is perhaps ideally – enacted in female form, the achievement of full adulthood requires the assumption and, apparently, brutal employment of the phallus. The helpless child is gendered feminine; the autonomous adult or subject is gendered masculine; the passage from child-hood to adulthood entails a shift from feminine to masculine. It is the male killer's tragedy that his incipient femininity is not reversed but completed (castration) and the Final Girl's victory that her incipient masculinity is not thwarted but realised (phallicisation). When De Palma says that female frailty is a predicate of the suspense genre, he proposes, in effect, that the lack of the phallus, for Lacan the privileged signifier of the symbolic order of culture, is itself simply horrifying, at least in the mind of the male observer. Where pornography (the argument goes) resolves that lack through a process of fetishisation that allows a breast or leg or whole body to stand in for the missing member, the slasher film resolves it either through eliminating the woman (earlier victims) or reconstituting her as masculine (Final Girl). The moment at which the Final Girl is effectively phallicised is the moment that the plot halts and horror ceases. Day breaks, and the community returns to its normal order.

Casting psychoanalytic verities in female form has a venerable cinematic history. Ingmar Bergman has made a career of it, and Woody Allen shows signs of following his lead. One immediate and practical advantage, by now presumably unconscious on the part of the makers as well as viewers, has to do with a preestablished cinematic 'language' for capturing the moves and moods of the female body and face. The cinematic gaze, we are told, is male, and just as that gaze 'knows' how to fetishise the female form in pornography (in a way that it does not 'know' how to fetishise the male form),[53] so it 'knows', in horror, how to track a woman ascending a staircase in a scary house and how to study her face from an angle above as she first hears the killer's footfall. A set of conventions we now take for granted simply 'sees' males and females differently.

To this cinematic habit may be added the broader range of emotional expression traditionally allowed women. Angry displays of force may belong to the male, but crying, cowering, screaming, fainting, trembling, begging for mercy belong to the female. Abject terror, in short, is gendered feminine, and the more concerned a given film with that condition – and it is the essence of modern horror – the more likely the femaleness of the victim. It is no accident that male victims in slasher films are killed swiftly or offscreen, and that prolonged struggles, in which the victim has time to contemplate her imminent destruction, inevitably figure female. Only when one encounters the rare expression of abject terror on the part of a male (as in I Spit on Your Grave) does one apprehend the full extent of the cinematic double standard in such matters.[54]

It is also the case that gender displacement can provide a kind of identificatory buffer, an emotional remove, that permits the majority audience to explore taboo subjects in the relative safety of vicariousness. Just as Bergman came to realise that he could explore castration anxiety more freely via depictions of hurt female bodies (witness the genital mutilation of Karin in Cries and Whispers), so the makers of slasher films seem to know that sadomasochistic incest fantasies sit more easily with the male viewer when the visible player is female. It is one thing for that viewer to hear the psychiatrist intone at the end of Psycho that Norman as a boy (in the backstory) was abnormally attached to his mother; it would be quite another to see that attachment dramatised in the present, to experience in nightmare form the elaboration of Norman's (the viewer's own) fears and desires. If the former is playable in male form, the latter, it seems, is not.

The Final Girl is, on reflection, a congenial double for the adolescent male. She is feminine enough to act out in a gratifying way, a way unapproved for adult males, the terrors and masochistic pleasures of the underlying fantasy, but not so feminine as to disturb the structures of male competence and sexuality. Her sexual inactivity, in this reading, becomes all but inevitable; the male viewer may be willing to enter into the vicarious experience of defending himself from the possibility of symbolic penetration on the part of the killer, but real vaginal penetration on the diegetic level is evidently more femaleness than he can bear. The question then arises whether the Final Girls of slasher films – Stretch, Stevie, Marti, Will, Terry, Laurie, and Ripley – are not boyish for the same reason that the female 'victims' in Victorian flagellation literature – 'Georgy', 'Willy' – are boyish: because they are transformed males. The transformation, Steven Marcus writes, 'is itself both a defense against and a disavowal of the fantasy it is simultaneously expressing – namely, that a *boy* is being beaten – that is, loved – by another man'.[55] What is represented as male-on-female violence, in short, is figuratively speaking male-on-male sex. For Marcus, the literary picture of flagellation, in which *girls* are beaten, is utterly belied by the descriptions (in *My Secret Life*) of real-life episodes in which the persons being beaten are not girls at all but 'gentlemen' dressed in women's clothes ('He had a woman's dress on tucked up to his waist, showing his naked rump and thighs. . . . On his head was a woman's cap tied carefully round his face to hide whiskers') and whipped by prostitutes. Reality, Marcus writes, 'puts the literature of flagellation out of the running . . . by showing how that literature is a completely distorted and idealised version of what actually happens'.[56] Applied to the slasher film, this logic reads the femaleness of the Final Girl (at least up to the point of her transformation) and indeed of the women victims in general as only apparent, the artifact of heterosexual deflection. It may be through the female body that the body of the audience is sensationalised, but the sensation is an entirely male affair.

At least one director, Hitchcock, explicitly located thrill in the equation victim = audience. So we judge from his marginal jottings in the shooting instructions for the shower scene in *Psycho*: 'The slashing. An impression of a knife slashing, as if tearing at the very screen, ripping the film.'[57] Not just the body of Marion is to be ruptured, but also the body on the other side of the film and screen: our witnessing body. As Marion is to Norman, the audience of *Psycho* is to Hitchcock; as the audiences of horror film in general are to the directors of those films, female is to male. Hitchcock's 'torture the women' then means, simply, torture the audience. De Palma's remarks about female frailty likewise contemplate a male-on-'female' relationship between director and viewer. Cinefantastic horror, in short, succeeds in the production of sensation to more or less the degree that it succeeds in incorporating its spectators as 'feminine' and then violating that body – which recoils, shudders, cries out collectively – in ways otherwise imaginable, for males, only in nightmare. The equation is nowhere more plainly put than in David Cronenberg's *Videodrome*. Here the threat is a mind-destroying video signal and the victims television viewers. Despite the (male) hero's efforts to defend his mental (and physical) integrity, a deep, vagina-like gash appears on his lower abdomen. Says the media conspirator as he thrusts a videocassette into the victim's gaping wound, 'You must open yourself completely to this.'

If the slasher film is 'on the face of it' a genre with at least a strong female presence, it is in these figurative readings a thoroughly strong male exercise, one that finally has very little to do with femaleness and very much to do with phallocentrism. Figuratively seen, the Final Girl is a male surrogate in things oedipal, a homoerotic stand-in, the audience incorporate; to the extent she 'means' girl at all, it is only for purposes of signifying phallic lack, and even that meaning is nullified in the final scenes. Our initial question – how to square a female victim-hero with a largely male audience – is not so much answered as it is obviated in these readings. The Final Girl is (apparently) female not despite the maleness of the audience, but precisely because of it. The discourse is wholly masculine, and females figure in it only insofar as they 'read' some aspect of male experience. To applaud the Final Girl as a feminist development, as some reviews of *Aliens* have done with Ripley, is, in light of her figurative meaning, a particularly grotesque expression of wishful thinking.[58] She is simply an agreed-upon fiction, and the male viewer's use of her as a vehicle for his own sadomasochistic fantasies an act of perhaps timeless dishonesty.

For all their immediate appeal, these figurative readings loosen as many ends as they tie together. The audience, we have said, is predominantly male; but what about the women in it? Do we dismiss them as male-identified and account for their experiences as an 'immasculated' act of collusion with the oppressor?[59] This is a strong judgment to apply to large numbers of women; for while it may be that the audience for slasher films is mainly male, that does not mean that there are not also many female viewers who actively like such films, and of course there are also women, however few, who script, direct, and produce them. These facts alone oblige us at least to consider the possibility that female fans find a meaning in the text and image of these films that is less inimical to their own interests than the figurative analysis would have us believe. Or should we conclude that males and females read these films differently in some fundamental sense? Do females respond to the text (the literal) and males the subtext (the figurative)?[60]

Some such notion of differential understanding underlies the homoerotic reading. The silent presupposition of that reading is that male identification with the female as female cannot be, and that the male viewer/reader who adjoins feminine experience does so only by homosexual conversion. But does female identification with male experience then similarly indicate a lesbian conversion? Or are the processes of patriarchy so one-way that the female can identify with the male directly, but the male can identify with the female only by transsexualising her? Does the Final Girl mean 'girl' to her female viewers and 'boy' to her male viewers? If her masculine features qualify her as a transformed boy, do not the feminine features of the killer qualify him as a transformed woman (in which case the homoerotic reading can be maintained only by defining that 'woman' as phallic and retransforming her into a male)? Striking though it is, the analogy between the Victorian flagellation story's Georgy and the slasher film's Stretch falters at the moment that Stretch turns on her assailant and unmans him. Are we to suppose that a homoerotic beating fantasy suddenly yields to what folklorists call a 'lack-liquidated' fantasy? Further: is it simple coincidence that this combination tale – trials, then triumph – bears such a striking resemblance to the classic (male) hero story? Does the standard hero story featuring an anatomical female 'mean' differently from one featuring an anatomical male?

As Marcus perceived, the relationship between the Georgy stories of flagellation literature and the real-life anecdote of the Victorian gentleman is a marvellously telling one. In his view, the maleness of the latter must prove the essential or functional maleness of the former. What his analysis does not come to full grips with, however, is the clothing the gentleman wears – not that of a child, as Marcus's 'childish' reading of the scene contemplates, but explicitly that of a woman.[61] These women's clothes can of course be understood, within the terms of the homoerotic interpretation, as a last-ditch effort on the part of the gentleman to dissociate himself from the (incestuous) homosexuality implicit in his favored sexual practice. But can they not just as well, and far more economically, be explained as part and parcel of a fantasy of literal femaleness? By the same token, cannot the femaleness of the gentleman's literary representatives – the girls of the flagellation stories – be understood as the obvious, even necessary, extension of that man's dress and cap? The same dress and cap, I suggest, haunt the margins of the slasher film. This is not to deny the deflective convenience, for the male spectator (and film-maker), of a female victim-hero in a context so fraught with taboo; it is only to suggest that the femaleness of that character is also conditioned by a kind of imaginative curiosity about the feminine in and of itself.

So too the psychoanalytic case. These films do indeed seem to pit the child in a struggle, at once terrifying and attractive, with the parental Other, and it is a rare example that does not directly thematise parent-child relations. But if Freud stressed the maternal source of the *unheimlich*, the Other of our films is decidedly androgynous: female/feminine in aspects of character and place (the 'intrauterine' locale) but male in anatomy. Conventional logic may interpret the killer as the phallic mother of the transformed boy (the Final Girl), but the text itself does not compel such a reading. On the contrary, the text at every level presents us with hermaphroditic constructions – constructions that draw attention to themselves and demand to be taken on their own terms.

For if we define the Final Girl as nothing more than a figurative male, what do we then make of the context of the spectacular gender play in which she is emphatically situated? In his essay on the uncanny, Freud rejected out of hand

Jentsch's theory that the experience of horror proceeds from intellectual uncertainty (curiosity?) – feelings of confusion, induced by an author or a coincidence, about who, what, and where one is.[62] One wonders, however, whether Freud would have been quite so dismissive if, instead of the mixed materials he used as evidence, he were presented with a coherent story corpus – forty slashers, say – in which the themes of incest and separation were relentlessly played out by a female character, and further in which gender identity was repeatedly thematised as an issue in and of itself. For although the factors we have considered thus far – the conventions of the male gaze, the feminine constitution of abject terror, the value for the male viewer of emotional distance from the taboos in question, the special horror that may inhere, for the male audience, in phallic lack, the homoerotic deflection – go a long way in explaining why it is we have Pauline rather than Paul as our victim-hero, they do not finally account for our strong sense that gender is simply being played with, and that part of the thrill lies precisely in the resulting 'intellectual uncertainty' of sexual identity.

The 'play of pronoun function' that underlies and defines the cinefantastic is nowhere more richly manifested than in the slasher; if the genre has an aesthetic base, it is exactly that of a visual identity game. Consider, for example, the by now standard habit of letting us view the action in the first person long before revealing who or what the first person is. In the opening sequence of *Halloween I*, 'we' are belatedly revealed to ourselves, after committing a murder in the cinematic first person, as a six-year-old boy. The surprise is often within gender, but it is also, in a striking number of cases, across gender. Again, *Friday the Thirteenth I*, in which 'we' stalk and kill a number of teenagers over the course of an hour of screen time without even knowing who 'we' are; we are invited, by conventional expectation and by glimpses of 'our' own bodily parts – a heavily booted foot, a roughly gloved hand – to suppose that 'we' are male, but 'we' are revealed, at film's end, as a woman. If this is the most dramatic case of pulling out the gender rug, it is by no means the only one. In *Dressed to Kill*, we are led to believe, again by means of glimpses, that 'we' are female – only to discover, in the denouement, that 'we' are a male in drag. In *Psycho*, the dame we glimpse holding the knife with a 'visible virility quite obscene in an old lady' is later revealed, after additional gender teasing, to be Norman in his mother's clothes.[63] *Psycho II* plays much the same game. *Cruising* (in which, not accidentally, transvestites play a prominent role) adjusts the terms along heterosexual/homosexual lines. The tease here is whether the originally straight detective assigned to the string of murders in a gay community does or does not succumb to his assumed homosexual identity; the camerawork leaves us increasingly uncertain as to his (our) sexual inclinations, not to speak of his (our) complicity in the crimes. Even at film's end we are not sure who 'we' were during several of the first-person sequences.[64]

The gender-identity game, in short, is too patterned and too pervasive in the slasher film to be dismissed as supervenient. It would seem instead to be an integral element of the particular brand of bodily sensation in which the

Dressed to Kill (Brian de Palma, 1980)

genre trades. Nor is it exclusive to horror. It is directly thematised in comic terms in the recent 'gender benders' *Tootsie* (in which a man passes himself off as a woman) and *All of Me* (in which a woman is literally introjected into a man and affects his speech, movement, and thought). It is also directly thematised, in the form of bisexual and androgynous figures and relations, in such cult films as *Pink Flamingos* and *The Rocky Horror Picture Show*. (Some version of it is indeed enacted every few minutes on MTV.) It is further thematised (predictably enough, given their bodily concerns) in such pornographic films as *Every Woman Has a Fantasy*, in which a man, in order to gain access to a women's group in which sexual fantasies are discussed, dresses and presents himself as a woman. (The degree to which 'male' pornography in general relies for its effect on cross-gender identification remains an open question; the proposition makes a certain sense of the obligatory lesbian sequences and the phenomenal success of *Behind the Green Door*, to pick just two examples.[65]) All of these films, and others like them, seem to be asking some version of the question: what would it be like to be, or to seem to be, if only temporarily, a woman? Taking exception to the reception of *Tootsie* as a feminist film, Elaine Showalter argues that the success of 'Dorothy Michaels' (the Dustin Hoffman character), as far as both plot and audience are concerned, lies in the veiling of masculine power in feminine costume. *Tootsie*'s cross-dressing, she writes,

> is a way of promoting the notion of masculine power while masking it.
> In psychoanalytic theory, the male transvestite is not a powerless man;

according to the psychiatrist Robert Stoller, in *Sex and Gender*, he is a 'phallic woman' who can tell himself that 'he is, or with practice will become, a better woman than a biological female if he chooses to do so'. When it is safe or necessary, the transvestite 'gets great pleasure in revealing that he is male-woman .... The pleasure in tricking the unsuspecting into thinking he is a woman, and then revealing his maleness (e.g., by suddenly dropping his voice) is not so much erotic as it is proof that there is such a thing as a woman with a penis'. Dorothy's effectiveness is the literal equivalent of speaking softly and carrying a big stick.[66]

By the same literalistic token, then, Stretch's success must lie in the fact that in the end, at least, she 'speaks loudly' *even though* she carried *no* 'stick'. Just as 'Dorothy's' voice slips serve to remind us that her character really is male, so the Final Girl's 'tits and scream' serve more or less continuously to remind us that she really is female – even as, and despite the fact that, she in the end acquits herself 'like a man'.[67] Her chainsaw is thus what 'Dorothy Michaels's' skirt is: a figuration of what she *does* and what she *seems*, as opposed to – and the films turn on the opposition – what she *is*. The idea that appearance and behavior do not necessarily indicate sex – indeed, can misindicate sex – is predicated on the understanding that sex is one thing and gender another; in practice, that sex is life, a less-than-interesting given, but that gender is theater. Whatever else it may be, Stretch's waving of the chainsaw is a moment of high drag. Its purpose is not to make us forget that she is a girl but to thrust that fact on us. The moment, it is probably fair to say, is also one that openly mocks the literary/cinematic conventions of symbolic representation.

It may be just this theatricalisation of gender that makes possible the willingness of the male viewer to submit himself to a brand of spectator experience that Hitchcock designated as 'feminine' in 1960 and that has become only more so since then. In classic horror, the 'feminization' of the audience is intermittent and ceases early. Our relationship with Marion's body in *Psycho* halts abruptly at the moment of its greatest intensity (slashing, ripping, tearing). The considerable remainder of the film distributes our bruised sympathies among several lesser figures, male and female, in such a way and at such length as to ameliorate the Marion experience and leave us, in the end, more or less recuperated in our (presumed) masculinity. Like Marion, the Final Girl is the designated victim, the incorporation of the audience, the slashing, ripping, and tearing of whose body will cause us to flinch and scream out in our seat. But unlike Marion, she does not die. If *Psycho*, like other classic horror films, solves the femininity problem by obliterating the female and replacing her with representatives of the masculine order (mostly but not inevitably males), the modern slasher solves it by regendering the woman. We are, as an audience, in the end 'masculinized' by and through the very figure by and through whom we were earlier 'feminized'. The same body does for both, and that body is female.

The last point is the crucial one: the same *female* body does for both. The Final Girl 1) undergoes agonising trials, and 2) virtually or actually destroys the antagonist and saves herself. By the lights of folk tradition, she is not a heroine, for whom phase 1 consists in being saved by someone else, but a hero, who rises to the occasion and defeats the adversary with his own wit and hands. Part 1 of the story sits well on the female; it is the heart of heroine stories in general (Red Riding Hood, Pauline), and in some figurative sense, in ways we have elaborated in some detail, it is gendered feminine even when played by a male. Odysseus's position, trapped in the cave of the Cyclops, is after all not so different from Pauline's position tied to the tracks or Sally's trapped in the dining room of the slaughterhouse family. The decisive moment, as far as the fixing of gender is concerned, lies in what happens next: those who save themselves are male, and those who are saved by others are female. No matter how 'feminine' his experience in phase 1, the traditional hero, if he rises against his adversary and saves himself in phase 2, will be male.

What is remarkable about the slasher film is that it comes close to reversing the priorities. Presumably for the various functional or figurative reasons we have considered in this essay, phase 1 wants a female: on that point all slashers from *Psycho* on are agreed. Abject fear is still gendered feminine, and the taboo anxieties in which slashers trade are still explored more easily via Pauline than Paul. The slippage comes in phase 2. As if in mute deference to a cultural imperative, slasher films from the 1970s bring in a last-minute male, even when he is rendered supernumerary by the Final Girl's sturdy defense. By 1980, however, the male rescuer is either dismissably marginal or dispensed with altogether; not a few films have him rush to the rescue only to be hacked to bits, leaving the Final Girl to save herself after all. At the moment that the Final Girl becomes her own savior, she becomes a hero; and the moment that she becomes a hero is the moment that the male viewer gives up the last pretense of male identification. Abject terror may still be gendered feminine, but the willingness of one immensely popular current genre to re-represent the hero as an anatomical female would seem to suggest that at least one of the traditional marks of heroism, triumphant self-rescue, is no longer strictly gendered masculine.

So too the cinematic apparatus. The classic split between 'spectacle and narrative', which 'supposes the man's role as the active one of forwarding the story, making things happen', is at least unsettled in the slasher film.[68] When the Final Girl (in films like *Hell Night, Texas Chainsaw II*, and even *Splatter University*) assumes the 'active investigating gaze', she exactly reverses the look, making a spectacle of the killer and a spectator of herself. Again, it is through the killer's eyes (I-camera) that we saw the Final Girl at the beginning of the film, and through the Final Girl's eyes that we see the killer, often for the first time with any clarity, towards the end. The gaze becomes, at least for a while, female. More to the point, the female exercise of scopic control results not in her annihilation, in the manner of classic cinema, but in her triumph; indeed, her triumph *depends* on her assumption of the gaze. It is no surprise, in light of these developments, that the Final Girl should show signs of boyishness. Her symbolic phallicisation, in the last scenes, may or may not proceed at root from the horror of lack on the part of audience and maker. But it certainly proceeds from the need to bring her in line with the epic laws of Western narrative tradition – the very unanimity of which bears witness to the historical importance, in popular culture, of the literal representation of heroism in male form – and it proceeds no less from the need to render the reallocated gaze intelligible to an audience conditioned by the dominant cinematic apparatus.

It is worth noting that the higher genres of horror have for the most part resisted such developments. The idea of a female who outsmarts, much less outfights – or outgazes – her assailant is unthinkable in the films of De Palma and Hitchcock. Although the slasher film's victims may be sexual teases, they are not in addition simple-minded, scheming, physically incompetent, and morally deficient in the manner of these film-makers' female victims. And however revolting their special effects and sexualised their violence, few slasher murders approach the level of voluptuous sadism that attends the destruction of women in De Palma's films. For reasons on which we can only speculate, femininity is more conventionally elaborated and inexorably punished, and in an emphatically masculine environment, in the higher forms – the forms that *are* written up, and not by Joe Bob Briggs.

That the slasher film speaks deeply and obsessively to male anxieties and desires seems clear – if nothing else from the maleness of the majority audience. And yet these are texts in which the categories masculine and feminine, traditionally embodied in male and female, are collapsed into one and the same character – a character who is anatomically female and one whose point of view the spectator is unambiguously invited, by the usual set of literary-structural and cinematic conventions, to share. The willingness and even eagerness (so we judge from these films' enormous popularity) of the male viewer to throw in his emotional lot, if only temporarily, with not only a woman but a woman in fear and pain, at least in the first instance, would seem to suggest that he has a vicarious stake in that fear and pain. If it is also the case that the act of horror spectatorship is itself registered as a 'feminine' experience – that the shock effects induce bodily sensations in the viewer answering the fear and pain of the screen victim – the charge of masochism is underlined. This is not to say that the male viewer does not also have a stake in the sadistic side; narrative structure, cinematic procedures, and audience response all indicate that he shifts back and forth with ease. It is only to suggest that in the Final Girl sequence his empathy with what the films define as the female posture is fully engaged, and further, because this sequence is inevitably the central one in any given film, that the viewing experience hinges on the emotional assumption of the feminine posture. Kaja

Silverman takes it a step further: 'I will hazard the generalisation that it is always the victim – the figure who occupies the passive position – who is really the focus of attention, and whose subjugation the subject (whether male or female) experiences as a pleasurable repetition from his/her own story', she writes. 'Indeed, I would go so far as to say that the fascination of the sadistic point of view is merely that it provides the best vantage point from which to watch the masochistic story unfold.'[69]

The slasher is hardly the first genre in the literary and visual arts to invite identification with the female; one cannot help wondering more generally whether the historical maintenance of images of women in fear and pain does not have more to do with male vicarism than is commonly acknowledged. What distinguishes the slasher, however, is the absence or untenability of alternative perspectives and hence the exposed quality of the invitation. As a survey of the tradition shows, this has not always been the case. The stages of the Final Girl's evolution – her piecemeal absorption of functions previously represented in males – can be located in the years following 1978. The fact that the typical patrons of these films are the sons of marriages contracted in the 1960s or even early seventies leads us to speculate that the dire claims of that era – that the women's movement, the entry of women into the workplace, and the rise of divorce and woman-headed families would yield massive gender confusion in the next generation – were not entirely wrong. We may prefer, in the eighties, to speak of the cult of androgyny, but the point is roughly the same. The fact that we have in the killer a feminine male and in the main character a masculine female – parent and Everyteen, respectively – would seem, especially in the latter case, to suggest a loosening of the categories, or at least of the equation sex = gender. It is not that these films show us gender and sex in free variation; it is that they fix on the irregular combinations, of which the combination masculine female repeatedly prevails over the combination feminine male. The fact that masculine males (boyfriends, fathers, would-be rescuers) are regularly dismissed through ridicule or death or both would seem to suggest that it is not masculinity per se that is being privileged, but masculinity in conjunction with a female body – indeed, as the term victim-hero contemplates, masculinity in conjunction with femininity. For if 'masculine' describes the Final Girl some of the time, and in some of her more theatrical moments, it does not do justice to the sense of her character as a whole. She alternates between registers from the outset; before her final struggle she endures the deepest throes of 'femininity'; and even during that final struggle she is now weak and now strong, now flees the killer and now charges him, now stabs and is stabbed, now cries out in fear and now shouts in anger. She is a physical female and a characterological androgyne: like her name, not masculine but either/or, both, ambiguous.[70]

Robin Wood speaks of the sense that horror, for him the by-product of cultural crisis and disintegration, is 'currently the most important of all American [film] genres and perhaps the most progressive, even in its overt nihilism'.[71] Likewise Vale and Juno say of the 'incredibly strange films', mostly low-budget horror, that their volume surveys: 'They often present unpopular – even radical – views addressing the social, political, racial, or sexual inequities, hypocrisy in religion or government.'[72] And Tania Modleski rests her case against the standard critique of mass culture (stemming from the Frankfurt School) squarely on the evidence of the slasher, which does *not* propose a spurious harmony; does *not* promote the 'specious good' (but indeed often exposes and attacks it); does *not* ply the mechanisms of identification, narrative continuity, and closure to provide the sort of narrative pleasure constitutive of the dominant ideology.[73] One is deeply reluctant to make progressive claims for a body of cinema as spectacularly nasty towards women as the slasher film is, but the fact is that the slasher does, in its own perverse way and for better or worse, constitute a visible adjustment in the terms of gender representation. That it is an adjustment largely on the male side, appearing at the furthest possible remove from the quarters of theory and showing signs of trickling upwards, is of no small interest.

I owe a special debt of gratitude to James Cunniff and Lynn Hunt for criticism and encouragement. Particular thanks to James (not Lynn) for sitting with me through not a few of these movies.

NOTES

1 Films referred to in this essay are included in the Index of Film and Video Titles.

2 Morris Dickstein, 'The Aesthetics of Fright', *American Film* 5, 1980, p. 34.

3 'Will Rogers said he never met a man he didn't like, and I can truly say the same about the cinema', Harvey R. Greenberg says in his paean to horror, *The Movies on Your Mind* (New York, 1975); yet his claim does not extend to the 'plethora of execrable imitations [of *Psycho*] that debased cinema', p. 137.

4 William Schoell, *Stay Out of the Shower* (New York, 1985).

5 'Joe Bob Briggs' was evidently invented as a solution to the *Dallas Times Herald*'s problem of 'how to cover trashy movies'. See Calvin Trillin's 'American Chronicles: The Life and Times of Joe Bob Briggs, So Far'. *The New Yorker*, 22 December 1986, pp. 73–88.

6 Lew Brighton, 'Saturn in Retrograde; or, The Texas Jump Cut', *The Film Journal* 7, 1975, p. 25.

7 Stephen Koch, 'Fashions in Pornography: Murder as Cinematic Chic', *Harper's*, November 1976, pp. 108–9.

8 Robin Wood, 'Return of the Repressed', *Film Comment* 14, 1978, p. 30.

9 Robin Wood, 'Beauty Bests the Beast', *American Film* 8, 1983, p. 63.

10 Dickstein, 'The Aesthetics of Fright', p. 34.

11 'The "Uncanny" ', in *The Standard Edition of the Complete Psychological Works of Sigmund Freud*, (ed.) and trans. James Strachey, 24 vols. (London: Hogarth Press, 1953–66), vol. 17, p. 244. Originally published in *Imago* 5/6, 1919, p. 317.

12 Steven Marcus, *The Other Victorians: A Study of Sexuality and Pornography in Mid-Nineteenth-Century England* (New York, 1964), p. 278.

13 William Castle, *Step Right Up! I'm Gonna Scare the Pants Off America* (New York, 1978).

14 Given the number of permutations, it is no surprise that new strategies keep emerging. Only a few years ago, a director hit upon the idea of rendering the point of view of an infant through use of an I-camera at floor level with a double-vision image (Larry Cohen, *It's Alive*). Nearly a century after technology provided a radically different means of telling a story, film-makers are still uncovering the possibilities.

15 Mick Martin and Marsha Porter, in reference to *Friday the Thirteenth I*, in *Video Movie Guide: 1987* (New York, 1987), p. 690. Robin Wood, 'Beauty Bests the Beast', p. 65, notes that the first-person camera also serves to preserve the secret of the killer's identity for a final surprise – crucial to many films – but adds: 'The sense of indeterminate, unidentified, possibly supernatural or superhuman Menace feeds the spectator's fantasy of power, facilitating a direct spectator-camera identification by keeping the intermediary character, while signified to be present, as vaguely defined as possible.' Brian De Palma's *Blow-Out* opens with a parody of just this cinematic habit.

16 On this widely discussed topic, see especially Kaja Silverman, *The Subject of Semiotics* (New York, 1983), pp. 194–236; and Lesley Stern, 'Point of View: The Blind Spot', *Film Reader* 4, 1979, pp. 214–36.

17 In this essay I have used the term *identification* vaguely and generally to refer both to primary and secondary processes. See especially Mary Ann Doane, 'Misrecognition and Identity', *Cine-Tracts* 11, 1980, pp. 25–32; also Christian Metz, 'The Imaginary Signifier', in his *The Imaginary Signifier: Psychoanalysis and the Cinema* (Bloomington, Ind., 1982).

18 Mark Nash, '*Vampyr* and the Fantastic', *Screen*, vol. 17 no. 3, Autumn 1976, p. 37. Nash coins the term *cinefantastic* to refer to this play.

19 Rosemary Jackson, *Fantasy: The Literature of Subversion* (London: Methuen 1981), p. 31.

20 As Dickstein puts it, 'The "art" of horror film is a ludicrous notion since horror, even at its most commercially exploitative, is genuinely subcultural like the wild child that can never be tamed, or the half-human mutant who appeals to our secret fascination with deformity and the grotesque'; 'The Aesthetics of Fright', p. 34.

21 James B. Twitchell, *Dreadful Pleasures: An Anatomy of Modern Horror* (New York, 1985), p. 84.

22 Donald Spoto, *The Dark Side of Genius: The Life of Alfred Hitchcock* (New York, 1983).

23 Wood, 'Return of the Repressed', p. 26. In Wes Craven's *Nightmare on Elm Street*, it is the nightmare itself, shared by the teenagers who live on Elm Street, that is fatal. One by one they are killed by the murderer of their collective dream. The one girl who survives does so by first refusing to sleep and then, at the same time that she acknowledges her parents' inadequacies, by conquering the feelings that prompt the deadly nightmare. See, as an example of the topic dream/horror, Dennis L. White, 'The Poetics of Horror', *Cinema Journal* 10, 1971, pp. 1–18.

24 It is not just the profit margin that fuels the production of low horror. It is also the fact that, thanks to the irrelevance of production values, the initial stake is within the means of a small group of investors. Low horror is thus for all practical purposes the only way an independent film-maker can break into the market. Add to this the film-maker's unusual degree of control over the product and one begins to understand why it is that low horror engages the talents of such people as Stephanie Rothman, George Romero, Wes Craven, and Larry Cohen. As V. Vale and Andrea Juno put it, 'The value of low-budget films is: they can be transcendent expressions of a single person's individual vision and quirky originality. When a corporation decides to invest $20 million in a film, a chain of command regulates each step, and no person is allowed free rein. Meetings with lawyers, accountants, and corporate boards are what films in Hollywood are all about'; *Incredibly Strange Films*, (eds.) V. Vale and Andrea Juno, *Re/Search* 10, San Francisco, 1986, p. 5.

25 Despite the film industry's interest in demographics, there is no in-depth study of the composition of the slasher-film audience. Twitchell, *Dreadful Pleasures*, pp. 69–72 and pp. 306–7, relies on personal observation and the reports of critics, which are remarkably consistent over time and from place to place; my own observations concur. The audience is mostly between the ages of twelve and twenty, disproportionately male. Some critics remark on a contingent of older men who sit separately and who, in Twitchell's view, are there 'not to be frightened, but to participate specifically in the "stab-at-female" episodes'. Roger Ebert and Gene Siskel corroborate the observation.

26 The development of the human-sausage theme is typical of the back-and-forth borrowing in low horror. *Texas Chainsaw Massacre I* hints at it; *Motel Hell* turns it into an industry ('Farmer Vincent's Smoked Meats: This is It!' proclaims a local billboard); and *Texas Chainsaw Massacre II* expands it to a statewide chili-tasting contest.

27 'The release of sexuality in the horror film is always presented as perverted, monstrous, and excessive, both the perversion and the excess being the logical outcome of repressing. Nowhere is this carried further than in *Texas [Chainsaw] Massacre [I]*. Here sexuality is totally perverted from its functions, into sadism, violence, and cannibalism. It is striking that there is no suggestion anywhere that Sally is the object of an overtly sexual threat; she is to be tormented, killed, dismembered, and eaten, but not raped'; Wood, 'Return of the Repressed', p. 31.

28 With some exceptions: for example, the spear gun used in the sixth killing in *Friday the Thirteenth III*.

29 Stuart Kaminsky, *American Film Genres: Approaches to a Critical Theory of Popular Film* (New York, 1977), p. 107.

30 The shower sequence in *Psycho* is probably the most echoed scene in all of film history. The bathtub scene in *I Spit on Your Grave* (not properly speaking a slasher, though with a number of generic affinities) is to my knowledge the only effort to reverse the terms.

31 Schoell, *Stay Out of the Shower*, p. 35. It may be argued that *Blood Feast* (1963), in which a lame Egyptian caterer slaughters one woman after another for their bodily parts (all in the service of Ishtar), provides the serial-murder model.

32 This theme too is spoofed in *Motel Hell*. Farmer Vincent's victims are two hookers, a kinky couple looking for same (he puts them in room #1 of the motel), and Terry and her boyfriend Bo, out for kicks on a motorcycle. When Terry (allowed to survive) wonders aloud why someone would try to kill them, Farmer Vincent answers her by asking pointedly whether they were married. 'No', she says, in a tone of resignation, as if accepting the logic.

33 Further: 'Scenes in which women whimper helplessly and do nothing to defend themselves are ridiculed by the audience, who find it hard to believe that anyone – male or female – would simply allow someone to kill them with nary a protest.' Schoell, *Stay Out of the Shower*, pp. 55–6.

34 *Splatter University* (1984) is a disturbing exception. Professor Julie Parker is clearly established as a Final Girl from the outset and then killed just after the beginning of what we are led to believe will be the Final Girl sequence (she kicks the killer, a psychotic priest-scholar who keeps his knife sheathed in a crucifix, in the groin, runs for the elevator – and then is trapped and stabbed to death). So meticulously are the conventions observed, and then so grossly violated, that we can only assume sadistic intentionality. This is a film in which (with the exception of an asylum orderly in the preface) only females are killed, and in highly sexual circumstances.

35 This film is complicated by the fact that the action is envisaged as a living dream. Nancy finally kills the killer by killing her part of the collective nightmare. See note 23 above.

36 Spoto, *Dark Side of Genius*, p. 454. See also William Rothman, *Hitchcock: The Murderous Gaze* (Cambridge, Mass., 1982), pp. 246–341.

37 'The Philosophy of Composition', in *Great Short Works of Edgar Allan Poe*, (ed.) G. R. Thompson (New York, 1970), p. 55.

38 As quoted in Schoell, *Stay Out of the Shower*, p. 56.

39 As quoted in Schoell, p. 41.

40 Spoto, *Dark Side of Genius*, p. 483.

41 Silvia Bovenschen, 'Is There a Feminine Aesthetic?' *New German Critique* 10, 1977, p. 114. See also Doane, 'Misrecognition and Identity'.

42 Ann Kaplan, *Women and Film: Both Sides of the Camera* (London and New York: Methuen, 1983), p. 15. The discussion of the gendered 'gaze' is lively and extensive. See above all Laura Mulvey, 'Visual Pleasure and Narrative Cinema', *Screen* vol. 16 no. 3, Autumn 1975, pp. 6–18; reprinted in *Film Theory and Criticism: Introductory Readings*, eds. Gerald Mast and Marshall Cohen, 3rd ed. (New York, 1985), pp. 803–16; also Christine Gledhill, 'Recent Developments in Feminist Criticism', *Quarterly Review of Film Studies* (1978); reprinted in Mast and Cohen, *Film Theory and Criticism*, pp. 817–45.

43 Wood, 'Beauty Bests the Beast', p. 64.

44 The locus classicus in this connection is the view-from-the-coffin shot in Carl Dreyer's *Vampyr*, in which the I-camera sees through the eyes of a dead man. See Nash, '*Vampyr* and the Fantastic', esp. pp. 32–3. The 1987 remake of *The Little Shop of Horrors* (itself originally a low-budget horror film, made the same year as *Psycho* in two days) lets us see the dentist from the proximate point of view of the patient's tonsils.

45 Two points in this paragraph deserve emending. One is the suggestion that rape is common in these films; it is in fact virtually absent, by definition (see note 27 above). The other is the characterization of the Final Girl as 'sexy'. She may be attractive (though typically less so than her friends), but she is with few exceptions sexually inactive. For a detailed analysis of point-of-view manipulation, together with a psychoanalytic interpretation of the dynamic, see Steve Neale, '*Halloween*: Suspense, Aggression, and the Look', *Framework* 14 (1981).

46 Wood is struck by the willingness of the teenaged audience to identify 'against' itself, with the forces of the enemy of youth. 'Watching it [*Texas Chainsaw Massacre 1*] recently with a large, half-stoned youth audience, who cheered and applauded every

one of Leatherface's outrages against their representatives on the screen, was a terrifying experience'; 'Return of the Repressed', p. 32.

47 'I really appreciate the way audiences respond', Gail Anne Hurd, producer of *Aliens*, is reported to have said. 'They buy it. We don't get people, even rednecks, leaving the theater saying, "That was stupid. No woman would do that." You don't have to be a liberal ERA supporter to root for Ripley'; as reported in the *San Francisco Examiner Datebook*, 10 August 1986, p. 19. *Time*, 28 July 1986, p. 56, suggests that Ripley's maternal impulses (she squares off against the worst aliens of all in her quest to save a little girl) give the audience 'a much stronger rooting interest in Ripley, and that gives the picture resonances unusual in a popcorn epic'.

48 Further: 'When she [the mother] referred to the infant as a male, I just went along with it. Wonder how that child turned out – male, female, or something else entirely?' The birth is understood to be parthenogenetic, and the bisexual child, literally equipped with both sets of genitals, is figured as the reborn Christ.

49 Linda Williams, 'When the Woman Looks', in *Re-Vision: Essays in Feminist Film Criticism*, eds. Mary Ann Doane, Patricia Mellencamp, and Linda Williams, American Film Institute Monograph Series (Los Angeles: The American Film Institute/ Frederick, Maryland: University Publishers of America, 1984), p. 90. Williams's emphasis on the phallic leads her to dismiss slasher killers as a 'non-specific male killing force' and hence a degeneration in the tradition. 'In these films the recognition and affinity between women and monster of classic horror film gives way to pure identity: she *is* the monster, her mutilated body is the only visible horror' (p. 96). This analysis does not do justice to the obvious bisexuality of slasher killers, nor does it take into account the new strength of the female victim. The slasher film may not, in balance, be more subversive than traditional horror, but it is certainly not less so.

50 Freud, 'The "Uncanny"', p. 245. See also Neale, '*Halloween*', esp. pp. 28–9.

51 'The woman's exercise of an active investigating gaze can only be simultaneous with her own victimization. The place of her specularization is tranformed into the locus of a process of seeing designed to unveil an aggression against itself'; Mary Ann Doane, 'The "Woman's Film"', in *Re-Vision*, p. 72.

52 John Carpenter interviewed by Todd McCarthy, 'Trick and Treat', *Film Comment* 16, 1980, pp. 23–4.

53 This is not so in traditional film, nor in heterosexual pornography, in any case. Gay male pornography, however, films some male bodies in much the same way that heterosexual pornography films female bodies.

54 Compare the visual treatment of the (male) rape in *Deliverance* with the (female) rapes in Hitchcock's *Frenzy* or Wes Craven's *Last House on the Left* or Ingmar Bergman's *The Virgin Spring*. The latter films study the victims' faces at length and in closeup during the act; the first looks at the act intermittently and in long shot, focusing less on the actual victim than on the victim's friend who must look on.

55 Marcus, *The Other Victorians*, pp. 260–61. Marcus distinguishes two phases in the development of flagellation literature: one in which the figure being beaten is a boy, and the second, in which the figure is a girl. The very shift indicates, at some level, the irrelevance of apparent sex. 'The sexual identity of the figure being beaten is remarkably labile. Sometimes he is represented as a boy, sometimes as a girl, sometimes as a combination of the two – a boy dressed as a girl, or the reverse.' The girls often have sexually ambiguous names, as well. The beater is a female, but in Marcus's reading a phallic one – muscular, possessed of body hair – representing the father.

56 Marcus, pp. 125–27.

57 Further: 'Suspense is like a woman. The more left to the imagination, the more the excitement.... The perfect "woman of mystery" is one who is blonde, subtle, and Nordic.... Movie titles, like women, should be easy to remember without being familiar, intriguing but never obvious, warm yet refreshing, suggest action, not impassiveness, and finally give a clue without revealing the plot. Although I do not profess to be an authority on women, I fear that the perfect title, like the perfect woman, is difficult to find'; as quoted by Spoto, *Dark Side of Genius*, p. 431.

58 This would seem to be the point of the final sequence of Brian De Palma's *Blow-Out*, in which we see the boyfriend of the victim-hero stab the killer to death but later hear the television announce that the woman herself vanquished the killer. The frame plot of the film has to do with the making of a slasher film ('Co-Ed Frenzy'), and it seems clear that De Palma means his ending to stand as a comment on the Final Girl formula of the genre. De Palma's (and indirectly Hitchcock's) insistence that only men can kill men, or protect women from men, deserves a separate essay.

59 The term is Judith Fetterly's. See her *The Resisting Reader: A Feminist Approach to American Fiction* (Bloomington, Ind., 1978).

60 On the possible variety of responses to a single film, see Norman N. Holland, 'I-ing Film', *Critical Inquiry* 12, 1986, pp. 654–71.

61 Marcus, *The Other Victorians*, 127. Marcus contents himself with noting that the scene demonstrates a 'confusion of sexual identity.' In the literature of flagellation, he adds, 'this confused identity is also present, but it is concealed and unacknowledged'. But it is precisely the femaleness of the beaten figures that does acknowledge it.

62 Freud, 'The "Uncanny"', esp. pp. 219–21 and pp. 226–27.

63 Raymond Durgnat, *Films and Feelings* (Cambridge, Mass., 1967), p. 216.

64 Not a few critics have argued that the ambiguity is the unintentional result of bad film-making.

65 So argues Susan Barrowclough: The 'male spectator takes the part not of the male, but of the female. Contrary to the assumption that the male uses pornography to confirm and celebrate his gender's sexual activity and dominance, is the possibility of his pleasure in identifying with a "feminine" passivity or subordination'. See her review of *Not a Love Story* in *Screen* vol. 23, 1982, pp. 35–6. Alan Soble seconds the proposal in his *Pornography: Marxism, Feminism, and the Future of Sexuality* (New Haven, 1986), p. 93. Porn/sexploitation film-maker Joe Sarno: 'My point of view is more or less always from the woman's point of view; the fairy tales that my films are based on are from the woman's point of view; I stress the efficacy of women for themselves. In general, I focus on the female orgasm as much as I can'; as quoted in Vale and Juno, *Incredibly Strange Films*, p. 94. 'Male identification with women,' Kaja Silverman writes, 'has not received the same amount of critical attention [as sublimation into professional "showing off" and reversal into scopophilia], although it would seem the most potentially destabilizing, at least as far as gender is concerned.' See her discussion of the 'Great Male Renunciation' in 'Fragments of a Fashionable Discourse', in *Studies in Entertainment: Critical Approaches to Mass Culture*, (ed.) Tania Modleski (Bloomington, Ind., 1986), p. 141.

66 Elaine Showalter, 'Critical Cross Dressing: Male Feminists and the Woman of the Year', *Raritan* 3, 1983, p. 138.

67 Whatever its other functions, the scene that reveals the Final Girl in a degree of undress serves to underscore her femaleness. One reviewer of *Aliens* remarks that she couldn't help wondering why in the last scene, just as in *Alien*, 'we have Ripley

wandering around clad only in her underwear. A little reminder of her gender, less we lost sight of it behind all that firepower?'; Christine Schoefer, *East Bay Express*, 5 September 1986, p. 37.

68 Mulvey, 'Visual Pleasure and Narrative Cinema', p. 12.

69 Kaja Silverman, 'Masochism and Subjectivity', *Framework* 12, 1979, 5. Needless to say, this is not the explanation for the girl-hero offered by the industry. *Time* magazine on *Aliens*: 'As Director Cameron says, the endless "remulching" of the masculine hero by the "male-dominated industry" is, if nothing else, commercially shortsighted. "They choose to ignore that 50% of the audience is female. And I've been told that it has been proved demographically that 80% of the time it's women who decide which film to see"'; 28 July 1986. It is of course not Cameron who established the female hero of the series but Ridley Scott (in *Alien*), and it is fair to assume, from his careful manipulation of the formula, that Scott got her from the slasher film, where she has flourished for some time with audiences that are heavily male. Cameron's analysis is thus both self-serving and beside the point.

70 If this analysis is correct, we may expect horror films of the future to feature Final Boys as well as Final Girls. Two recent figures may be incipient examples: Jesse, the pretty boy in *A Nightmare on Elm Street II*, and Ashley,. the character who dies last in *The Evil Dead* (1983). Neither quite plays the role, but their names, and in the case of Jesse the characterization, seem to play on the tradition.

71 For the opposite view (based on classic horror in both literary and cinematic manifestations), see Franco Moretti, 'The Dialectic of Fear', *New Left Review* 136, 1982, pp. 67–85.

72 Vale and Juno, *Incredibly Strange Films*, 5.

73 Tania Modleski, 'The Terror of Pleasure: The Contemporary Horror Film and Post-modern Theory', in *Studies in Entertainment*, pp. 155–66. (Like Modleski, I stress that my comments are based on many slashers, not all of them.) This important essay (and volume) appeared too late for me to take it into full account in the text.

II
THE *MISE EN SCÈNE* OF DESIRE

Introduction

As I noted in the general introduction, there has been in recent years something of a 'turn to fantasy' in cultural theory. The editors of *Formations of Fantasy* explain the impulse behind this move – the attempt to understand the *articulation* of the psychic and the social without seeing either side of the equation as wholly contingent on, or reducible to, the other.

> Psychoanalysis does not intend to uncover objective causes *in* reality so much as it seeks to change our very attitudes *to* that reality. This it achieves by effectively deconstructing that positivist dichotomy in which fantasy is simply *opposed* to 'reality', as an epiphenomenon. Psychoanalysis dismantles such a 'logic of the supplement' to reveal the supposedly marginal operations of fantasy at the centre of all our perceptions, beliefs and actions. The object of psychoanalysis is not the 'reality' of common sense, and (in a prevalent view) of empirical science; it is what Freud termed 'psychical reality'. Contrary to psychologism, psychoanalysis recognises no state of totally unambiguous and self-possessed lucidity in which an external world may be seen for, and known as, simply what it *is*. There is no possible 'end to ideologies'. Unconscious wishes, and the fantasies they engender, are as immutable a force in our lives as any material circumstance.[1]

This emphasis on fantasy as an organising force both within psychic life and within a variety of cultural forms – literary narratives, poetry, photography and even the figure of 'Margaret Thatcher' as well as films have been studied from this perspective – is clearly quite different from many more orthodox forms of Freudian interpretation.[2] All too often, those involved a hunt for sexual symbolism, spotting a penis and a breast here or a mouth and a womb there, searching out such bodily parts in apparently the most innocent texts. Fantasy, as it has been taken up in the study of film – particularly by feminist theorists – could not be more different from this banal reductionism. On the contrary, it has been used as a way of moving forward some of the most interesting theoretical and political debates of the 1970s and 80s, and of getting out of certain impasses within them.

One of the most extensively discussed of these problems has been that of the female spectator. Laura Mulvey's influential 1975 article 'Visual pleasure and narrative cinema' explored the way that mainstream film form is structured around a controlling male gaze – a perspective that entails not only a 'masculinised' address, but also (and only) the masculine pleasures of voyeurism and fetishism.[3] This seemed to leave the female spectator caught between the Scylla of identification with the sadistic male gaze and the Charybdis of being lumbered with the passive or masochistic position of the female characters. As an alternative to this uninviting Catch-22, with its emphasis on cinema's power to fix or 'position' both the female characters within a narrative and also the female spectator in the cinema, articles like Elisabeth Lyon's 'The cinema of Lol V. Stein' and Elizabeth Cowie's 'Fantasia' stress the *shifting* subject positions for female protagonists and the *multiple* points of identification for the spectator. Starting from a definition of fantasy as 'the mise en scène of desire',[4] for example, Cowie demonstrates through an analysis of *Now Voyager* and *The Reckless Moment* that:

> ... in each film the subject-positions shift across the boundary of sexual difference but do so always in terms of sexual difference. Thus while subject-positions are variable the terms of sexual difference are fixed. It is the form of tension and play between the fixing of narrative – the secondary elaboration – and the lack of fixity of the subject in the original fantasies which would seem to be important, and not any already-given privileging of one over the other.[5]

What is being proposed, in other words, is less an account of how the spectator is 'positioned' by cinema than an account of a play between fixity and mobility (we shall return to the concept of 'the original fantasies' in a moment.) Lyon makes a similar argument about *India Song*: that there is a continual shifting between, and merging of, the positions of 'the I/eye of the camera – the beggarwoman – Ann-Marie Stretter – the Vice-Consul – death' in which the spectator is caught up (this volume, p. 165). And, in 'The sexual differentiation of the Hitchcock text', Donald Greig illustrates his critique of the tunnel vision of Raymond Bellour's textual analysis, which sees only for the male Oedipal scenario, by revealing the textual fluidity and contradictoriness of a number of Hitchcock's films.

In a similar vein of critical reappraisal, Constance Penley has proposed fantasy – that is, *the staging and imaging of the subject and its desire* – as an alternative conceptual framework to the apparatus theories of Baudry and Metz. This would retain their dual focus on both the institution cinema and the psychic economy of spectatorship but, claims Penley, it would avoid their tendency to depict cinema as a 'bachelor machine'. By that she means that their emphasis on homogeneity and closure tends to efface the question of sexual difference and – if the cinematic machine is as efficient as they claim – to rule out the possibility of its subversion. She therefore invokes fantasy to suggest a relationship between film text and spectator that is less stable and more complex; she claims three major advantages for her alternative. First, it makes it possible 'to describe not only the subject's desire for the filmic image and its reproduction, but also the structure of the fantasmatic relation to that image, including the subject's belief in its reality'. Second, it presents a more accurate description of the spectator's shifting and multiple identifications and a more comprehensive account of these same movements within the film: the perpetually changing configurations of the characters, for example, are a formal response to the unfolding of a highly organised fantasy that is the filmic fiction itself.

And, finally, 'the model of fantasy would allow us to retain the ... stress on the cinema as an *institution*: in this light, all films, and not just the products of Hollywood, would be seen and studied in their fully historical and social variety as *dream-factories*.'[6]

FANTASY IN PSYCHOANALYSIS

Such approaches to fantasy, which see it not as simple wish-fulfilment, but as a more complex, defensive process which involves the organisation of desire, lack and repression, owe much to two key texts by Jean Laplanche and J.-B. Pontalis, the entry on 'Phantasy (or fantasy)' in *The Language of Psychoanalysis* and their article 'Fantasy and the origins of sexuality'.[7] It is well worth reading these to contextualise many of the arguments made in the articles reprinted in this section; here I can offer only a thumbnail sketch of this conceptualisation.

Freud's interest in the formative power of fantasy and psychic reality is usually attributed to his realisation that the tales of paternal seduction or rape told by many of his women patients did not necessarily refer to a real event. Such events, he argued, could be as decisive on their psychic life if they were imagined or fantasised as when they actually happened (which he did not deny). Elizabeth Cowie argues the relevance of this controversial claim for feminists:

> What Freud came to understand ... was not that the woman was making something up, pretending, or trying to fake, dupe us/Freud, but that since the event had not happened, then sexuality in the women could not be thought of as simply the 'effect' of outside events, of the seduction or rape, whether pleasurable or traumatic. Rather sexuality was already there, in play. The fantasy and its attendant traumas were not the *result* of a seduction but of the *wish* for a seduction, implying a sexuality already there motivating the wish. Freud is then concerned to elaborate on *how* it is already there ... What Freud shows is that it is irrelevant to consider whether the event was fantasised or real, or whether the woman wishes it to be real, for the fantasy refers not to physical reality but to psychical reality.[8]

What is important about fantasy, then, is not its fictional or illusory quality – the commonsense opposition between fantasy and reality – but its role in organising and representing sexuality.

One thing that struck Freud in many case studies was the persistence and recurrence of a small number of fantasy scenarios, which he referred to as the primal, or original, fantasies of the primal scene, seduction and castration. These 'emerge' in the history of the individual subject, yet they always seem already to have been in place – so much so that Freud, who never entirely renounced his detective's search for an originating event that would explain such phenomena, suggested in *Totem and Taboo* that they might be the sedimented memory-traces of the murder of the tribal father by the rebellious sons in the primal horde.[9] Laplanche and Pontalis reinterpret this now rather scandalous, or at least embarrassing, phylogenetic argument in more structuralist terms. It should be read, they suggest, 'as a prefiguration of the "symbolic order" defined by Lévi-Strauss and Lacan in the ethnological and psychoanalytic fields respectively', the function of which is 'to assign limits to the "imaginary" which contain its own principle of organization'.[10] The primal fantasies thus provide subjective myths of origins:

> Like myths, they claim to provide a representation of, and a solution to, the major enigmas that confront the child. Whatever appears to the subject as something needing an explanation or theory, is dramatised as a moment of emergence, the beginning of a history.
>
> Fantasies of origins: the primal scene pictures the origin of the individual; fantasies of seduction, the origin and upsurge of sexuality; fantasies of castration, the origin of the difference between the sexes . . . There is convergence of theme, of structure, and no doubt of function: through the scenarios constructed, the varied quest for origins, we are offered in the field of fantasy, the origin of the subject himself.[11]

Fantasy – the primal or original fantasies, that is – appears as 'given' for the subject because of this convergence of theme, structure and function; this is also what structures the apparently endless variety of secondary, imaginary fantasies. This distinction between primal and secondary fantasies is not a division between unconscious and conscious. The same nucleus is at work in unconscious dreams, in daydreams, in the secondary revision of dreams (our conscious attempts to give them some narrative coherence and meaning) – and also in such public forms of fantasy as novels and films. What is at issue, then, is not a question of original *content*, but a particular structuring of representations and narratives, the *rhetoric* through which the fantasies are made manifest:

> . . . the unity of the fantasy whole depends . . . on their mixed nature, in which both the structural and the imaginary can be found, although to different degrees. It is with this in mind that Freud always held the model fantasy to be the reverie, that form of novelette, both stereotyped and infinitely variable, which the subject composes and relates to himself in a waking state.[12]

What is it that determines both this stability and this variety? In *The Language of Psychoanalysis*, Laplanche and Pontalis define fantasy as 'an imaginary scene in which the subject is a protagonist, representing the fulfilment of a wish (in the last analysis, an unconscious wish) in a manner that is distorted to a greater or lesser extent by defensive processes'.[13] This differentiates their conception once again from the idea of a simple wish-fulfilment: what is evident in fantasies is not just the wish, but the setting out of the wish in a way that always also incorporates the prohibitions, censoring, and defences that surround the wish. 'Fantasy never articulates desire alone. And even more complexly, it may express conflicting desire and the law in a single ensemble.'[14]

This complexity is possible largely because of the form in which the subject is present in the imaginary scene. This need not involve the subject being a protagonist 'in person', as it were, nor identification with one of the actors in the scene. Laplanche and Pontalis cite Freud's brief essay on the fantasy 'A child is being beaten', in which he notes how both the sex of the child being beaten and the person doing the beating oscillate in the different stages of the scenario. The original fantasy, they deduce, 'is characterised by the absence of subjectivisation'. In fantasy, the subject does not pursue the desired object or its sign, but itself appears caught up in the sequence of signs. If the seduction fantasy is summarised as 'A father seduces a daughter', for Laplanche and Pontalis this provides 'a scenario with multiple entries, in which nothing shows whether the subject will be immediately located as *daughter*; it can as well be fixed as *father*, or even in the term *seduces*'. This lack of fixity, this mobility of identification, means that 'the subject, although always present in the fantasy, may be so in a desubjectivised form, in the very syntax of the sequence in question.'[15]

The complexity of secondary fantasies is not simply a question of the malleability of the protagonists within the scenario or the multiple points of entry for the subject. As I have noted, it also involves the articulation of wish and prohibition in the *mise en scène* of desire (which itself originates as prohibition). Indeed, fantasy provides a way of understanding that desire is not purely an upsurging of the drives. For Laplanche and Pontalis, desire comes to exist as sexual only through its articulation in fantasy. Reinterpreting Freud's concept of the experience of satisfaction, they locate the origin of fantasising in auto-eroticism – not, for them, a stage of development, but the moment of a repeated disjunction of sexual desire and non-sexual functions. Thus the suckling infant who experiences hunger tries to recreate the original satisfaction of being fed in hallucinatory form. 'The first wishing seems to have been a hallucinatory cathecting of the memory of satisfaction,' writes Freud. Victor Burgin draws out the implications of this observation.

> We may see in this scenario the Lacanian schema according to which 'desire' insinuates itself between 'need' and 'demand': the infant's *need* for nourishment is satisfied when the milk is provided; the infant's *demand* that its mother care for it is also met in the same instant. *Desire*, however, is directed neither to an object (here the substance, 'milk') nor to a person, but to a *fantasy* – the mnemic traces of the lost satisfaction. It should be noted here that the origins of fantasy are inseparable from the origins of *sexuality* ... Thus, the act of sucking, initially functionally associated with the ingestion of food, becomes enjoyed as 'sensual sucking', an activity in its own, erotic, right ... It is at this stage that the

infant must construct out of the primal flux of its earliest perceptions that primitive hierarchy in which the breast can emerge as 'object'. Hardly has this been achieved, however, than the object is 'lost' with the realisation that the breast, in real terms, belongs to the mother. The first fantasy then is most fundamentally motivated by the desire to fill the gap thus opened between the infant and the maternal body, but a body already fantasmatically displaced in relation to the real.[16]

However, Burgin warns against too simple a parallelism between *need* directed towards an object, and *desire* directed towards a fantasy object – precisely because, to return to Laplanche and Pontalis's axiom, fantasy 'is not the object of desire but its setting . . . the subject does not pursue the object or its sign: he appears caught up himself in the sequence of images'.[17]

> . . . the fact that the infant may be observed making sucking motions even after its hunger has been satiated is not to be construed as the outward manifestation of the intentional aim of a desiring subject towards a fantasy object. Rather, what we are witnessing is the display of auto-erotic pleasure in the *movement* itself, to which we must assume an accompanying fantasy not of *ingestion* (functional), but of *incorporation* (libidinal). The fantasy-precipitating sequence *having/losing* the object, then, also institutes *autoeroticism*.[18]

Burgin therefore follows Laplanche and Pontalis in identifying 'the "origin" of auto-eroticism' as 'the moment when sexuality, disengaged from any natural object, moves into the field of fantasy and by that very fact becomes sexuality.'[19]

FANTASY IN FILM

How do these mechanisms of setting out and containing desire operate within film texts? In his 1974 article, 'The fugitive subject', Paul Willemen discussed fantasy and repression in Raoul Walsh's *Pursued*.[20] In her analysis of *Now Voyager* in 'Fantasia', Elizabeth Cowie also looks at the complex dynamic of desire and the law in fantasy. Here the structuring fantasy is that of the phallic mother. Having finally displaced her own repressive mother, Charlotte Vale becomes a surrogate mother to her lover's daughter by taking her in and caring for her in a way Tina's mother never has. She denies herself a sexual relationship with Jerry, however, and so enables his unhappy marriage to continue: 'Don't let's ask for the moon when we can have the stars.' Thus Charlotte's initial transgressions, her enactment of homosexual and aggressive impulses, are indirectly punished and thereby legitimated. By retaining a part of Jerry – Tina – while not marrying him, she is able both to become the phallic mother and to abide by patriarchal law: hence the *articulation* (both combination and expression) of desire and prohibition. Cowie stresses that she is not analysing Charlotte as character or analysand, but the film's *mise en scène* of a dynamic of desire. The fantasy is not Charlotte's wish for independence, social success and sexual satisfaction, but an effect of the film's narration for the spectator.

> If we identify simply with Charlotte's desires, the series of social and erotic successes, then the final object, the child Tina, will be unsatisfactory. But if our identification is with the playing out of a desiring, in relation to the opposition (phallic) mother/child, the ending is very much more satisfying ... A series of 'day-dreams' fantasies enfold an Oedipal, original fantasy. The subject of this fantasy is then the spectator; inasmuch as we have been captured by the film's narration, its *énonciation*, we are the only place in which all the terms of the fantasy come to rest.[21]

The emphasis, then, is on fantasy as desiring rather than on wish-fulfilment through getting a desired object: 'the fantasy is the support of the desire,' insisted Lacan, 'it is not the object that is the support of the desire.'[22] The mobility of character positions within the narration and the multiple points of identification for the spectator in fantasy are so organised as to perpetuate the setting out of desire. Elizabeth Cowie exemplifies this through her reading of Max Ophuls' *The Reckless Moment* in which the main protagonists, Lucia and Donnelly, move through a shifting network of positions and relationships. Lucia is variously Donnelly's lover and mother and, in her own family in the absence of her husband, father of the household. Donnelly, in turn, acts as lover, son, father and mother. 'The staging of desire emerges through the series of figures, the exchanges and equivalences set up, produced, by the narrative.' When Donnelly finally dies, this only brings the tensions produced by these shifts and transformations to a halt: it does not resolve them.[23]

From these two films, Cowie concludes that the 'fixing' produced by the narrative may not reproduce the fixed positions of sexual difference. In *Now Voyager*, Charlotte Vale achieves a transgressive position as wife and mother. In *The Reckless Moment*, the final image, when Lucia takes a phone call from her absent husband, frames her ironically behind the bar-like bannisters on the staircase. Cowie suggests that this restates a wish presented in the film for the eviction of the Father in his symbolic function. The moral seems to be that 'while the terms of sexual difference are fixed, the places of characters and spectators in relation to those terms are not'.[24] The degree of this play in narration and identification – and how it may be constrained – have subsequently been explored in articles like Stephen Neale's 'Fantasy and sexual difference' and Barbara Creed's 'A journey through *Blue Velvet*'.[25]

Finally, to complement Donald Greig's account of the operation of fantasy in Hitchcock films and to underline the *activity* implicit in the model of the text-spectator relationship being developed in this section, it is worth quoting at length Victor Burgin's account of his response to *Vertigo*. Taken from his essay 'Diderot, Barthes, *Vertigo*', which argues that the art-historical concept of *tableau* can be read as an indication of the organising function of fantasy in paintings and photographs, this deals in part with the relationship between moving image and still image that Constance Penley also touches on in her discussion of *La Jetée*. It not only suggests the displacements and transformations through which an original fantasy is rendered in textual form; it also suggests how the act of memory and interpretation – Burgin's 'secondary elaboration' of his experience of the film – is itself intertextually structured by the same nucleus of fantasy.

When I first read a short essay by Freud called, 'A special type of choice of object made by men', I was struck by the similarities between the syndrome of male desire Freud describes and the pattern of behaviour Scottie (James Stewart) exhibits in Hitchcock's film *Vertigo* (1958). The first condition determining the choice of love-object by the type of man discussed in Freud's essay is that the woman should be already attached to some other man – husband, fiancé, or friend: in the film, Scottie falls in love with the woman he is hired to investigate, the wife of an old college friend. The second precondition is that the woman should be seen to be of bad repute sexually: Madeleine (Kim Novak), the college friend's wife, suffers from a fixated identification with a forbear whose illicit love-affair and illegitimate child brought her to tragic ruin. The type of man described by Freud is 'invariably moved to rescue the object of his love', and prominent amongst the rescue fantasies of such men is the fantasy of rescue from water: Scottie rescues Madeleine from San Francisco Bay. Finally Freud observes, 'The lives of men of this type are characterised by a repetition of passionate attachments of this sort: ... each is an exact replica of the other', and he remarks that it is always the same physical type which is chosen: following Madeleine's death, Scottie becomes obsessed by Judy (Kim Novak), a woman who physically resembles Madeleine and whom he sets about 'remaking' into an exact replica of Madeleine. Behind the pattern of repetitious behaviour he describes, Freud identifies a primary scenario of male Oedipal desire for the mother – already attached to the father, her sexual relations with whom bring her into ill repute in the eyes of the little rival for her love. The ubiquitous fantasy of rescue from water represents a conflation of 'rescue' and 'birth'. Just as he was, at birth, 'fished from the waters' and given life, so will he now return this gift to his mother in a reciprocal act of recovery from water. Finally, the adult man's love-attachments form an endless series of similar types for the simple reason that, as mother surrogates, they can never match the irreducibly unique qualities of the original.

When I fish Hitchcock's film from the depths of my memory it surfaces in the form of two images superimposed as one: Madeleine's face above the shadow of her lifeless body below the waters of the bay; Judy's face floating through the green-tinged gloom of the hotel room where she has just emerged from her final transformation, in the bathroom, into the image of the dead Madeleine. I can, of course, recall many other images, actions, snatches of dialogue, and so on, but the first, composite, image comes as if unbidden, spreading itself as if to form the very screen upon which my memory of the *reel*-film is projected ... Away from the cinema now, away from the insistence of the film's unreeling, this privileged image opens on to that skeletal narrative I find both in *Vertigo* and in Freud's paper on men's desire; but a narrative whose substance is undecidedly (n)either text (n)or tableau; and this in turn immediately dissolves into a myriad other delegates from a history of Western representations flooded with watery images of women – from the *Birth of Venus* to the *Death of Ophelia*. For example, in pursuit of these last two, I am returned to *Vertigo* by way of the bridge over the bay, in whose shadow Madeleine casts flowers on the water as she prepares to jump, leaping the gap between Hitchcock's and Botticelli/Millais' images of woman/water/flowers. As I now recall that Botticelli's *Birth of Venus* depicts the goddess at the moment of her *landfall* at Paphos, eliding the circumstances of her birth out at sea from the bloody foam produced when Saturn casts the genitals of the newly castrated Uranus into the ocean, I find that my re-entry into the text of the film is by a different route – one destined to take me through a different sequence of images, until I have traversed the text again, to regain another exit into the intertext, from which I shall be returned again ... and again, until the *possible* passages have been exhausted, or until I find that the trajectory of associations has become attracted into the orbit of some other semantically/affectively dense textual item, some other fantasy.[26]

In the perpetual motion not only of the narrative's *mise en scène* and the spectator's oscillating points of identification, but also in the endless chain of cultural associations that the spectator brings to bear in elaborating those engagements, there is no arrival at a point of origin either in 'the world' or 'the subject'. The subject emerges in the negotiation of this realm of representations – a symbolic order whose form, function and authority are at least partially organised and reproduced through the operation of the original fantasies. This returns us to the point I made at the beginning: the importance of this conception of fantasy is not that it offers just one more technique of reading films. It implies the more ambitious claim that films – along with other forms of mass-circulation fantasy scenarios – help to construct our psychic reality in ways that bear the imprint of Oedipal structures.

It is this bringing together of the psychoanalytic, the cultural and the political that opens up new questions and possibilities. Feminist theory, observes Laura Mulvey:

> ... has drawn attention to the area of contact between the unconscious and its manifestation in collective fantasy: roughly speaking, popular culture and representations. Freud, too, saw layers and levels to the human psyche, but the scars and traces that emerge symptomatically in language, images and symbolisations, as well as cultural phenomena, were to him primarily a means of interpreting and curing the present by means of the past. Feminism, on the other hand, as a political movement, must endeavour to deconstruct, to question, to re-invent this terrain in which women's secondary status is sealed.[27]

NOTES

1 Victor Burgin, James Donald and Cora Kaplan (eds.), *Formations of Fantasy* (London: Methuen, 1986), p. 2.

2 See, for example, Cora Kaplan, 'The Thorn Birds: fiction, fantasy, femininity'; John Fletcher, 'Poetry, gender and primal fantasy'; Victor Burgin, 'Diderot, Barthes, *Vertigo*', all in *Formations of Fantasy*; Laura Mulvey, 'Impending time', *Mary Kelly: Interim (Part 1)*, Catalogue (Edinburgh: Fruitmarket Gallery/Cambridge: Kettle's Yard/London: Riverside Studios, 1986); Jacqueline Rose, 'Margaret Thatcher and Ruth Ellis', *New Formations*, no. 6, Winter 1988/9.

3 Laura Mulvey, 'Visual pleasure and narrative cinema', *Screen*, vol. 16, no. 3, Autumn 1975. Mulvey has herself had second, and third, thoughts on her original formulations. See 'Afterthoughts on "Visual pleasure and narrative cinema" inspired by *Duel in the Sun*', *Framework*, nos. 15–16–17, 1981; 'Changes: thoughts on myth, narrative and historical experience', *History Workshop Journal*, no. 23, Spring 1987.

4 Jean Laplanche and J.-B. Pontalis, *The Language of Psychoanalysis* (London: Hogarth Press, 1973), p. 318.

5 Elizabeth Cowie, 'Fantasia', *m/f*, no. 9, 1984, p. 102.

6 Constance Penley, 'Feminism, film theory and the bachelor machines', *m/f*, no. 10, 1985, pp. 53–4.

7 Laplanche and Pontalis, 'Fantasy and the origins of sexuality', in Burgin, Donald and Kaplan (eds.), *Formations of Fantasy*.

8 Cowie, 'Fantasia', p. 76.

9 See Burgin, p. 97 and Fletcher, pp. 111–13 in *Formations of Fantasy*.

10 'Fantasy and the origins of sexuality', p. 17. This reading suggests a similar orientation and ambition to Dadoun's account of fetishism in the horror film.

11 'Fantasy and the origins of sexuality', p. 19.

12 Ibid., p. 22.

13 Laplanche and Pontalis, *The Language of Psychoanalysis*, p. 314.

14 Robert Lapsley and Michael Westlake, *Film Theory: an introduction* (Manchester: Manchester University Press, 1988), p. 91.

15 'Fantasy and the origins of sexuality', pp. 22/3, 26.

16 Burgin, 'Diderot, Barthes, *Vertigo*', p. 93.

17 'Fantasy and the origins of sexuality', p. 26.

18 Burgin, pp. 93/4.

19 'Fantasy and the origins of sexuality', p. 26.

20 Paul Willemen, 'The fugitive subject', in *Raoul Walsh*, Edinburgh Film Festival, 1974.

21 Cowie, 'Fantasia', p. 91. I have drawn here on Lapsley and Westlake's succinct summary in *Film Theory*, pp. 91/2.

22 Jacques Lacan, *Four Fundamental Concepts of Psychoanalysis* (London: Hogarth Press, 1977), p. 185. Cinema's most refined figuring of the Lacanian view of desire as the pursuit of an eternally lost object (as well as the funniest) may be found in the relationship between Wile E. Coyote and Road Runner in Chuck Jones's 1950s Warner Brothers cartoons.

23 Cowie, 'Fantasia', p. 101.

24 Ibid., p. 102.

25 Stephen Neale, 'Sexual difference in cinema', *Sexual Difference: Oxford Literary Review*, vol. 8, 1986; Barbara Creed, 'A journey through *Blue Velvet*: film, fantasy and the female spectator', *New Formations*, no. 6, 1988.

26 Burgin, pp. 101–3.

27 Mulvey, 'Impending time', p. 5.

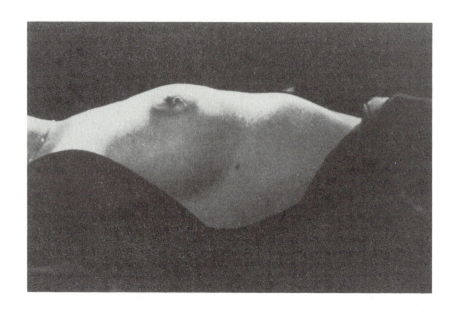

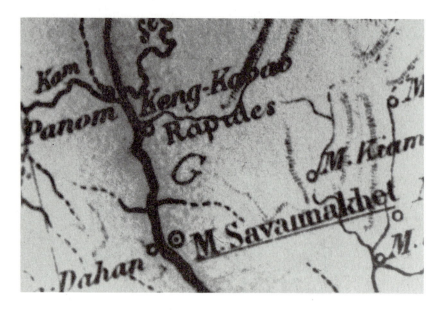

The Cinema of Lol V. Stein

ELISABETH LYON

I   ... this word, which does not exist, is none the less there: it awaits you
just around the corner of language, it defies you – never having been
used – to raise it, to make it arise from its kingdom, which is pierced on
every side and through which flows the sea, the sand, the eternity of the
ball in the cinema of Lol V. Stein.   LE RAVISSEMENT DE LOL V. STEIN

India Song is part of what has been called in Marguerite Duras's work the
'Indian' cycle,[1] a group of three novels and three films which all transform and
repeat a single story. That story, like the 'cinema of Lol V. Stein' (from the
novel in which it first appears), turns around a scene which is at once an
'eternity' and eternally absent: the ball at S. Tahla. Although the novels (*Le
Ravissement de Lol V. Stein, Le Vice-Consul, L'Amour*) were written first, in
Duras's work perhaps more than in other film-makers similarly engaged, the
films (*La Femme du Gange, India Song, Son nom de Venise dans Calcutta désert*)
are not reducible simply to translations into cinematic terms of those fictions.
Both the novels and the films are taken in the same effort of remembering –
through the imaginaries of the characters, narrators, Duras, and the spectator
or reader – making it impossible to find a real event from which the imaginary
stories would follow. The scene of the ball, although it becomes a kind of
signifying knot across which the fantasy of *India Song* is later put into play,
never attains the status of a true event or an original trauma. It is always
already fantasmic as it is told by the narrator at the beginning of *Le Ravissement
de Lol. V. Stein* (1964):

> Here then in full and all mixed together, both this false impression
> [*faux semblant*] which Tatiana Karl tells about and what I have been
> able to imagine about that night at the town beach casino. Following
> which I shall relate my own story of Lol Stein.[2]

The story begins then already shot through with the holes and gaps of
someone else's memory. But the transformations and repetitions within *Le
Ravissement de Lol. V. Stein* and the subsequent novels and films do nothing to
fill these gaps, but rather open up new ones or enlarge those already there.

The story of Lol V. Stein recedes somewhat to the background of

Duras's next novel in this cycle. *Le Vice-Consul* (1966), on which *India Song* is partially based, takes place in Calcutta and focuses primarily on Anne-Marie Stretter and Michael Richardson. Lol's story circulates through the novel in fragmented references to *Le Ravissement de Lol. V. Stein* and is taken up in some ways by the figures of the mad beggar-woman and the Vice Consul, whose stories also become mixed and identified with that of Anne-Marie Stretter. The novel *L'Amour* (1971) reopens the story of Lol V. Stein in S. Tahla with the return of Michael Richardson many years later to the fantasmic scene of the ball. It is from this matrix of madness and fantasy that Duras later drew the film *La Femme du Gange* (1972).[3]

The story of Anne-Marie Stretter and Michael Richardson as it is first told in *Le Vice-Consul* was subsequently developed in several different kinds of work: besides the novel, Duras wrote a play (*India Song, texte-théâtre-film*, 1973) and directed two films, *India Song* (1975) and *Son nom de Venise dans Calcutta désert* (1976) which plays the same sound track as *India Song*, but replaces the image track with scenes of a deserted mansion, its ruined facades and rooms emptied of people until the very end. As in *Le Vice-Consul*, the story of Lol V. Stein continues to circulate through the films: off-screen, the voices of two young women in the beginning tell the story of the ball at S.Tahla, echoing and at some points actually citing, in a *mise en abyme* of memory, both *La Femme du Gange* and *Le Ravissement de Lol. V. Stein*.

The scene of the ball at the beginning of *Le Ravissement de Lol. V. Stein* describes a kind of substitution operated through an exchange of looks in which the couple Lol V. Stein and her fiancé Michael Richardson is replaced by the couple Anne-Marie Stretter and Michael Richardson. At the moment of that substitution, however, the couple becomes a threesome, Lol being inextricably bound to them by her look, as the spectator in the scene, a witness to her own no-longer-being-there, her own absence. It is the fantasy of being able to see herself not being there in precisely that play of substitutions set up at the ball that Lol seeks to repeat throughout the rest of the novel. But like the repetitions and transformations that occur elsewhere intertextually in this cycle of novels and films, repetition is not therapeutic: it leads to neither resolution nor cure, but rather to an uncanny effect of familiarity and difference.

What is fascination if not, so to speak, the temperate or mild form of the feeling of strangeness or of unbelievable familiarity (*Unheimlichkeit*) which is called forth when there is before me (or in what there is before me, in the *Gegenstand*) something unknown but nevertheless at the root of my identity, like a stranger to my self?   *Moustapha Safouan*

Duras was once asked why the character of Anne-Marie Stretter fascinated her. She replied that when she was very young and living in Indochina, a new embassy official, perhaps named Stretter, moved into town with his wife and two little girls. A short time after their arrival, Duras learned that a young man had committed suicide because of his love for this woman.

> In any case, it's like the primal scene that Freud talks about. Perhaps this is my primal scene, the day I learned of the death of the young man. You see, this woman was a mother – good, sensible – and the two little girls always in white were her children, and this man, this husband, was a father. I had no father and my mother lived like a nun. This woman, the mother of these two little girls who were my age, possessed a body which had the power of death.[4]

Duras describes being attracted by the extraordinary paleness of this woman, 'invisible' yet seen by Duras riding around in her limousine and at the embassy tennis courts where Duras's brother used to play because 'he was handsome and played well', but from which she was excluded.

The interest of Duras's response to a question of fascination lies less in its final explanatory value than in its suggestiveness – her comments are less proof of an origin of her fascination than of another scene in which it is replayed. Her references here to original fantasies,[5] of which the primal scene is one, finds a certain resonance in the rest of her work. In many ways the ball scene has the status of an original fantasy, a kind of primal scene of the Indian cycle, in which a scene is reconstructed *après coup* across the imaginary registers of seen and heard, by people who may or may not have seen or heard anything. Like the primal scene, then, the ball scene is first of all a fantasy. And like the ball scene, the original fantasy analogously marks a vanishing point in psychoanalytic theory. For psychoanalysis, like the subject it describes, is tempted by a fantasy of origins, wishing as it does to construct an origin or an original moment in the history of the subject, a moment which lies at once beyond that history and in it.

The question of the origin of the fantasy is one which is difficult to settle. Jean Laplanche and J.-B. Pontalis have addressed this question in, among other places, an article which appeared in *Les Temps modernes* whose title indicates the complexity of the problem: 'Fantasme originaire, fantasmes des origines, origine du fantasme.'[6] If, from the beginning of his work on hysteria and on the origins of hysterical fantasies, Freud finds himself repeatedly caught between the oppositions real-imagined, objective-subjective, it is not necessarily due to an inadequate conceptualisation of the problem, but to the complex and ambiguous relationship of real to imagined in the fantasy.

Freud first mentions the primal scene in a case history entitled 'A Case of Paranoia Running Counter to the Psychoanalytic Theory of the Disease' (1915). In a remarkable condensation, the patient, a young woman, claimed to have been photographed while making love, hearing what she imagined to be the click of a camera while in a compromising position with her lover. Freud concludes that she probably never heard a noise, having projected as the perception of an external object what was in all probability the beat of her clitoris. Earlier in this same paper, however, leading to a discussion of 'primal fantasies', Freud decides that the actual status of the noise, real or imagined, is unimportant.

> I do not for a moment imagine, of course, that if the unlucky noise had not occurred the delusion would not have been formed; on the contrary, something inevitable is to be seen behind this accidental circumstance, something which was bound to assert itself compulsively in the patient just as when she supposed that there was a *liaison* between her lover and the elderly superior, her mother-substitute. Among the store of unconscious phantasies of all neurotics, and probably of all human beings, there is one which is seldom absent and which can be disclosed by analysis: this is the phantasy of watching sexual intercourse between the parents. I call such phantasies – of the observation of sexual intercourse between the parents, of seduction, of castration, and others – 'primal phantasies'....[7]

Freud goes on to correct himself, saying that 'it is doubtful whether we can rightly call the noise "accidental"' since such noises are an integral part of the fantasy of listening and an indication of the primal scene – the noise of parental intercourse which wakes the child and/or the noise by which the child is afraid he will betray himself. Here, the oppositions real-imagined have become displaced, as the question of the origin of the fantasy becomes circular. What is imagined to be at the source of the fantasy, the origin of its subsequent elaboration – in this case, a noise – is at once an integral part of the original fantasy, a mark of the primal scene: '... the origin of the fantasy is integrated in the very structure of the original fantasy.'[8]

In psychoanalytic theory, the origin of the notion of fantasy comes about through Freud's work on hysteria. It was through his analysis of hysterical fantasies that the categories of real and imagined began to be displaced and, at the same time, where he was forced to attempt an account of the desire of the hysteric. From a theory of sexual seduction by a father or a father-figure, a more realist conception of primal scenes, Freud, in a long and complex development, began to elaborate a theory of primal fantasies which were not reducible to the lived experience of the subject. In a letter to Fliess on 21 September 1897, Freud confesses 'the great secret that has been slowly dawning on me in the last few months: I no longer believe in my *neurotica*....'[9] He had begun to question whether the scenes of seduction, systematically and pervasively recounted by hysterics, had actually taken place. Although Freud remained convinced that seduction did in fact occur in a number of cases, he was equally convinced that it was not as frequently real as he had first thought.

The question of the desire behind the fantasy and of the role of the subject in it remain, but are taken up again in '"A Child is Being Beaten": A Contribution to the Study of the Origin of Sexual Perversions' (1919). Basing his analysis on the case of four women, Freud reconstructs the syntactical permutations of the fantasy 'a child is being beaten'.

> The little girl's beating-phantasy passes through three phases, of which the first and third are consciously remembered, the middle one remaining unconscious. . . . In the first and third phantasies the child who is being beaten is always someone other than the subject, in the middle phase it is always the child herself; in the third phase it is almost invariably only boys who are being beaten. The person who does the beating is from the first her father, replaced later on by a substitute taken from the class of fathers.[10]

The child, then, is not only the subject looking but takes up positions *in the scene*. This kind of slipping of the subject among various positions, various identifications, is characteristic of the structure of the fantasy and of the complexity of the desire it stages. Returning to Laplanche and Pontalis and to the fantasy of seduction of the hysteric,

> . . . 'A father seduces a daughter' might perhaps be the summarized version of the seduction fantasy. The indication here of the primary process is not the absence of organization, as is sometimes suggested, but the peculiar character of the structure, in that it is a scenario with multiple entries in which nothing shows whether the subject will be immediately located as *daughter*; it can as well be fixed as *father*, or even in the terms *seduces*.[11]

The fantasy of seduction is only one of the original fantasies, but it has in common with the others its relation to origins, a claim to represent a response to those major enigmas which confront the child. Original fantasies are at the same time, then, fantasies of origins. They dramatize moments of emergence: the primal scene replays the origin of the individual; the fantasy of seduction pictures the emergence of sexuality; and fantasies of castration represent the origin of sexual difference.

Analogously, the ball scene, as the original fantasy, the fantasy of origins and the origin of the fantasy of the Indian cycle, marks the beginning of a history.

The principle of classical film is well known: the end must reply to the beginning; between one and the other something must be set in order; the last scene frequently recalls the first and constitutes its resolution.

Raymond Bellour

Although *India Song* is not a classical film, it does conform in certain important aspects to the classical model: it is composed, rather classically, of three parts, three large movements; there is, also along the lines of the classical model as Bellour has described it, a symbolic folding of the last part onto the first, but one which here, instead of constituting the resolution of the first scene, continues the narrative circulation it puts into play.

The story of *India Song* is that of the last days/weeks/months of Anne-Marie Stretter's life and of her love affair with Michael Richardson in India during the 1930s. It takes place in Calcutta, where Anne-Marie Stretter is living as the wife of the French ambassador to India, and on an island in the Delta during the season of the summer monsoon. The story is told by voices whose faces are never seen, gradually taking shape through what they remember, 'having known or read of this love story long ago. Some of them remember it better than others. But none of them remembers it completely. And none of them has completely forgotten it.'[12] Around this story, but off-screen, is another – that of the misery of Calcutta, hunger and leprosy. There are two characters who are explicitly part of this off-screen story: the mad beggar-woman, who is heard but never seen; and the Vice Consul, who is both seen and heard, but remains in social and diplomatic exile.

The three-part composition of the film traces a story which is always already history when the film begins: embedded in the telling of the story of Anne-Marie Stretter is the triple inscription of her death – spoken by the voices in the past tense at the beginning, as part of the *already-there* (*déjà-là*) of the space of the film; in the recurring image of an 'altar' to a recent death – flowers, a photograph, incense; and finally at the end of the film when the voices tell of Anne-Marie Stretter's suicide.

India Song is the *mise en scène* of what could be called a *fantasmatic* – that structuring activity which shapes and orders the life of the subject.[13] It is the work of the fantasy which gives the story its contours, its structure:

- in the *mise en abyme* of beginnings, endings, origins;
- in the slipping and mixing, the circulation, of identification;
- in its answer to the question of desire.

The first part of the film (shots 1–27) puts into play a circulation of positions and identities, beginning with the I/eye who is looking and the beggarwoman and ending with the Vice Consul and an idea of death. The voices of two young women, at times indistinguishable from one another, tell the stories – the *already-there* of the fiction – of the beggarwoman, Anne-Marie Stretter,

Michael Richardson, Lol V. Stein and the Vice Consul. The identities are mixed in a kind of fantasmic blend across the registers of seen and heard (*entendu*),[14] projecting – here recalling Freud's study of 'A Case of Paranoia . . .' (see above) – one onto the other, one into the other.

IV

Shot 1 (5″).
White credits on black.

Shot 2 (3′52″).
Credits continue over an image of the setting sun, then stop. A woman is singing in an Asian language – the song of Savannakhet sung by the beggarwoman. The song stops and the voices begin.[15]

Voice 1: *A beggarwoman.*
Voice 2: *Mad.*
V1:   *Yes.*
V2:   *Yes, I remember. She stays around the riverbanks. She comes from Burma.*

The beggarwoman begins to sing again, then stops.

V1:   *She's not Indian. She comes from Savannakhet. Born there.*

The song begins again and continues intermittently.

V2:   *She's been walking for ten years. One day, she comes to the Ganges.*
V1:   *Yes. She stays.*
V2:   *That's right . . . Twelve children die while she walks to Bengal.*
V1:   *Yes. She leaves them, sells them, forgets them. Becomes barren on the way to Bengal.*

The beggarwoman sings alone, then the voices begin again.

V2:   *Savannakhet, Laos.*
V1:   *Yes, Seventeen years. She's pregnant, seventeen years old. She's driven away by her mother. She leaves. She asks how to get lost. No one knows.*

The beggarwoman continues to sing intermittently, then begins to babble, stops and the voices begin again.

V1:   *They were together in Calcutta.*
V2:   *The white woman and the other one?*
V1:   *Yes. During the same years . . .*

The first position taken up by the I/eye of the camera during the second shot – the look toward the setting sun – is one which is off-screen: that of the beggarwoman and the voices of the two women which identify her and tell her story, both excluded from the scene and on the side of seeing, as are we. The stories of Anne-Marie Stretter and the beggarwoman also begin to be woven together, ('They were together in Calcutta. . . .') beginning a series of positions taken up, linked in a play of identity and difference.

Shot 3 (56").
'India Song' is heard, played on the piano. An interior at night. On a black piano, a lamp and a photograph of a young girl. On the keyboard a musical score. A servant in Hindu dress enters and places a bouquet of flowers next to the photograph, lights a candle and some incense, leaves.

Shot 4 (59").
Slow pan from right to left over some black cloth, jewels, a red dress, a red hair piece. 'India Song' continues.

V1:   *He had followed her to India.*
V2:   *Yes. He left everything for her. In one night.*
V1:   *The night of the ball?*
V2:   *Yes.*
V1:   *Michael Richardson was engaged to a girl from S. Tahla, Lola Valérie Stein ...*
V2:   *They were to have been married in the autumn.*
      Then there was the ball, the ball at S. Tahla.
V1:   *She had arrived at the ball late in the middle of the night, dressed in black ...*

'India Song' continues on the piano.

Shot 5 (10").
Photograph of a young girl in black, some flowers, incense, three half-filled champagne glasses. The smoke from the incense rises.

V1:   *What love at the ball, what desire.*

These three shots begin to trace the *already-there* of the fiction: we see, for the first time, what will be the recurring image of the 'altar' – the photograph, flowers, incense; and we hear, also for the first time, the story of what is already in this cycle a recurring scene: the fantasy of the ball at S. Tahla.

The image of the photograph introduces another dimension into the temporal *mise en abyme* of the fiction. In the logic of the film, it comes to represent the death of Anne-Marie Stretter (metonymically, as part of the 'altar'), marking that death as ever-present through repetition in the present, the *being-there* of the film. A little later however, the voices tell us about her death in the past tense, making it part of the *already-there* of the fiction.

Although still caught up in the present of the film (the *being-there*), the photograph is a condensation of the two temporalities at work in *India Song*: 'What we have is a new space-time category: spatial immediacy and temporal anteriority, the *here-now* and the *there-then*.'[16] The time of the photograph, then, its *having-been-there*, joins the fantasmic *already-there*, the past of the fiction, to the present of the film.

Between the shots of the photographs (shots 3 and 5), the voices begin to remember the story of the ball, looping the film once again back onto the *already-there* of the fiction. The fantasy of the ball is accompanied by music, 'India Song', and is told over a slow, lingering pan of Anne-Marie Stretter's *things*, personal things – clothing, hair pieces, jewels – detached from her body and strewn about as if she no longer had any use for them. This image, somewhere between voyeurism and melancholia, is one of a series in the film which, through an activity of looking in relation to loss, wants to shape the story into a fantasy of looking.

Shot 6 (15″).
On the right, a lighted chandelier, reflected in a rectangular mirror placed behind it on a mantle. In front of the mirror, a small clock with red flowers on either side. 'India Song' continues on the piano.

V2:   *That light.*
V1:   *The monsoon.*
V2:   *The dust . . .*
V1:   *Central Calcutta.*

Shot 7 (17″).
Reframing of the clock in the center, the mirror behind it (reflecting another mirror) and the red flowers on either side; the reverse of the previous shot. Above, a chandelier whose reflections play off one another in a *mise en abyme* between the mirrors. 'India Song' stops.

V2:   *Isn't there a smell of flowers?*
V1:   *Leprosy.*
V2:   *Where are we?*

Shot 8 (1′29″).
Blue sky, then a pan of the exterior of a mansion, scaffolding under a window, crumbling walls, shuttered windows; pan left to right to a dark green forest, framed at the end of the shot in a low angle against the blue sky.

V1:   *The French Embassy in India.*
V2:   *That distant noise . . .*
V1:   *The Ganges.*

Silence.

V1:   *After her death, he left India?*
V2:   *Yes . . .*
V1:   *Her tomb is in the English cemetery?*
V2:   *Yes:*

Silence.

V1:   *She died there, in the islands. One night, found dead . . .*

Silence.

V2:   *A black Lancia speeds along the road to Chandernagor.... It was then that she first ...*
V1:   *Yes.*

Shots 6 to 8 return to the play of identification and substitution being set up in this part, linking in a series of questions and answers: the light – the monsoon; the dust – central Calcutta; the smell of flowers – leprosy; a distant noise – the Ganges. These terms recur throughout the film and are mixed and blended by the voices with the identities of Anne-Marie Stretter and the beggarwoman. This mirroring effect, the play of identity and difference set up by the voices, has a counterpart in the image: shots 6 and 7, both framed across mirrors, present the same objects, reframed and reflected. In the middle of the next shot, the voices talk about Anne-Marie Stretter's death, her tomb in the English cemetery, over an image of the ruined façades and broken windows of what appears to be an abandoned mansion, but is identified as the French Embassy ('Where are we?' 'The French Embassy in India.').

Shot 9 (3′2″).
Semi-circular pan, right to left, of the drawing room; beginning in a corner with a rose-colored sofa, panning across some French doors opening onto a park, the piano with the lamp, flowers, photograph and incense. A young man in a white suit, looking toward off-screen right, is reflected in a mirror against which he is leaning and which also reflects the piano, the objects on it and the French doors. The camera stops panning at the mirror, where a young man and  woman are reflected dancing (Anne-Marie Stretter and Michael Richardson). The couple stops dancing. The young man in white turns his head to the right and the woman of the couple moves away slightly and turns.

V1:   *What are you afraid of?*

Long silence.

V2:   *Anne-Marie Stretter.*

Long silence.

V2:   *They used to dance at night?*
V1:   *They're dancing.*

'India Song' begins again, played on the piano.

V1:   *Why are you crying?*
      I love you so much I can't see anymore, can't hear, can't live....

Shot 10 (21″).
The stone steps of a stairway in the park, brightly lit. A shadow comes and goes near the bottom step, then disappears. 'India Song' continues.

Shot 11 (11'5").
Anne-Marie Stretter, Michael Richardson and the young man in white all looking to the right towards the park, through the open French doors, Anne-Marie Stretter exits through the doors, the two men follow her.

V1: *You know, lepers burst like sacks of dust.*
V2: *[They] don't suffer?*
V1: *No. Not a thing. Laugh.*

Long silence.
Voice of the beggarwoman: *Savannakhet! Savannakhet!*

V1: *She's there, on the banks of the Ganges, under the trees. She has forgotten.*

Uncannily, the dialogue of the voices over shot 9 recalls *La Femme du Gange*, where the voices of two young women speak to each other, occasionally commenting on the image, but more frequently trying to reconstruct, to remember the scene of the ball and the stories of Anne-Marie Stretter, Lol V. Stein, and Michael Richardson. Also like *La Femme du Gange*, the voices here speak of their love for each other in words which seem to float between the stories they are telling and their own.

With shot 9, we see a pan of the drawing room, a glimpse of the couple dancing (Anne-Marie Stretter and Michael Richardson), caught in a paradoxical past-present moment ('They used to dance in the evenings'/ 'They're dancing'), a moment complicated by being also a filmed reflection, introducing the possibility of an absent or displaced presence into the already complex temporal scheme.

This absent presence is continued in the next shot (shot 10) with a shadow approaching the stairs then retreating – the beggarwoman? – recalling, again, a very similar shot in *La Femme du Gange*, with the difference that in the earlier film the 'shadow' revealed itself to be Lol V. Stein.

During shot 11, the voices once more take up the play of substitutions – 'lepers burst like sacks of dust' – and introduce a phrase ('[they] don't suffer')[17] which becomes a refrain linking the various positions set up in the first movement. Meanwhile, Anne-Marie Stretter, Michael Richardson and the young man – the spectator in the scene – move outside, their attention drawn by the cries of the beggarwoman.

Shot 12 (56").
Anne-Marie Stretter, Michael Richardson and the young man outside in front of the Embassy residence. They walk slowly toward the camera and exit to the left.

Shot 13 (12").
In the distance, a man in white, standing near a small lake in the park.

V2: *The French Vice Consul in Lahore.*
V1: *Yes, in disgrace in Calcutta.*

Shot 14 (28").
Anne-Marie Stretter, Michael Richardson, the young man walk down the stairs; in the background, the façade of the Embassy residence.

Shot 15 (41").
Return to *13*. The man in white (the Vice Consul) walks slowly along the edge of the lake, stops, then leaves.

V1:   *Has he come back into the park?*
V2:   *Yes, he comes every night.*

Shot 16 (28").
The deserted tennis courts, some benches, a red bicycle seen through a wire mesh fence. The Vice Consul enters from the left, passes the bicycle, stops to look at it, then exits to the right.

V2:   *The deserted tennis courts.*
V1:   *Anne-Marie Stretter's red bicycle.*

Shot 17 (24").
The Vice Consul walking in the park. The camera pans left to right with his movement. He stops and looks to the right.

Shots *12* to *17* present a series of exterior shots, the only ones in the film in which Anne-Marie Stretter appears. The first four form an alternation between the three characters walking (Anne-Marie Stretter, Michael Richardson, the young man, in shots *12* and *14*) and the Vice Consul (shots *13* and *15*), who is introduced by the voices during shot *13*. This alternation sets up spatial parallels between Anne-Marie Stretter and the Vice Consul which will converge, briefly, at the end of the first movement. Their eventual meeting is prefigured, metonymically, in shot *16* where we see the Vice Consul walking by the deserted tennis courts and lingering over Anne-Marie Stretter's red bicycle, an object which is invested with some of the same value as the more personal effects seen in shot *4*.

Shot 18 (3'1").
Reflected in a large rectangular mirror, the piano (with musical score, flowers, lamp, photograph) and three open French doors. A servant, dressed in white, enters and lights the lamp on the piano. He walks toward the mirror, which still reflects him, and then enters the frame at the right, doubled by his reflection. He lights another lamp next to the mirror, then exits. From the left, Anne-Marie Stretter enters, closing her black peignoir around her. She exits at the right edge of the frame and reappears, reflected in the background by the mirror, walking toward the open doors. She goes outside, then re-enters, still seen reflected in the mirror, stops near the piano where she looks for a long time at the photograph. She then looks at herself in the mirror and exits to the left.

V2:   *Where is the one dressed in black?*
V1:   *Out, every evening. She comes back when it's dark. The Embassy's black Lancia has just*
      entered the park.

The beggarwoman begins to sing.

V2:   *You know, she hunts at night in the Ganges, for food.*

Long silence.

V1:   *Dead in the islands.*
V2:   *Her eyes blinded with light, dead.*
V1:   *Yes, there under a stone. Around her, a bend in the Ganges.*

Silence, then Beethoven's variation #14 on a theme by Diabelli begins on the piano.

Shot 19 (1'27").
From a high angle, Anne-Marie Stretter in her black peignoir, stretched out on her
stomach on the floor. Reflected in the mirror, in the background, a man in white comes
down the stairs, stops. The Beethoven variation continues on the piano.

V1:   *Four o'clock. Black night.*
V2:   *No one can sleep.*
V1:   *No one.*
V2:   *The heat ... impossible ... terrible.*
V1:   *Another storm ... approaching Bengal.*
V2:   *Coming from the islands.*
V1:   *The mouth of the river. Inexhaustible.*
V2:   *What's that sound?*
V1:   *Her weeping.*
V2:   *[She] doesn't suffer, does she?*
V1:   *She neither. A leper ... of the heart.*

Shot 20 (54").
The camera pans over a fragment of a red dress against some rose-colored material, a red
hair piece, a silver belt, then in a sweeping movement, it pans over black, obscuring the
edges of the frame, then back to the red dress. The Beethoven variation continues.

Shot 21 (4'45").
Return to *19*. The man seen in
shot *19*, Michael Richardson, is
now stretched out next to Anne-
Marie Stretter, leaning on his
elbow, looking at her. She turns
over onto her back, uncovering
her breast. In the background,
the young man seen in shots *9*,
11, etc. enters through a
doorway, walks in front of the
mirror, leaves, then re-enters
and sits down near Anne-Marie
Stretter and Michael Richardson
on the floor. The Beethoven
variation continues.

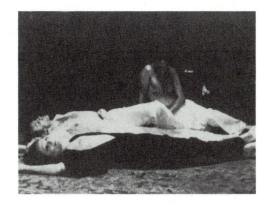

V2:   *[She] can't bear it.*
V1:   *No, she can't bear it ... can't bear India.*

The voices are silent.

V1:   *She's sleeping.*
V2:   *He loved her more than anything in the world.*
V1:   *Even more.*

The music stops.

V1:   *Michael Richardson started a marine insurance company in Bengal so that he could stay in India.*
V2:   *Listen … Ganges fisherman …*

Silence.

V1:   *What darkness, what heat, relentless, deathly.*

Silence.

V1:   (As if reading) *From behind the indoor plants in the bar, she watches them. It was only at dawn, when the lovers were going towards the door of the ballroom, that Lola Valérie Stein uttered a cry.*

Sounds of water.

V1:   *Couldn't hear anymore, couldn't see.*
V2:   *With this crime behind them …*

Sounds of water continue. A siren can be heard in the background.

V1:   *Yes.*
V2:   *Rain …*
V1:   *Yes … cool …*

Silence. The piano begins to play Beethoven's variation again.

V1:   *The music, it was in Venice. A hope in music …*
V2:   *She never gave up playing?*
V1:   *No.*

Silence. The music continues.

V2:   (Pronouncing each syllable) *Anna Ma-ri-a Guar-di.*
V1:   *Yes …*

Silence.

V2:   *The first marriage, the first post …?*
V1:   *Savannakhet, Laos. She's married to a French colonial official. She's eighteen.*
V2:   *Ah yes … a river … she's sitting by a river. Already. Looking at it.*
V1:   *The Mekong.*
V2:   *She's silent, crying?*
V1:   *Yes. They say: 'She can't get acclimatised. She'll have to be sent back to Europe.'*
V2:   *[She] couldn't bear it, even then?*
V1:   *Even then.*
V2:   *Those iron gates around her?*
V1:   *The park of the chancellery.*
V2:   *The sentries?*
V1:   *Official.*
V2:   *Even then, [she] couldn't bear it.*
V1:   *No.*

The music stops.

V1:   *One day, a government launch stops: Monsieur Stretter is inspecting the posts on the Mekong.*

V2: *He takes her away from Savannakhet?*
V1: *Yes. Takes her with him.*

Shot 22 (33").
Anne-Marie Stretter's nude
breast, surrounded by the black
peignoir. Beads of sweat form
on the skin as she breathes.

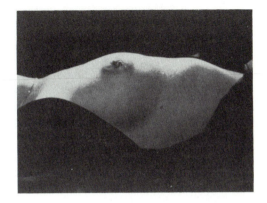

V1: (Continuing) *Takes her*
      with him for seventeen years
      through the capitals of Asia.
      You find her in Peking, then
      in Mandalay, in Rangoon,
      Sydney. You find her in
      Lahore. Seventeen years.
      You find her in Calcutta.
      Calcutta: she dies.

During shots *18* and *19*, the voices continue the work of substitution, linking through almost imperceptible alternations, the identities of Anne-Marie Stretter and the beggarwoman: shifting from 'the one dressed in black' to 'she hunts at night' to 'Dead in the islands'. The refrain '[She] doesn't suffer' returns to link Anne-Marie Stretter with leprosy: 'A leper . . . of the heart'.

There are several levels of redundancy between the spatial and temporal schemes at work in shot *18*: the uncanniness of watching Anne-Marie Stretter looking at the photograph which has been associated with the 'altar' to her death and then at herself in the mirror; the voices meanwhile speak of her in the past tense ('Dead in the islands'). This effect of absent presence has a spatial counterpart produced by the placement of the mirror in the room, in which Anne-Marie Stretter disappears from the view of the camera, reappearing seconds later, caught as a reflection.

Shots *20* and *22* continue the series that began with shot *4*, shaping a fantasy of looking. The first (shot *20*) is very similar to shot *4*: a pan over Anne-Marie Stretter's *things* – the jewels, the hair piece, the red dress, black cloth (the peignoir we saw earlier?). But here, after panning over the objects strewn against a rose-colored sofa, there is a sweeping movement of the camera over black, blending the edges of the frame with the object, confusing the looked at with the frame of the look. Then, in an upward sweep, the frame is regained against the rose of the sofa and the red dress.

Shot *21* returns us to the heat, 'relentless, deathly' of Calcutta while the voices take up again the *already-there* of the fiction (the ball – 'this crime behind them'), at times seeming to slip back to that past, seeing Lol *looking* ('From behind the indoor plants in the bar, she watches them'), seeing Anne-Marie Stretter in Savannakhet, sitting by the Mekong, or surrounded by the iron gates of the chancellery. The story of Anne-Marie Stretter is more explicitly linked here to that of the beggarwoman – both of them beginning their trajectories across Asia at Savannakhet.

Anne-Marie Stretter's movement from Savannakhet to Calcutta is traced in the next shot (shot 22) over the image of her nude breast, an image which marks the deathly heat by the beads of sweat forming on her skin. The stories of the beggarwoman and Anne-Marie Stretter have become parallel: one, eighteen years old, married, unhappy; the other, seventeen years old, pregnant, driven away; both beginning in Savannakhet and ending in Calcutta.

Like the two shots (4 and 20) which precede it in this series, the image of Anne-Marie Stretter's breast, although on a more abstract level, is about a fantasy of looking, a slipping of subject and object, of the look and the looked at. The breast, as a signifier in psychoanalytic theory, has in common with both the look and the fantasy a relation to loss. In the history of the subject, the object of the infant's 'primal hallucination', in which he seeks to reproduce the experience of satisfaction in the absence of the real object (the milk), is in fact not the *real* object but the *lost* object 'linked with the very earliest experiences of the rise and resolution of desire'[18] – the breast as a signifier.

It is the work of the fantasy to try to 'cover the moment of *separation* between *before* and *after*, … between the two stages represented by real experience and its hallucinatory revival, between the object that satisfies and the sign [the breast] which describes both the object and its absence….'[19] The fantasy originates in the continually renewed and repeated moment of separation, making its appearance along with sexuality which, split off from the non-sexual functions (such as feeding) which provided its object, becomes auto-erotic.

The fantasy not only has its origins at the same time as auto-eroticism, in loss, but is the *mise en scène* of the subject in relation to loss – to the experience of separation and to an impossible desire for a lost object. Both the look and the breast have in common their status as signifiers of loss (*l'objet petit a* in the Lacanian algebra), those objects which have been separated from or have fallen off from the body and which stand for the experience of separation. Within this, both the fantasy and the look permit a kind of reciprocity, a circulation and return: the fantasy, in the slipping among positions of subject and object, blurs those distinctions within its own structure; and the look always includes not only *seeing* but *being seen*.[20]

The fantasy of looking, then, could be said to be the desire to see loss, to see what is by definition that to which the subject can have no access, but through which, at the same time, the subject is marked. In the context of a reading of the other two shots in this series – somewhere between voyeurism and melancholia – the image of the breast traces out that middle ground. The distinctions between looking and looked at that began to be confounded in shot *20*, here find a mythical moment of reciprocity – recalling in a singularly overdetermined way, Lol's desire to see herself not being there.

Shot 23 (18″).
From a high angle, Anne-Marie
Stretter, Michael Richardson and
the young man stretched out on
the floor. In the extreme
foreground, half off-screen, the
back of a man in a white jacket.

V2: *The other man who's*
     sleeping?
V1: *Passing through. A friend of*
     the Stretters.

The piano begins playing the
Beethoven variation again.

V1: *She belongs to whoever*
     wants her. Gives her to
     whoever will have her.
V2: *Love.*

Shot 24 (25″).
Against a black background, the
Vice Consul stands facing the
camera, looking. The piano
music continues.

V1: *Yes ... splendor.*
V2: (Pronouncing each
     syllable) *An-ne Marie Stret-*
     ter written on her tomb?
V1: *An-na Ma-ria Guar-di,*
     erased.

The music stops.

Shot 25 (27″).
Return to 23. The Vice Consul,
seen again from the back, exits.
Anne-Marie Stretter sits up and
looks beyond the camera.

V1: *Every night ... looks at her.*

Piano music begins again softly.

V2: *He never spoke to her?*
V1: *No. Never went near ...*

Shot 26 (37").
The deserted tennis courts and
the red bicycle leaning against
the fence. The Vice Consul
enters from the left and stops
near the bicycle, touches it, and
turns to face the camera.

V2: *The male virgin of Lahore.*
V1: *Yes.*

The music stops.

Shot 27 (1'22").
Return to 25. Anne-Marie
Stretter, sitting up, continues to
look off-screen in the direction
of the camera. She lies down
again. The light dims and goes
out. The bodies are vaguely
outlined in the darkness. The
beggarwoman's song can be
heard in the distance.

V2: *Those flickering lights?*
V1: *The crematories.*
V2: *They're burning those who've*
     starved to death?
V1: *Yes. It's going to be daylight*
     soon. (Pause) He fired a gun.
     One night, from his balcony in Lahore, he fired at the lepers in the Shalimar gardens.
V2: *[He] couldn't bear it.*
V1: *No.*
V2: *India – couldn't bear India?*
V1: *No.*
V2: *What couldn't he bear about it?*
V1: *The idea.*

The last term to be brought into the play of identification and difference,
which began with shot 2, is the Vice Consul in a series of five alternating shots.
This manipulation of a classic instrument of identification, shot/reverse shot,
in which the look of the camera is placed in an axis identical to that of the
spectator, occurs only once in the film, at the end of the first movement. After
the image of the breast, we see, from a high angle, Anne-Marie Stretter,
Michael Richardson and the friend stretched out on the floor (shot 23). In the
extreme foreground, half off-screen is the Vice Consul. The next shot is a
medium close-up of his face, looking beyond the camera (shot 24). Shot 25
goes back to the camera set-up of 23, the Vice Consul turning and leaving at
the edge of the frame. Anne-Marie Stretter then sits up and looks beyond the

camera, in the direction of his exit (shot 25). The Vice Consul is then seen wandering around the deserted tennis courts, lingering near Anne-Marie Stretter's red bicycle (shot 26). The last shot (shot 27) of this series, the last in the first movement of the film, goes back to the set-up of shots 25 and 23 – Anne-Marie Stretter is looking off-screen then lies down again. The voices talk of the crematories where they burn the bodies of those who have died of starvation. They then tell the story of the Vice Consul (already begun over shot 13). Through the voices, the Vice Consul becomes identified with death: Anne-Marie Stretter's tomb (shot 24); the generalized death permeating India, but never seen – the crematories (shot 27 which, like shots 23 and 25, is identified with the Vice Consul's look, his point of view); and an act of death – firing on the lepers in Lahore (shot 27).

The look of the camera which coincides with the axes of the looks of Anne-Marie Stretter and the Vice Consul establishes a relation of doubling, ensuring their eventual substitution, underlined by the cries of the beggarwoman, the references to death, and the refrain '[she] doesn't suffer' and its slightly displaced opposite '[he/she] can't bear it'. In this final, fatal condensation the last term is put into play in the series of positions taken up during this first movement of the film. The trajectory might be written as follows, keeping in mind that each moment along the way is less precisely located than it is continually repeated and blended with the others: the I/eye of the camera – the beggarwoman – Anne-Marie Stretter – the Vice Consul – death.

For us, the most important thing about the reception, its essence as it were, was the pursuit of Anne-Marie Stretter, her hunting down by death, by the bearer of that feminine element, the Vice Consul of Lahore.   *Marguerite Duras*

The first part of the film sets up a circulation among positions of subject and object, the look and looked at, characteristic of the structure of the fantasy where the subject is at once included in the scene and excluded from it. Each of the terms put into play during the first movement, from the I/eye who is looking to death, has the status of an absent presence complicated by the temporal scheme – the relation of the *already-there* of the fiction to the *being-there* of the film. This absent presence is the mark of a kind of reciprocity, of a joining of inclusion/exclusion: Anne-Marie Stretter and the Vice Consul are literally present in the scene, but they are also linked with those positions which are literally absent, excluded from the scene – the beggarwoman and the I/eye who is looking. Each term, then, is both present and absent, in the scene and excluded from it, an exemplary version being Anne-Marie Stretter's death and the image of the photograph which is its emblem.

This play of inclusion/exclusion is written into the very structure of the fantasy, as Lacan has formulated it: $\mathcal{S} \lozenge a$ (which reads: the barred subject; desire of/for/to; *petit objet a*).[21] The lozenge (*le poinçon*, the 'punch' in the middle of the formula), even on the level of its *shape*, includes the possibility of a circulation which links inclusion/exclusion. To indicate that circular process, Lacan provides the lozenge with a 'vectorial direction': $\curvearrowleft$.[22] But the lozenge can also be read as the joining of the signs for inclusion and exclusion (< and >) signifying, then, the circulation among positions of subject and object in the fantasy, where the subject plays a role not only as an observer but as a participant in his own fantasy.

The second part of *India Song* (shots *28–59*), the center of the film, is the reception scene. The voices of the guests, men and women, talk about what they observe at the reception and tell what they remember of the stories, the backgrounds, of Anne-Marie Stretter, Michael Richardson, the Vice Consul and the beggarwoman. The guests remain off-screen throughout the reception which takes place in a drawing room of the Embassy residence. We see Anne-Marie Stretter, Michael Richardson, the Vice Consul, the friend of the Stretters (from part one) and a young attaché passing through or dancing, accompanied by various kinds of music and the voices of the unseen guests speaking among themselves. From time to time, we hear conversations taking place among some of the five characters we see on the screen – between Anne-Marie Stretter and the young attaché or the Vice Consul, for example – but we never see them speaking: 'while they are speaking, their lips remain silent.'[23]

The reception scene continues the work of the fantasmatic, continuing that circulation which began in the first part, and at the same time, carving out in the center of the film, like the lozenge of the fantasy, an absent presence. The entire scene is an alternation from shot to shot between images of the exterior of the Embassy – the façades, the park, tennis courts – and the drawing room. Within this, all of the scenes of the drawing room are organised around a mirror placed at one end of the room, opposite the camera (similar to shot 9). The position of the mirror in the scene produces a temporal and spatial gap in the image into which the characters disappear as they enter and dance across the room, leaving the field of the camera only to reappear a few seconds later reflected in the mirror. An absence, then, is written into the filmed present in the actual filming of the scene by the triangulation of the look of the camera: camera – mirror – object.

This part of the film is organized in a pattern of alternation: from shot to shot and interior to the image, the mirror in the drawing room effecting a kind of alternation *manqué*. As in the first movement, the alternation here between inside and outside (one might as easily say inclusion and exclusion) leads to the final encounter at the end of the evening (at the end of the second movement) between Anne-Marie Stretter and the Vice Consul, an encounter that has been in preparation from the beginning. But unlike the encounter at the end of the first part of the film, where Anne-Marie Stretter and the Vice Consul are linked together by a manipulation of shot/reverse shot, the scene (shot 52) is filmed in a long, slow pan of the camera, re-tracing in reverse the movement of shot 9, where we first saw Anne-Marie Stretter dancing, reflected in the mirror, with Michael Richardson. The alternation which leads to this final encounter, between the interior shots of the drawing room and the exterior tracking shots or pans of the buildings and the park, rep-

52

resents not only the literal alternation interior/exterior, but also the positions that Anne-Marie Stretter and the Vice Consul have taken up in the fiction: each included in the scene of the fiction, but each at the same time linked with positions in 'exile' – the Vice Consul, in diplomatic and social exile in Calcutta for his crime, yet still invited by Anne-Marie Stretter to the reception; and Anne-Marie Stretter herself, linked by her history to that of the beggarwoman who is in her own form of exile as an 'untouchable'. The scene of their encounter, filmed in a single shot across the kind of repressed alternation that the mirror produces, fuses Anne-Marie Stretter and the Vice Consul in a common space of exile.

Anne-Marie Stretter's 'exile' – which has come to mean her death by her identification with 'the bearer of that feminine element, the Vice Consul' – is prefigured again in the last shot of the second movement (shot 59). Surrounded by the guest, the young attaché, Georges Crawn and Michael Richardson, Anne-Marie Stretter is sitting partially stretched out on a sofa. The Vice Consul, who horrified the guests during the reception by his presence and by his encounter with Anne-Marie Stretter, has been driven away. With her, he had been the center of attention during the reception; at the end he is present only by the sound of his voice, off-screen, crying: Anna Maria Guardi. During the shot, his cries become more and more distant, the Beethoven variation that was heard in the first movement of the film is heard again, and two voices, a man's and a woman's, describe the scene. The trajectory which began in the first part of the film with the I/eye who is looking and ended with an identification with death, here finds those two points condensed in the *fascinum*: 'it is that which has the effect of arresting movement and, literally, of killing life'.[24] Anne-Marie Stretter is fixed by the look in a pose, like a still-life where nothing moves but the light which dims and brightens again like slow breathing.

The second movement of the film continues the circulation that began in the first, at the same time condensing even further the play of identity and difference set up among the I/eye who is looking, the beggarwoman,

Anne-Marie Stretter, the Vice Consul and death, which has become their common denominator. Like the lozenge in Lacan's formulaic designation of the fantasy – ◊ – this circulation turns around an empty center which in the film takes the shape of an absent presence: in the *mise en scène* effected by the mirror; in the temporal disjunction produced by characters who are *heard* speaking, but never *seen* speaking; in the complicated status of each of the successive positions taken up in the first part; and, finally, in the (almost) literal center of the second movement, an image of the photograph (shot 40), a mark of the absent presence of Anne-Marie Stretter and of the two temporalities of the film – the *already-there* and the *being-there*.

59

40

VI The third movement (shots *60–74*) of the film responds in some ways to the first: if the first movement puts into play a fantasmatic, the third both continues that circulation and is its signature. There are similarities between the two: two voices – this time a man's and a woman's – talk about what they are seeing and about what they remember of Anne-Marie Stretter's story; the 'mood' of the last part is also similar to that of the first – the long nights, the heat, flowers, incense – but this time situated at the ambassador's residence on an island in the Delta.

The work of signature begins with the voices: the man's voice (Dionys Mascolo) asks questions, can't remember at first, while the woman's seems to know, sees what we and he can't see, seems to remember it all. Duras has called these two voices 'the authors, the motors, ... of the story',[25] a particularly appropriate comment because that distinctive voice, marked by its difference from other voices heard in the film, is her own.

There is also an effect of symbolic folding of the last part onto the first, forming a frame around the empty center, giving the film the shape of the lozenge of the fantasy: ◊. The folding of the last part onto the first is constructed across four specific shots, two in each part.

Shot 2
The look toward the setting sun during which the voices tell the story of the beggarwoman: born in Savannakhet, begins walking ten years ago (west, it's easy to figure, toward the setting sun) and has twelve children who die along the way. By the time she reaches the Ganges she is barren.

Shot 22
The image of Anne-Marie Stretter's nude breast; the voices speak of her trajectory across Indochina to India, for seventeen years through the capitals of Asia: Savannakhet, Peking, Mandalay, Rangoon, Sydney, Lahore, Calcutta.

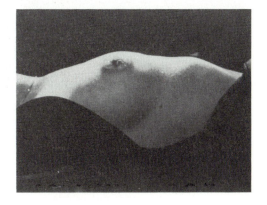

Shot 62
A blinding white light is coming in through a window next to which Anne-Marie Stretter is sitting with her entourage. The voices of two women (one is Duras) tell the story:

V1:   *It was a September evening during the summer monsoon on the islands in 1937. In China the war was continuing. Shanghai had just been bombed. The Japanese were still advancing. In the Asturias the battle was raging, they were still fighting.*

V2:   (Duras) *The throat of the Republic has been cut. In Russia, the revolution is betrayed.*

V1:   *The Nuremberg Congress had just taken place.*

Shot 73
The last shot before the credits at the end: a tracking shot of a map of India and Indochina. There are no voices, but 'India Song' is played on the piano. The shot begins at some islands on the coast of India (where the last part of the film takes place) and moves to Rangoon, Mekong and finally Savannakhet.

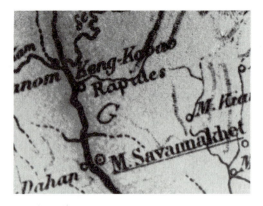

The trajectories of Anne-Marie Stretter and the beggarwoman, told in the present tense by the voices at the beginning of the film, are then retraced in reverse as history at its end. Within that join, *India Song*, like the fantasy, dramatises an imaginary history of the subject, but one which, nevertheless, is marked by traces of time. The geographical and historical notations make of *India Song* a dated scene, providing a symbolic structure, a frame in which subjectivity and history meet in the scene of the fantasy. By the end of the last part the fiction has folded back onto itself, the two temporalities of the film condensing – the *already-there* of the fiction joining the *being-there* of the film as Anne-Marie Stretter leaves (shot 71) to accomplish that death that has been at once inexorably present in the film and the condition of its *mise en scène*.

VII

That is precisely what I recognize in the ravishing of Lol V. Stein, where Marguerite Duras turns out to know without me what I teach.

Jacques Lacan

To return to dreams and hysteria, isn't this exactly the question which reveals itself in the dream of the hysteric ... who dreams that her own wish was not fulfilled, through an identification with the woman she posited as her sexual rival? Her desire, therefore, being the desire of an unsatisfied desire ...

Jacqueline Rose

Returning briefly to the formula of the fantasy, we have seen how the lozenge signifies the circulation of the subject through positions inside and outside the scene of his fantasy. However, the lozenge not only marks that circulation, but in relation to the other terms in the formula $\$ \lozenge a$) is the screen which radically separates the subject from the lost object. The fantasy is not only the *mise en scène* of desire, but the *mise en scène* of an impossible desire – the desire for that to which the subject can have no access. It is in this impossibility that any moment of reciprocity (as in shot 22) has to be mythical and, further, why it is said that desire and prohibition go hand in hand.[26]

It is in the *mise en scène* of this impossibility – the desire for an unsatisfied desire – that the structure of the fantasy again rejoins the fantasy of *India Song*. The film replays that circulation around an absence, an empty center, a circulation which even in the moments it rejoins itself – the folding of the last part onto the first – it has simply accomplished that which was always already there (Anne-Marie Stretter's death), but lost to itself.

Although it is not here a question of hysteria or of desire and identification in hysteria, it was from a matrix of hysterical fantasies – Lol, Dora – that the question of desire was opened in the film and in psychoanalytic theory, but it is in their difference that our fascination with *India Song* derives. The film does not propose itself as a corrective to psychoanalysis, but it does take up and interrogate, within the terms of psychoanalytic theory, within the structure of a fantasmatic, the question of desire. If *India Song* proposes to us a reading of psychoanalytic theory, it is insofar as the film, like the fantasy, is the *mise en scène* of desire, not its object, displacing the question of the content of that desire back onto the question itself.

NOTES

1   This analysis is indebted to the meticulous work of Marie-Claire Ropars-Wuilleumier who is responsible for the complete découpage of *India Song* (and *Son Nom de Venise dans Calcutta désert*), including a transcription of the sound track, published in *L'Avant Scène Cinéma*, no. 225 (April 1979).

2   Marguerite Duras, *The Ravishing of Lol Stein*, trans. Richard Seaver (New York: Grove Press, 1966), p. 4.

3   For a brief discussion/description of the film, see Elisabeth Lyon, 'Woman of the Ganges', *Camera Obscura*, no. 2, Fall 1977.

4   François Barat and Joël Farges (eds.), *Marguerite Duras* (Paris: Editions Albatros, 1975), p. 85.

5   The decision in this article (apart from citations) to use the word 'fantasy' instead of 'phantasy', the term sometimes employed in English to translate a distinction between conscious and unconscious fantasies, has been made for the reasons outlined by Jean Laplanche and J.-B. Pontalis, quoted in the Preface of this volume, p. 2.

6   This article first appeared in French in *Les Temps modernes* 19, 1964, no. 215.

7   Sigmund Freud, 'A Case of Paranoia Running Counter to the Psychoanalytic Theory of the Disease', in *The Standard Edition of the Complete Psychological Works of Sigmund Freud* (hereafter *SE*), (ed.) and trans. James Strachey (London: The Hogarth Press, 1958), vol. 14, p. 269.

8   Laplanche and Pontalis, 'Fantasy and the Origins of Sexuality' in Victor Burgin, James Donald and Cora Kaplan (eds.), *Formations of Fantasy* (London and New York: Methuen, 1986), p. 8.

9   Freud, *SE*, vol. 1, p. 259.

10 Freud, '"A Child is Being Beaten": A Contribution to the Study of the Origin of Sexual Perversions', *SE*, vol. 17, p. 195–6.

11 Laplanche and Pontalis, 'Fantasy and the Origins of Sexuality', pp. 22/3.

12 Marguerite Duras, *India Song*, trans. Barbara Bray (New York: Grove Press, 1976), p. 145. Originally published in French as *India Song – texte-théâtre-film* (Paris: Gallimard, 1973).

13 '... It is the subject's life as a whole which is seen to be shaped and ordered by what might be called, in order to stress this structuring action, "a phantasmatic" (*une fantasmatique*). This should not be conceived of merely as a thematic – not even as one characterised by distinctly specific traits for each subject – for it has its own dynamic, in that the phantasy structures seek to express themselves, to find a way

out into consciousness and action.' Jean Laplanche and J.-B. Pontalis, *The Language of Psycho-Analysis*, trans. Donald Nicholson-Smith (New York: Norton, 1973), p. 317.

14 In French, *entendu* has the sense of both heard and understood: '. . . Hearing is also . . . the history or the legends of parents, grandparents, and the ancestors: the family *sounds* or *sayings*, this spoken or secret discourse, going on prior to the subject's arrival, within which he must find his way. Insofar as it can serve retroactively to summon up the discourse, the noise . . . can acquire this value.' Laplanche and Pontalis, 'Fantasy and the Origins of Sexuality', pp. 18–19.

15 All the dialogue is taken from Marie-Claire Ropars-Wuilleumier's découpage of the film (see note 1). The translation is at times my own and, where possible, taken from *India Song*, trans. Barbara Bray.

16 Roland Barthes, 'Rhetoric of the Image', in *Image, Music, Text*, trans. Stephen Heath (New York: Farrar, Straus & Giroux, Hill & Wang, 1977), p. 44.

17 The dialogue in French is '*Ne souffrent pas?*' and is later replaced by '*Ne supporte pas*' (see shot 21). Both verbs – *souffrir* and *supporter* – can be translated in English as to suffer: the former in a more literal sense of suffering and the latter in the sense of enduring. The translation is complicated by the fact that in the French there is no subject designated, permitting each phrase as it is repeated to refer to a number of different subjects. To indicate this play in English, I have put what seem to be the implied subjects in brackets.

18 Laplanche and Pontalis, 'Fantasy and the Origins of Sexuality', p. 24.

19 Ibid, pp. 24–5.

20 'I must, to begin with, insist on the following: in the scopic field, the gaze is outside, I am looked at, that is to say, I am a picture.
    This is the function that is found at the heart of the institution of the subject in the visible. What determines me, at the most profound level, in the visible, is the gaze that is outside. It is through the gaze that I enter light and it is from the gaze that I receive its effects. Hence it comes about that the gaze is the instrument through which light is embodied and through which – if you will allow me to use a word, as I often do, in a fragmented form – I am *photo-graphed*.' Jacques Lacan, *The Four Fundamental Concepts of Psycho-Analysis*, trans. Alan Sheridan (London: The Hogarth Press and the Institute of Psycho-Analysis, 1977), p. 106.

21 Jacques Lacan, 'Kant avec Sade', in *Ecrits* (Paris: Seuil, 1966), p. 774.

22 Lacan, *The Four Fundamental Concepts*, p. 209.

23 Marguerite Duras, 'Notes on *India Song*', p. 48.

24 Lacan, *The Four Fundamental Concepts*, p. 118.

25 Nicole-Lise Bernheim, *Marguerite Duras tourne un film* (Paris: Editions Albatros, 1974), p. 122.

26 'From the beginning Freud rejected the banal thesis which attributed the unpleasure provoked by sexuality to a purely external prohibition. Whether they are of internal or external origin, desire and prohibition go hand in hand.' Laplanche and Pontalis, 'Fantasy and the Origins of Sexuality', p. 30, footnote 23.

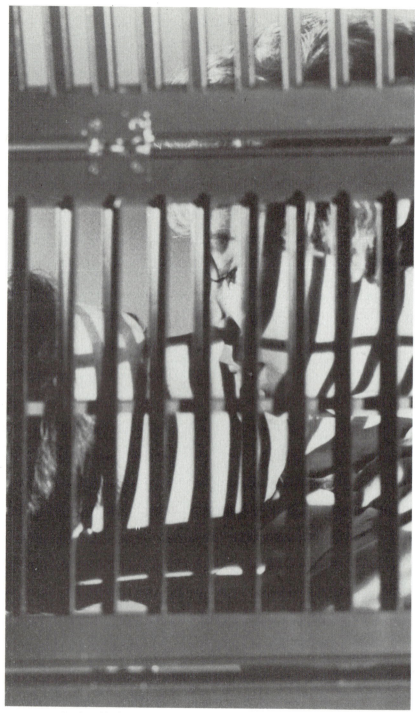

Psycho (Alfred Hitchcock, 1958)

The Sexual Differentiation of the Hitchcock Text

DONALD GREIG

> It is part of the theory of the Text to plunge any enunciation,
> including its own, into crisis.   *Roland Barthes*[1]

Much textual analysis in the 70s, most notably that of Raymond Bellour, proposed and demonstrated a model of the classical Hollywood cinema in which sexual difference occupied a central position. Sexual difference served as both the problematic of the text, inaugurating narrative through its introduction of difference to the stability of repetition, and as the final goal of the text, its resolution and negation of that difference through, more often than not, the establishment of the heterosexual couple. Within this model the figure of the woman functioned as the term of difference, the crucial pivot for both text and analysis; inversely, the desire of the man, a masculine desire, constituted the enunciation of the film. The correlative to this model was the spectator, the unwitting final resting place of this textual activity, marshalled *for* this enunciation by the film text, desired by the text in order to desire like the text. And throughout this process, pursuing a parallel enunciation, distanced through the text of critical activity, was the (male) critic, apologising for the results while offering a table of rhymes and repetitions as evidence.

It is only recently that this methodology has come to be questioned, most notably in recent feminist work around the notion of fantasy. While accepting the demonstration of certain formal characteristics of classical editing (alternation, repetition-resolution, etc.) and noting ideology's appropriation of such textual effects for its own ends, it is specifically the political value of the critical repetition of the workings of patriarchy that has been foregrounded. Textual analysis may well demonstrate the *tendency* of the text, may well trace the dominant obsessions of the text and its efforts to implicate the spectator in a male Oedipal itinerary but, as Barthes and others have been at pains to show, the fluidity and contradictoriness of the text makes any unified reading open to question. Work on fantasy has allied itself with this approach in its stress upon the interchangeability of roles, for spectator and character, *across* the terms of sexual difference – the possibility for the spectator, ultimately, of positions, rather than the one (male) subject position that the text seems to favour. This is to assert not only multiple entries into the text, but also multiple identities within the text.

It is through the films of Alfred Hitchcock, and readings of those films, that I wish to confront the issues of sexual difference within the Hollywood machine, and to question sexual difference within a critical practice. The Hitchcock text has the advantage of being both obsession and testing ground for the methodology of textual analysis (the films displaying something of the 'open-codedness' that drew Heath to his analysis of *Touch of Evil*[2]) but also, in popular opinion, Hitchcock seems to stand as a kind of index of the fatal inevitability of sexual difference. And it is at this conjuncture that I wish to situate the enquiry, at the moment at which any critical methodology, however ideologically sound its premises, rejoins the ideological activity of the text and endorses it through the fascinated, and fascinating, revelation of its internal mechanisms. To this end I shall take up some recent work on fantasy in an attempt at re-reading, to shift the emphasis on the films as elaborate machines for the endorsement of sexual differentiation, towards new proposals for the basis of their continued popularity.

It is necessary, then, to give an account of the underlying methodology of textual analysis and its application to the Hitchcock text. This inevitably involves consideration of a series of articles by Raymond Bellour, written across several years. In the interests of coherence they will be taken as a whole, thereby producing an image of a coherent strategy behind what was undoubtedly a far less knowing moment of critical hermeneutics. My argument is not with the validity of the methodology or its findings but with the way in which that critical machine may be and has been appropriated, for a dangerous popularisation of pre-set truisms of the nature of sexual difference and a concomitant assertion of a masochistic attitude of the female spectator. (An obvious example is Robin Wood's analysis of *Rear Window* and *Vertigo* in which, following his reading of Bellour, the spectator is 'unambiguously male'.[3])

THE HOLLYWOOD MACHINE & HITCHCOCK

The following is by no means an exhaustive account of either Bellour's work in textual analysis or the underlying theory of textual analysis as elaborated, in literature, by Roland Barthes and others. There is a comparative wealth of material on this subject[4] and I do not intend to add to this list. But the reduction of such a corpus necessitates a certain censoring of the critical activity. The experience of working closely on a film on the editing table is, itself, always reduced in the transcription of that work into writing. (It is that loss of the experience of the text which leads to an easy account of the findings of textual analysis, at the expense of its contradictions.) But there is always a marginal recuperation of that activity in the writing, usually at moments when it becomes almost impossible to follow the line of argument, juggling a multiplicity of codes. It is at these moments that analysis demonstrates most clearly Barthes' theory of the potentially infinite continuation of textual activity (*the Text is experienced only in an activity of production*[5]). My focus here is the reduced account of the Hitchcock text as a demonstration of sexual difference which leaves itself open to theoretical and popular recuperation such that its potential for transgression is foreclosed. I begin, then, with an account of Bellour's model of Hollywood cinema and the particular relationship that Hitchcock enjoys with that machine.

For Bellour, Hitchcock is the exceptional case who proves the rule, the *auteur* who works within the paradigm of classic Hollywood cinema but always slightly askance to it. Speaking of *Psycho*:

> ... the film, in a sense, contravenes the classical model of narrative – as well as that more singular model which is both an eccentric and exemplary version of it: the Hitchcockian system.[6]

Hitchcock is part of the system, subject to the same rules and regulations, but with Hitchcock there is always something knowing, a nod in the direction of the enunciation of the text, more coded than obvious. Lang is similar in this respect, both directors noted for their insistence upon vision and the look, marking, through this emphasis, something specifically cinematic.

Narrative and narration are similarly resonant in the Hitchcock text. Narration produces narrative but is, itself, the product of an oscillation, a balance, between terms of repetition and terms of difference. From stasis (A) through a rupture into difference (B) and, then, to the recontainment of that difference in a term of repetition (A'): an Aristotelian model of narrative (A-B-A') in microcosm, something like a fundamental unit of narration. Narrative is the result of this careful oscillation, always weighted towards difference through the course of the story (the film's 'acceleration') and slowed up at the end through the return of repetition (hence, often, the film's rhyme between opening and closing scenes).[7] Hitchcock works according to the same principle but goes to the limit of possible balance: repetition is deeply insistent, for example, the sequence in *The Birds*[8] providing and producing an imbalance whose final rupture is the attack. Similarly, the repetition of the oscillation of looks in the crop-duster sequence in *North by Northwest*[9] or, on a grander scale, the suggestion made by both Bellour and Peter Wollen[10] that the Hitchcock text is an endless repetition of the same basic narrative. And also, as we shall see, there is the implication that this very narrative repetition is the mark of a specific psychic structure – the male Oedipal scenario – which is the repetition of Hollywood's and Hitchcock's own symbolic régime, that of Western patriarchy.

Within this scenario it is the figure of the woman which is simultaneously codified as different and which functions as the term of difference

nich inaugurates the narrative. There is a double movement here which
scues Bellour from any suggestion of a supposed essentialism. Woman is not
different (from man) when introduced into the narrative, but it is her function
as a term of difference, as inaugurator of the narrative movement which
retroactively codifies her as difference. The closure of the narrative, ultimately
the containment of difference, is then the containment of the woman, either
through her negation (wounding as symbolic castration or death), or through
her denial of independence in the socially sanctioned institution of marriage.

The amplification of this system into the Hitchcockian system is
manifest in the organisation of looks in specific films. The analysis of *The Birds*
has already been noted and it is clear in this instance that the look of the
woman at the man is transgressive (and, hence, punishable) insofar as it
introduces a term of difference in the place of a term of repetition. That is to
say that the look of the man at the woman is acceptable within the scenario
outlined above: the term of repetition is that of the man looking, and the term
of difference – the woman looked at – is contained by this structure. But the
look of the woman at the man is a reversal that cannot be tolerated, hence the
symbolic castration through the wound inflicted by the gull on Melanie
Daniels.

In the same way that the analysis of *The Birds* demonstrates the
regulation of the scopic drive according to the symbolic pressure of patriarchy,
so the analysis of the opening of *Marnie*[11] traces a chain of (male) looks around
the imag(in)ing of the heroine. In this, Marnie is contained as a term of
difference by the repetition of looks of male characters and the look of the
camera across the sequence. And central to this analysis is the figure of
Hitchcock, the male director, who uses the male characters as 'fictional delegates' in order to fulfil Hitchcock's own desire. It is Hitchcock's own appearances in his films that is the index of the particular relationship between
Hitchcock's films and the larger corpus of Hollywood cinema. The appearance
is the ironic underlining, a cinematic tic, which suggests the set of (patriarchal)
suppositions which the Hollywood system is forever at pains to disguise
beneath the mask of the Natural. But Bellour's analysis of Hitchcock's appearances is also a claim that *Marnie* and other films in the Hitchcock text are all
ordered by a logic of masculine desire, and that pleasure within this system is
to be found only at the expense of the woman and through identification with
the man.

HITCHCOCK THE ENUNCIATOR

The starting point for much textual analysis in the 70s was the
theory of the text outlined by Roland Barthes. A series of early
polemical essays[12] argued for a new methodological field in opposition to a reductive, author-based, reflection criticism, principally in the field
of literature. Against the search for the unified reading, against the final

signified, Barthes foregrounded the very activity of signification, and argued for a general theory of signification and of the subject's place within that production. Ultimately, the theory of the text was a refusal of the metalingualism of traditional criticism and for the promotion of criticism itself to the level of literary production.

This approach demanded the death of the author as source and guarantor of the meaning of the statement (énoncé) and insisted upon the site of enunciation (énonciation) as the locus of the production of meaning. Traditional criticism's mistake was in insisting that there was only ever one enunciation, that of the author, and that his/her intentions were the guarantee of meaning of the statement. But Emile Benveniste demonstrated that any statement is to a lesser or greater degree dependent upon its context for its meaning. The point is made clear in his study of 'deictics' or shifters, words which have no fixed meaning but which are context dependent. A word like 'I', for example, is dependent upon who utters it for its meaning. Equally, the word 'now', at the time at which I write it, has a different signified from that at the time at which you read it. What such examples demonstrate is the split between the moment of uttering the statement (the enunciation) and the statement itself (the enounced) as an 'independent' structure.[13]

In the same way that a shifter like the word 'I' is dependent for its meaning upon the moment at which it is uttered and who utters it, so the text could be thought of as context-dependent. The readerly text could be made writerly[14] by the textual critic, could be made to speak that which it tried to keep silent (and which traditional criticism endeavoured to keep silent) – sexuality, economics, contradiction. *S/Z* is the obvious text-case, an elaborate critical machine for the re-production of Balzac's novella *Sarrasine*, a sort of *hommage* to the complexity of signification in its proportion of textual reading to text.

For Bellour *S/Z* is exemplary. His reading of *North by Northwest* follows two codes suggested by Barthes (the Hermeneutic and the Symbolic[15]), and his article, 'The Unattainable Text',[16] is a treatise on that aspect of Barthes' theory which film so readily yields – the continual spiralling away of enunciation, of signification. Again, it is enunciation as a concept derived from linguistics which occupies a central position. Enunciation is viewed as a dynamic of the text, as the site of the production of meaning and, inversely, as the point around which all activity coheres. For certain cases this locus is realised as an actual figure in the text. The figure is termed 'the Enunciator' by Bellour[17] and is identified in Dumas' novels as the character Balsamo and, in the Hitchcock text, as the figure of Hitchcock and his fictional delegates. Importantly, the figure of Hitchcock is not the author for, at its simplest, the figure is part of the text, part of the enounced as opposed to the enunciation. But, as a result of this critical account, Hitchcock, author and myth, comes to reclaim that text, to reappropriate the film as the mark of his obsessions. This movement is clear in the popular reception of Hitchcock movies where his appearances, together with the desire to see a Hitchcock film (where 'he' will manipulate you) and to recognise stylistic tics, are all part of the shared experience of seeing a 'Hitchcock film'. There is a strong argument against Bellour's repetition of this pattern in 'Hitchcock the Enunciator', but less convincing is the argument against the reduction of these texts to one symbolic trajectory: Hitchcock the Enunciator – Fictional Delegates – Spectator.

These are the terms of the argument, and the unifying thread of these terms is an enunciatory drive, or a 'film wish', which is manifestly a masculine desire. Hitchcock the man employs/is employed by male fictional delegates whose desire, in the case of *Marnie*, is for the possession of the woman, for her containment. And, as a further link in the chain, there is the spectator, positioned as male for this enunciation, invited to play the game of possession and dispossession of the image of Marnie. The same schema is in operation in Bellour's analysis of *North by Northwest* where the enunciation of the film text is shown to be, unequivocally, the male Oedipal trajectory, and this enunciatory drive is again linked to Hitchcock through his appearance. *North by Northwest* is also cited in a section of 'Hitchcock the Enunciator' in which Bellour discusses several other films to show how Hitchcock's appearances serve as an ironic condensation of the particular obsession of the enunciation, inevitably a male problematic. The circle is complete: from enunciation as a male concern, through male fictional delegates, to the (male) spectator.

But is the text so contained and so containing? Is this demonstration of the enunciation, however impressive, incontrovertible? On a purely linguistic level, there is never only one possible enunciation, marking the potential of infinite variation, repetition, inflection and reproduction. The point has been made by Mary Ann Doane in a slightly different form.[18] She argues for a dialogical text, a text of irony where two potential enunciations continually confront each other in the production of a subtle contradiction. In a discussion of 'Hitchcock the Enunciator' she provides a credible alternative to Bellour's reading, suggesting that the play of possession and re-possession of Marnie marks a hesitancy of the patriarchal hand, a resistance to such analytic closure centred on the figure of the woman. The re-viewing of the film in this light throws the previous viewing experience against the present one and produces an ironic distance from the male obsession that the text seemed to display. The bounded film is unsettled, the male bonding questioned and the grain of the text revealed.

What this consideration also reveals is the way in which Bellour's analyses of Hitchcock's films tend to cohere around one issue, that of male psychosis, which pushes textual analysis into the sphere of a final signified. In other words, these textual analyses depart from a Barthesian account of the text at the moment at which they discover a principle of consistency. Certainly, Bellour's project is not that of a happy pluralism, but, instead, evidences a more political concern for an understanding of patriarchal culture and its operation in popular texts (principally the nineteenth-century novel and the Hollywood film). Given the nature of enunciation and the potential of any text for oppositional readings, however, it is important to examine in more detail this principle of consistency and its derivation.

SYMBOLIC DETERMINATION

It is the symbolic as a psychoanalytic category which is the principle methodological constituent of the Bellourian system, the symbolic as it is found in the work of Lévi-Strauss, Lacan and, particularly, Rosolato. The notion is a complex one[19] which, somewhat simplistically, we might define as that system or structure of differences constitutive of language into which the child is born(e) and within which the child must take his/her place in order to be identified/to gain identity. The symbolic is conceived as a network of pre-existent signifiers, an existent order, within which the child/adult must situate itself throughout existence in order to attempt a stable subject position. Equally, though, any consideration of the symbolic will be concerned with signification itself, with any meaning production (and this is particularly true of Metz's consideration of the symbolic), rather than simply with the description of existent symbolic systems such as kinship and marriage laws, systems of art and economic relations. For it is simultaneously the entry into the symbolic and the acquisition of language which is the production for the subject of meaning.

Bellour's consideration of the symbolic and his use of it as a category is limited, in the main, to a consideration of its function as the locus for the establishment and sustenance of a stable and staple masculine identity. The symbolic, for Bellour, is focused upon the male Oedipal myth and upon a consideration of that myth as the nucleus of male identity and male neuroses. In one sense, at least, the relationship between the Oedipus complex and the symbolic is highly privileged for, in anthropology, it is the direct representation of a universal marriage prohibition and, in psychoanalysis, it represents the universal experience of the male child in his quest for understanding, for identity and for his position within the family. Bellour's essay on *North by Northwest* is an elaborate and highly detailed account of the enunciation of the film as a male Oedipal trajectory. The passage of the hero from the security of the family into his mistaken flight as 'wrong man' from the law is, Bellour suggests, the same Oedipal scenario outlined by Freud and Lacan in which the boy child must find his place in relation to desire and the law.

The analysis draws on Guy Rosolato's account of the various figures of the Father within a classic Oedipal scenario,[20] an account which is then used by Rosolato in his own analysis of the enunciation of three religious myths and its relation to the male Oedipus complex.[21] Rosolato's implicit argument, after Lévi-Strauss, is that the dominant religious myths of a society are the direct representation of a shared psychic problematic, shared, that is, not on the basis of any mysticism or telepathy, but on the basis of the dominant group's regulation of their common obsessions through repetition in re-presentation. As Lévi-Strauss succinctly puts it, 'Myths get thought in man unbeknownst to him'.[22]

The analysis of *North by Northwest* appears, in this light, as a decoding of another religious myth (Hollywood as non-denominational church) and this observation is supported by Bellour's reading of Wyler's *The Westerner* in *Le cinéma américain*,[23] a further account of the centrality of the male Oedipal trajectory in American cinema. Hollywood is seen as a machine for the circulation and regulation of a stable male identity. Given this outline it is not surprising that the marginality of woman simply conceals her centrality to this regime. And it is in the latter half of the article on *The Westerner* that Bellour shows, through an analysis of Curtiz' *The Mystery of the Wax Museum*, a further refinement of the Hollywood machine as the locus of a stable male identity. The account is one of the pivots of Bellour's work and occurs in many articles:

> ... the difference which appears due to woman is nothing but the mirror effect of the narcissistic doubling that makes possible the constitution of the male subject through the woman's body, ordered by a double play of differential identity, based on an effect of imaginary projection subjected to the constitutive pressure of symbolic determination.[24]

In other words, that difference which is attributed to woman, which codifies her as the mark of sexual difference, is the result of what Bellour terms symbolic determination, a symbolic pressure, which can be found at work in myth and in the Hollywood cinema. This symbolic pressure works upon the original moment of the imaginary, the moment of recognition of self in the mirror which gives way, almost immediately (the mother granting the image to the child) to the recognition of difference. This recognition of (sexual) difference, the moment of the symbolic, is achieved within the same 'reflective' moment ('the mirror effect of a narcissistic doubling'). This recognition is made on the basis of a reflected comparison for the male child, the pos(ition)ing of the mirror-image as different in relation to the world. This moment of self-differentiation is a moment of identification (the mirroring of self in other) and differentiation (the mark of the failure of that identification: 'differential identity') which is played out by the Hollywood system as a form of symbolic pressure. Hollywood asserts: 'Look at the woman – she's different' in order to promote 'Look at yourself – you're the same (as us)'. Hollywood here is conceived as the patriarchal machine which reflects, refracts and promotes the patriarchal society.

Again, for Bellour, the symbolic is concerned with the stability of male identity, is even constitutive of it. The two moments, nuclei which are present at all times, are that of the male Oedipal scenario and that of the recognition of sexual difference, moments which are weighted, in the Hollywood machine, towards the issue of male identity. The problem with such an account is in its critical repetition, the repetition of a specific symbolic organisation bearing all the characteristics and all the fixity of myth itself. And the application of such a model to a set of texts produces a restriction upon transgression of the symbolic organisation that that very description might be arguing against. Such, I think, is the problem with Bellour's argument in 'Psychosis, Neurosis, Perversion', a further article on the Hitchcock text, here focused on *Psycho* but, again, encompassing several other texts. It is in this article that he refines the argument that the image of woman in Hollywood is the repetition of the constitutive moment of male identity and here that he outlines what, for him, is the conspicuous organisation of sexual difference in the Hitchcock text: 'woman, the subject of neurosis, becomes the object of psychosis of which man is the subject. ...'[25] This summation asserts the importance of sexual difference as the underlying logic of the Hitchcockian system, although the use of the Hitchcock text as an amplification of Hollywood and patriarchy is qualified later to the effect that the argument is only valid 'given a certain regime of fiction, and a certain order of civilization'.[26]

The consideration of the symbolic and its use in Bellour's and others' work is concerned with the elaboration of insistent and repetitive narrative structures and their place within a dominant cultural order. The symbolic, then, is the term used to denote and describe the play of sexual difference and its centrality to the classical narrative system, specifically the skewing of sexual difference towards the maintenance of a stable male identity. The components of this conception of the symbolic are, primarily, the positive male Oedipus[27] and an 'earlier' narrative wherein the male is constituted as male through a double understanding of differentiation in the image of the woman. And these two scenarios are, decisively, narratives; they are instances not of determinant moments in the history of the subject but accounts of such constitutive moments as they come to be fixed in myth. The symbolic is seen and found not as a structuring movement but as structure. In one sense this is quite apposite, for the child comes to find his/her place within a structure ordained and ordered for it by the parents, a structure anterior to the child and composed of the parents' individual histories and fantasies. But this existent structure is never entirely pre-set or entirely determinate of the child's behaviour, for it is only through the existence of the child that the structuration necessary to sustain the Oedipal scenario is set in play. The symbolic, then, is never simply structure (indeed, if it were there would be no possibility of ever overcoming its questioned universality) and must be considered as the potential of structure – as structuration – as a play of signifiers bearing all the potential of the pluralism of signification.

The symbolic as employed by Bellour and others may well describe the most likely resultant structure for the male child ('given a certain regime of fiction, and a certain order of civilisation'), but the text must maintain its potential for the transgression of such systems, must be seen as dynamic structuration. If the text is closed on the order of the symbolic then the overlay of myth is complete: from religious myth to Hollywood myth to critical myth. And it is here that the symbolic enjoins a popular conception of the Hollywood myth, binds text and spectator into the replaying of the most insistent ideological operations, which is to confuse the aim of the text, its symbolic pressure, with its actual and potential transgression. Woman is, otherwise, the simple expenditure of the text, its cost margin, and the experience of the female spectator is similarly marginalised: entry to the text by any other route than that described by textual analysis is barred.

TEXTUAL ANALYSIS & TRANSGRESSION

A methodology which might unsettle a certain orthodoxy of textual analysis[28] is one that I have developed elsewhere[29] in an analysis of Dorothy Arzner's film, *Dance, Girl, Dance*. (The choice of film was in no way determined by any simple matrix of 'Hitchcock/male director: Arzner/female director', but by the far more banal requirements of print availability.) My project was to investigate 'at first hand' the methodology of textual analysis and, if possible, to open up the space within that analysis for a transgressive reading. The terms of the analysis were, somewhat cavalierly, the categories of the psychic and the social, the psychic considered as the site of the unconscious and the social as the representation of a patriarchal society and its values. The psychic was concerned with the elaboration of a *female* Oedipal trajectory and, as a necessary concomitant, with work on various manifestations of figures of the mother and the relationship of the girl child with the mother. The analysis produced a provocative confrontation: on the one hand, the film promotes an enunciation concerned with female Oedipality in which the end of the film marks the 'successful' psychic resolution; on the other, it represents an unsatisfactory and ridiculous containment of the heroine in the embrace of a patronising patriarch. It is the collision of these two readings that offers the space for a transgressive reading much like that of category 'E' proposed by *Cahiers du Cinéma*, where the stranglehold of ideology is more apparent than real.[30] It is the psychic trajectory of the heroine which offers a transgressive identification (transgressing the insistence of patriarchy in the social and in the symbolic as it functions within textual analysis), and also acts as a demonstration of the mechanisms of patriarchy. Irigaray:

> The female oedipus complex realises, ultimately, the entry of the woman into a system of values that is not her own and where she can only 'become visible' and mingle caught up in the needs, desires and fantasies of others – Men.[31]

The importance of what I have termed a transgressive textual analysis is its ability to unsettle earlier assertions of the dominance of text over spectator in its marshalling of the spectator for one particular enunciation. The insistence of the above approach is upon the possibility of several enunciations within a single text, each 'verifiable' according to the methodology of textual analysis and each in conflict with another. This is at the same time to promote the continuing activity of the text (and here we are close to what Barthes refers to as the radically symbolic nature of the text[32]), and to argue for different spectatorial identifications running against the grain of patriarchal imposition (be it practical or theoretical).

More specifically, and as a kind of condensation of the issues involved, such an approach radically undermines critical, theoretical and popular discourses of the films of Hitchcock which figure here under the rubric of the Hitchcock text, for although traces of the female Oedipal trajectory have been located in analyses of *Rebecca*[33] and *The Birds*,[34] the twin moons of textual analysis and other Hitchcock films still assert the dominance of the male spectator. In this respect there is an evident lack of consideration of those films of Hitchcock in which there is a central female figure (*Rebecca*, *Marnie*, *Spellbound*, *Suspicion*, etc.) and the approach outlined above would seem well equipped to deal with such texts.

As has been noted, though, such an approach maintains the binarism of sexual difference in the interests of unsettling a new critical orthodoxy. It is to the notion of fantasy as elaborated in recent feminist work[35] that we must turn to escape such an impasse. And, in order to rescue the text from its existent symbolic trap, I will turn to the theory of primal or original fantasy elaborated in a seminal essay by Laplanche and Pontalis.[36]

FANTASY & THE TEXT

Recent work on fantasy has responded directly to work in textual analysis in the 70s and what has been seen as its self-referentiality in its analysis of patriarchy.[37] The problem for feminist criticism has been the role of the female spectator (and, indeed, of the feminist critic) which has been, if not discarded, at least de-centred in a subtle mimesis of the Hollywood text. This account does little to explain the pleasure for the female spectator except in terms of masochism, an account that is all too readily recuperable by traditional criticism. Behind this argument is an often unspoken agreement that the enunciation of the text necessarily marshals the unwitting spectator along the same trajectory of desire that textual analysis displays: the text as powerful ideological tool, the spectator as its gullible victim. The autonomy of the spectator and, indeed, his/her own individual history and set of associations and personal resonances is, by implication, limited to secondary elaboration *after* the humiliating experience of being picked up by the scruff of the text and carried through this alienating psychic trajectory. Fantasy, it has been implicitly argued, is the precise psychoanalytic concept which, in relation to the text, provides the spectator with a 'relative autonomy', with a series of possible entries and identifications with characters according to their different roles and functions within a network of character relations. Elizabeth Cowie has demonstrated this kind of sliding of positions in her analysis of *The Reckless Moment* in which: 'the diverse positions mother, father, child, lover, wife, husband ... are never finally contained by any one character.'[38]

What this provides for the spectator is a series of possible subject-positions according to the particular ordering of these oppositions in relation to one another, the possibility of reordering the 'fantasy' in much the same way that Freud's 'A Child Is Being Beaten' reveals a complex palimpsest of possible narratives (rearrangements of the terms subject/object/verb), all of which display potential and pleasurable subject positions for the fantasist within and outside the text.

'A Child Is Being Beaten' is an analysis of a fantasy articulated by several of Freud's patients, most notably those suffering from obsessional neurosis and hysteria.[39] It was common enough for Freud to treat it as almost universal and the object of my enquiry is not so much the nature of perversion (as Freud proposes) but the mechanism of fantasy that is so clearly outlined. Freud's first concern is to find out what lies behind the manifest text and, as with the dream, there are several different 'layers', which vary according to the gender of the subject. Beneath the first text, for the female patient only, is found 'My father is beating the child (whom I hate)' – the bracketed part being discovered in analysis – and beneath this text, for both sexes, is the text 'I am being beaten by my father'. In turn there is a third layer, differentiated by gender: for the boy, 'I am being beaten by my mother', for the girl, 'My "authority figure" is beating the (masculine) child'.

Freud's (problematic) distribution of fantasies by gender is dis-cussed in detail elsewhere by D. N. Rodowick.[40] But for the purposes of this study, the *mechanism* of fantasy which he outlined can be retained. The manifest text, 'A Child Is Being Beaten', produces a high degree of pleasure (usually accompanied by masturbation), but the pleasure differs according to the varying forms of the fantasy (in one case sadistic, in another masochistic). What is particularly interesting in this respect is that the original text can be made to yield up at least two different enunciations, enunciations which partake of different modes of pleasure. The crucial thing to note here is that the pleasure is not limited or fixed to the specific mode of the fantasy under analysis. The subject does not 'know' the source of pleasure, is only aware of a text that repeats itself with all the characteristics of an obsession. The subject may derive pleasure from this one disguised text equal to that pleasure that may be felt when the fantasy is specifically confronted in the analysis of another 'layer', but the subject may not choose the pleasure just as the fantasist cannot choose the particular mode of fantasy to be enjoyed. All that is available to view is one, manifest text: a child is being beaten. And the pleasure that that text produces is due to its potential enunciations, enunciations that Freud demonstrates through analysis.

In this light it is worth considering the formal characteristics of the manifest fantasy upon which Freud begins his textual analysis, characteristics which, I would suggest, bear more than a passing resemblance to those of what has been called the classic realist text. (The following comparisons should be considered, ideally, in the light of Christian Metz's observations on the meta-psychological status of the cinema spectator and the particular propensity for the cinema to offer a regulated space for the indulgence of fantasy.[41])

First, then, we might note that a common characteristic of manifest fantasy text and the classic realist text (CRT) is in the masking of the enuncia-tion(s) behind the enounced, the denial of an immediate source of utterance of the statement (indeed, for the child recounting the fantasy it is not a question of the source being identifiable, but of finding a scene running on perpetually inside the head). There is a comparative mechanism, then, in both CRT and fantasy for the denial of the source of the text. Secondly, the role of the child in relation to the text and the reader/spectator of the CRT is that, suitably enough, of a passive spectator (and Freud even uses the term 'spectator' in his account). There is, in this respect, no control over the unwinding of the event (an obvious correlative to the lack of identifiable source). Thirdly, here refer-ring to the CRT in cinema, the action or event is a focused part – a close-up – a synechdoche and, as such, part of a metonymic movement giving onto a series of other possible scenarios. Again, in relation to cinema, the event unfolds in an eternal present tense ('being beaten'), a loop repeating the event, always within the paradox of present absence, never quite a screen memory but bearing several common characteristics with that as well.

As such, and returning to a more strictly Barthesian account, the first version of the fantasy bears important characteristics of the 'readerly' which is to say that fantasy, as a mechanism, tends towards this impersonal form. The subject positions that this text can yield are then demonstrated by Freud through the elaboration of the various possible enunciations of that text, positions in which the subject can be subject of the narrative, object of a sequence or 'outside' in the form of spectator. And this in itself is a demon-stration of what has so far been called the possibility of different entries into the text. That is, I think, what Barthes is working on in a somewhat different form, most notably in S/Z where, in an analysis of the readerly (in the form of Balzac's Sarrasine), he reveals the possibility of different entries into the text. And it is through the notion of the symbolic that he suggests this, the symbolic conceived as a major axis of oppositions, castrating/castrated and active/passive. These are the same terms, clearly, as those in Freud's analysis of 'A child is being beaten', and, like Freud, Barthes is engaged in an account in which sexual difference is itself unsettled. Hence: '... the symbolic field is not that of the biological sexes. ...'[42] The logic of Barthes' textual analysis seems to follow that outlined by Freud in his interpretation of dreams and fantasy: 'the logic of the symbolic field is characterised, like the dream, by atemporality, substitution, reversibility.'[43] Their aims and theoretical fields are, of course, significantly different (not least because Freud is reliant upon the patient's associations to provide a continuation of the manifest text), but both assert the autonomy of the spectator from textual effects.

Central to this argument is the implicit proposition that the dynamic of the text – its potential enunciations – is not specifically ordered according to the law of sexual difference (for, in Freud's analysis, there are different enunciations – masculine and feminine – for the same enounced) and that, as a result, the same text is equally accessible and pleasurable for all readers. This is in contrast to Bellour's particular theory of the text in which there is only one dynamic of the text – one enunciation – the male Oedipal trajectory.

It is a contrast which is apparent in a useful and interesting interview conducted by Bellour with Barthes in 1970 where, discussing *S/Z*, two opposing considerations of the text are outlined. The argument centres upon Bellour's observation of an Oedipal problematic within the novella *Sarrasine*, a problematic which draws no comment from Barthes in his analysis and which, in interview, he deems of secondary importance, given what he sees as a questioned centrality of the importance of the Oedipal within psychoanalytic theory: 'Moreover, can you be sure that Lacan, in his recent work, attributes as decisive a role to the Oedipus as you suggest?'[44]

Conversely, Barthes prioritises the castration complex as determinant for the subject, the castration complex as a series of moments across a lifetime which is never dealt with and never lived through.[45] The Oedipus complex, by contrast, is something which is surpassed, dealt with, mastered[46] and, through its status as myth, promotes itself as a sort of secondary manifestation of the *before* of the castration complex; the castration complex as enunciation and the Oedipus complex as the enounced. For Barthes the symbolic code is concerned particularly with the axis of castration/castrated in *Sarrasine*, yet Bellour attempts to promote the Oedipal trajectory itself as the symbolic code and, from there, to insist upon the symbolic as the very sight/site of the structuration of the text.[47] Barthes rejects this suggestion on the basis that there is more than one 'entry' into the text, more than one enunciation. His theory of the text is committed to the continuation of textual reading, as a practice opposed to the halting on a final signified. It is a proposition which supports the assertion that there is more than one enunciation to any text and which argues for potentially contradictory readings within the same text, an argument which highlights the various functions of criticism as a meta-text.

ORIGINAL FANTASY & THE HITCHCOCK TEXT

Original fantasies, as the name suggests, are directly concerned with the first enigmas that confront the child and, in answer to those questions, original fantasies are among the earliest representations. They can be reduced to three in number, unified by their explicit thematic of origin:

> Fantasies of origins: the primal scene pictures the origin of the individual; fantasies of seduction, the origin and upsurge of sexuality; fantasies of castration, the origin of the difference between the sexes.[48]

Consideration of fantasy can offer a different conception of the site of enunciation as a continual structuration (and here I am repeating Elizabeth Cowie's description of fantasy as the *mise en scène* of desire[49]), a structuration based upon original enigmas providing models of fictional pleasure which are in no way gender specific. The initial link between the notion of primal fantasy and the Hitchcock text lies in the recurrence of a form of the primal scene as the central hermeneutic of several films. The primal scene is the moment, constructed by the child on the basis of noises and observations provided by reality, at which the child 'sees' for the first time sexual intercourse between the parents. This knowledge and the production of the scene is always based upon the action of the child's investigative and projective capabilities, in the employment of a variety of scenes and fantasies against each other (the testing of hypotheses) in order to come to a 'satisfactory' conclusion. That conclusion is the imagining of the parents' coupling. Central to this investigation, the point at which the child is unable fully to master the information, is the perception of the scene as one of violence, by the father against the mother. Sexuality, violence and investigation are, then, the components of the primal scene, the terms of the original fantasy and its origin. These are the concerns of many films, but in the Hitchcock text the particular condensation of these issues marks the primal scene as a structuring principle.

In *Rear Window*, for example, Jeffries, the arch voyeur/investigator, pursues an obsessive investigation into the couplings around the courtyard while himself remaining curiously unaware of the potential for his own sexual life with Lisa. The focal point, the actual hermeneutic of the film, is the Thorwald couple and an investigation into the supposed murder of wife by husband, a particularly violent vision of the primal scene. *Rebecca*, in which the Joan Fontaine character (an unnamed orphan) leads an investigation into the marital scene of De Winter and Rebecca, culminates in the description of Rebecca's murder by De Winter. In *Marnie* the central trauma, the narrative hermeneutic, is the child's witnessing of a violent primal scene. In these examples, and in others, it is the coupling, often violent, which produces what might be called the trauma of the film (inevitably also its hermeneutics) and its structuring principle. The primal scene is, as Lacan suggests, always too much

Rebecca (Alfred Hitchcock, 1940)

or too little, always conducive to trauma[50] and the Hollywood text's consistent release is in the displacement of its violence into death (a displacement well served by western culture's condensation of sex, orgasm and death).

The most obvious example in this respect is *Psycho*, in which the primal scene is both the text's dynamic and its obsession. The opening scene offers no obvious problem in this respect: the forward movement of the camera from the roof through the window and venetian blinds underlines the voyeuristic perception of the coupling and, at the same time, acts as a displacement of the violence of the scene. And it is this violence which comes to figure throughout the film in the murders, acting as a kind of obscene condensation of the primal scene, facilitated by the oscillation between male and female accomplished through Norman's portrayal of Mother. The murder of Marion becomes the violent enactment of Norman's perception of the primal scene, a scene in which he both plays a part (as man/murderer beneath the disguise) and as observer. This is to imply a retroactive knowledge across the film (by which we come to know that it is Norman beneath the disguise) but, even without that, there is a strong underlining of the murder as a projection of Bates' desire through the assertion of his point of view immediately preceding the shower scene. The murder of Arbogast is another enactment of the primal scene, this time with the Mother playing the dominant role and Arbogast abseiling backwards down the bannister, arms flailing, in a grotesque parody of orgasm.

Finally, and centrally, comes the account of the primal scene which, for the fiction, inaugurated Norman's trauma and, for the film, the hermeneutic which is the structuring principle of the text. The murder, reported by the psychiatrist, is recounted in obviously Oedipal terms: Mother married another man, rejecting Norman, who killed them both. Indeed, this scenario is *too* Oedipal – its obviousness and acceptability smacks more of Hollywood's assimilation of the subversive science of psychoanalysis than of clinical practice. But the 'clues' to the original trauma, the trauma of the primal scene as in *Marnie*, still remain. The poisoning must have taken place in the home, for the lovers were found 'dead together. In bed.' Dead together. The very condensation of violence, sexuality and death that I have outlined. The implication is that Norman killed them in bed or elsewhere and dragged their bodies upstairs to re-enact a bizarre version of the primal scene as *Liebestod*. It is the moment of the primal scene as violence and death, which recurs throughout the film, marking an enunciatory concern with the trauma of the primal scene.

Within this schema the end rhymes with and resolves the beginning (Bellour's problematic in 'Psychosis, Neurosis, Perversion'), the last three shots of the film marking a condensation of, and a release from, the trauma of the primal scene. The body of Norman dissolves into the body of the mother and the voice-over (Mother's voice) renounces violence in her refusal to swat the fly: the union of man and woman is achieved without the accompanying associations of violence. And as V. F. Perkins has noted,[51] the hoisting of the car out of the swamp marks a formal release from repeated downward movements of knife and water: crude post-coital withdrawal, devoid of the violence of the murder it contains.

The structuration of *Psycho* then, is based upon varied moments of the primal scene, different stagings of desire, ultimately ordered and revised through the central hermeneutic of Bates' misconception of the significance of the primal scene.

To date, work on fantasy in film has been concerned with the possibility of different identifications facilitated by the shift of characters in relation to each other within the text, thereby allowing the spectator the possibility of taking up new positions. The problem is succinctly put by Janet Bergstrom who, after describing the argument proposed by Bellour in 'Neurosis, Psychosis, Perversion', notes that:

... this exchange and/or doubling of roles is not restricted to psychosis; it is *characteristic of* the structure of the phantasy. Bellour begins to approach the question of partial or changing identifications, but only in terms of Norman's psychosis (or, even more sketchily, Marnie's 'split personality').[52]

If such readings seem to rely heavily upon consideration of character, they do so only in relation to the work of the film in marshalling those characters for a desire which is then structured across the film. The tendency of the Bellourian critique is to read such characters according to the very stereotypes which support patriarchy in its cultural superiority, rather than through a conception of the film text as an existent dynamic which employs symbolic organisations finally to halt that dynamic. It is this proposition, that the film and the work of the film is an autonomous structuration revolving around primal fantasies that comes close to what Laplanche and Pontalis, speaking of the human subject, term the 'fantasmatic'.[53] In the same way that the subject is found in a sort of infinite play of fantasy, at rest in a dynamic structuration, so the film text might be seen as a continuous interaction of fantasies and enunciations – and any resultant structure is dependent upon the individual position taken up in relation to that text. And that final resting point is the spectator.

NOTES

1 Roland Barthes, 'Theory of the Text', in Robert Young (ed.), *Untying the Text* (London: Routledge and Kegan Paul, 1981).

2 See Stephen Heath, 'Film and System, Terms of Analysis', *Screen*, Spring and Summer 1975, vol. 16 nos. 1 and 2, pp. 7–77 and 91–113.

3 Robin Wood, 'Fear of Spying', *American Film*, November 1983, p. 31.

4 For an account of Bellour's work see Janet Bergstrom, 'Enunciation and Sexual Difference' and 'Alternation, Segmentation, Hypnosis: Interview with Raymond Bellour', *Camera Obscura* 3/4, Summer, 1979, pp. 71–103.

5 Roland Barthes, 'From Work to Text', in Stephen Heath (ed.), *Image, Music, Text* (London: Fontana, 1977), p. 157.

6 Raymond Bellour, 'Psychosis, Neurosis, Perversion', *Camera Obscura* 3/4, Summer 1979, pp. 105–6

7 See Raymond Bellour, 'The Obvious and the Code', *Screen*, Winter 1974/75, vol. 15 no. 4, pp. 7–17.

8 Raymond Bellour, 'Les Oiseaux: analyse d'une séquence', *Cahiers du Cinéma*, no. 219, October 1969.

9 Raymond Bellour, 'Le blocage symbolique', *Communications* 23 (Paris: Editions de Seuil, 1975).

10 See Raymond Bellour in 'Psychosis, Neurosis, Perversion', op. cit., and Peter Wollen, 'Hybrid Plots in *Psycho*', *Framework* no. 13, 1980.

11 Raymond Bellour, 'Hitchcock the Enunciator', *Camera Obscura* 2, Fall 1977.

12 See Roland Barthes, 'The Death of the Author' and 'From Work to Text' in *Image, Music, Text*, op. cit., and 'Theory of the Text', in Robert Young (ed.), *Untying the Text*.

13 See Emile Benveniste, 'Man and Language' in *Problems in General Linguistics* (University of Miami Press, 1971).

14 See Roland Barthes, *S/Z* (New York: Hill and Wang, 1974), for a working account of the distinctions between readerly and writerly.

15 Barthes deploys five codes, described as 'voices' within the text, in his analysis of Balzac's novella, *Sarrasine*: the Symbolic, the Hermeneutic, the Proairetic, the Semic and the Cultural/Reference code. Bellour employs the Symbolic and Hermeneutic codes. The former is originally defined as the voice of the Symbol and the latter is defined as the voice of Truth. The Hermeneutic code covers the scene of enigmas, questions, suspensions and answers in the realist text, in which there are no narrative 'loose ends' to disturb the flow and the completion of the narration.

16 Raymond Bellour, 'The Unattainable Text', *Screen*, Autumn 1975, vol. 16 no. 3, pp. 19–27.

17 Bellour develops this theory in 'L'Enonciateur' in *Recherches Poïétiques I* (Paris: Klinsieck, 1975), and 'Un jour, la castration' in *L'Arc* no. 71, 1978. The assertion of 'Hitchcock the Enunciator' is not one supported by the original French article but was the compromise agreed by the *Camera Obscura* collective for the untranslatable 'énoncer'. Literally, this means 'to enounce', but the verb in this infinitive form suggests the common root for both *énoncé*, the enounced, and *énonciation*, the enunciation. I am indebted to Constance Penley for this point.

18 Mary Ann Doane, *The Dialogical Text: Filmic Irony and the Spectator*, unpublished PhD thesis, Iowa, 1979.

19 See, for example, Anika Lemaire's commentary, *Jacques Lacan* (London: Routledge and Kegan Paul, 1977); Jacqueline Rose's introduction to Juliet Mitchell and Jacqueline Rose (eds.), *Feminine Sexuality* (London: Macmillan, 1982) and her article, 'The Imaginary' in Colin MacCabe (ed.), *The Talking Cure* (London: Macmillan, 1981).

20 See Guy Rosolato, 'Du Père' in *Essais sur le symbolique* (Paris: Gallimard, 1969).

21 Guy Rosolato, 'Trois générations d'hommes dans le mythe réligieux et la généalogie' in *Essais sur le symbolique*.

22 Claude Lévi-Strauss, *Myth and Meaning* (London: Routledge and Kegan Paul, 1978), p. 3.

23 Raymond Bellour, 'Symboliques', in *Le cinéma américain I* (Paris: Flammarion, 1979).

24 Raymond Bellour, 'Psychosis, Neurosis, Perversion', op. cit., p. 119.

25 Ibid., p. 112.

26 Ibid., p. 116.

27 The positive male oedipus complex is counterposed with its negative counterpart, the former involving desire for the parent of the opposite sex and rivalry with the same sex parent, the latter, desire for the same sex parent and rivalry with that of the opposite sex.

28 I think it is fair, in this context, to talk of a Bellourian tradition of textual analysis. The early work, endorsed through Metz's work on codification in *Language and Cinema* (The Hague: Mouton, 1974), has led to a formal orthodoxy best illustrated

by the issue of *Enclitic* (vol. 5 no. 2/vol. 6 no. 1, Fall 1981/Spring 1982) devoted to its International Conference on the Textual Analysis of Film. Subsequent work in this field has been dominated by this tradition and the popularisation of textual analysis has focused on Bellour's work in particular.

29 See Donald Greig, MA thesis, *Textual Analysis and Transgression*, University of Kent, 1983.

30 Jean-Louis Comolli and Jean Narboni, 'Cinema/Ideology/Criticism', *Screen Reader 1*, Society for Education in Film and Television, London, 1977, pp. 2–11.

31 Luce Irigaray, *Ce sexe qui n'en est pas un* (Paris: Editions de Minuit, 1977), p. 132 (my translation).

32 See Roland Barthes, 'From Work to Text', pp. 158–9.

33 See Tania Modleski, '"Never To Be Thirty-Six Years Old": Rebecca as Female Oedipal Drama', *Wide Angle*, vol. 5 no. 1, 1982, pp. 34–41.

34 See Margaret M. Horwitz, 'The Birds: A Mother's Love', *Wide Angle*, vol. 5 no. 1, 1982, pp. 42–8, and Jacqueline Rose, 'Paranoia and the Film System', *Screen*, vol. 17 no. 4, Winter 1976/7, pp. 85–104, both of which *suggest*, rather than trace, a female Oedipus.

35 See Elisabeth Lyon, 'The Cinema of Lol V Stein', reprinted in this volume, pp. 147–174; Elizabeth Cowie, 'Fantasia', *m/f* 9, 1984, pp. 71–104, and Constance Penley, 'Feminism, Film Theory and the Bachelor Machines', *m/f* 10, 1985, pp. 39–56.

36 J. Laplanche and J-B. Pontalis, 'Fantasy and the Origins of Sexuality', *The International Journal of Psycho-Analysis* vol. 49, 1968, Part 1. (Reprinted in Victor Burgin, James Donald and Cora Kaplan (eds.), *Formations of Fantasy*, London: Methuen, 1986, pp. 5–34.)

37 See, in particular, Constance Penley, 'Feminism, Film Theory and the Bachelor Machines'.

38 Cf. Elizabeth Cowie, 'Fantasia', p. 101.

39 Sigmund Freud, '"A Child Is Being Beaten" (A Contribution to the Study of the Origin of Sexual Perversions)', *On Psychopathology* (Harmondsworth: Pelican Freud Library vol. 10, 1979), pp. 163–193.

40 See D. N. Rodowick, 'The Difficulty of Difference', *Wide Angle*, vol. 5 no. 1, 1982, pp. 4–15.

41 Christian Metz, 'The Fiction Film and its Spectator: A Metapsychological Study', *Psychoanalysis and Cinema* (London: Macmillan, 1982).

42 Roland Barthes, *S/Z*, p. 36.

43 Roland Barthes, interview with Raymond Bellour in *Le livre des autres*, p. 216: '[La logique du champ symbolique] se definit, comme la logique du rêve, par des caractères d'intemporalité, de substitution, de réversibilité.'

44 Ibid., p. 225, my translation.

45 Jaques Lacan, 'The Signification of the Phallus', *Ecrits: A Selection* (London: Tavistock, 1977), p. 281.

46 'Every new arrival on this planet is faced by the task of mastering the Oedipus complex ...': Sigmund Freud, 'Three Essays on Sexuality', *On Sexuality* (Harmondsworth: Pelican Freud Library vol. 7, 1977), footnote added 1920, p. 149.

47 Raymond Bellour, *Le livre des autres*, p. 219.

48   Laplanche and Pontalis, 'Fantasy and the Origins of Sexuality', p. 11.

49   Elizabeth Cowie, 'Fantasia'.

50   '... why is the primal scene so traumatic? Why is it always too early or too late?
     Why does the subject take either too much pleasure in it – at least, that is how we
     conceived the traumatising causality of the obsessional neurotic – or too little, as in
     the case of the hysteric?' – Jaques Lacan, *The Four Fundamental Concepts of Psycho-
     Analysis* (Harmondsworth: Penguin, 1979).

51   V. F. Perkins, *Film as Film* (Harmondsworth: Penguin, 1972).

52   Janet Bergstrom, 'Enunciation and Sexual Difference', p. 58.

53   '... it is the subject's life as a whole which is seen to be shaped and ordered by what
     might be called, in order to stress this structuring action, "a phantasmatic".... This
     should not be conceived of merely as thematic – not even as one characterised by
     distinctly specific traits for each subject – for it has its own dynamic, in that the
     phantasy structures seek to express themselves, to find a way out into consciousness
     and action, and they are constantly drawing in new material' – J. Laplanche and J-B.
     Pontalis, *The Language of Psycho-Analysis* (London: Hogarth Press, 1980).

Arnold Schwarzenegger

Time Travel, Prime Scene and the Critical Dystopia
CONSTANCE PENLEY

If the sure sign of postmodern success is the ability to inspire spin-offs, *The Terminator* was a prodigy. The film was quickly replicated by *Exterminator*, *Re-animator*, *Eliminators*, *The Annihilators*, and the hard-core *The Sperminator*, all sound-alikes if not look-alikes. It then went on to garner one of popular culture's highest accolades when a West Coast band named itself *Terminators of Endearment*. And just to show that postmodernity knows no boundaries, national or otherwise, an oppressively large (2 ft. × 3 ft.) and trendy new Canadian journal has appeared, calling itself *The Manipulator*.

For some science fiction critics, Fredric Jameson among them, *The Terminator*'s popular appeal would represent no more than American science fiction's continuing affinity for the dystopian rather than the utopian, with fantasies of cyclical regression or totalitarian empires of the future. Our love affair with apocalypse and Armageddon, according to Jameson, results from the atrophy of utopian imagination, in other words, our cultural incapacity to imagine the future.[1] Or, as Stanislaw Lem puts it, in describing the banality and constriction of most American science fiction, 'The task of the SF author today is as easy as that of the pornographer, and in the same way.'[2] But surely there are dystopias and dystopias, and not all such films (from *Rollerball* to *The Terminator*) deserve to be dismissed as trashy infatuations with an equally trashy future. While it is true that most recent dystopian films are content to revel in the sheer awfulness of The Day After (the Mad Max trilogy and *A Boy and His Dog* come readily to mind), there are others which try to point to present tendencies that seem likely to result in corporate totalitarianism, apocalypse, or both. Although *The Terminator* gives us one of the most horrifying post-apocalyptic visions of any recent film, it falls into the latter group because it locates the origins of future catastrophe in decisions about technology, warfare and social behavior that are being made today. For example, the new, powerful defense computer that in *The Terminator* is hooked into everything – missiles, the defense industry, weapons design – and trusted to make all the decisions, is clearly a fictionalised version of the burgeoning Star Wars industry. This computer of the near future, forty years hence, gets smart – a new order of intelligence. It 'began to see all people as a threat,' Reese tells Sarah as he tries to fill her in on the future, 'not just the ones on the other side. It decided our fate in a microsecond. Extermination.

A film like *The Terminator* could be called a 'critical dystopia' inasmuch as it tends to suggest causes rather than merely reveal symptoms. But before saying more about how this film works as a critical dystopia, two qualifications need to be made. First, like most recent science fiction from *V* to *Star Wars*, *The Terminator* limits itself to solutions that are neither individualist nor bound to a romanticized notion of guerilla-like small-group resistance. The true atrophy of the utopian imagination is this: we *can* imagine the future but we *cannot* conceive the kind of collective political strategies necessary to change or ensure that future. Second, the film's politics, so to speak, cannot be simply equated with those of the 'author', James Cameron, the director of *The Terminator*, whose next job, after all, was writing *Rambo* (his disclaimers about Stallone's interference aside, he agreed to the project in the first place). Instead *The Terminator* can best be seen in relation to a set of cultural and psychical conflicts, anxieties and fantasies that are all at work in this film in a particularly insistent way.

TECH NOIR

What are the elements, then, of *The Terminator*'s critical dystopian vision? Although the film is thought of as an exceptionally forward-thrusting action picture, it shares with other recent science fiction films, like *Blade Runner*, an emphasis on atmosphere or 'milieu', but not, however, at the price of any flattening of narrative space. (In this respect it is closest to *Alien*.) *The Terminator* is studded with everyday-life detail, all organised by an idea of 'tech noir'. Machines provide the texture and substance of this film: cars, trucks, motorcycles, radios, TVs, time clocks, phones, answering machines, beepers, hair dryers, Sony Walkmen, automated factory equipment. The defense network computer of the future which decided our fate in a microsecond had its humble origins here, in the rather more innocuous technology of the film's present. Today's machines are not, however, shown to be agents of destruction because they are themselves evil, but because they can break down, or because they can be used (often innocently) in ways they were not intended to be used. Stalked by a killer, Sarah Connor cannot get through to the police because the nearest phone is out of order. When she finally reaches the LAPD emergency line, on a phone in the Tech Noir nightclub, it is predictably to hear, 'All our lines are busy . . . please hold. . . .' Neither can she get through to her room-mate, Ginger, to warn her because Ginger and her boyfriend have put on the answering machine while they make love. But Ginger wouldn't have been able to hear the phone, in any case, because she'd worn her Walkman to bed. Tech turns noir again when the Terminator, not Ginger, takes the answering machine message that gives away Sarah's location. Later Sarah will again reveal her whereabouts when the Terminator perfectly mimics her mother's voice over the phone. And in one of the film's most pointed gestures toward the unintentionally harmful effects of technology, the police psychiatrist fails to see the Terminator entering the station when his beeper goes off and distracts him just as their paths cross. Lacking any warning, scores of policemen are killed and the station destroyed. The film seems to suggest that if technology can go wrong or be abused, it will be. To illustrate this maxim further, Kyle Reese is shown having a nightmare of his future world where laser-armed, hunter-killer machines track down the few remaining humans; he wakes to hear a radio ad promoting laser-disk stereos. It comes as no surprise, finally, to see that his futuristic concentration camp number is the ubiquitous bar code stamped on today's consumer items.

That tech turns noir because of human decision-making and not something inherent in technology itself is presented even more forcefully in the 'novelization' of *The Terminator* by Randall Frakes and Bill Wisher.[3] The novelization adds a twist, perhaps one that originally appeared in the script but was discarded because it would have generated a complicated and digressive subplot. Or perhaps the authors of the book made it up on their own, unable to resist pointing out, once again, that it is humans, not machines, that will bring on the apocalypse. Near the end of the book, after the Terminator has been destroyed, a man named Jack, a Steve Wozniak-like computer prodigy, discovers a microchip in the debris. His entrepreneur friend, Greg, decides that they will go into business for themselves, once they figure out how to exploit what they take to be a new kind of microprocessing unit. Sixteen months later, they incorporate under the name Cyberdyne Systems . . . the company that goes on to make the same defense network computer that will try to destroy humanity in Reese's day. Here the case is being made not so much against the tunnel vision of corporate greed, but against the supposedly more benign coupling of golly-gosh tech-nerd enthusiasm with all-American entrepreneurship.

The film, moreover, does not advance an 'us against them' argument, man versus machine, a Romantic opposition between the organic and the mechanical, for there is much that is hybrid about its constructed elements. The Terminator, after all, is part machine, part human – a cyborg. (Its chrome skeleton with its hydraulic muscles and tendons of flexible cable looks like the Nautilus machines Schwarzenegger uses to build his body.) And Kyle's skills as a guerilla fighter are dependent upon his tech abilities – hot-wiring cars, renovating weapons, making bombs. If Kyle has himself become a fighting machine in order to attack the oppressor machines, Sarah too becomes increasingly machine-like as she acquires the skills she needs to survive both the Terminator and the apocalypse to come. The concluding irony is that Kyle and Sarah use machines to distract and then destroy the Terminator when he corners them in a robot-automated factory. At the end of one of the most harrowing, and gruellingly paced, chase scenes on film, Sarah terminates the Terminator between two plates of a hydraulic press. This interpenetration of human and machine is seen most vividly, however, when Sarah is wounded in the thigh by a piece of exploding Terminator shrapnel. Leaving aside the rich history of sexual connotations of wounding in the thigh,[4] part of a machine is here literally incorporated into Sarah's body ("a kind of cold rape," the novelization calls it). While the film addresses an ultimate battle between humans and machines, it nonetheless accepts the impossibility of clearly distinguishing between them. It focuses on the partial and ambiguous merging of the two, a more complex response, and one typical of the critical dystopia, than the Romantic triumph of the organic over the mechanical, or the nihilistic recognition that we have all become automata (even if those automata are better than we are, more human than human, as in *Blade Runner*).[5]

TIME TRAVEL

The Terminator, however, is as much about time as it is about machines. Because cinema itself has the properties of a time machine, it lends itself easily to time travel stories, one of the staples of science fiction literature. Surprisingly, however, there have been relatively few attempts in film to create stories around the idea of time travel. Hollywood, to be sure, has always been more drawn to conquering space and fighting off alien invaders than thinking through the heady paradoxes of voyaging through time. The exceptions have been very successful, however, and so it is curious that the industry has not made more effort to produce such stories. George Pal's *The Time Machine* (1960) was so exquisite (it brought the MGM look to science fiction film) that one even forgave the film's suppression of H. G. Wells's kooky class analysis of the Eloi and the Morlocks, which was, after all, the conceptual centre of the original tale. And the runaway success of the banal and clumsily made *Back to the Future* should have convinced Hollywood that there is something commercially attractive about the idea of time travel. Indeed, *The Terminator*'s appeal is due in large part to the way it is able to put to work this classical science fiction theme.

Compared to the complexity of many literary science fiction time travel plots, *The Terminator*'s story is simple: in 2010 a killer cyborg is sent back to the present day with the mission of exterminating Sarah Connor, a part-time waitress and student, and future mother of John Connor, the man who will lead the last remnants of humanity to victory over the machines which are trying to rid the world of humans. John Connor chooses Kyle Reese, a young and hardened fighter, to travel back in time to save Sarah from the Terminator. If the Terminator succeeds in his mission, John Connor, of course, will never be born, and the humans will never be able to fight back successfully against the machines. Kyle has fallen in love with Sarah through her photograph, given to him by John Connor. He says he always wondered what she was thinking about when the photo was taken for she has a faraway look on her face and a sad smile. 'I came across time for you,' he professes. 'I love you. I always have.' They make love, he is killed soon after, Sarah destroys the Terminator and leaves for the mountains to give birth to her son and wait out the holocaust to come. The film ends South of the Border with a Mexican boy taking a Polaroid of Sarah as she is thinking of Kyle. It is the photograph that John Connor will give to Kyle, forty years later, knowing that he is sending his own father to his death.

This sort of story is called a time-loop paradox because cause and effect are not only reversed but put into a circle: the later events are caused by the earlier events, and the earlier by the later.[6] If John Connor had not sent Kyle Reese back in time to be his father, he would never have been born. But he was born, so Kyle Reese must *already* have travelled back to the past to impregnate Sarah Connor. As another instance of paradox, John Connor's fighting skills were taught him by his mother. Sarah Connor, however, learned those skills from Kyle Reese, who had himself learned them while fighting at John Connor's side. (The novelization adds another time-loop paradox in locating the origin of the defense network computer in the microchip found in the Terminator debris.) Small wonder then that Sarah looks slightly bewildered when Kyle says he has 'always loved' her. How could this be true when, from the perspective of her point in time, he hasn't been born yet?

What is the appeal of time loop paradox stories? They are so fascinating that many people who used to read science fiction but have long since given it up will usually remember one story in particular, Ray Bradbury's 'A Sound of Thunder', even if they can no longer recall the author or the title (others have also noted this phenomenon). In this famous story, big-game hunters from the future travel back to the age of the dinosaurs. They don't have to fear that their shooting and bagging will affect the future, however, because dinosaurs will soon be extinct anyway. They are strictly warned, though, not to step off the walkway that has been prepared for them over the primeval jungle. One hunter disobeys and in doing so crushes a tiny butterfly under his boot. When the hunting party returns to the future, everything is ever so slightly different, the result of killing one small insect millions of years earlier.

PRIMAL SCENE

The essential elements of time travel and its consequences are witnessed in a very succinct way in 'A Sound of Thunder'. That is why the story is remembered. But when plots of this kind become more complex, one theme tends to predominate: what would it be like to go back in time and give birth to oneself? Or, what would it be like to be one's own mother and father? Robert Heinlein has given us the seminal treatment of this paradoxical situation in 'All You Zombies'. A time traveller who has undergone a sex-change operation not only encounters both earlier and later versions of himself but turns out to be his own mother and father. Similarly, in David Gerrold's *The Man Who Folded Himself*, each time the protagonist travels in time, he reduplicates himself. Eventually this results in a large group of identical men who find each other to be ideal lovers. One of them goes very far back in time and meets a lesbian version of himself. They fall in love, have children, and then break up, to return to their copy-lovers. (As the narrator says in 'All You Zombies', 'It's a shock to have it proved to you that you can't resist seducing yourself.') The appeal of *Back to the Future* should now be apparent – it is only a more vulgar version of the desire manifested in these stories. There is of course a name for this desire; it is called a primal scene fantasy, the name Freud gave to the fantasy of overhearing or observing parental intercourse, of being on the scene, so to speak, of one's own conception. The desire represented in the time travel story, of both witnessing one's own conception and being one's own mother and father, is similar to the primal scene fantasy in which one can be both observer or one of the participants. (The possibility of getting pregnant and giving birth to oneself is echoed in *Back to the Future*'s TV ad: 'The first kid to get into trouble before he was ever born.') The reconstruction of a patient's primal scene assumes, in fact, a great deal of time travel. (Freud said the most extreme primal scene fantasy was that of observing parental intercourse while one is still an unborn baby in the womb.)[7] The Wolf-Man, supine on the analytic couch, is sent further and further back in time to 'remember' the moment when, as a child, he saw his parents having sex. Although Freud's interpretation depends upon the Wolf-Man witnessing such a scene, he decides, finally, that it was not necessary for the event to have *actually occurred* for it to have had profound effects on the patient's psychical life. A patient can consciously fabricate such a scene only because it has been operative in his or her unconscious, and this construction has nothing to do with its actual occurrence or nonoccurrence. The idea of returning to the past to generate an event that has already made an impact on one's identity, lies at the core of the time-loop paradox story.

What is *The Terminator*'s primal scene? The last words that Kyle Reese throws at the Terminator, along with a pipe bomb, are 'Come on, motherfucker!' But in the narrative logic of this film it is Kyle who is the mother fucker. And within the structure of fantasy that shapes the film, John Connor is the child who orchestrates his own primal scene, one inflected by a family romance, moreover, because he is able to choose his own father, singling out Kyle from the other soldiers. That such a fantasy is an attempted end-run around Oedipus is also obvious: John Connor can identify with his father, can even *be* his father in the scene of parental intercourse, and also conveniently dispose of him in order to go off with (in) his mother.

Recent film theory has taken up Freud's description of fantasy to give a more complete account of how identification works in film.[8] An important emphasis has been placed on the subject's ability to assume, successively, all the available positions in the fantasmatic scenario. Extending this idea to film has shown that spectatorial identification is more complex than has hitherto been understood because it shifts constantly in the course of the film's narrative, while crossing the lines of biological sex; in other words, unconscious identification with the characters or the scenario is not necessarily dependent upon gender. Another element of Freud's description of fantasy that also deserves attention, particularly in discussing fantasy in relation to popular film, is the self-serving or wish-fulfilling aspect of fantasy. In 'The Paths to the Formation of Symptoms', Freud constructs two analogies between the creation of fantasy and instances drawn from 'real life'. He begins by saying that a child uses fantasies to disguise the history of his childhood, 'just as every nation disguises its forgotten prehistory by constructing legends' (p. 368). A fantasy is thus not 'just a fantasy' but a story *for* the subject. The fantasy of seduction, for example, serves to deny the subject's acts of auto-eroticism by projecting them onto another person. (Such fantasy constructions, Freud says, should be seen separately from those real acts of adult seduction of children that occur more frequently than is acknowledged.) Similarly, in the 'family romance' the subject creates another parent, an ideal one, to make up for the perceived shortcomings of the real mother or father. Thus a film like *The Terminator* that is so clearly working in relation to a primal fantasy, is also working in the service of pleasure (already a requirement for a mass audience film), a pleasure that depends upon suppressing conflicts or contradictions. (Because such suppression does not always work, and because desire does not always aim for pleasure – the death drive – much recent film analysis is devoted to examining those aspects of film that go distinctly 'beyond the pleasure principle'.)[9]

Take, for example, the seemingly contradictory figure of Kyle Reese. The film 'cheats' with his image in the same way that *The Searchers* 'cheats' with Martin Pauley's image, which is, variously, wholly Indian, 'half-breed', 'quarter-blood' Cherokee, one-eighth Cherokee, or wholly white, depending upon the unconscious and ideological demands of the narrative at any given moment.[10] In *The Terminator* Kyle is the virile, hardened fighter barking orders to the terrified Sarah, but alternately he is presented as boyish, vulnerable, and considerably younger in appearance than her. His childishness is underscored by Sarah's increasingly maternal affection for him (bandaging his wounds, touching his scars), and in the love scene, he is the young man being initiated by the more experienced, older woman. Kyle is thus both the father of John Connor and, in his youth and inexperience, Sarah's son, John Connor. The work of fantasy allows the fact of incest to be both stated and dissimulated. It is only in fantasy, finally, that we have our cake and eat it too. Or as the French equivalent puts it, even more aptly, that we can be and have been – *peut être et avoir été*.

Freud also compared the mental realm of fantasy to a 'reservation' or 'nature reserve', a place set aside where 'the requirements of agriculture, communication and industry threaten to bring about changes in the original face of the earth which will quickly make it unrecognizable' (almost a description of a post-apocalyptic landscape). 'Everything, including what is useless and even what is noxious, can grow and proliferate there as it pleases. The mental realm of fantasy is just such a reservation withdrawn from the reality principle' (p. 372). Can a film like *The Terminator* be similarly dismissed as merely escapist, appealing as it does to a realm of fantasy 'withdrawn from the reality principle', where even our incestuous desires can be realized? For one possible answer we can turn to the end of Freud's essay on symptom formation, where he tells us that there is 'a path that leads back from fantasy to reality – the path, that is, of art'. An artist, he says, has the ability to shape a faithful image of his fantasy, and then to depersonalise and generalise it so that it is made accessible to other people. Even if we do not have as much faith in 'art' or the 'artist' as Freud has, we can still draw some useful conclusions from what he says.

One could argue that *The Terminator* treads the path from fantasy back to reality precisely because it is able to generalize its vision, to offer something more than this fully, though paradoxically, resolved primal fantasy. This *generalizing* of the fantasy is carried out through *The Terminator*'s use of the topical and everyday: as we have seen, the film's texture is woven from the technological litter of modern life. But this use of the topical is not, for example, like *E.T.*'s more superficial referencing of daily life through brand name kid-speak, that is, topicality for topicality's sake. Rather, it is a dialogue with Americana that bespeaks the inevitable consequences of our current technological addictions. To give another example, the shopping mall in George Romero's *Dawn of the Dead* is more than a kitsch ambience, it is a way of concretely demonstrating the zombification of consumer culture. By exposing every corner of the mall – stores, escalators, public walkways, basement, roof – the location becomes saturated with meaning, in a way that goes far beyond *E.T.*'s token gesturing toward the commodification of modern life. If *The Terminator*'s primal scene fantasy draws the spectator into the film's paradoxical realization of incestuous desire, its militant everydayness throws the spectator back out again, back to the technological future.

SCIENCE FICTION & SEXUAL DIFFERENCE

In the realm of the unconscious and fantasy, the question of the subject's origin, 'Where do I come from?' is followed by the question of sexual difference, 'Who am I (What sex am I)?' It is by now well-known that the narrative logic of classical film is powered by the desire to establish, by the end of the film, the nature of masculinity, the nature of femininity, and the way in which those two can be complementary rather than antagonistic.[11] But in film and television, as elsewhere, it is becoming increasingly difficult to *tell the difference*. As men and women are less and less differentiated by a division of labor, what, in fact, makes them different? And how can classical film still construct the difference so crucial to its formula for narrative closure? Ironically, it is science fiction film – our hoariest and seemingly most sexless genre – that alone remains capable of supplying the configurations of sexual difference required by the classical cinema. If there is increasingly less practical difference between men and women, there is more than enough difference between a human and an alien (*The Man Who Fell to Earth, Starman*), a human and a cyborg/replicant (*Android, Blade Runner*), or a human from the present and one from the future (*The Terminator*). In these films the question of sexual difference – a question whose answer is no longer 'self-evident' – is displaced onto the more remarkable difference between the human and the other. That this questioning of the difference between human and other is sexual in nature, can also be seen in the way these films reactivate infantile sexual investigation. One of the big questions for the viewer of *Blade Runner*, for example, is 'How do replicants *do it*?' Or of *The Man Who Fell to Earth*, 'What is the sex of this alien who possesses nothing that resembles human genitals (its sex organs are in its hands)?'

But if recent science fiction film provides the heightened sense of difference necessary to the classical narrative, it also offers the reassurance of difference *itself*. In describing one important aspect of the shift in the psychical economy from the nineteenth century to the twentieth century, Raymond Bellour maintains that in the nineteenth century men looked at women and feared they were different, but in the twentieth century men look at women and fear they are the same.[12] The majority of science fiction films work to dissipate that fear of the same, to ensure that there is a difference. A very instructive example is the NBC mini-series *V*, broadcast during the 1983–84 season. A rare instance of science fiction on television (*Star Trek* to the contrary, the television industry insists that science fiction does not work on television), *V* tried to be as topical and up-to-date as possible, particularly in the roles it gave to women. The Commander of the alien force that takes over Earth's major cities, the Supreme commander of the aliens, the leader of the Earthling guerrillas, and the leader of the alien fifth column aiding the Earthlings, are all played by women. They are seen performing the same activities as the men (planning, fighting, counterattacking, infiltrating, etc.), thus removing the most important visible signs of difference. The only difference remaining in *V* is that between the aliens (scaly, green reptiles in human disguise) and the humans. That difference, however, comes to represent sexual difference, as if the alien/human difference were a projection of what can no longer be depicted otherwise.[13] The leader of the guerrillas is captured and brainwashed by the alien commander. Although she is eventually rescued by her comrades, it is feared that the brainwashing has turned her into an alien. She even begins using her left hand rather than her right one, a reptile-alien characteristic. Thus when she and her boyfriend, the second in command of the guerillas, are shown making love, we realize, as they do, that this could be interspecies sex – the blonde, all-American Julie may be a lizard underneath it all, whether in fact or in mind. It gives the otherwise banal proceedings a powerful source of dramatic tension, while it reassures TV-viewing audiences everywhere that there is a difference. (Such a radical disposition of difference always risks, of course, tipping over into the horror of *too much* difference.)

Similarly, it is instructive to see how *Aliens*, directed by James Cameron following his success with *The Terminator*, cracks under the strain of trying to keep to the very original *lack* of sexual differentiation in its precursor, Ridley Scott's *Alien* (not counting, of course, the penultimate scene of Ripley in her bikini underwear). Dan O'Bannon's treatment for the first film was unique in writing each role to be played by either a man or a woman.[14] Ridley Scott's direction followed through on this idea, producing a film that is (for the most part) stunningly egalitarian. In attempting to repeat the equal-opportunity camaraderie of the first film, Cameron's sequel includes a mixed squad of marines, in which the women are shown to be as tough as the men, maybe

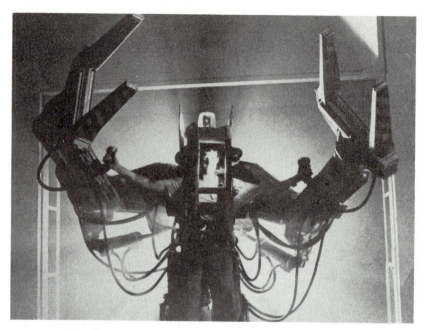

Aliens (James Cameron, 1986)

tougher. And Ripley is, again, the bravest and smartest member of the team. But this time there is a difference, one that is both improbable and symptomatic. Ripley 'develops' a maternal instinct, risking her life to save the little girl who is the only survivor of a group of space colonists decimated by the aliens. Tenaciously protective, she takes on the mother alien, whose sublime capacity for destruction is shown nonetheless to result from the same kind of maternal love that Ripley exhibits. Ripley is thus marked by a difference that is automatically taken to be a sign of femininity. (We do not see Hicks, for example – played by Michael Biehn, who was Kyle Reese in *The Terminator* – acting irrationally in order to rescue a child who is probably already dead.) *Aliens* reintroduces the issue of sexual difference, but not in order to offer a newer, more modern configuration of that difference. Rather, by focusing on Ripley alone (Hicks is awkwardly 'disappeared' from the film in the closing moments), the question of the couple is supplanted by the problem of the woman as mother. What we get finally is a conservative moral lesson about maternity, futuristic or otherwise: mothers will be mothers, and they will *always* be women. We can conclude that even when there is not much sex in science fiction, there is nonetheless a great deal about sexuality, here reduced to phallic motherhood: Ripley in the robot-expediter is simply the Terminator turned inside out.

Just as it is ironic that science fiction film can give us the sharper notion of sexual difference lost from contemporary classical film, so too it is ironic that when this genre does depict sexual activity, it offers some of the most effective instances of eroticism in recent film. The dearth of eroticism in current film-making is pointed up by Woody Allen's success in providing the paradigm of the only kind of sexual difference we have left: the incompatibility of the man's neuroses with the woman's neuroses. Understandably, this is not very erotic. But science fiction film, in giving us an extreme version of sexual difference, coincides with the requirements of the erotic formula, one which describes a fantasy of absolute difference and absolute complementarity (the quality of being complementary, of course, depending upon the establishment of difference). Unlike in classical cinema, the science fiction couple is often not the product of a long process of narrative differentiation; rather, the man and the woman are different *from the very beginning*. The narrative can then focus on *them together* and the *exterior* obstacles they must overcome to remain a couple. The erotic formula has, in fact, two parts: first, the two members of the couple must be marked as clearly different. (In non-science fiction film, for example, she is a nun, he is a priest; she is white, he is black, she is a middle-class widow, he is a young working-class man; she is French, he is German/Japanese, etc.) Second, one of the two must die or at least be threatened by death. If the man and the woman, in their absolute difference, are absolutely complementary, then there is nothing left to be desired. Something has to be taken away to regenerate desire and the narrative. Thus, although the lovemaking scene in *The Terminator* is not a very distinguished one in terms of the relatively perfunctory way that it was filmed, it nonetheless packs a strong erotic charge, *in its narrative context* because it is a kiss across time, a kiss between a man from the future and a woman from the present, an act of love pervaded by death. For Kyle has to die in order to justify the coda, in which Sarah ensures the continuity of the story, now a legend, of their love for each other.

TIME TRAVEL AS PRIMAL SCENE: *LA JETÉE*

If time travel stories are fantasies of origins, they are also fantasies of endings. Mark Rose has pointed out that many of the narratives that deal with time travel tend to be fictions of apocalypse.[15] (As in *The Terminator*, however, these visions of endings may also be visions of new beginnings – in the Genesis version, after God destroys the world by flood, it is Sarah who is anointed 'mother of all nations'.) Rose cites Frank Kermode's *The Sense of an Ending* to show that we create fictions of endings to give meaning to time, to transform *chronos* – mere passing time – into *kairos*, time invested with the meaning derived from its goal. History is given shape, is made understandable by spatializing time, by seeing it as a line along which one can travel. Such spatialization of time, however, introduces the paradox of time travel. 'Much of the fascination of the time loop is related to the fact that it represents the point at which the spatialization of time breaks down.'[16] If I could travel back into the past, I could (theoretically) murder my own grandmother. But I would cease to exist. How then could I have murdered her?

If this example illustrates the collapse of time as we know it, it also shows that it is impossible to separate ourselves from time. (The time traveller who murders her grandmother ceases to exist.) Thus time travel paradox narratives typically explore either the question of the end of time or the reciprocal relation between ourselves and time. Although *The Terminator* is concerned with both apocalypse and the question of time in relation to personal identity, another film which preceded it by more than twenty years, Chris Marker's *La Jetée*, weaves the two together in a way that still haunts the spectator of this stunning film. *The Terminator*, in fact, bears such an uncanny resemblance to *La Jetée* that Cameron's film could almost be its mass-culture remake. Marker's film too is about a post-apocalyptic man who is chosen to be a time traveller because of his fixation on an image of the past. It too involves a love affair between a woman from the present and a man from the future, and an attempt to keep humanity from being wiped out.

A crucial difference between *The Terminator* and *La Jetée*, however, is that Marker's film explicitly addresses the paradox of time travel. After being sent on numerous journeys through time, *La Jetée*'s time traveller attempts to return to the scene from his childhood that had marked him so deeply. On that day, a Sunday afternoon before a third World War which will drive the few remaining survivors underground, his parents had brought him to Orly to watch the planes take off. He remembers seeing the sun fixed in the sky, a scene at the end of the jetty, and a woman's face. Then, a sudden noise, the woman's gesture, a crumbling body, the cries of the crowd. Later, the voice-over tells us, he knew that he had seen a man die. When he tries to return to that Sunday at Orly, he is killed by one of the scientists from the underground camp who had sent him voyaging through time; they no longer have any use for him. The moment, then, that he had been privileged to see as a child and which had never stopped him, was the moment of his own death. In the logic of this film he has to die, because such a logic acknowledges the temporal impossibility of being in the same place as both adult and child. In *La Jetée* one cannot be and have been.

The film goes even further when it insists on the similar paradox at work in the primal scene fantasy by depicting the psychical consequence of attempting to return to a scene from one's childhood: such a compulsion to repeat, and the regression that it implies, leads to the annihilation of the subject.[17] But the subject is also extinguished in another way, this time through a symbolic castration depicted as a very real death. The woman he is searching for is at the end of the jetty, but so is the man whose job it is to prevent him from possessing her, the man and the woman on the jetty mirroring the parental (Oedipal) couple that brought the little boy to the airport. (This film's version of the Terminator succeeds in its mission.) While *The Terminator* gives us a time travel story that depends upon a primal scene fantasy for its unconscious appeal, its fantasmatic force, *La Jetée* shows that the two are one and the same: the fantasy of time travel is no more nor less than the compulsion to repeat that manifests itself in the primal scene fantasy. Moreover, since *La Jetée*'s circular narrative is wholly organized as a 'beginning toward which [one] is constantly

La Jetée (Chris Marker, 1962)

moving',[18] it suggests that all film viewing is infantile sexual investigation.

The Terminator, in many respects, merely abstracts and reifies *La Jetée*'s major elements. Marker's film, for example, is composed almost entirely of still images, photographs that dissolve in and out of one another in a way that constantly edges toward the illusion of 'real' filmic movement. As Thierry Kuntzel has pointed out,[19] such a technique allows *La Jetée* to be a film about movement in film, and our desire for movement. Using still images to make a film is also a perfect way to tell a time travel story because it offers the possibility of mixing two different temporalities: the 'pastness' of the photographic image and the 'here-nowness' of the illusionistic (filmic) movement.[20]

Although I suggested that *The Terminator* could be seen as the industry remake of *La Jetée*, it should now be clear that Marker's film could not be remade because in its very structure it is *unrepeatable*. Inasmuch as it acknowledges the paradox of the time loop and rejects the rosy nostalgia of a wish-fulfilling version of the primal scene fantasy, it is not likely remake material with respect to popular film's demand for pleasure without (obvious) paradox. Similarly, one could not imagine a *sequel* to *La Jetée* because of the way the film collapses time in its rigorous observance of the fatalistic logic of time travel. But one can be sure that *Terminators* is already more than a gleam in a producer's eye. After all, what is to stop John Connor, in another possible future, from sending Kyle Reese back in time again, but at a later date, perhaps so that he could rendezvous with Sarah in her South of the Border hide-out?

Would it not be too easy, however, to conclude by pitting *La Jetée* against *The Terminator*? To end by falling back on less-than-useful dichotomies like the avant garde versus Hollywood or even the Symbolic versus the Imaginary? It is true that *La Jetée* is governed by 'the laws of recollection and symbolic recognition' (in Lacan's terms) while *The Terminator* is ruled by 'the laws of imaginary reminiscence.'[21] But it is precisely the way *The Terminator* harnesses the power of 'imaginary reminiscence' (the primal scene fantasy of time travel) that allows it to present one of the most forceful of recent science fiction tales about the origins of techno-apocalypse. The film is able to do so, as I have argued, by generalizing its core of fantasy through the systematic use of the topical and everyday, reminding us that the future is now. As a critical dystopia, *The Terminator* thus goes beyond the flashy nihilism of apocalypse-for-the-sake-of-apocalypse to expose a more *mundane* logic of technological modernity, even if it is one that is, finally, no less catastrophic.

NOTES

1 Fredric Jameson, 'Progress Versus Utopia; or Can We Imagine the Future', *Science Fiction Studies* 9, 1982.

2 Stanislaw Lem, 'Cosmology and Science Fiction', trans. Franz Rottenstein, *Science Fiction Studies* 4, 1977, p. 109.

3 Randall Frakes and Bill Wisher, *The Terminator* (a novel based on the screenplay by James Cameron with Gale Anne Hurd) (New York: Bantam Books, 1984).

4 See Jessie L Weston, *From Ritual to Romance: An Account of the Holy Grail from Ancient Ritual to Christian Symbol* (Cambridge: Cambridge University Press, 1920), pp. 42–8.

5 For a full and very interesting discussion of the political dimensions of the cyborg, see Donna Harraway, 'A Manifesto for Cyborgs: Science, Technology, and Socialist Feminism in the 1980s', *Socialist Review*, no. 80 March/April, 1985.

6 Useful essays on time travel and its paradoxes include Stanislaw Lem, 'The Time-Travel Story and Related Matters of SF Structuring', *Science Fiction Studies* 1, 1974; Monte Cook, 'Tips for Time Travel', *Philosophers Look at Science Fiction* (Chicago: Nelson-Hall, 1982); and David Lewis, 'The Paradoxes of Time Travel', *Thought Probes*, (eds.) Fred D. Miller, Jr. and Nicholas D. Smith (New Jersey: Prentice Hall, 1981).

7 Sigmund Freud, *Introductory Lectures on Psychoanalysis, The Standard Edition of the Complete Psychological Works of Sigmund Freud*, (ed.) and trans. James Strachey (London: Hogarth Press, 1958), vol. 16, p. 370.

8 See, among others, Elisabeth Lyon, 'The Cinema of Lol V. Stein' (reprinted in this volume, pp. 147–173); Elizabeth Cowie, 'Fantasia', *m/f* no. 9, 1984; and Steve Neale, 'Sexual Difference in Cinema', *Sexual Difference*, special issue of *The Oxford Literary Review* 8, nos. 1–2, 1986.

9 For the best formulation of this idea, see Joan Copjec, '*India Song/Son nom de Venise dans Calcutta désert*: The Compulsion to Repeat', *October* 17, Summer 1981.

10 Brian Henderson, 'The Searchers: An American Dilemma', *Film Quarterly* 34, no. 2, Winter 1980–81; reprinted in *Movies and Methods* vol. II, (ed.) Bill Nichols (Berkeley: University of California Press, 1985).

11 There are, of course, important exceptions to this standard narrative logic, as Jacqueline Rose has shown, for example, in her analysis of *The Birds*, in which Mitch's 'successful' attainment of a masculine and paternal identity comes at the price of regression and catatonia for Melanie. 'Paranoia and the Film System', *Screen* vol. 17, no. 4, Winter 1976–7.

12 Raymond Bellour, 'Un jour, la castration', *L'Arc*, special issue on Alexandre Dumas, no. 71, 1978.

13 This wholly unremarkable series seems surprisingly capable of taking on a great deal of cultural resonance in its radical presentation of 'difference'. Andrew Kopkind (*The Nation* 243, no. 17, 22 November 1986) reports that *V* is currently one of the most popular shows in South Africa. He speculates that the show's success lies in the unconsciously ironic, allegorical reading that it allows. Kopkind cites the newspaper description of the week's episode (broadcast on the state-controlled television channel): TV 4: 9:03. 'Visitor's Choice'. The Resistance Stages a daring attack at a convention of Visitor Commanders where Diana intends to show off the ultimate device in processing humans for food.

Robit Hairman in *The Voice* (13 January 1987) also reports on the cult that has grown up around *V* in South Africa because of the allegorical readings that escaped the government censors. Before the series was over, anti-government forces were spraying slogans from the series on walls in Johannesburg and Soweto, and T-shirts with a large

V painted on front and back became a feature on the streets: '*V* joined the mythology of the resistance.' There are also at least two fanzines devoted to *V*, the newest of which, *The Resistance Chronicles*, describes its first issue in terms that evoke infantile sexual investigation: 'This volume will contain the answers to the following burning questions – Why is that blue Chevy with the fogged up windows rocking back and forth??? How does Chris Farber feel about virtue . . . and boobs? What color underwear does Ham Tyler wear? What do Ham and Chris keep in their medicine cabinet? Plus a musical *V* parody, "We're off to See the Lizard. . . ."'
Description taken from *Datazine*, no. 44 (October–November 1986).

14 Danny Peary reports this on his interview with Sigourney Weaver, 'Playing Ripley in *Alien*', *OMNI's Screen Flights/Screen Fantasies: The Future According to Science Fiction Cinema*, (ed.) Danny Peary (Garden City, N.Y.: Doubleday, 1984), p. 162.

15 Mark Rose, *Alien Encounters: Anatomy of Science Fiction* (Cambridge, Mass.: Harvard University Press, 1981), p. 99.

16 Ibid., p. 108.

17 My discussion of primal scene fantasy in *La Jetée* is indebted to Thierry Kuntzel's lectures on that topic in his 1975–76 seminar at the American University Center for Film Studies in Paris.

18 Ned Lukacher's formulation of the primal scene fantasy in *Primal Scenes: Literature, Philosophy, Psychoanalysis* (Ithaca: Cornell University Press, 1986), p. 42. This book contains the best recent discussion of the structure of the primal scene fantasy.

19 In his lectures on *La Jetée* at the American University Center for Film Studies.

20 The distinction is made by Roland Barthes in 'Rhetoric of the Image', in *Image–Music–Text*, trans. Stephen Heath (New York: Hill and Wang, 1977), p. 45.

21 Jacques Lacan, *Ecrits: A Selection* (New York: Norton, 1977), p. 141. A distinction cited by Lukacher, p. 43.

Issues of Difference
Alien and *Blade Runner*
STEPHEN NEALE

Two of the most successful science-fiction films of the past decade, *Alien* (1979) and *Blade Runner* (1982), are both centrally concerned with issues of difference – the difference between the human and the non-human, sexual difference and (in *Blade Runner*) racial difference. Here I want to explore the extent to which these three distinct types of difference become intertwined in the films, and whether one set of differences can be substituted for another. This is my starting point. I also want to consider certain questions that *Alien* and *Blade Runner* raise about genre. Both films are, in a loose sense, instances of 'the fantastic'. As such, they might conventionally be categorised as films of 'fantasy', in implicit opposition to some notion of 'realism'. Against this view, my argument is that such films are no more or less marked by fantasy in its psychoanalytic sense than any others. Nevertheless, if this genre and these films *are* marked by a consistent concern with particular kinds of difference and particular issues of difference, then that does raise the question of the relationship between *fantasies* and difference and *the fantastic* and difference.

ALIEN

In her article on *The Terminator*, Constance Penley discusses how the problematic of sexual difference is inscribed in recent sci-fi and horror films.[1] 'In postmodern film and television, she suggests, the classical narrative logic which established masculinity and femininity as opposite-but-complementary has begun to break down: 'it is becoming increasingly difficult to *tell the difference*'. Sexual difference does not disappear, however. It is displaced onto other differences: between human and alien (*The Man Who Fell to Earth*, *Starman*), between a human from the present and one from the future (*The Terminator*), or – in a case like *Blade Runner* – between humans and replicants. Elsewhere, there may be increasingly less practical difference between men and women, but in these figures there is still 'more than enough difference'. Later, Penley also refers to *Alien*. Here, she suggests, sexual difference appears more centrally at issue because, paradoxically, it is treated with apparent indifference.

> Dan O'Bannon's treatment for [*Alien*] was unique in writing each role to be played by either a man or a woman. Ridley Scott's direction followed through on this idea, producing a film that is (for the most part) stunningly egalitarian.[2]

I would argue that the issue of difference in both *Alien* and *Blade Runner* is more complex than these remarks indicate. Furthermore, I would tend to reverse the way Constance Penley characterises their treatment of it. *Alien*, it seems to me, works quite systematically towards *establishing* a difference between the sexes, whereas *Blade Runner* works to establish a male/female couple, but at the cost of *erasing* certain differences between humans and replicants.

An important preliminary point is that both films (and most of the others Penley mentions) touch on issues of difference as a matter of generic necessity. As sci-fi/horror hybrids, *Alien* and *Blade Runner* are obliged by the conventions of generic verisimilitude to establish narrative equilibrium and disequilibrium, diegetic order and disorder, in terms of differences between, on the one hand, 'the human' and 'the natural' and, on the other, the 'non-human', the 'unnatural' and the 'monstrous'.[3] One way of approaching these films, therefore, is to examine how these categories of difference are deployed across the process of the narrative and, in particular, how the categories are inscribed within the films' definitions of diegetic order and disorder.

In *Alien* one fundamental difference, of course, is that between the alien monster and the crew of the space-ship *Nostromo*. But there are also differences between the various crew members: gender difference (to which I shall return) and the difference between the humans and its robot member, Ash. Ash, unlike the alien monster, cannot be *recognised* as different: the revelation of his robot identity (his decapitation reveals bits of wire and machinery instead of flesh and blood) is one of the film's most shocking and disorienting set-pieces, along with the scene in which the monster rips its way out of Kane's stomach while the crew are breakfasting. Ash and the monster, despite *their* differences, are thus linked in terms of the threats they pose to the humans (Ash is prepared to sacrifice the crew to get the alien back to Earth) and also in the staging of the discovery of their true identities.

They are linked, too, by a third element – the element of *sexual* difference that runs as a thread through *Alien*. This finds its neuralgic focus in the figure or image or idea of the Mother.

Most discussions of sexual difference in *Alien* have focused on the character of Ripley, her functions within the human crew and her relations with them. Constance Penley's (qualified) view of the film as 'stunningly egalitarian' in terms of gender is echoed by James H. Kavanaugh:

> The film ... presents a rather complex feminist version of the strong woman who must mobilise all her autonomous intellectual and emotional strength ... the film can be seen as almost postfeminist in its image of the relations between the men and women of the *Nostromo*'s crew. There are strong and weak women and men on the ship, but the woman's right to assume authority is not even an issue; authority and power are ceded to persons irrespective of sex, solely in regard to their position and function.[4]

This needs to be qualified, I think. Ripley's 'autonomous intellectual and emotional strength' is signalled primarily in her confrontations with Ash and the alien monster. She alone seems to be suspicious of Ash and challenges his suggestions and wishes; she alone manages to rid the *Nostromo* of the alien. This is what differentiates her from the rest of the human crew, and the fact that she is female is part of the differentiation. Perhaps more importantly, it is also these functions and characteristics that mark her femininity: within the film's wider symptomatic system, she is the figure most implacably counterposed to the two 'unnatural' forms of motherhood associated with Ash and the alien.

Ash is subservient to the *Nostromo*'s computer, Mother. Mother, as Kavanaugh notes, 'is the filmic presence that gives both life and death – freezing and resurrecting the crew in one womblike chamber'. Mother also 'assigns absolute priority to the alien' and is thus, like the alien, the enemy of the human crew.[5] As a computer, a machine, this Mother is different from any human mother; as the crew's enemy, this difference constitutes a threat. It is Ripley (again as Kavanaugh remarks) who ultimately confronts not just Ash but also Mother, and who succeeds in eliciting her secret plans.

This Mother – this image of motherhood – is 'unnatural' and 'inhuman' not only because she is a machine but also because she tries to destroy her human charges instead of protecting them. Her final act of treachery is to ignore Ripley's attempts to countermand the *Nostromo*'s self-destruct programme. Ripley sees her for what she is: 'Mother, you bitch.' Kavanaugh points out that this is also the curse addressed to the alien. Alien and computer are linked through the notion of motherhood. Although Mother fails to protect the humans, she *does* protect the alien – even though it is not her child. It is, rather, the child of Kane, a child delivered of a human male impregnated by a non-human organism. Its monstrosity is confirmed by these reversals of gender (as well as by this miscegenation of species) at both its conception and its birth. This is Kavanaugh's description:

> The three clumsy seekers find, in one chamber, death gigantic, and in another, the expectant egg of a new life grotesque. This conception – in which male and female, life and death are confused – is then reversed as the egg forces its own tenacious fertilising instrument on the man, who as passive receptacle must ingest its seed. Finally, the particularly horrifying confusion of the sexual-gynecological with the gastrointestinal is patched onto the life-death, male-female confusions as Kane dies in agony enduring the forced 'birth' of the razor-toothed phallic monster that gnaws its way through his stomach into the light.[6]

This 'unnatural' act of impregnation – and the 'unnatural' birth that ensues – constitute the disruption which inaugurates the narrative of *Alien* and which the narrative must resolve if it is to achieve closure. A secondary disorder is figured in the 'inhuman' human, Ash, and the 'inhuman' mother, the computer. The order initially disturbed and finally re-established is thus implicitly defined as the obverse of these monstrous disorders: a 'natural', 'human' order centred on gender and gender difference in which female and male are securely differentiated in terms of biological functions. It is men who impregnate women, women who give birth, and women, therefore, who are 'natural' mothers. It is no accident that it is Ripley, a human female, who restores this order – nor that her woman's body is emphasised in her final encounter with the alien. Thinking she is safe in the *Nostromo*'s capsule, she takes off her uniform only to discover the monster lurking in the background. As Constance Penley's parenthetical reference to it suggests, this sequence has always bothered those claiming *Alien* as in some sense feminist or egalitarian. But it does fit logically into the symbolic economy of the film. *Alien* systematically distinguishes 'the natural' from 'the unnatural' and 'the human' from 'the non-human' on the basis of a difference between male and female defined in terms of the anatomical and biological aspects of reproduction and, crucially, motherhood.

BLADE RUNNER

The difference most overtly at issue in *Blade Runner* is that between humans and the Nexus 6 replicants. In addition, though, two other important forms of difference interweave with this in a variety of ways: the Oriental/Occidental and the male/female. Their varied combinations are distributed unevenly across the primary human/replicant distinction. There are male and female human Orientals, male human Occidentals but no female human Occidentals. There are both male and female replicants, but they are all Occidentals.

Replicant	*Human*
Occidental/(Oriental)	Occidental/Oriental
(Oriental male)/(Oriental female)	Oriental male/Oriental female
Occidental male/Occidental female	Occidental male/(Occidental female)

Although the gaps and absences in this taxonomy are not absolutely symmetrical, there is a rough structural equivalence between the lack of racial difference on the replicant side (no Orientals) and the lack of sexual difference on the human side (no Occidental women). By the end of the film, all the replicants except Rachel have been destroyed. One half of the equation, one form of difference is thus eradicated, because Rachel has been incorporated into the human by becoming partner to the hero, Deckard. This switch is justified narratively by Deckard's discovery that she is 'special', that unlike the other replicants she has no in-built termination date; the symptomatically unmotivated nature of this discovery contributes to the awkwardness and arbitrariness of the film's ending. Rachel's transition not only sees the disappearance of the final replicant, however. More importantly, it restores the one gap on the human side of the taxonomy, it makes good the lack of Occidental females.

The category 'human' is neither absolute nor immutable in the film.

It is true, as Constance Penley points out, that the replicants are 'more human than human' – at least in the terms of a rather diffuse ideology of 'humanism'. The replicants look after one another and feel for one another, whereas the humans have created a messy, impersonal and 'inhumane' world. Deckard feels himself contaminated by his human environment and especially by his job. 'Sushi. That's what my wife called me. Cold fish.'

Deckard's disquiet about his job, his detestation of Bryant, the policeman who hires him to destroy the Nexus 6 replicants, and his growing feelings for Rachel mark him out as different from all the other humans in the film – apart from Sebastian, the model-maker who gave the replicants their human appearance. As Deckard comments when he realises how unhappy Rachel has become on discovering that her 'memories' are a fiction: 'Replicants weren't supposed to have feelings; neither were blade runners. What the hell was happening to me?' There is thus a parallel between Deckard and Rachel. They both become 'more human'. As the film progresses, there is at this level an erosion of difference. (This also affects other characters: the replicant Roy is at his most human when, just before dying, he saves Deckard and delivers his valediction; Gaffe, the Oriental detective, in the end allows Rachel and Deckard to escape together.)

The qualities that constitute this version of 'the human' are suggested by the use of the Empathy Tests, which are 'designed to provoke an emotional response' and so to differentiate humans from replicants. Humans also cling to their memories, a symptom of a desire to transcend mortality that is also felt particularly keenly by the replicants. Indeed, the group of replicants in the film risk returning to earth to find out from their inventor and manufacturer, Tyrrell, whether their termination dates can be extended or abolished.

Tyrrell clearly occupies the position of Father and Law vis-à-vis the replicants in general and Roy in particular. He is the object of their quest, the one who holds the answers to their questions, and the one responsible for their mortality and their awareness of their mortality. His function is therefore in part to focus a narcissistic fantasy or immortality, the wish to live forever, and at the same time to act as a barrier to the fulfilment of that wish. When Roy finally kills him, it is an act of classic Oedipal vengeance.

> Roy: *'It's not an easy thing to meet your maker.'*
> Tyrrell: *'What seems to be the problem?'*
> Roy: *'Death.'*
> Tyrrell: *'The fact of life.'*

As Tyrell tells Roy: 'you are the prodigal son.'

The shifting of Rachel's position (and the 'humanisation' of the various other characters) begins after Tyrrell is killed, after the elimination of the Father. When Roy, the last replicant, finally dies, Deckard and Rachel ride away together from the city into a happy ending across the border, beyond the reach of the Law. In all such endings, as Raymond Bellour has noted, the establishment of the couple contains both a recognition and a disavowal of sexual difference.[7] Here the element of disavowal is registered in the couple's defiance of the Law and in the shift in Rachel's status. In addition, the convention of the happy ending and the establishment of the couple combine to affirm a fantasy of love as perfect union. This involves narcissism both in terms of the two characters constituting the couple and also in terms of a further component of the fantasy – the idea that their love will *last*, that it will defy time and even, perhaps, death.[8] The death of the Father thus allows – and produces – a disavowal of difference and a restoration of narcissism. This contrasts both with the figures of difference and mortality that elsewhere dominate the film and also with its previous insistence on the fact of Symbolic castration.[9]

If this reading is right, why does Roy have to die along with the other replicants? Indeed, if the replicants are 'more human than human', why do they fail the Empathy Tests? What ultimately makes the difference? When the replicant Leon is tested at the beginning of the film, the point at which he fails, panics and shoots his tester is when he is asked about his mother: 'My mother? Let me tell you about my mother.' Of course, replicants have no mothers: that (and only that?) is the difference. Looking through Leon's pictures, Deckard comments: 'And family photos? Replicants didn't have families either.' But to a degree, they do. Not only do they share human emotions of 'hate, love, fear, anger' (Deckard), they are also related to each other through their common 'father', Tyrrell. What they lack is a mother. Rachel, beginning to suspect that she may be a replicant after her Empathy Test, shows Deckard a photograph of a child and an older woman: 'Look, it's me with my mother.' His reply is worth quoting in full:

> Remember when you were six. You and your brother snuck into an empty building through a basement window. You were gonna play doctor. He showed you his. When it got to be your turn, you chickened and ran. Remember that? You ever tell anybody that? Your mother? Tyrrell? Anybody?
>
> You remember the spider that lived in a bush outside your window? Orange body. Green legs. Watched her build a web all summer. Then one day there was a big egg in it. The eggs hatched. Yeah. And a hundred baby spiders came out and ate her.
>
> Implants. Those aren't your memories. They're somebody else's. They're Tyrrell's niece's.

The importance of the issue of motherhood – and the figure of the Mother – could not be more clearly or poignantly presented. And in the first of these 'memories', the recollection of the mother is specifically linked to the discovery of (sexual) difference.

The replicants, lacking a mother, are part of the disorder that inaugurates the narrative of *Blade Runner*; their eradication helps to make its closure possible. Also eradicated is Tyrrell – the original source of the disrup-

Blade Runner (Ridley Scott, 1979)

tion, the immaculate Father of the replicants and the incarnation of the law of mortality. Once disorder is eliminated to this extent, as we have seen, the humanisation of Rachel and the other characters can begin and the loving heterosexual couple can be formed. But that couple and that love are still counterposed against the Law – represented in the character of Bryant and located in the city. Hence the escape to the country completes a chain of equivalences – the couple, the couple's love, Rachel's humanity, the values represented by the couple (and endorsed by the film) – which exists in defiant opposition to the Law and so to the Father. The unstated term that links them is the figure of the Mother.

At the beginning of the narrative, difference is presented as disruptive, a problem (or series of problems) articulated around the Law (through Bryant and Tyrrell), the Father (through Tyrrell) and the Symbolic (through the film's concern with language: its jargon and the Cityspeak Deckard describes as 'a mishmash of Japanese, Spanish, German, what have you', and the difficulties in communication they occasion). By the end, difference has been pretty well eradicated, at least as a problem. The Law and the Father have been left behind or destroyed. The couple commune effortlessly and silently with one another as they fly across the border. From domination by the Law and the Father, the narrative of *Blade Runner*, in what is at its dénouement almost overtly a process of wish-fulfilment, progressively displaces them in favour of the values and qualities associated in fantasy with the Mother.

This filling of the lack and the establishment of a new narrative equilibrium at the end of the film are achieved primarily through the eradication of the replicants, the destruction of the Father, the evasion of the Law and, crucially, the shift in Rachel's status, the filling of the gap on the human side of the taxonomy I sketched earlier. But they are achieved at a cost: the repression of one of the categories of difference present at the beginning, the category of *racial* difference. The opposition between Oriental and Occidental, far from being worked through and resolved, simply disappears, to return momentarily at the end in the person of Gaffe, the Oriental cop, whose sudden change of heart enables Deckard and Rachel to escape. Gaffe's presence here, and the awkwardly unmotivated nature of his actions, point to a failure, finally, in the film's attempt to displace the issue of racial difference onto the opposition between human and replicant. This attempt is most clearly marked in Deckard's gloss on Bryant's use of the term *skin-job*: 'Skin-jobs. That's what Bryant called replicants. In history books he's the kind of cop used to call black men niggers.' This has a dual function. It makes explicit the link between racial difference and human/replicant difference, which is a precondition for the displacement. And at the same time it attempts to mark the issue of race as a 'dead' issue, one relegated to the past and to history books. This strategy cannot succeed completely, though, because the very category of being onto which the displacement is attempted, the replicants, are not themselves racially differentiated. If *they* are eliminated, as they are, the issue of racial

difference itself is not, because it is an issue pertinent only to the humans –
and the humans still remain.

Blade Runner (Ridley Scott, 1979)

GENRE & FANTASY

In this reading of *Alien* and *Blade Runner*, I have concentrated on the deployment within them of several categories of difference – male/female, human/non-human and, in the case of *Blade Runner*, Occidental/Oriental. These categories seem to be pertinent inasmuch as they are motivated by being repeatedly marked across a number of different codes traversing the two film-texts.[10]

Important among these are the codes of genre. As I have noted, the genres of the fantastic often deal with issues of difference – especially the boundaries between the human and the monstrous. Here I have tried to show how, in *Alien* and *Blade Runner*, such differences interact with sexual and racial categories of difference. One conclusion I would draw is that although particular categories can sometimes function metaphorically as symptomatic signs of other categories, they are nonetheless irreducible to one another. That is why I would not altogether go along with Constance Penley's view that 'in these films the question of sexual difference ... is displaced onto the more remarkable difference between the human and the other.' I would say instead that there is a constant *interaction* between the categories of difference – an interaction which in all three cases is focused insistently on the body.

This leads to a final question: why is it that distinct categories of differences are often reduced to a single category – usually *sexual* difference – or thought solely in terms of that category? One reason might be the tendency to conflate *the fantastic* (an aesthetic category) with *fantasy* (a psychoanalytic concept) which I also mentioned in my introduction. Recent discussions of fantasy in cinema have generally attempted to take the theorisation of sexual differences beyond the paradigm of 'ideology' and 'visual pleasure' that emerged in the 1970s.[11] No surprise, then, if this focus on one category of difference sometimes results in other categories that may also be in play in a film or a genre being underestimated or overlooked. The problem is compounded when this sort of approach is addressed to films of the fantastic, because the genre does seem – at least semantically – to be a peculiarly apt vehicle for the study of the textual inscription of fantasy. I am not suggesting that the issue of sexual difference is in any way of secondary importance or that the concept of fantasy cannot illuminate the generic logic of the fantastic. My point is simply to underline the need to take account of the ways in which – in films of the fantastic as elsewhere – sexual difference interrelates with other categories of difference without reducing the latter to the former. As to the form such studies might take, it would be interesting to investigate further the representations of the body that figure so centrally in *all* the categories of difference I have discussed. I am thinking in particular of the special fascination with the body which characterises the fantastic – an ambivalent and highly erotic compound of attraction and repulsion. It may well be at *this* level that the issue of sexual difference is key.

NOTES

1 Constance Penley, 'Time travel, primal scene, and the "critical dystopia"', reprinted in this volume, pp. 197–212.

2 Ibid., pp. 204–5.

3 See Stephen Neale, *Genre* (London: BFI, 1980), esp. pp. 21–2.

4 James H. Kavanaugh, '"Son of a bitch": feminism, humanism and science in *Alien*', *October*, no. 13 (Summer 1980), pp. 95–6.

5 Ibid., pp. 94–5.

6 Ibid., pp. 93–4.

7 Raymond Bellour, 'Psychosis, neurosis, perversion', *Camera Obscura*, nos. 3/4, 1979, esp. pp. 118–19. See also a number of remarks in his interview with Janet Bergstrom in the same issue. As Bergstrom points out, closure and the establishment of the couple both involve and inscribe a 'massive, imaginary reduction of sexual difference to a narcissistic doubling of the masculine subject' (Janet Bergstrom, 'Enunciation and sexual difference', ibid., p. 55).

8 For an elaboration of the foundations and components of this fantasy in the context of melodrama see Stephen Neale, 'Melodrama and tears', *Screen*, vol. 27, no. 6, November/December 1986.

9 An imagery of castration runs through the film: Roy breaks Deckard's fingers, Roy pierces his own hand with a nail; the neon dragon outside the nightclub has a phallic tongue which constantly flicks on and off.

10 On the concepts of pertinence, motivation and codic doubling in the reading of a film text, see Ben Brewster, 'Notes on the text "Young Mr Lincoln" by the editors of *Cahiers du Cinema*', *Screen*, vol. 14, no. 3, Autumn 1973.

11 See, for example, Elizabeth Cowie, 'Fantasia', *m/f*, no. 9, 1984; Constance Penley, 'Feminism, film theory and the bachelor machines', *m/f*, no. 10, 1985; Stephen Neale, 'Sexual difference in cinema – issues of fantasy, narrative and the look', *Oxford Literary Review*, nos. 8/9, 1986.

III
CARNIVAL

Introduction

The assault on the hegemony of Hollywood-Mosfilm was never just a question of academic theorising. Equally important was the production of different types of films in a non-commercial context – in short, the anti-realist avant-garde of the 1970s. In its more politically self-conscious forms, this was generally premised on the definition of the relationship between film and spectator as *ideological*. Film's 'suturing' of the spectator was held to sustain broader social relations of power. The corollary of this seemed to be that to break this link by exposing the illusionist conventions of cinema narrative and the contamination of the pleasures it offers might throw at least a small spanner into the ideological works of capitalism and patriarchy.

Well, these mighty edifices seem to have withstood the challenge. The power of cinema turns out not to be just a matter of texts and subjects, but to be bound up in a much extensive network of 'cultural technologies' which (in Foucault's sense) police modern populations and their pleasures.[1] But even in trying to understand the fascination of films as texts, the questions about the fantastic and fantasy raised in the previous sections of this book suggest a greater complexity than the ideology model sometimes allowed. They reveal the depth and pervasiveness of the *ambivalence* of film narratives, and the mobility and fragmentation of the fantasmatic dynamics both within these narratives and also in spectators' investment in them. Such perceptions have led to a reassessment of earlier cultural and cinematic strategies, and to a search for new ones. It is in this self-critical – but far from apologetic – spirit that Laura Mulvey, in her 1987 article 'Changes', looks back on the conjuncture of feminist politics, psychoanalytic theory and avant-garde aesthetics which shaped the work she did both as a film-maker and theorist in the 1970s, and takes a distance from it.

> After the 1983 election and into 1984, I began to feel that work I considered to be on-going, in the present tense, had shifted into the past to become identified with the previous decade. My formative experiences, desires, and failures involved with cultural struggle, seemed gradually to be relegated to a closed epoch. The avant-garde was over. The Women's Movement no longer existed as an organisation, in spite of the widespread influence of feminism. And the changed political and economic climate marked the 1980s off from the 1970s. It was tempting to accept a kind of natural entropy: that eras just did come to an end.[2]

Having distrusted the recuperative or domesticating powers of narrative closure as an avant-garde feminist film-maker, Laura Mulvey also expresses her unease with this sense of an era having ended. Her mistrust was confirmed as she witnessed the orchestration of the 'trial of strength' between Thatcherism and the miners in the British coal strike of 1985/6 around a rhetoric of oppositions which turned on the same trope: 'the "end of an era" opposition conjures up a phantasmagoric polarisation between past and future in which the catastrophic present and the complex processes of class struggle are repressed.'[3]

This has led her to reconsider the binarisms shaping her own ideas and films. However accurate in diagnosing the existing state of things, she now feels that the argument in 'Visual pleasure and narrative cinema'

> ... hinders the possibility of change and remains caught ultimately within its own dualistic terms. The polarisation only allows an 'either/ or'. As the two terms (masculine/feminine, voyeuristic/exhibitionist, active/passive) remain dependent on each other for meaning, their only possible movement is into inversion ... [T]he either/or binary pattern seemed to leave the argument trapped within its own conceptual frame of reference, unable to advance politically into a new terrain or suggest an alternative theory of spectatorship in the cinema.[4]

Similarly, Mulvey calls into question the aesthetic 'scorched earth policy' of the 1970s avant-garde – including the films like *Penthesilea*, *Riddles of the Sphinx*, and *Amy!* that she made with Peter Wollen – insofar as their aim was to *negate* the 'deadly sins' of mainstream film by deploying the 'cardinal virtues' of a revolutionary, materialist counter-cinema.

In 'Changes', then, Laura Mulvey addresses the same impasses and aporias of the realism/anti-realism debates identified in my general introduction. How might the focus on fantasy and the fantastic offer alternatives not trapped within the dualistic principles of avant-garde opposition and negation?

BEYOND NEGATION

The articles in this section suggest different perspectives and practices that might contribute to a critical cinema. Although still concerned with questions of textuality and representation, their proposals are no longer for a 'politics of interruption' focussing exclusively on the text-spectator relationship – gone are the days of film students with their Super-8 in one hand and their *Screen* or Noel Burch in the other, trying to translate the theory into pictures. In contrast to the teleologies of negation and progress, they suggest a more open-ended temporality – in 'Changes', Laura Mulvey quotes Bakhtin's definition of carnival as 'the feast of becoming, change and renewal' which was 'hostile to all that was immortalised and completed'. Instead of thinking in terms of dominant versus oppositional, mainstream versus avant-garde, or realism versus anti-realism, they try to prevent such polarities from becoming fixed.

These concerns are also evident in the current enthusiasm for Third Cinema – not just the cinemas of the 'third world', but a cinema outside such dualities, or not constrained by them at least. Third Cinema, according to Teshome Gabriel, 'includes an infinity of subjects and styles as varied as the lives of the people it portrays'.[5] The search for a perspective 'somewhere else' by western theorists can sometimes run the risk of setting up its own polarities of inside and outside, the one and the other.[6] But it does chime with many of the concerns evident in much current writing not just about cinema, but also about many aspects of 'postmodernism'. It can be seen, for example, as a response to what Fredric Jameson diagnoses as perhaps its central malaise: 'the enormity of a situation in which we seem increasingly incapable of fashioning representations of our own current experience.'[7] For Jameson, of course, this *experience* refers ultimately to a Lukacsian, big-H History. That is the narrative which we have lost, to our cost. In its place we are offered, in the cinema, *la mode rétro*, the colonisation of the past as glossy, depthless, commodified spectacle in films like *American Graffiti*, *Chinatown*, or *The Conformist*. The nostalgia of their film language is incompatible with 'genuine historicity'; the *noir* style of a film like *Body Heat* 'displaces "real" history'.[8]

The 'third force' that Jameson proposes as an alternative to this 'narrative logic of contemporary postmodernism' is *magic realism*.[9] This idea, derived from Latin American writers like Alejo Carpentier and Gabriel García Márquez, may, he suggests, point to an emerging cinematic mode that allows at least some purchase on History. Taking as examples three films that have had little if any distribution in the United Kingdom – *Fever* (Poland, Agnuszka Holland, 1981), *La Casa de Agua* (Venezuela, Jacobo Penzo, 1984), and *Condores no entierran todos los dias* (Colombia, Gustavo Alvarez Gardearzabel, 1984) – he traces through three elements he considers them to have in common. First, they are all *historical* films, although what they offer is not the totalising narratives of classic realism nor the past as 'lost object of desire' in nostalgia films, but a 'history with holes, perforated history' (p. 303). Their reality is itself already 'the articulated superposition of whole layers of the past within the present' (p. 311); it is in this sense that magic realism both demands and constitutes a transfiguration of the object world. The other features they share are a use of colour which constitutes 'a unique supplement and the source of a particular pleasure, or fascination, or *jouissance*, in its own right', and a narrative dynamic which is 'reduced, concentrated, and simplified' by their attention to violence and, to a lesser degree, sexuality (p. 303).

These aspects of his argument are reminiscent of Thomas Elsaesser's approach to discovering the way that 'history' is inscribed in German silent cinema.

> If one … wants to avoid making criticism a self-fulfilling prophecy, any reasoning about the social or political meaning of films of the fantastic has to respect both the autonomy of the historical dimension and the

autonomy of the textual level, and seek structures – not where they overlap or mirror each other, but at the points of contact where there is evidence that the text has seized, worked over, displaced or objectified elements of the historical or the social sphere in order to bring them to representation within the text's own formal or generic constraints. The model sketched here is therefore not aimed at discovering homologies, but to valorise imbalances, excesses, intensities – that is to say, the very figures of fantastic discourse.
(This volume, p. 29)

For Jameson, it seems, there is a homology between nostalgia films and the social reality of postmodernity. The critical edge of the magic realist films, their 'constitutive and privileged relationship with history', stems from their ability to subject us as spectators to 'a present of uncodified intensities' (p. 321). These intensities are partly conveyed through their use of colour. This involves a 'de-psychologising' and an 'un-theatricalising of their subjects'; the relevant contrast here is not between the by now universal use of colour as against black-and-white, but between the fashion-plate colour of nostalgia films and this magic realist deployment. It is also through colour that the films produce their uncanny effect. It acts as the trace of an older and archaic fantasy: 'This "return of the repressed" makes itself felt by the garish and technicolour representation of what is given as an essentially black-and-white reality.'[10] In their narrative strategies, the magic realist films reveal a tendency to 'de-narrativisation' which Jameson compares to the novelistic strategies of Robbe-Grillet – a 'reduction to the body and an attendant mobilisation of as yet unexploited resources and potentialities of pornography and violence' (p. 319).

> A whole range of subtle or complicated forms of narrative attention, which classical film (or, better still, sound film) laboriously acquired and adapted from earlier developments in the novel, are now junked and replaced by the simplest minimal reminders of a plot that turns on immediate violence. Narrative has not here been subverted or abandoned, as in the iconoclasm of experimental film, but rather effectively neutralised, to the benefit of a seeing or a looking in the filmic present. (p. 321)

Jameson's account of postmodernism as the cultural logic of late capitalism, although widely influential, remains highly contentious, not least because it seems to want to have its postmodernist theoretical cake and critique it from a historicist angle too. What is particularly interesting, and perhaps symptomatic, about his championing of a magic realist cinema as a critical strategy is the way that it assumes that neither progressive realism nor avant-garde experimentation any longer offers a radical alternative cinema. Like the advocates of Third Cinema, he seeks mobile and diffused angles of vision – the 'somewhere else' I mentioned earlier – that can reveal and accelerate the instability of discourse, of culture, of the social. This is the crucial link to questions of the fantastic and fantasy, for their starting point too is the instability of narrative and of identification. That, I would say, explains the recurrence, not only in

Jameson's account of magic realism but also in the articles in this section, of notions like carnival, the popular, the uncanny, the grotesque, the magical, the surreal, and the sublime – a strikingly different cultural and political language from that of the 70s.

CARNIVAL

In place of one old avant-garde's death-or-glory resistance to the Hollywood juggernaut and the other's utopian search for the 'progressive text' that would hasten the revolution,[11] then, the emphasis now seems to be on experimentation, the multiplication of different narratives, and the narration of differences. The aim is no longer the silence of negation, but the noise of negotiation and dialogue.[12] This implies neither a predisposition to compromise and quiescence, nor the pluralist assumption that 'anything goes'. Dialogue, in this view, equals conflict. Such conflict is neither an embarrassment nor a sign that the process is not working, that there is a failure of communication. On the contrary, the discord is essential. It demonstrates the aspiration to community, a community whose form and direction cannot be determined in advance, but only in the process of the dialogue. Hence this conception runs counter to Richard Rorty's dismissal of Lyotard's call for an art of the sublime on the grounds that it is 'wildly irrelevant to the attempt at communicative consensus which is the vital force which drives [liberal democratic] culture'.[13] It recognises that no representation is going to be adequate to the complexity of the present, let alone to an imagined future that would be (again alluding to Lyotard's terms) both different from what we already know, but also just. This aspiration and this self-awareness – the 'measuring up' of discourse to the ideal – are the mark of an aesthetic of the sublime. Films made in this spirit are also likely to be fundamentally dialogic, interrogating their own narration or discourse in their critical, intertextual contingency on other narratives, other voices.

This is why carnival may be the most appropriate image for this idea of cinema. For Bakhtin, carnival was the highest point of dialogism. It captures not only the loss of innocence and the absence of earnestness in the new approach, but also its wit, its seriousness and its critical relationship to the institutions within which it operates.

> The carnival is the repeated affirmation of the possibility of alternative relations in the midst of order and control; it is the model for a society that is not slavishly determined by any one structure or conceived in terms of any one model or theory ... The carnivalesque is an unreal, fictive, theatrical element within history and society (within discourse) that serves to give critical perspectives on social reality, on 'things as they are'.[14]

From this perspective, even the idea of *cinema* as a self-sufficient institution can appear anachronistic. 'The dream factory' is an unmistakably Fordist image which, however appropriate to Hollywood in its heyday, scarcely conveys the variety of media, techniques and institutions that now contribute to the production and dissemination of moving images and sounds. The uses of video from art gallery experimentation to home viewing to advertising on the London underground are just the most visible symptom of this; hence the inclusion here of an article on a video artist, Cecelia Condit.

A carnivalesque cinema – or whatever collective term should replace it – suggests neither a new formula for making avant-garde films, nor a new canon of postmodern radicalism. Of course, it is too much fun to speculate on what this might include to be able to resist. At least three possible, overlapping, canons might be proposed. One would be the magic realism which Jameson opposes to *la mode rétro*. A second strand would be postmodern in Lyotard's sense of exploring the materiality of film in a revival of a modernist avant-garde: this might include Eggeling, Richter, Fischinger, Lye, Breer, Snow, Gidal, the co-op movement and so forth.[15] In recent years, this avant-garde seems to have taken on a distinctly fantastic tinge. 'It is perhaps no accident,' writes Michael O'Pray in his introduction to an exhibition of recent film and video work, 'that the fragmentation, the need for "relevance" and "content" and the desperate flight into fantasy felt so strongly at times in avant-garde film-making, should occur in the uncertain climate of Britain in the 80s.'[16] The third canon would certainly include many of the films included in the *Elusive Sign* exhibition, but it would not be limited to any notion of an avant-garde. Rather, its criterion of inclusion would be that the films and tapes make dialogism a structuring principle of their narration – Condit's tapes, Marker's *Sunless*, many of the films of Raul Ruiz (a magic realist if ever there was one), Vera Neubauer's *The Decision* and *The Mummy's Curse*, Lizzie Borden's *Born in Flames*, Sankofa's *Territories* and the Black Audio Film Collective's *Handsworth Songs*, David Lynch's *Blue Velvet* are some examples that come to mind.

Just as the notion of a carnivalesque canon is in the end a contradiction in terms, so there can be no single 'postmodern perspective' on regimes of representation. Certainly no such thing is to be found in the articles in this section. Rather, they advocate a variety of styles and arguments engaged in critical disputes that open up the possibility of movement and change; not, as in pluralism, heterogeneity as an end, but a heterogeneity of ends. They also recognise that, within the institution of cinema, only a temporary and licensed disruption of categories and hierarchies can be achieved – like in carnival, as many critics have pointed out. But at least this new modesty signals an awareness of the limits of cinema, and a refusal of the lazy, self-deluding substitution of film-making or theorising (or carnival, or culture) for politics. The articulation of cinematic radicalism to other cultural and political narratives is another question.

NOTES

1 See, for example, Colin Mercer, 'That's entertainment: the resilience of popular forms', in Tony Bennett, Colin Mercer and Janet Woollacott (eds), *Popular Culture and Social Relations* (Milton Keynes: Open University Press, 1986); and 'Entertainment, or the policing of virtue', *New Formations*, no. 4, 1988.

2 Laura Mulvey, 'Changes: thoughts on myth, narrative and historical experience', *History Workshop Journal*, no. 23 (London: Routledge and Kegan Paul, Spring 1987) p. 3.

3 Ibid., p. 5.

4 Ibid., pp. 6–7.

5 Quoted in Paul Willemen, 'The Third Cinema question: notes and reflections', *Framework*, no. 34, 1987, p. 21.

6 Another danger, not entirely absent from Willemen's article, is of old guard theorists, bored and embarrassed by the priggish consumerism they have spawned, turning to Third Cinema as a way of enlivening a moribund metropolitan film culture – a curiously eugenic idea of theory and cinema. Also relevant here, of course, are the current debates about the relationship between postmodernism and feminism (especially those initiated by Craig Owens's article 'The discourse of others', in Hal Foster (ed.), *The Anti-Aesthetic* [Port Townsend, Washington: Bay Press, 1983]) and about 'male feminism' (see, for example, Alice Jardine and Paul Smith (eds.), *Men in Feminism* [London: Methuen, 1987]).

7 Fredric Jameson, 'Postmodernism or the cultural logic of late capitalism', *New Left Review*, no. 146, July–August 1984, p. 68.

8 Ibid., p. 67.

9 Fredric Jameson, 'On magic realism in film', *Critical Inquiry*, vol. 12, no. 2, Winter 1986. Page references are given in the text.

10 Ibid., p. 317. Jameson is here quoting from his own *Fables of Aggression: Wyndham Lewis, the modernist as fascist* (Berkeley: University of California Press, 1979), pp. 57–8.

11 The idea of the 'progressive text' is brilliantly lampooned in John O. Thompson's image of an Effectometer, plugged into the Conjuncture. Films or schools of film-making would then be fed into this machine, and positive or negative readings taken on a scale of Progressive Effects. Work by work, though, the Effectometer keeps reading roughly zero. 'Up aporia creek', *Screen Education*, no. 31, 1979, p. 36.

12 On 'negotiation', see Homi Bhabha, 'The commitment to theory', *New Formations*, no. 5, 1988.

13 Quoted in Robert Lapsley and Michael Westlake, *Film Theory: an introduction* (Manchester: Manchester University Press, 1988), p. 213.

14 David Carroll, 'Narrative, heterogeneity, and the question of the political: Bakhtin and Lyotard', in Murray Krieger (ed.), *The Aims of representation: subject/text/history* (New York: Columbia University Press), pp. 91, 95.

15 For Lyotard's tastes in film, see his 'Acinema', in Philip Rosen (ed.), *Narrative, Apparatus, Ideology: A film theory reader* (New York: Columbia University Press, 1986).

16 Michael O'Pray, 'The elusive sign: from asceticism to aestheticism', in David Curtis (ed.), *The Elusive Sign: British avant-garde film and video 1977–1987* (London: Arts Council of Great Britain/British Council, 1987), p. 10.

The Fantastic, the Sublime and the Popular
Or, What's at Stake in Vampire Films?
JAMES DONALD

Learn to go and see the 'worst' films; they are sometimes sublime,

Ado Kyrou, Le Surréalisme au cinéma, 1963

A typical American film, naive and silly, can – for all its silliness and even *by means of* it – be instructive. A fatuous, self-conscious English film can teach one nothing. I have often learnt a lesson from a silly American film.

Ludwig Wittgenstein, 1947

Say 'mass culture' and images of a manipulative utopianism and a blandly delusory wish-fulfilment spring to mind. Say 'popular culture' and that might invoke more heroic notions of 'the people' expressing their values and aspirations. In either case, what often seems to be overlooked, or perhaps disavowed, is the insistent display of anxiety, violence and uncertainty in popular cultural forms – horror movies have a long pre-history. Does it matter that the dream factories have often produced nightmares? I think it does. As Freud wrote to Fliess in January 1897, 'the story of the Devil, the vocabulary of popular swear-words, the songs and habits of the nursery – all these are now gaining significance for me.'[1] The interest of a despised form like the horror film is not just that it might offer a certain corrective to the partial and distorted perception of cultural formations allowed by an exclusive concern with 'legitimate' canons. More intriguing, in my view, is the apparently paradoxical overlap between this very 'lowness' and what seems to be its contrary, the sublime – a concept whose reappearance centre stage in the aesthetics and politics of postmodernism is another enigma I want to investigate here. 'The abject is edged with the sublime,' observes Julia Kristeva. 'It is not the same moment on the journey, but the same subject and speech bring them into being.'[2]

    It is this uneasy affinity between the vulgarity of the popular vampire movie and the sublime dissolution of aesthetic and perceptual norms that guides the tortuous route of my journey here. Along the way, I want to explore three questions. First, what might ideas about the fantastic and the uncanny familiar from literary and film theory reveal about some of the tackier forms of popular culture? Second, could they contribute anything to a rethinking of the concept of 'the popular', as it has been used within cultural studies, so that it would take account of the fragmentation and instability of subjectivity? Although often

Dracula (Tod Browning, 1946)

waved aside as a flight of Lacanian or Derridian fancy, it seems to me that the persistence of tales about vampires, doubles, golems and cyborgs within popular culture tells a different story: simply, that this version of subjectivity is closer to the insistent, everyday reality of how we experience ourselves in the world than the myth of autonomous, self-conscious agency.

My third question is more topical, perhaps even idiosyncratic. Reading about politics in Britain or the United States these days, I have noticed a number of writers turning to images of the monstrous in trying to explain the dynamics and appeal of Thatcherism and Reaganism. In 1984, for example, after the Brighton bombing, Sarah Benton commented on the dark side of the mystical Tory faith in national community: 'Such a belief can only derive coherence from the conjuring up of the Alien, a force whose shape you never quite see but which lurks in every unlit space ready to destroy you; and is incubated, unnoticed, in the healthy body politic.' For Laura Mulvey, the official narration of the British miners' strike of 1984–5 was more ambivalent, but still monstrous: 'Like the Frankenstein monster, the miners struggled for control of their own story, and like the monster, were cast simultaneously as evil and tragic.' Michael Rogin contextualises Ronald Reagan's view of the world in a history of 'demonology' and 'countersubversion' in American politics:

> The demonologist splits the world in two, attributing magical, pervasive power to a conspiratorial centre of evil. Fearing chaos and secret penetration, the countersubversive interprets local initiatives as signs of alien power. Discrete individuals and groups become, in the countersubversive imagination, members of a single political body directed by its head. The countersubversive needs monsters to give shape to his anxieties and to permit him to indulge his forbidden desires. Demonisation allows the countersubversive, in the name of battling the subversive, to imitate his enemy.

Similarly, Jacqueline Rose quotes instances of Margaret Thatcher's rhetoric of 'power in the adversarial mode', the opposition between identity and that which threatens it. 'The decline of contemporary thought has been hastened by the misty phantom of Socialism,' Thatcher asserted in 1976; two years later came one of her most notorious utterances: 'The British character has done so much for democracy, for law, and done so much throughout the world that if there is any fear that it might be swamped people are going to react ...' Here, suggests Rose, she seems to be repeating 'one of the fundamental psychic tropes of fascism, which acts out this structure of aggressivity, giving name and place to the invisible adversary which is an inherent part of it, and making fear a central component of strategy.'[3] My question is, why this imagery now, at the end of the 1980s, and can its appearance be explained at all by representations of the monstrous and the terrifying in other cultural forms? For what we are dealing with, I think, is a history of popular fears – fears that are not only given expression in horror films, but which also drive this paranoid political style.

THE FANTASTIC & THE UNCANNY

The usual way of trying to explain tales of horror and terror in literature and the cinema is to ask: what does the monster mean? In 'Dialectic of fear', for example, Franco Moretti invokes Marx and Freud to diagnose what is inscribed in the monstrous *metaphors* of Frankenstein and Dracula – he argues that it is specific economic, psychic and sexual fears. These metaphors also transform the fears. The relationship between capitalist and proletariat becomes that between Frankenstein and his creation. For Frankenstein's monster read 'a Ford worker', says Moretti; *this* is the fear of a dependent, exploited yet dangerously *in*dependent creation. As for Dracula, Moretti perceives in him the fear of, on the one hand, the blood-sucking financiers of monopoly capital and, on the other, the castrating mother. Perhaps to cloak the baldness of this translation, he suggests that these meanings are subordinated to the literal presence of the Count, to his metaphoric status. That is the point of transforming the original fears: 'so that readers do not have to face up to what might really frighten them.'[4] In 'An introduction to the American horror film', Robin Wood takes a similar line. The basic formula of Hollywood horror films of the 1960s and 70s, he argues, is: 'normality is threatened by the Monster'. The figure of the Monster *dramatises* 'all that our civilization *re*presses or *op*presses' – that means, for him, female sexuality, the proletariat, other cultures, ethnic groups, alternative ideologies, homosexuality and bisexuality, and children.[5]

My summaries inevitably sacrifice the sophistication and nuances of these analyses. Even so, both articles do flirt with a certain functionalism and a certain reductionism. For Moretti, the fear provoked by fictional horror is 'a fear one *needs*: the price one pays for coming contentedly to terms with a social body based on irrationality and menace'. For Wood, the real monster turns out to be the 'dominant ideology', that 'insidious all-pervasive force capable of concealment behind the most protean disguises'.[6] The meaning of these fictions can be unscrambled confidently enough once you find the right code. History? Here's Marx with the answer. Repression? Wheel on Freud. What Moretti and Wood offer as an interpretation of the monstrous is, in the end, a *sociologising of the Other* – also evident perhaps in this formulation by Fredric Jameson in his essay on 'Magical narratives':

> Evil ... continues to characterise whatever is radically different from me, whatever by virtue of precisely that difference seems to constitute a real and urgent threat to my own existence. So from the earliest times, the stranger from another tribe, the 'barbarian' who speaks an incomprehensible language and follows 'outlandish' customs, but also the woman, whose biological difference stimulates fantasies of castration and devoration, or in our own time, the avenger of accumulated resentments from some oppressed class or race, or else that alien being, Jew or Communist, behind whose apparently human features a malignant and preternatural intelligence is thought to lurk: these are some of the

archetypal figures of the Other, about whom the essential point to be made is not so much that he is feared because he is evil; rather he is evil because he is Other, alien, different, strange, unclean, and unfamiliar.[7]

Certainly Jameson – like Moretti and Wood – is onto something important here. But again the coincidence between the psychic, the historical and the 'mythic' strikes me as just too neat. It presents the Other as a threat to identity; it ignores the *need* for an Other to define the terms and limits of identity. 'Whatever is radically different from me' essentialises both self and other. The image of an apparently coherent self repressing the irrational, the evil, the different disavows the fragmentation of subjectivity entailed by the very idea of repression and the unconsious.

What seems to be missing from such acccounts is any sense of eeriness, that disorientation of perception that Tzvetan Todorov identifies as the key to the literary 'fantastic'.

> In a world which is indeed our world, the one we know, a world without devils, sylphides, or vampires, there occurs an event which cannot be explained by the laws of this same familiar world. The person who experiences the event must opt for one of two possible solutions: either he is the victim of an illusion of the senses, of a product of the imagination – and laws of the world then remain what they are; or else the event has indeed taken place, it is an integral part of reality – but then this reality is controlled by laws unknown to us.[8]

For Todorov, the fantastic lasts as long as that hesitation. In contrast to realism's illusion of knowledge and coherence, works of the fantastic insist upon the delusory nature of perception – What's going on here? How can I be sure? Within this aura of uncertainty, Todorov identifies some of the fantastic themes of the self: 'the fragility of the limit between matter and mind'; the 'multiplication of the personality; collapse of the limit between subject and object; and lastly, the transformation of time and space . . .'[9] The fantastic, in short, plays upon the *insecurity* of the boundaries between the 'I' and the 'not-I', between the real and the unreal.

This seems obviously relevant to horror movies – the fracturing of the self in doubles and monsters like Dr Jekyll and Mr Hyde, Frankenstein, werewolves, and the rest; the terror of its invasion by vampires, zombies, or aliens. Yet Todorov's approach has not been widely taken up in relation to film; presumably because most popular films of the fantastic stick firmly within the conventions of cinematic verisimilitude. Also, although Todorov suggests that fantastic tales in the nineteenth century represented 'the bad conscience of this positivist [nineteenth-century] era',[10] his focus on formal questions does tend to leave many questions about 'history' and 'ideology' begging.

Is it possible to combine Todorov's stress on the textual mecha-nisms of uncertainty, and on the 'fragility of limits' and the 'multiplication of the personality', with Moretti and Wood's more materialist concern with the historical specificity of monstrous figures? This is what Thomas Elsaesser attempts in his article on German silent cinema, 'Social mobility and the fantastic'.[11] He is as interested in the inscription of 'history' as Moretti or Wood, but he insists that this is a question of *enunciation*. History cannot be reduced to a set of social and/or psychic fears that are metaphorised or dramatised in the films. The inadequacy of any formal representation to this idea of history produces effects that are fantastic or uncanny. Whereas Todorov restricts his usage of the uncanny to strange events for which there is a rational explanation not immediately apparent to the deceiving mind of the spectator, however, Elsaesser uses the term more broadly to indicate the anxiety that is both invoked and contained by *The Student of Prague, Caligari,* or *Nosferatu*. His usage is thus closer to Freud's definition of the uncanny as 'that class of the frightening which leads back to what is known of old and long familiar'; that is, something 'old-established in the mind', but 'alienated from it only through the process of repression'.

This idea shifts the focus away from the symbolic equation 'the monster stands for social and psychic anxieties that have been repressed' towards an explanation of the frisson of the uncanny in terms of the dynamics of fantasy. Nevertheless, Freud's essay on 'The Uncanny', published in 1919, does give some warrant to Moretti and Wood's attempts to tie down the meaning of the monstrous as well as to Todorov's emphasis on structural hesitation. Freud notes several times – particularly with reference to fairy tales – that the fictional representation of uncanny events is not in itself sufficient to produce the effect of the uncanny: 'that feeling cannot arise unless there is a conflict of judgment as to whether things which have been surmounted and are regarded as incredible [archaism and animism, for example] may not, after all, be possible; and this problem is eliminated from the outset by the postulates of the world of fairy tales.'[12] Although Freud here insists on uncertainty as a requirement of the uncanny, critics have repeatedly shown how, in the reading of Hoffmann's story *The Sandman* which forms the backbone of the essay, he consistently represses most of its uncanny aspects in order to identify a single, coherent meaning and to justify this interpretation.[13] Its narrative complexity, the intensity of its rhetoric, and its repeated scenes of violence are all left out of account so that he can establish the 'scientific' truth of his thesis that uncanniness is attributable to 'the *anxiety* belonging to the castration complex of childhood'.

At the same time, observes Hélène Cixous, the partiality of this reading reveals Freud's own anxieties and repetition compulsions; it's impossible to tie down the meaning of the uncanny as neatly as he wants to. What is at stake are the instability of the boundaries between human/automaton or live/dead, and the fragility of the limits of identity. The double should therefore be seen not as 'counterpart or reflection, but rather the doll that is neither dead nor alive'.

> It is the *between* that is tainted with strangeness ... What is intolerable is that the Ghost [or the Vampire] erases the limit which exists between two states, neither alive nor dead; passing through, the dead man returns in the manner of the Repressed. It is his coming back which makes the ghost what he is, just as it is the return of the Repressed that inscribes the repression.

And (recalling for us the hero witnessing his corpse being confined in its casket in *Vampyr* or Dracula sleeping in his coffin of native earth) Cixous conjures up 'the supremely disquieting idea: the phantasm of the man buried alive: his textual head, shoved back into the maternal body, a horrible pleasure'.

> Why is it that the maternal landscape, the *heimisch*, and the familiar become so disquieting? The answer is less buried than we might suspect. The obliteration of any separation, the realisation of the desire which in itself obliterates a limit ...

It is in this 'confusion of life and death', suggests Cixous, that castration takes on its significance.

> It is the notch and also the other self of the man buried alive: a bit too much death in life; a bit too much life in death, at the merging intersection. There is no recourse to an inside/outside. You are there permanently. There is no *reversal* from one term to another. Hence, the horror: you could be dead while living, you can be in a dubious state.[14]

Vampyr (Carl Dreyer, 1931)

THE SUBLIME

This sense of being in a dubious state connects the uncanny not only to Todorov's fantastic, but also to the idea of the sublime. The sublime too involves uncertainty and vertigo: Can this be true? This defies imagination! Some critics have therefore suggested that in 'The Uncanny' Freud stumbled upon a partial psychology of the sublime: *partial* because he attempts to exert his control over the sublime by reducing the uncanny to an infantile and/or archaic complex.[15]

What then distinguishes the sublime from the fantastic and the uncanny? The usual starting point for attempts to understand the sublime, at least in its post-Enlightenment forms, is Edmund Burke. He not only made the crucial distinction between the beautiful and the sublime, he also insisted that the sublime is a theory of terror: 'terror is in all cases whatsoever, either more openly or latently the ruling principle of the sublime'.[16] It shares this with Todorov's fantastic and Freud's uncanny; it differs from them in identifying the *source* of terror. For Burke, this lies not in the perceptual uncertainties of the fantastic or the disquietingly ill-defined boundaries of the uncanny but in the sheer immensity of Nature – and metonymically of divinity. He invokes stormy oceans, wild cataracts, dark towers and demons to convey the forces that overwhelm human reason and imagination and produce a response of awe and terror: his sublime involves powerful emotions ultimately reducible to visceral processes of pleasure and pain.

At least two paths lead out from Burke's ideas. One, concerned primarily with the beautiful/sublime opposition as a key to questions of taste, leads first to Kant, who rejected Burke's physiologism and reformulated the sublime not in terms of the emotions it provokes, but in terms of the limits of representation and the need to test its adequacy to the Idea to be expressed. Whereas the beautiful consists in ordering and limiting representation – the illusion of closure through the framed picture or the complete narrative – the sublime points to limitlessness and infinitude. But what is most important for Kant is the possibility of conceptualising the sublime in rational terms even if we cannot grasp it through our senses. We can conceptualise *infinity*, even though we cannot see it or even imagine it. Thus the sublime, even though it may be provoked by what threatens to overpower us, confirms our status as rational and moral beings in the positive moment of rational comprehension or moral confrontation – this is its pedagogic aspect. For Kant, what is sublime is not the vast or powerful object but the supersensible cast of mind which enables us to deal with it.[17]

Kant ruled out the products of human artifice as sources of the sublime – perhaps because art could entail the beautification, and hence the containment of *management*, of the sublime. Already in Kant, the sublime was what resists the tendency to a closed, definitive system that is inherent in the idea of the beautiful. This argument was taken up by people like Schiller and Kleist, who saw the merely beautiful (and the sublime's true antithesis, *kitsch*) as collusive with the value-less world of bourgeois modernity in providing a mask of order and value for its real disorder. Hence the monstrous – along with terror, barbarity and tyranny – continues to appear in nineteenth-century art of the sublime as a tactic for transgressing the compensatory illusions of beauty, grace and reason.

There is a complex history as the idea runs from Kant through Schiller, Schelling and Hegel to Schopenhauer, for whom the sublime meant the Will contemplating itself, and finally to Nietzsche's distinction between the Apollonian and the Dionysian in art. Before following that through to Lyotard's formulation of a postmodern sublime, I want to trace my other history of the sublime. This runs not through Reason, Romance and Philosophy, but through a gaudier and more vulgar route.

The initial move here is to the Gothic novel (where, of course, we meet up again with the vampire[19]). Like the sublime, the Gothic attempts to provoke awe and terror. Like the uncanny, its principal themes are death and the supernatural: this may be one way in which it provides a bridge between Burke and Freud. What the Gothic *adds* – especially through the absurdity and excess of its paraphernalia – is a new relationship to representation. By heightening the artificiality of its supernatural elements, claims David Morris, the Gothic sublime of *The Castle of Otranto* foreshadows Freud's view that terror does not depend on a belief in the reality of what frightens us: 'Walpole goes beyond Burke in composing a fiction which – however intermittently or awkwardly – employs representation as a means of expressing and of evoking what cannot be represented' (in this case, the materials of the unconscious).[19]

In his classic study of *The Romantic Agony*, Mario Praz plotted the high road from this anti-allegorical Gothic as its emphasis on the arbitrariness of signification was incorporated into the work of the Romantics, the symbolists and the decadence. That offers another route to a properly modernist, abstracting sublime. But again I take the low road, where the romantic fascination with horror and perversity feeds upon, and reanimates, more popular traditions. The tale of how Mary Shelley's *Frankenstein* and Polidori's Byronic *Vampyre* were written is well enough known by now, but it is worth noting how quickly they were absorbed into the popular theatre. The fact that by the mid-1820s it was possible to see a double bill of dramatic adaptations of *Frankenstein* and *The Vampire* at the English Opera House in London suggests the next milestone in this history of a vulgar sublime: *melodrama*.

Like Kant's sublime and the Gothic novel, melodrama too can be interpreted as a characteristically modern form of imagination. It gives expression to 'the anxiety brought by a frightening new world in which the traditional patterns of moral order no longer provide the necessary social glue'.[20] The force of that anxiety is registered in the apparent triumph of villainy, and then dissipated in the eventual victory of virtue. To this extent, melodrama seems to perform the same optimistic function as kitsch. But it also shares with the sublime – and with certain forms of realism – the aspiration to get beyond surfaces. It attempts to reveal the underlying drama of what Peter Brooks calls 'the "moral occult", the domain of operative spiritual values which is both indicated within and masked by the surface of reality'.[21] As in the Gothic novel, the unreality, the excess and the irrationality are functional: they enable us to conceive the unpresentable.

In its more realist mode – in the serials of Eugène Sue or G. M. W. Reynolds, in many thrillers and 'women's pictures', even in *Dallas* and *Dynasty* – melodrama highlights the strangeness, the traces of this irrationality, in the familiar and the normal. This resonates with Schiller's view of the underlying irrationality of modern society, seen here not as a field of opportunities to be manipulated by the young heroes of the *Bildungsroman*, but as a cultural repressed. In its more monstrous forms – in Frankenstein, in tales of terror, in today's splatter movies – melodrama also figures the irruption of that terrifying irrationality into the everyday world. In making these links from melodrama to contemporary popular forms, it is worth recalling Freud's comments on fairy tales for the well established moral categories and theatrical conventions of the melodrama and its successors increasingly work against the possibility of producing an uncanny or fantastic effect. In this world of virtue threatened by evil, the *mise en scène* usually ensures that we know exactly where we are. So where should we look for a modern sublime?

A MODERN SUBLIME

Once again the distinction is between popular genres which display mysterious or shocking events within the conventions of a naturalistic dramaturgy – the Universal Frankensteins and Draculas of the 1930s, Hammer from the 50s to the 70s, films by Cronenberg, Craven and Hooper today – and a modernism which calls such conventions into question through its forms of enunciation. This raises the question whether there are *any* links to be drawn between, for example, horror films and a postmodern sublime – the neo-Nietzscheanism of Kristeva, Foucault or Lyotard – whose slogan is 'represent the unpresentable'.

Although Kristeva's contrast between the semiotic and the symbolic might be read as a reformulation of the sublime/beautiful distinction, it is the ideas she develops about abjection in *Powers of Horror* that relate more directly to my earlier discussion of Todorov and Cixous's accounts of horror and liminality. Like Cixous's uncanny, abjection is that which does not 'respect borders, positions, rules', that which reveals the 'fragility of the law'. It is 'the place where meaning collapses':

> We may call it a border; abjection is above all ambiguity. Because, while releasing a hold, it does not radically cut off the subject from what threatens it – on the contrary, abjection acknowledges it to be in perpetual danger. But also because abjection itself is a composite of judgment and affect, of condemnation and yearning, of signs and drives.

The affinity between the abject and the sublime, which I noted earlier, is that neither has a representable object, that both disturb identity, system and order.

> The 'sublime' object dissolves in the raptures of a bottomless memory … Not at all short of but always with and through perception and words, the sublime is a *something added* that expands us, overstrains us, and causes us to be both *here*, as dejects, and *there*, as others and sparkling. A divergence, an impossible bounding.[22]

Foucault's work on exclusion and transgression, dating mostly from the 1960s, also touched on aspects of the sublime. Like Kristeva, he uses a spatial model of Same and Other, in which the Other is inhabited by figures of madness, sexuality, death and the diabolical. This space lies between discourse and the unconscious, and these figures become visible in the form of a non-discursive language which transgresses its limit and invades the space of discourse and rationality. Although they may seem familiar from the Gothic novel, melodrama and the horror film, it is the form of enunciation that is important here. In non-discursive writing, language takes on an opacity, an 'ontological weight' which subverts the transparency of discursive language. It is within the *pli* or fold created by non-discursive language that the post-modern sublime is constituted.[23]

Foucault and Kristeva are less likely to invoke folk devils like Frankenstein and Dracula, zombies and master criminals, pod people and blade runners, than the modernist pantheon of Nietzsche, Dostoyevsky, Artaud, Blanchot, Bataille, Céline and Klossowski. Although the popular tradition of horror and terror gestures towards the abject, the transgressive, the sublime, or whatever it is, its representation as morality tale or melodrama places it squarely on the side of a moralistic mass culture, of petit bourgeois kitsch. In an article from the mid-1970s, Kristeva did acknowledge its appeal – 'from the most "sophisticated" to the most "vulgar", we cannot resist vampires or the massacres of the Western'. Moreover, in such films 'the sillier the better' because the gunplay of a routine Western or 'the alternation between horror and prettification found in porno films' may bear, both referentially and formally, relatively unmediated traces of the drive – the aggression – which motivates them. But the terrifying aspect of this terror/seduction node is soon domesticated in popular cinema; only the regulatory catharsis remains – 'in mediocre pot-boilers, … in order to remain within the range of petty bourgeois taste, film plays up to narcissistic identification, and the viewer is satisfied with "three-buck" seduction'.[24] Once again, with a saving clause for the authentically vulgar and silly, Kristeva displays the contempt and condescension for kitsch which has always been the mark of the modernist sublime.[25]

Nowhere is this more explicit than in Lyotard.[26] His aesthetic of the sublime is a response to his vision of the radical incommensurability and heterogeneity of our 'world' – the ungraspability to which artists should bear witness. The mimetic conventions of realist art and literature are not just inadequate to this. Insofar as they embody a constraining consensus of taste, they are part of the problem. It is to challenge this consensus and these conventions that painting should always pose anew the question, 'what is painting?' But what is the unpresentable that this avant-garde art of the sublime is supposed to represent?

This becomes clearer in Lyotard's distinction between two types of modernist sublime. In the sublime of *nostalgia*, the unpresentable is an absent *content* – a lost presence experienced by the human subject – which is presented in reassuringly familiar *form*. Lyotard gives the literary example of Proust, along with artists like Fuseli, Friedrich, Delacroix, Malevich, the German Expressionists and de Chirico. (So if my 'popular' sublime could sneak in anywhere, it would be here.) *Novatio* – the genuine sublime sentiment – presents the unpresentable in the form itself, emphasising 'the increase of being and the jubilation which result from the invention of new rules of the game, be it pictorial, artistic, or any other'. Thus, *contra* Proust, Joyce; and in the visual arts, Cézanne, Picasso and Braque, Lissitsky, Mondrian and Duchamp. Such works of novatio are postmodern not because they fit into some art-historical periodisation, but because they refuse art's institutional tendency to domesticate the sublime.

Why all this postmodernist fuss about the sublime? Does it represent anything more than the elevation of modernism's frisson of newness to an aesthetic principle? For Lyotard it clearly does – as his displacement of the force of the sublime/beautiful opposition onto novatio and nostalgia hints. For him, the beautiful lingers on only as a term of abuse with which to berate Habermas and his dreams of art as a culturally healing force. The implication is that Lyotard's sublime always has a political as well as an aesthetic dimension. This is evident, for example, in the tantalising call at the end of *The Postmodern Condition* for 'a politics that would respect both the desire for justice and the desire for the unknown'.[27] Here the 'desire for the unknown' is the political sublime that contrasts with Habermas's utopian desire to legislate the good society.

But can Lyotard escape the hold of norms so easily? Doesn't his 'desire for justice' itself imply acceptance of rules, of laws and of order? He claims not, because he inhabits a political landscape of discourse-genres cut off from each other by abysses. In this context, any claims to consensus or to identity – like the aesthetics of beauty or the politics of utopianism –constitute not just an unwarranted totalisation, but a form of totalitarianism. And yet, Lyotard acknowledges, despite the absence of universal norms or agreed criteria of judgment, one has to act politically, to make critical choices. It is in this disenchanted desire for justice that Lyotard's aesthetic argument takes on its political force. The sublime suggests a way of bridging the gap between the aesthetic and the historical-political: for if the sublime resides less in the artwork itself than in speculation on it, then it can become a model for political judgment. If aesthetic thought is characterised by the need to judge in the absence of determinable laws, and if you agree with Lyotard that there are no determinable laws in ethics and politics either – a whopping *if*, that – then the question of the *authority* for calculation within these spheres itself becomes the nub of the problem.

The sublime thus comes to indicate a tension between the joy of having a feeling of the totality and the inseparable sorrow of not being able to present an object equal to the Idea of that totality. As David Carroll explains, the terms in which Lyotard addresses this problem derive from Kant's conception of community.

> Central to the feeling of the sublime is the limitlessness of its determination, its aesthetic and political formlessness; in it there is a *demand* for universality, for community, and not the projection of a particular form of community as if it were universal ... The advantage of Kant's indirect presentation of the Idea of community for Lyotard is that the demand for community is felt even more strongly and can be considered universal (and thus just) only because it remains a *demand* and is not motivated or determined by any knowledge or intuition of the *form* such a community should take. The demand is there and is constant without, however, any rules determining it; the demand reveals the limitation of all rules, the necessity to go beyond them. In this way, the differences of opinion, the conflicts and disputes over the form community should take could themselves be taken as signs of the demand for community and not necessarily a threat to it. The real threat to community is when a state, society, class, party, or group pretends to know what true community is and acts to impose this ideal on society.[28]

For Lyotard, this projection of community constitutes terror. And that brings me, circuitously, back to the popular.

THE POPULAR

Not that Lyotard has much to say about the sort of popular culture I have been talking about. He is as unremittingly hostile, or uncomprehending, towards it as Adorno at his grumpiest.[29] More interesting is the way he worked through the tension he identifies between the *demand* for universality and the *imposition* of identity in relation to the idea of 'the popular', for this echoes the equivocal currency of 'the popular' in British cultural studies. In *Au Juste*, for example, he uses the popular tradition of narration among the Amazonian Cashinahua as an example of the pragmatic basis for ethics which he sees as an alternative to the classic Western explanation in terms of law and autonomy. The Cashinahua narrator is not autonomous in that he must first be a narratee; he has to hear his story before he can tell it. He thus becomes a relay in the tradition, only identifying himself at the end of the narration: 'when he gives his proper name, the teller designates himself as someone who has been narrated by the social body'.[30] For Lyotard this is a *popular* tradition insofar as the narrative does not become codified, but constantly has to be reinvented as it is repeated. It imposes an obligation to narrate, but this is not the same as the imposition of a particular content – what we might call an identity.

> The relevant feature is not faithfulness: it is not because one has pre-served the story well that one is a good narrator, at least as far as profane narratives are concerned. On the contrary, it is because one 'hams' it up, because one invents, because one inserts novel episodes that stand out as motifs against the narrative plot line, which, for its part, remains stable, that one is successful. When we say tradition, we think identity without difference, whereas there actually is very much difference: the narratives get repeated but are never identical.[31]

More recently, Lyotard has taken a greater critical distance from this example of traditional, myth-based narratives because the authority of the narrator derives from his submission to the tradition, and so eventually to an archaic 'we'.[32] This leads Lyotard to deploy the same instance to make almost a contrary case. Rather than illustrating the demand of community through the obligation to narrate, it now suggests to him the problem of what happens when a 'politics of myth' is imposed in modernity, claiming legitimacy from a mythic national tradition and distant origin. 'We respect the Amazon peoples to the extent they are not modern,' he has said in an interview, 'but when modern men make themselves into Amazons, it is monstrous.'[33]

Lyotard's example of this monstrous politics of myth is Nazi Germany. But the imposition of a universal identity in the name of an origin that should define the form of community – *the people* in the sense of a *Volk* – also takes us back to the terroristic kitsch of Mrs Thatcher's 'British character' with which I began. Nor is this solely a feature of her 'authoritarian populism' – think, for example, of less obviously malevolent cases like Ealing cinema's 'projection of Britain' or the Communist historians' epic narratives of 'the free-born Englishman'.[34]

At the same time, however, *the popular* also connotes the heteroge-neity in any social formation which remains intractable to such normative demands. Bakhtin's carnival is still the most forceful image of this, but it is also one to which Lyotard comes close when he characterises his Idea of 'the people' as 'the name of heterogeneous phrases that contradict each other and are held together by their contrariety itself.'[35]

This ambiguity between normativity and heterogeneity can be seen in the deployment of 'the popular' not only in political rhetoric, but also in aesthetic or cultural arguments. Its mobility is something else 'the popular' shares with 'the sublime'. Perhaps, in a Lyotardian gesture, we might regard both these terms as naming possible moves within the two language games of politics and aesthetics. Their juxtaposition then becomes a kind of knight's move, an advance that sidesteps the given categories of either game and shifts between the two, using the rules of one game as a principle of judgment and calculation in the other.

In aesthetics, approaching the sublime through the popular immediately undermines the Kantian differentiation of spheres by highlighting the institutions of cultural production, the sociological aspects of taste communities and the political clout of cultural capital. It also casts a new light on Lyotard's investment in the modernist sublime: judged from the perspective of, say, Bourdieu's sociology of taste, isn't this as authoritarian an aesthetic as any other?[36]

Try that the other way round:how would a popular aesthetic appear from the perspective of the Lyotardian sublime? At first sight, no doubt, it seems to be its polar opposite: a demand for kitsch, for the domestication of aesthetic experience as an adjunct of everyday life. Whereas the sublime attempt to grasp the ungraspable requires experimentation and distance, the popular demands the familiar and the delimited – even when, as in melodramas and horror films, it is dealing with anxiety, irrationality and death. But the popular always denotes a centrifugal force as well as, and in tension with, its centripetal pull towards consensus; that is why some popular forms – especially the more offensive ones – *share* with the sublime a transgression of aesthetic boundaries and decorum. So isn't it possible to argue, with the surrealists, that bad taste should take its place alongside the fantastic, the uncanny and the sublime in a carnival of resistance to the hegemony of the beautiful?

This could be one version of what's at stake in vampire films. They are not just ideological mechanisms for domesticating terror and repression in popular culture, as critics like Moretti and Wood sometimes suggest, although they are no doubt some sort of 'defence' against the violence that is the root of the socio-symbolic bond. They can therefore be seen also as symptoms of the instability of culture, the impossibility of its closure or perfection. The dialectic of repulsion and fascination in the monstrous reveals how the apparent certainties of representation are always undermined by the insistent operations of desire and terror. The lurid obsession with archaism and liminality in horror films, and their play on the uncanny ambivalences of *heim* and *unheimlich*, highlight the fragility of any identity that is wrought from abjection.

From here, another knight's move may suggest what is at stake politically in rethinking the popular through the sublime. Although Gramsci was actually concerned with fascism's 'crisis of authority' in the 1930s when he remarked that it 'consists precisely in the fact that the old is dying and the new cannot be born; in this interregnum a great variety of morbid symptoms appear',[37] he might almost have been describing those murky aspects of popular culture I have been looking at here. Gramsci's conception of crisis also recalls Lyotard's sublime insofar as both point to the way that established political categories periodically fall apart: 'the great masses have become detached from their traditional ideologies, and no longer believe what they used to believe previously'. It is this dissolution of boundaries and identities that produces the 'morbid symptoms'. These might include not only vampire films, Mussolini's 'youth question' (Gramsci's example), the hysterical misogyny of the *Freikorps* novels studied by Klaus Theweleit in *Male Fantasies*,[39] or Lyotard's example of the monstrous myths of Nazism. They would again extend to the familiar figures of contemporary political rhetoric – Thatcher's 'individuals', 'families' and 'nation', or the Left's 'people', that Golem whose inert clay awaits animation by the inscription of the arcane Word. These figures too are fictions that both express and manage the fragmentation of subjectivity and the alterity of culture.

Lyotard's 'sublime' and Gramsci's 'crisis' do not just undermine the status of political identities. They actually pose the question of politics differently, focusing less on *identity* than on *authority*. Any claim to speak in the name of 'the people' should thus be judged not in terms of the supposed accuracy or authenticity with which the interests, desires or nature of a given population are being represented, but as the assertion of a particular mode of authority. And because this entails the claim to represent the known political *form* of community – its identity – it pre-empts the agonistic negotiations that could sustain the aspiration to communality. From this point of view, new, improved 'identities' cannot provide a real alternative to the radical imperatives of a normative political culture. So could a popular politics perhaps learn from Lyotard to find new forms of calculation and mobilisation modelled on the particularising forms of aesthetic judgment – a politics concerned less with the people as an archaic myth of origins than with a pragmatics of the popular as an endless, disorderly dialogue?

Any proposal that mixes politics and aesthetics should set off alarm bells. To aestheticise politics without at the same time politicising aesthetics and so revaluing both terms is, as Walter Benjamin taught us, a move to fascism – it is what made Nazism monstrous. But the step I am trying to imagine leads in a different direction, towards a cultural politics and a political culture that take heterogeneity and fragmentation, those blunt and comic facts of life, seriously. In this future, will-o'-the-wisp 'identities' would still be conjured up by the dynamics of fantasy and desire, by the operation of cultural technologies, governmental disciplines and systems of representation, and by the interaction between them – just as they always have been. The mistake is to found a politics on the expression or perfection of such identities. Instead, as Frantz Fanon insisted in a phrase that recalls the uncertainties and hesitations of Todorov's fantastic, 'it is to the zone of occult instability where the people dwell that we must come'.[39] What would a politics appropriate to such a shadowy borderland look like? It would still require worldly political calculation – always that. From the 'sublime' it might learn an attention to the materiality and limits of representation, and to their inevitable inadequacy to the idea of totality; and so also a certain pragmatic modesty. And, not least, form the transgressive and creative aspects of popular culture it might learn not only the impossibility of political closure but also the critical possibilities of social and cultural heterogeneity for an aspiration towards community that always remains to be brought into being. Maybe, taking our cue from what Wittgenstein learnt in his afternoons at the cinema, this could be one line of thought opened up by a despised and silly popular form like the vampire film.

NOTES

1 Sigmund Freud, *The Standard Edition of the Complete Psychological Works of Sigmund Freud*, ed. and trans. James Strachey (London: The Hogarth Press, 1953–66), vol. I, p. 243 (cit. Roger Dadoun, 'Fetishism in the horror film', this volume, p. 44.).

2 Julia Kristeva, *Powers of Horror: an essay on abjection* (New York: Columbia University Press, 1982), p. 11.

3. Sarah Benton, 'Monsters from the deep', *New Statesman*, 19 October 1984 (quoted in Jacqueline Rose, below, p. 27.); Laura Mulvey, 'Changes: thoughts on myth, narrative and historical experience', *History Workshop Journal*, no. 23 (London: Routledge & Kegan Paul, Spring 1987), p. 5; Michael Rogin, *Ronald Reagan, the Movie, and Other Episodes in Political Demonology* (Berkeley: University of California Press, 1987), p. xiii; Jacqueline Rose, 'Margaret Thatcher and Ruth Ellis', *New Formations*, no. 6, Winter 1988/9, p. 17.

4 Franco Moretti, 'Dialectic of fear', in *Signs Taken for Wonders* (London: Verso, 1983), p. 105.

5 Robin Wood, 'An introduction to the American horror film', in Bill Nichols (ed.), *Movies and Methods, vol. II* (Berkeley: University of California Press, 1985), pp. 201, 203.

6 Moretti, 'Dialectic of fear', p. 108; Wood, 'American horror film', p. 196.

7 Fredric Jameson, 'Magical narratives: on the dialectical use of genre criticism', in *The Political Unconscious: narrative as a socially symbolic act* (London: Methuen, 1981), p. 115.

8 Tzvetan Todorov, *The Fantastic: a structural approach to a literary genre* (Ithaca: Cornell University Press, 1973), p. 25.

9 Ibid., p. 120.

10 Ibid., p. 168.

11 Thomas Elsaesser, 'Social mobility and the fantastic: German silent cinema', reprinted in this volume, pp. 23–38.

12 Freud, 'The "uncanny"', *Art and Literature, The Penguin Freud Library*, vol. 14 (Harmondsworth: Penguin, 1985), p. 373.

13 For a useful summary, see Elizabeth Wright, *Psychoanalytic Criticism: theory in practice* (London: Methuen, 1984), p. 142ff.

14 Hélène Cixous, 'Fiction and its phantoms: a reading of Freud's "Das Unheimliche" ("The 'uncanny'")', *New Literary History*, vol. 7, Spring 1976, pp. 540, 543, 544, 545.

15 See Harold Bloom, 'Freud and the sublime: a catastrophe theory of creativity', in *Agon* (Oxford: Oxford University Press, 1982).

16 Edmund Burke, *A Philosophical Enquiry into the Origin of our Ideas of the Sublime and Beautiful* [1757], ed. James T. Boulton (London: Routledge & Kegan Paul), 1958, p. 58.

17 Here and in the following paragraphs I draw extensively on Paul Crowther, 'The Kantian sublime, the avant-garde, and the postmodern: a critique of Lyotard', *New Formations*, no. 7, Spring 1989.

18 On the Gothic novel, see Mario Praz, *The Romantic Agony* [1933] (London: Oxford University Press, 1970); on its relationship to horror films, see David Pirie, *A Heritage of Horror: the English Gothic cinema 1946–1972* (London: Gordon Fraser, 1973) and S. S. Prawer, *Caligari's Children: the film12as tale of terror* (Oxford: Oxford University Press, 1980).

19 David Morris, 'Gothic sublimity', *New Literary History*, vol. XVI, no. 2, Winter 1985, p. 311.

20 Peter Brooks, *The Melodramatic Imagination* (New York: Columbia University Press, 1985), p. 20.

21 Ibid., p. 5.

22 Kristeva, *Powers of Horror*, pp. 4, 2, 9–10, 12.

23 See Scott Lash, 'Postmodernity and desire', *Theory and Society*, no. 14, 1985, pp. 4, 8.

24 Julia Kristeva, 'Ellipsis on dread and the specular seduction', *Wide Angle*, vol. 3, no. 3, 1979, pp. 44, 46.

25 John Rajchman, *Michel Foucault: the freedom of philosophy* (New York: Columbia University Press, 1985), pp. 17–18.

26 My account of Lyotard's sublime borrows from Crowther, 'The Kantian sublime'; Meaghan Morris, 'Postmodernity and Lyotard's sublime', *Art & Text*, no. 16, Summer 1984/5; and David Carroll, 'Rephrasing the political with Kant and Lyotard: from aesthetic to political judgments', *Diacritics*, Fall 1984.

27 Jean-Francois Lyotard, *The Postmodern Condition: a report on knowledge* (Manchester: Manchester University Press, 1984), p. 67.

28 Carroll, 'Rephrasing the political', pp. 83–4.

29 See, for example, his rather bemused response to three papers on popular culture at an ICA event in London, 1985. He suggests they are 'a little hasty with their concessions to what is positive in these forms of pop culture or mass culture' and suggests as an alternative television programmes or whatever which 'produce in the viewer or the client in general an effect of uncertainty and trouble.' Lisa Appignanesi (ed.), *Postmodernism: ICA Documents 4/5* (London: Institute of Contemporary Arts, 1986), p. 58.

30 Jean-Francois Lyotard and Jean-Loup Thébaud, *Just Gaming* (Mancester: Manchester University Press), 1985, p. 32.

31 Ibid., p. 33.

32 See David Carroll, 'Narrative, heterogeneity, and the question of the political: Bakhtin and Lyotard', in Murray Krieger (ed.), *The Aims of Representation: subject/text/ history* (New York: Columbia University Press, 1987), pp. 100–1.

33 Cit. in ibid., p. 101.

34 As a *mea culpa*, I could add as a further example the Open University's *Popular Cutlure* course, which elided significant differences in writing a genealogy of an English national-popular identity.

35 Cit. in Carroll, 'Narrative, heterogeneity, . . .', p. 106.

36 See, for example, Pierre Bourdieu, *Distinction: a social critique of the judgement of taste* (London: Routledge & Kegan Paul, 1984).

37 Antonio Gramsci, *Selections from the Prison Notebooks*, ed. and trans. Quintin Hoare and Geoffrey Nowell-Smith (London: Lawrence & Wishart, 1971), p. 276.

38 Klaus Theweleit, *Male Fantasies*, vol. 1 (Cambridge: Polity Press, 1987).

39 Frantz Fanon, *The Wretched of the Earth* (Harmondsworth: Penguin, 1967), pp. 182–3; quoted in Homi K. Bhabha, 'The commitment to theory', *New Formations*, no. 5, Summer 1988, p. 19.

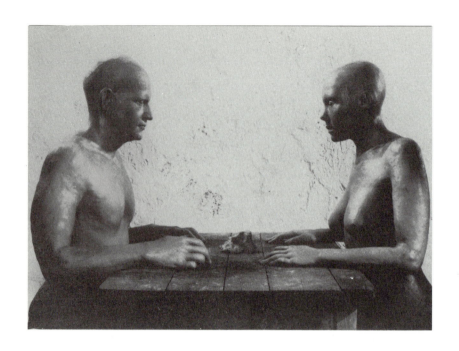

Dimensions of Dialogue (Jan Švankmajer, 1982)

Surrealism, Fantasy and the Grotesque
The Cinema of Jan Švankmajer
MICHAEL O'PRAY

'We are not concerned,' he said, 'with long-winded creations, with long-term beings. Our creatures will not be heroes of romances in many volumes. Their roles will be short, concise; their characters – without background. Sometimes, for one gesture, for one word alone, we shall make the effort to bring them to life ... our creations will be temporary, to serve for a single occasion. If they be human beings, we shall give them, for example, only one profile, one hand, one leg, the one limb needed for their role ...'

The strange, yet insightful, words of the bizarre father in Bruno Schulz's book *The Street of Crocodiles* are to be found in the section titled 'Treatise on Tailors' Dummies, or The Second Book of Genesis'.[1] In some other possible world, they could equally have been found in a film animation handbook, for they describe not only the art of animation but also its very nature. In trying to understand the elusive and hybrid character of animation, I would argue, more is to be gained from a study of writers like Schulz, Kafka, de Sade and Mikhail Bakhtin and of painters like Arcimboldo, Hieronymous Bosch and Max Ernst than from most contemporary film theory and criticism.

This, in any case, is the perspective from which I approach the work of Jan Švankmajer, which has only become well known outside Czechoslovakia in recent years.[2] Since he first encountered film-making as a member of the Laterna Magika Theatre in 1960, Švankmajer has made about twenty films – including *The Last Trick* (1964), *Punch and Judy* (1966), *Historia Naturae Suita* (1967), *The Flat* (1968), *Don Juan* (or *Don Shayn*) (1970), *Jabberwocky* (1971), *Dimensions of Dialogue* (1982) and *Down to the Cellar* (1983). Rich in imagination, strikingly theatrical and saturated by a black humour and the cruellest melancholy, these films combine animation – trick photography, marionettes, puppets and three-dimensional modelling – with live action to produce an overall collage effect. Technically, they are brilliant: in the speed and immaculate timing of the editing, for instance, and in Švankmajer's use of camera movement or movement within the frame in the transition from one shot to the next. In *Don Juan*, to take one example, the speed and immaculate timing of the editing are evident when the blur of a fast pan is brought to a heart-stopping halt with a completely static image; Švankmajer's use of camera movement is exemplified by its nervous exploration of the surfaces of walls, chairs and floors; his use of movement within the frame in the transition from one shot to the next is revealed when a slow tracking shot blocked by an intervening wall is used to cut closer to the object tracked; and so on.

What relates Švankmajer to the writers and painters mentioned above is his fascination with the grotesque and the morbid, and his explorations of surface materiality and texture. In trying to place his work, we can clearly set it against Hollywood's mainstream narrative genres and the naturalism or realism of much European art cinema. Although in many ways recognisably part of the same tradition of East European animation as Starevich and Trnka,[3] it remains unique in the way it combines its various elements. Švankmajer, I think, belongs above all among those film-makers whose work spills over forcibly into forms of representation – Gothic horror, Hollywood fantasy, sci-fi, vulgar comedy, grotesquerie and even modernism itself – which rupture or exceed the dominant cinematic conventions. The roll-call of such film-makers – the *alchemists of the surreal* as I have called them – would include Georges Méliès, Joseph Cornell, Zbigniew Rybczinski, Walerian Borowczyk, Luis Buñuel, Jeff Keen, the Brothers Quay, Jean Painlevé, David Lynch, Georges Franju, David Cronenberg, Peter Greenaway, Roger Corman, Juraj Herz, Roman Polanski and Harry Smith. They are alchemists in the sense that they blend disparate materials in the service of fantasy; they endow the real, the very materiality of the world – its objects, surfaces and textures – with an aura of strangeness and the fantastic.

Apart from these characteristics being evident in Švankmajer's films, the analogy is apt is another way, too. The fantastic elements in his work are firmly grounded in the materiality of substances and elements – just as alchemy was, despite its reputation as an unworldly and metaphysical practice. (Alchemy did, after all, become one of the foundations of modern western science in the seventeenth century.) In a similar way, the surrealism of these film-makers – and Švankmajer in particular – puts the emphasis on its *real* component. Surrealism, as his films admirably display, is not simply a matter of 'irrational' fantasy: it also involves a particular relationship to the real and its properties.

When Švankmajer proclaims himself a 'militant surrealist', he places himself in an established Czech tradition. A surrealist movement was first formed there about 1933, and it was formalised when André Breton visited Prague with Paul Eluard in 1935 (the year after Švankmajer was born there). It flowered in the years that followed, with Karel Teige as its leading theoretician, enthusiastically supported by Zavis Kalandra (who was also a member of the Communist Press Directorate). It declined in the 1940s and 50s under the impact of Stalinism: of its most prominent members, Teige was persecuted until his death in 1951, Kalandra was purged and Toyen moved to Paris. The present-day Czech surrealist group stresses its collective base and centres its activities around poetry and dream analysis. Švankmajer was introduced into it in 1969 by its theorist, Vratislav Effenberger; his wife, the painter and writer Eva Švankmajerova, is also a member.[5]

Although he adheres to the Breton orthodoxy, Švankmajer's surrealism is provocatively inflected by Czechoslovakian culture – and especially perhaps by Prague, which Breton thought had a major influence on surrealism. Using Apollinaire's phrase, he called it 'the magical capital of Europe' and he praised

> ... its magnificent bridge with the topiary statues, leading from yesterday to *forever*; its electric signs which were illuminated from within rather than on the surface – the Black Sun, the Golden Wheel, the Golden Tree ... its clock whose hands, cast from the metal of desire, turned anti-clockwise; its Alchemists' Streets and ... that intense unparalleled seething of ideas and hopes ... aspiring to wed poetry and revolution.[6]

Two artistic traditions in Czechoslovakia have also an important influence on Švankmajer's films. The first is its puppet and marionette tradition, from which much of their imagery is derived. His early training was in the Marionette Faculty at the Academy of Fine Arts in Prague, and he also worked as a theatre director in association with the Theatre of Masks and the famous Black Theatre. The other is the painting of Giuseppe Arcimboldo, whose bizarre portraits – made up of fish, fruit, vegetables and books – were produced in the Vienna and Prague courts of Maximilian II and Rudolf II respectively in the late sixteenth century, when it was the centre of Bohemian mannerism and Cabbalism.[7] Their unsettling merging of the concrete and fantasy, which is echoed in Švankmajer's films, no doubt accounts in part for the surrealists' fascination with him.

It is the integration of surrealism with these Czech cultural forms of puppetry and mannerist art that I want to explore in Švankmajer's films. I shall do so by looking particularly at their *humour*, their use of *effigies* and their modernist attention to the *materiality* of objects. This approach should make it possible to grasp their relationship to the idea of fantasy.

THE GROTESQUE & THE UNCANNY

The humour in Švankmajer's films is ambivalent: the laugh is often quickly stifled by a dramatic twist or image that resonates with the horrific, the macabre and repulsive. This ambivalence, which also threads through Kafka's novels and stories, is at the root of the black humour characteristic of much East European art. It is equally familiar, of course, to the child immersed in nursery tales and rhymes – so it is appropriate that there is a strong emphasis on the nursery in all its facets if Švankmajer's work. His version of Lewis Carroll's *Jabberwocky* is about a nursery in which all the objects – a suit of clothes, dolls, toy soldiers – come to life. *The Last Trick* involves marionettes and magicians who compete to perform the best trick and end up tearing each other to pieces; it is obviously based on puppet theatre. In

Down to the Cellar, a young girl has a series of nightmarish encounters on her way down to collect potatoes.

How should we understand this ambivalent humour? One starting point, I think, is a distinction that Rosemary Jackson makes in her book *Fantasy: the literature of subversion* between the grotesque and the uncanny. Following Wolfgang Kayser's definition, she suggests that the grotesque is a structure – 'it is the estranged world, our world, which has been transformed' – whereas the uncanny has no structure: 'it empties the "real" of its "meaning", it leaves signs without significance'.[8] Although hardly a model of clarity, the difference Jackson is getting at here is an interesting one in terms of Švankmajer's films – which on the whole seem closer to the grotesque than to the uncanny.

Freud, in his essay on the topic, argued that an uncanny effect cannot be achieved in a 'world of representation' which departs from 'the realities we are familiar with' – that is why, for him, the fairy-tale rarely evokes the uncanny. Equally, Freud pointed out that feelings associated with the uncanny – fear, horror, menace – can be undermined, transformed and neutralised by, for instance, comic effects. This suggests that Švankmajer's material, which constantly meshes humour and horror, is more likely to be identified with the grotesque – which is, in any case, a prominent feature of the Czech puppet tradition.

The grotesque shares with caricature both the quality of exaggeration and also this characteristic blend of the humorous and the horrific. Writing in collaboration with Ernst Gombrich, Ernst Kris notes that the 'double-edged character of our experience of the grotesque' is determined by the history of the form – as the 'sinister world of Bosch', for example, is transformed into the comic world of sixteenth-century woodcuts (such as those which appeared in 1569 under the name of Rabelais).[9] Etymologically, the term 'grotesque' refers to figurative decorations dating back at least as far as the first century AD, which were rediscovered in newly unearthed Roman grottos at the end of the fifteenth century. In these decorations, human, animal and vegetable forms were blended 'in bizarre but consistently elegant combinations.'[10] Although they inspired some aspects of the High Renaissance, their ambivalence was more in tune with the disconcerting artifice of Mannerism. 'By the word *grottesco*,' states Wolfgang Kayser, 'the Renaissance ... understood not only something playfully gay and carelessly fantastic, but also something ominous and sinister.'[11] Here the link to Švankmajer is clear. In *Dimensions of Dialogue*, he creates head-and-shoulder figures from household utensils, fruit and vegetables. These devour each other and then spew out more objects which metamorphose into a further figure – which then devours the other, and so forth until the various objects are reduced to a primeval sludge. The final figures are made of a clay-like material. The film's imagery and the 'composite heads' are self-consciously derived from Arcimboldo's grotesque portraits – as seen with a surrealist's eye.

Some of Švankmajer's other films seem closer to the uncanny – *Don Juan*, *The Fall of the House of Usher* and *Down to the Cellar*, for example – but even here any uncanny effect is generally outweighed both by formal devices, like the trick photography, and also by the grotesque elements within them. In *Don Juan*, these are represented by the marionettes, and in *The Fall of the House of Usher* by the battling trees and moving coffin. *Down to the Cellar* seems to be the closest that Švankmajer comes to the uncanny. This can be attributed to the use of a (live action) young girl as the central character, with whose terror we can identify, and also to its more naturalistic setting. (The girl meets other inhabitants of an apartment block on her way downstairs.) Even here, however, the reappearance of these figures in her journey through the cellar seems, in Freud's terms, more like a fairy tale than a genuine uncanny episode.

In this context, it is worth noting one of the most remarkable features of Freud's essay: its insight into the elements in a narrative which *prevent* it from producing an uncanny effect. He explicitly identifies humour as one. One might add another which seems to be implicit in his argument and which is particularly applicable to film – the presence of formal devices which distance the reader or spectator. Both these, as I have suggested, are relevant to Švankmajer.

Kris is in no doubt about the role of humour in the grotesque. What distinguishes the grotesque from the comic, he argues, is its reliance on the mechanism of relief from anxiety. The humour lies in a prior increase in tension, and in the grotesque that relief is sudden and surprising. This element of humour is notably absent from Kayser's account. His gloomily deterministic view of the grotesque as the 'alienated world' which expresses the id (which also underpins Jackson's summary) is challenged by Mikhail Bakhtin in *Rabelais and his World*.[12] This definition, claims Bakhtin, is inherently subjectivist – and it is also unable to account for either Romantic or Pre-Romantic versions of the grotesque.

In contrast, Bakhtin emphasises the freedom and laughter of the grotesque (thus recalling Ernst Kris's writings on caricature) and also its relationship to the carnivalesque and to what he calls the 'material bodily lower stratum'. Bakhtin is concerned with the public, the outer and the surface rather than the private, the interior and the psychologistic: his is primarily a social and historical account of the grotesque, in opposition to psychoanalytical interpretations. To this extent, his views remain within the classic marxist model. In contrast to Kayser, he denies any determining force to the unconscious. More importantly, Bakhtin sees in the history of the grotesque a degeneration from its medieval and renaissance forms to its twentieth-century descendants like surrealism, which he refers to as 'modernist' versions.

Both these aspects of Bakhtin's work raise interesting questions about the grotesque in Švankmajer's films. His use of puppets and marionettes is not only anti-realist, but also anti-psychologistic. In this context, the problem of *Down to the Cellar* can be seen as an ambiguity between a subjectivist narrative and an anti-psychologistic one, with the grotesque elements being neutralised by the identification with the internal states of the central character, the little girl. (It is in this sort of ambiguity that an uncanny effect can be created.)

His anti-psychologism also helps to define the particular nature of Švankmajer's surrealism. Although at least one of surrealism's main tendencies can be identified with the idea of projected internal, unconscious states – thus falling into Bakhtin's view of a degenerated 'modernist' grotesque – Švankmajer's refraction of surrealism through Czech cultural forms like puppetry and mannerist art curbs any such tendencies. In conversation, Švankmajer has dissociated himself from the East European art cinema of Wajda, Polanski and so forth that emerged in the 1960s in terms of his antipathy towards existentialist characters and narratives, with their projection of interior states. In this, Švankmajer shares the early surrealists' distrust of what they called 'bourgeois narrative' – along also with Buñuel, whose work focuses on the surfaces of social life, on symbols and the essential incoherence of conscious existence, without reducing the unconscious to the 'true' expression of some fundamental reality.

Bakhtin's account of the grotesque also suggests the nature of the political dimension to Švankmajer's work. Historically, according to Bakhtin, the grotesque liberated thought and imagination through degeneration, low humour (the marxian 'belly-laugh') and a celebration of the body's 'base' functions. The grotesque is thus a sign of resistance, a symbolic destruction of official culture. It is also a communal act of assertion and renewal. It is this original medieval and Renaissance conception that Švankmajer seems to share, rather than the Romantic and 'modernist' manifestations of the grotesque, which Bakhtin sees as subjectivist, deterministic and marginalised as 'high art'. Švankmajer has deplored the corruption of Western surrealism by its assimilation into capitalist advertising and popular imagery. His films should not be read as political allegories in any simple way – and certainly not through Cold War or ultra-leftist ideologies which would see the dehumanised puppets, marionettes and effigies in them as a metaphor for the status of people in Eastern Europe. This would be to ignore the presence of such figures, which is a key aspect of the grotesque in his work, in a much longer tradition of East European art. It would also fail to see the criticism (intended or not) of Western culture and values in Švankmajer's films. Like the grotesque and caricature – and also like Bakhtin's ideas about carnival – they do not push a particular political line. Instead, they reassert the freedom of imagination and the possibilities of art within a popular mode.

MARIONETTES, PUPPETS & OTHER EFFIGIES

The puppet tradition in Czechoslovakia dates from the sixteenth century, and its popularity was spread by touring troupes from England, Germany, Holland and Italy. Its repertoire was drawn less from fairy tales than from a wide range of sources that included Shakespeare, the Bible and the myths of Faustus and Don Juan; it also contained echoes of the *comedia dell'arte*. Between 1750 and 1848, one function of the wandering marionette theatres (a distinct tradition from that of puppetry) was to uphold the Czech language against the German widely used in urban areas. For a long time, argues Max von Boehn in his book *Puppets and Automata*, the marionette theatre formed 'the only dramatic art among nations without their own culture as, for example, the Czechs.'[13] As recently as the beginning of World War Two, there were still two hundred puppet theatres in Czechoslovakia (only fifty-three survived in its aftermath). As a relatively popular form which has produced artists like Karel Dodal, Hermina Tyrlova and Trnka and which is taken seriously by the art establishment (witness Švankmajer's early training), puppet theatre should perhaps be seen as part of a continuing need to protect Czech culture.

The best example of Švankmajer's use of puppets together with trick photography is probably *Punch and Judy*. The film ends with the hands of the puppeteer being revealed and disappearing under the stage, their work finished. Marionettes also appear in *Don Juan* and *The Last Trick*. Those in *Don Juan* are made to look antiquated, and their design seems to be based on the work of the eighteenth-century Czech woodcarver and puppeteer Frantisek Vida. In other films a variety of effigies are used – the animated photographs, dolls, toy soldiers and sailor's suit in *Jabberwocky* and the clay modelling or 'composite' constructions in *Dimensions of Dialogue* and *A Game with Stones*.

Punch and Judy (Jan Švankmajer, 1966)

Effigies have been used by many artists in this century, especially by surrealists like Hans Bellmer.[14] A particularly close parallel to Švankmajer, however, is the Belgian 'absurd' dramatist Michel de Ghelderode, whose work is imbued with the influence of pre-capitalist music and painting and by popular art forms. Part of his theatrical aesthetic is his fascination, shared by Švankmajer, with 'marionettes, dolls, puppets, little rag creatures that children of today scorn – also dummies with lovely mortal faces of wax, models of hands, adorable heads of young martyrs, severed by what executioner'.[15] Ghelderode suggests that such effigies of childhood were responsible for 'their disclosure of the theatre, the theatre in its pure state, the theatre in its violent state, the original theatre'. Implicit here is the idea of theatre as a repetitive reworking of childhood fantasies, themselves informed by primitive phantasies. Ghelderode remarks:

> ... the marionette was then my toy, my favourite toy, even my passion – other toys gave me no pleasure. But even then I believed – and this strange belief is not yet dead in me – that objects were sensitive, living.[16]

In the Bakhtinian sense, this can be seen as a modernist idea of the effigy as the location of the displaced phantasies which are often responsible for the appearance of the uncanny. The marionette, in theatre and animation, is an appropriately morbid and menacing figuration of the alienated being, at odds with the world and somehow soul-less, that one also finds in the writings of Kafka and Schulz or the films of the Quay Brothers.

This is partly due, no doubt, to the residual animism that Freud sees as one source of the uncanny – the projection of mental properties onto the world and its objects.[17] But the idea of the dehumanised self, of the subject at the mercy of some deterministic force or impulse, whether pathological or ideological, is also central to the uncanny scenario proposed both in Kayser's view of the grotesque and in Freud's analysis of Hoffmann's story *The Sandman*. The stiffness of wooden effigies recalls both the erect phallus and *rigor mortis* – and so neatly encapsulates the dual aspects of castratory anxiety. It also lends weight to the argument of writers like Hélène Cixous that the uncanny (and uncanny effigies like the animated doll in *The Sandman*) are representative not only of sexual anxiety but also of the ultimate encounter with death. And, like Freud, Cixous points out that 'our unconscious has as little use now as it ever had for the idea of its own mortality'.[18]

It would be wrong to press these arguments about the morbidity of marionettes in relation to Švankmajer's use of them. As Freud notes, the uncanniness of the animation of inanimate objects is often deflected in children's tales through explicitly fantasy scenarios or through humour. In a similar way, *Punch and Judy* and *Jabberwocky* display their anarchic wit and their techniques (rapid editing, close-ups, quick pans) to emphasise the more robust qualities of the comic, the grotesque and the ironic. In *Jabberwocky*, for example, it is objects like the wriggling maggots in the apple, the blood-flowing pocket-knife and the animated stones, bottles and irons which express the corruption and violence lurking in the real, rather than the effigies. It is true that dolls are seen to devour 'infant' dolls, that small dolls appear through the rips in a straw doll and that others are manically fed through a mechanical mincer. Even so, the central effigy in the film – a boy's sailor suit – is a joyful and innocent character.

Švankmajer's most perturbing use of effigies is to be found in *Don Juan*. Like *The Fall of the House of Usher* and *The Ossuary*, this opens with a hand-held camera shot entering a house – thus stressing spectator point-of-view. Then we are shown the marionettes with their ancient faces, their paint peeling and their wood worn with time and use, lined against a wall awaiting their human manipulators. The action begins with the marionettes in a theatre with mock strings and what are obviously actors in marionette-head props. To complicate the illusion and counter-illusions, Švankmajer turns the camera from the stage to reveal a marionette watching the play. The action then takes place in the streets, with the actor-marionettes plotting and fighting in real exterior locations. Through such devices, the film is made to balance ambiguously on a fine edge between puppetry and live-action, and the spectator's feelings towards the characters are not distanced in the same way they would be in purely animated film. Undoubtedly, however, they *are* distanced – but in ways more akin to the use of masks in certain forms of Japanese theatre or to Brecht's anti-naturalistic dramaturgy. When one of the characters is killed, the sword carves down through the head, leaving the smoothly split wood as a blank, featureless face. Equally macabre and grotesque is the image of a character pierced by a sword through the face, from which blood theatrically spurts. What might be a comic image here pushes the grotesque to the edge of the tragic. His skill in handling this uneasy concoction of the tragic and the grotesque is one of the things that distinguishes Švankmajer's films from the traditional puppet animation film.

THE TURMOIL OF THE MATERIAL

The grotesque qualities of Švankmajer's work and his use of effigies are both intimately connected with the *materiality* of his filmic universe. If any one process or any one kind of image dominates here, it is the animation of objects themselves – the magical transformation of things which gives an overwhelming sense of their textures and 'thingness'. The slicing away of the wooden face in *Don Juan* which I have mentioned already is just one example of this. The mud in which the tree stumps fight in *The Fall of the House of Usher* echoes the 'mud' pulp in *Dimensions of Dialogue*. In *The Flat* a bed is reduced instantly to shreds, and in *House of Usher* a coffin. The crushed fruit and vegetables in *Dimensions* recalls the instantly corrupted apple breaking up to reveal squirming maggots in *Jabberwocky*. An obsession with crumbling, decaying walls runs through *The Flat*, *House of Usher*, *Don Juan* and *The Ossuary*: Švankmajer's camera often moves in close-up over objects in a way that accentuates both the abstract patterns of decay and its strong tactile qualities.

At the same time, Švankmajer's work is an exceptional testament to the sheer resilient materiality of the world: the two most common elements in his films are wood and stone. This, perhaps surprisingly, can also be seen as an aspect of his surrealism. Although the surrealist movement has become identified with the irrationality of the imagination and the oozings of the unconscious, one might argue that 'the shock or trauma of the real' is just as central to it. Again, a comparison with Buñuel is apt. Part of the uniqueness of his first film, *Un Chien Andalou*, is its insistence on the physical qualities of objects. The bulbous liquidity of the eye provokes its attendant phantasies of vulnerability and horror as the razor slices through it, just as the ants crawling over the hands is a sign of the sensitivity of the skin and *its* attendant horrors. The monumentality and inertia of dead flesh is all too evident as the donkey carcases are dragged across the room. In *L'Age d'Or*, the cold eroticism of stone is emphasised by the man sucking the statue's toe.

In a similar way, Švankmajer uses the characteristic properties of objects as the basis for the animated life he gives them. (He has described objects as being sensitive and believes that we have an obligation to respect them. This reflects not some bizarre metaphysics, but an aesthetic principle – the idea that materials have qualities which should not be distorted by the artist's work on them.) Thus many of the fantasies expressed in Švankmajer's films operate not at the level of content: in the pure surrealist manner, they are simply extensions of the intrinsic nature of things – a material one always. In his version of Poe's *The Fall of the House of Usher*, Švankmajer creates a physical environment where the ground cracks and erupts, where a gnarled dead tree takes on a life of its own and crawls crab-like through mud and water, where a coffin explodes and where chairs and coffins move through the castle. *The Flat* likewise explores the violence of the world of objects through their material qualities.

Švankmajer shares this concern with surface, texture and physical properties with many forms of twentieth-century art. The tendency to abstraction in much avant-garde painting and sculpture, and their emphasis on the canvas, the paint, the stone and so forth, was the other side of the tendency towards actuality and the 'found object' in dada and surrealist art. Despite Dali's dislike of M. Mondrian's 'lozenges', in artists like Hans Richter and Marcel Duchamp the surrealist and dadaist project intermingled with a more formalist trait – mainly a constructivist one. At this highly general level, this materiality can be equated with modernity, even in surrealism where it is embroiled with questions of fantasy and symbolic figuration.

In this weak sense, Švankmajer's concern with materiality is a sign of his modernist aesthetic; so too is the reflexivity exemplified by the hands of the puppet master at the beginning and end of *Punch and Judy* or by the use of theatrical and filmic space in *Don Juan*. But another sort of materiality is also evident in his films. This is materiality in the sense of physicality – a fascination with Bakhtin's 'material bodily lower stratum'. Bakhtin discusses medieval man's familiarity with the grotesque body:

> Both in literature and pictorial art, the body of mixed parts and the strangest anatomical fantasies, the free play with the human limbs and interior organs were unfolded before him. The transgression of the limits dividing the body from the world became almost customary.[19]

Orifices were a central feature of these fantasies, especially the mouth. The 'gaping jaws' of hell were often a backdrop to the medieval mystery plays; in Rabelais the mouth and anus are the sites of transgressions – spitting, vomiting, farting, shitting, cannibalism and so forth. Švankmajer's work reveals the same obsession with orifices: the spewing out of the Arcimboldian figures after being devoured in *Dimensions of Dialogue* is the supreme example. But this grotesque view of the body is already there in his first film, *The Last Trick*, where the two duelling magicians are reduced to tearing each other apart until only an arm of each remains.

This aspect of Švankmajer's physicality is clearly linked to the persistent fragmentation of objects, which I have already described. These are not just instances of technical bravura: they are also a key to his humour, which turns largely on the battle between the human and an external world of animated and often hostile objects. Its significance can best be understood, perhaps, by seeing it in the context of what Petr Kral has to say in his article on the 'surrealism' of the silent Hollywood comic Larry Semon.[20] Semon, argues Kral, exploits an 'elementary violence'. Objects and bodies are violently conjoined so that a 'spiritual, human sense of this pitiless "settling of accounts" ' is represented 'in the name of repressed aggression'. This quality, which is lacking in the 'humanist coquetry' of Chaplin, can also be found in Mack Sennett.

> In the shorts produced by Mack Sennett a liberating *quantitative* squandering (entire companies of cops and bathing beauties chasing solitary heroes, not to mention the cataclysmic accumulation of catastrophies) is dialectically linked to a sense of the singular *quality* of certain elements and objects which perform a relatively constant role in Sennett's variable universe and give it the quality of an irrational *system* (custard pies, false beards, Model T Fords, hosepipes).[21]

Semon's 'fine sense of the materiality of things', claims Kral, enables him to make use of 'the singular facility cinema has of integrating the imaginary *directly* with the real'. In a Freudian vein, he identifies in Semon's work – and also in Harpo Marx's antics – an 'oral-sadistic' and cannibalistic relationship to reality. Such projection of aggressive phantasies comprising infantile impulses is not limited to Hollywood slapstick. It reappears in many of the things I have been discussing: the surrealist attitude to the world, the carnivals described by Bakhtin, the writing of Kafka – and, of course, Švankmajer's animation.

The same manic vision of a fundamentally malevolent external world which has to be defeated at all costs is also at the core of de Sade's writings. Here the conflict with Nature is also an attempt to *become* Nature, an impossible desire. The frantic cruelty of the *120 Days of Sodom* is in this sense the precursor of the Švankmajerian sensibility. Common to both is their physicality, their manic aggression, their reduction to lists, their mechanical means of achieving cruel ends and their pessimism shot through with the grotesque. Above all, they share the desire for a freedom which cannot be satisfied by the ends of government.

PHANTASY & FANTASY

So far, I have drawn out certain features, or conditions, of Švankmajer's work – surrealism, the grotesque, the puppetry tradition, a modernist aesthetic of materiality, and so on. Now I want to relate his work to the idea of fantasy – or, more precisely, to the Kleinian conception of phantasy developed by Adrian Stokes in his writings on art.

In modern art, Stokes argued, the 'massive illusionism' of the Renaissance period has been replaced by a new principle of collage – often characterised by a 'brassy element of shock, impact or arrest'. The Cubist collages saw the first literal importation of actuality (newspaper fragments, tickets and other objects or partial objects) into art; it then passed both into dadaism and also into the modernist school's veneration of the picture plane, canvas, paint and gesture. This importation of actuality has implications for the way phantasy is expressed in art.

> Actuality and phantasy can be regarded as partners, and equal partners at that. Reduce actuality and you are reducing the character of phantasy as such. Phantasy, projections, symbolic constructions, are no longer considered gratuitous, 'unreal', even imaginative. They reflect psychic structure and hence form the root of art. Phantasy and actuality do not only curb each other: 'straight' actuality is in fact the origin of 'straight' phantasy. Thus the modern sculptor does not begin to disguise the stone that he works. There is the stone and there is the stone that is made evocative.[22]

So in Švankmajer, for example, the edit is emphasised and allowed its part in the fantasies. In his films there is no easy distinction between form and content: the fragmentation celebrated in the imagery is part and parcel of the fragmentation of the editing itself. This encourages a view of his work in terms of Melanie Klein's ideas about part-objects.[23]

According to Klein, the primitive phantasies that dominate the paranoid-schizoid position in infancy contain concrete representations of part-objects: the breast, the penis, the mouth, the anus, the vagina. Their purpose is to provide a defence, primarily through mechanisms of denial and splitting, against the aggressive impulses of the early months of infancy – although these remain as psychical components throughout life. For Klein, phantasies saturate the physical activities of the body; at the same time, these activities lend structure and a mechanism to phantasy itself. Freud describes this process in his paper on 'Negation'.[24] He conceives affirmation and denial – that is, the mental acts of judgment which are the cornerstone of language – as being modelled on, respectively, the acts of swallowing and spitting, or for that matter any acts of taking-in or expelling (sucking, eating, vomiting, retaining faeces, urinating and so forth). From this, it follows that the fragmentation and aggressive nature of material involved in the paranoid-schizoid position are to be found in all forms of representation and perception.

In Stokes' writings, this aggressive fragmentation is associated with the 'invitation to art'[25] and its incantory drawing in of the spectator. Strong montage effects, highly delineated *mise en scène*, music overlay, point-of-view shots, close-ups and, in Švankmajer's case, overwrought and manic subject matter contribute to this envelopment of the spectator. Unlike certain kinds of realist and formalist cinema, his films are not experienced as separate and external. The point is that phantasy is not to be identified solely with diegetic characters and the complexities of narratives. It is embedded in the film as a whole, and especially in its form. As Stokes argues:

> Formal relationships themselves entail a representation or imagery of their own, though these likenesses are not as explicit as the images we obtain from what we call the subject-matter.[26]

The paradox is that the very familiarity and ritualism of the fantastic traditions on which Švankmajer draws – fairy tales, marionette theatre, grotesque paint- ing, the tales of Poe and Lewis Carroll – tend to alleviate the bizarreness, violence and cruelty of the primitive phantasies in which they are immersed. The same comfort is denied, in contrast, by the contemporary naturalistic settings of the part-object fantasies in David Cronenberg's films like *Shivers*, *Rabid* and *The Brood*.[27]

At the same time, Švankmajer's re-covery of grotesque and Manner- ist traditions raises different questions about the relationship between art and fantasy – not the unconscious phantasies that pervade all perception and all conscious mental life, but the desire to distance artistic representation from mimesis, to sustain a mode of trauma through images and materials associated with symbolic means of communication. Such fantasies, of course, are always in a determinate relationship to the historical body of social and cultural beliefs in which they find their place. The fantasies of religious painting, for example – the shocking depictions of horror, ecstasy and transgression – are mediated by the religious ideology within which they were produced and, importantly, consumed. It is for this reason that, when reproduced in this century, such imagery can evoke a traumatic effect probably missing in its own period. The absence of a sustaining religious culture leaves a space in which that imagery is allowed to return to its 'actuality' as fantasy, so to speak. The surrealist use of such imagery (for example by Dali), together with traditional *trompe l'oeil* techniques illustrates this point; so does the strategic use of 'quotation' in some post-modernist painting. It is in this context of the twentieth-century scepticism towards fantasies sustained in visual art through religious or political systems of ideology that Švankmajer's recuperation of earlier cultural traditions should be seen.

When Švankmajer quotes them in his films, Czech puppetry or the mannerism of Arcimboldo are stripped of the cultural and symbolic underpinnings which sustained their original status within a traditional mode of representation. And because the aesthetic principle of his work is not representation but a modernist collage – or its cinematic cousin, montage – what becomes most evident in these references is the materiality of objects and effigies and flesh and also, at the same time, their status as fantasies. The shock produced by these images is akin to the shock we face when Foucault describes a public execution in the period before the rise of the prison system in Europe: deprived of its symbolism, all that remains is the body and the brutality.[28]

One might argue that modern art, even in its constructivist guise, has provided a place for the unconscious retention of 'the body' (understood in its broadest sense) and the phantasies accruing to it. What has made this necessary is the destructive severity of the body as represented in the cultural imagery of advertising, film and the other mass media. Two polarities in the reaction against this gobbling up of the body in popular cultural forms might be the rise of abstract art (with its investment in the phantasies of materiality) and an often 'cruel' performance art. What is denounced as shocking in such modes are often their images or symptoms of fragmentation. But how shocking is the manic destruction of objects and figures in Švankmajer's films compared with the aggressive and facile fragmentation of, for example, the female body used to sell cars, fridges and perfume in Western advertising?

Švankmajer's films reveal the primitive phantasies embedded in culturally overt fantasies stemming from marionette theatre, mannerism, grotesque portraiture and so on. Perhaps more disturbingly, they extend our emotional relationship to what seem mundane objects in the world – furniture, wood, stone, household utensils, rooms – through an imaginative exploration of their ability to sustain primitive phantasies. It is in this way that we can understand Švankmajer's idea that objects have hidden memories, like persons, and that they contain a secret life of their own. The potency of objects to be immersed in fantasy is not simply the result of an arbitrary projection of phantasies onto them, but the art of judging which phantasies are appropriate to those objects given their physical, material qualities and their cultural associations. Švankmajer's depiction of scissors, for example, is an animation of their aggressive properties, something which is dialectically conditioned by their social use and their physical characteristics. In this exploration of the appropriateness of the film image to represent in a fertile and imaginative way, Švankmajer's work may thus provide a clue to the workings of animation and of cinema more generally.

This essay is a much extended version of the introduction to a touring programme *Alchemists of the Surreal: the films of Jan Svankmajer and the Brothers Quay* organised by the Film and Video Umbrella 1986–7. I would like to thank for their discussions and insight Jayne Pilling, Paul Taylor, and Keith Griffiths (who also provided valuable documentation on Švankmajer); and for their constructive criticism Jill McGreal, A. L. Rees and James Donald.

NOTES

1 Bruno Schulz, *The Street of Crocodiles* (London: Picador, 1963), p. 38.

2 *Monthly Film Bulletin* vol. 53, nos. 629–30, June/July 1986 contains: Michael O'Pray, 'In the capital of magic: the black theatre of Jan Švankmajer'; reviews by Julian Petley, Simon Field and Philip Strick; plus filmography. *Afterimage* no. 13, 1987, *Animating the Fantastic*, includes Michael O'Pray, 'A Švankmajer inventory'; two interviews with Švankmajer, plus three scenarios by him and his notes on *Alice*; and Vratislav Effenberger, 'Between idea and reality' and '*Jabberwocky*'.

3 For a bibliography which includes a section on East European animation, see Irene Kotlarz, 'Animation bibliography', *Undercut*, no. 13, Winter 1984/5.

4 These were the film-makers represented in the *Alchemists of the Surreal* touring programme noted above.

5 Little research or documentation on the Czech Surrealist Group, past or present, exists in English. See *Surrealism as a Collective Adventure: Surrealist Group in Czechoslovakia*, issue no. 4 of *dunganon* (Orkelljunga, Sweden: 1986/7[?]): this contains writings and scripts by Švankmajer and Švankmajerova, by Vratislav Effenberger and others. In French, see Petr Kral, *Le Surréalisme en Tchécoslovaquie*, (Paris: Gallimard, 1983).

6 André Breton, *What is Surrealism? Selected writings*, (ed.) Franklin Rosemont (London: Pluto Press, 1978), p. 375; Breton, 'Toyen', in *Surrealism and Painting* (London: Macdonald, 1972), pp. 207–214. (This is also published in a slightly different translation in Rosemont, op. cit, pp. 286–90.)

7 For the background to Rudolf II and Arcimboldo, see Jirina Horejsi, Jarmila Krcalova, Jaromir Neumann, Emanuel Poche and Jarmila Vackova, *Renaissance Art in Bohemia* (London: Hamlyn, 1979), p. 196 *et passim*; and *The Arcimboldo Effect: transformations of the face from the sixteenth to the twentieth century* (London: Thames & Hudson, 1987). On cabbalistic doctrine see Frances Yates, *The Occult Philosophy in the Elizabethan Age* (London: Ark, 1983), pp. 87–8 and *The Rosicrucian Enlightenment* (London: Ark, 1986).

8 Rosemary Jackson, *Fantasy: the literature of subversion* (London: Methuen, 1981), p. 68.

9 Ernst Kris, *Psychoanalytic Explanations in Art* (New York: Schocken, 1971), ch. 7.

10 See Jorg Krichbaum and Rein A. Zondergeld, *Dictionary of Fantastic Art* (London: Barron's, 1985); Georges Hugnet, *Fantastic Art, Dada, Surrealism*, (ed.) Alfred H. Barr, Jr. (New York: Museum of Modern Art, 1968).

11 Quoted in Krichbaum and Zondergeld, *Dictionary of Fantastic Art* pp. 231–2.

12 Mikhail Bakhtin, *Rabelais and his World* (Bloomington: Indiana University Press, 1984).

13 Max von Boehn, *Puppets and Automata* (New York: Dover, 1972), p. 56. On the background to puppetry in Czechoslovakia, see Jan Malik and Erik Kolar, *The Puppet Theatre in Czechoslovakia* (Prague: Orbis, 1970); Malik, *Puppetry in Czechoslovakia* (Prague: Orbis, 1948); and the catalogue *Laterna Magika: Experimental Playhouse of the National Theatre* (1973/4 season).

14 For examples of photographic work using effigies by Bellmer and Man Ray, see the Hayward Galley catalogue *L'Amour Fou: photography and surrealism* (London: Arts Council of Great Britain, 1986).

15 Michel de Ghelderode, 'The Ostend interviews', in *Seven Plays* (London: MacKibbon & Kee, 1960), p. 23.

16 Ibid., pp. 23–4.

17 Sigmund Freud, 'The "Uncanny"', in *Art and Literature, Pelican Freud Library (PFL)*, vol. 14 (Harmondsworth: Penguin, 1985). The psychoanalytic ideas I develop here are underpinned by the Kleinian position, particularly as mediated through Adrian Stokes's work. See *The Writings of Melanie Klein*, vols. I–IV (London: Hogarth Press, 1975); also Hanna Segal, *Klein* (London: Fontana, 1979) and *Introduction to the Work of Melanie Klein* (London: Heinemann, 1964).

18 Hélène Cixous, 'Fiction and its phantoms: a reading of Freud's *Das Unheimliche* ('The "uncanny"')', *New Literary History*, vol. 7, Spring 1976, p. 213.

19 Bakhtin, op. cit, p. 347.

20 Petr Kral, 'Larry Semon's message', in Paul Hammond (ed.), *The Shadow and its Shadow*, (London: BFI, 1978).

21 Ibid., p. 111.

22 Adrian Stokes, 'Reflections on the nude', in *The Critical Writings of Adrian Stokes*, vol. III, (ed.) Lawrence Gowing (London: Thames & Hudson, 1978), p. 315.

23 See Klein, 'Notes on some schizoid mechanisms', in *Envy and gratitude and other works, 1946–1963*, (London: Hogarth Press, 1975).

24 Freud, 'Negation', in *On Metapsychology*, PFL vol. 11.

25 See Stokes, 'The invitation to art', in Stokes, *Critical Writings*.

26 Stokes, 'Reflections . . .', p. 331.

27 See my 'Primitive phantasy in Cronenberg's films', in Wayne Drew (ed.), *David Cronenberg* (London: BFI Dossier 21, 1984), pp. 48–53. For further discussions of this primarily Kleinian view of cinema aesthetics, see also my 'On Adrian Stokes and film aesthetics', *Screen*, vol. 21, no. 4, 1980/1, and 'Modernism, phantasy and avant-garde film', *Undercut*, nos. 3–4, March 1982, pp. 31–3.

28 See Michel Foucault, *Discipline and Punish* (London: Allen Lane, 1977), pt. 1.

Uncanny Feminism
The Exquisite Corpses of Cecelia Condit
PATRICIA MELLENCAMP

> Thus traces of the storyteller cling to the story the way the handprints of the potter cling to the clay vessel.
>
> *Walter Benjamin*[1]

> The princess may very well have had an uncanny feeling, indeed she very probably fell into a swoon; but *we* have no such sensations, for we put ourselves in the thief's place, not in hers.
>
> *Sigmund Freud*[2]

Before analysing Cecelia Condit's videotapes – *Beneath the Skin* (1981) and *Possibly in Michigan* (1983), marvellous tales told from the princess's point of view – I will first wander through the metaphorical, treacherous forests of other stories, discovering 'invisible adversaries' along the path. The first is a handsome prince in a cautionary fable, 'The Twelve Dancing Princesses':[3]

> Once upon a time there was a king who had twelve daughters, each more beautiful than the other. They slept together in a hall where their beds stood close to one another. At night when they had gone to bed, the King locked the door and bolted it. But when he unlocked it in the morning, he noticed that their shoes had been danced to pieces, and nobody could explain how it happened.

Although imprisoned by patriarchy, these dancing daughters gleefully and confidently escaped the king's gaze of surveillance and power; together 'they danced, every night, on the opposite shore, in a splendid light, till three in the morning, when their shoes were danced into holes and they were obliged to stop'.

However, in this celebration of female adolescence and adventure – as in most of the 'once upon a time' of all fiction – something is wrong, and the youngest sister is suspicious: 'I don't know what it is. You may rejoice, but I feel so strange. A misfortune is certainly hanging over us.' For women, on a par with being scrutinised and contained by vision, the end is the dire, dreaded misfortune – in this fairytale, marriage to a prince, a quick and unhappy conclusion which separates the sisters and censors their nightly escapades. Anne Sexton's rewriting:

> Now the runaways would run no more and never again would their
> hair be tangled into diamonds, never again their shoes worn down to a
> laugh. He had won.[4]

A fellow had been given a cloak of invisibility by an old woman and had
secretly spied on their nightly pleasures and reported to the king. For his
voyeurism (and successful surveillance), he was given the kingdom and a
princess of his choice. The peril of being the visible, private object of desire
and the safe power of being the invisible, desiring, public subject are two
morals of this and contemporary theory's story. The undisciplined sisters had
transgressed the patrolled frontier between private and public – that demarcation line of power – and their passionate, dancing bodies were duly arrested.

Although the prince inadvertently revealed his presence through
touch and sound, eleven of the princesses paid no attention: 'And, as he broke
off a twig, a sharp crack came from the tree. The youngest cried out, "All is not
well! Did you hear that sound?"' No one else listened to these sounds which
made 'the youngest princess start with terror'. While many feminists are
proudly standing on opposite shores, watching the 'splendid light' of independent films and videotapes, and being invited to the intellectual dance of
postmodernism by scholars and the art world,[5] we might heed the alarm of the
youngest sister, for there are warnings in the academic air of godly wrath and
signs of virulent condescension, brazenly heralding a resurgence of reaction-
ary, anti-feminist positions – signalled by arguments for women's return to
private space, the home.

Lawrence Stone, Dodge Professor of History at Princeton, another
prince of a fellow and the second adversary of this essay, caused me to 'start
with terror' and conclude with furor at his patronising, biblical admonish-
ments in *The New York Review of Books* – at best a naked emperor when the
topic rarely turns to feminism; at worst, which is usually the case, a wolf
without the guise of sheep's clothing. In the first paragraph of 'Only Women', a
foreboding title, King Stone speaks to the princesses:

> I must first set out the ten commandments which should, in my
> opinion, govern the writing of women's history at any time and in any
> place.

– certainly a specious claim when discussing the writing of history. (Ruminous
sounds, awkwardly famous movie stars, and unearthly special effects restage
this spectacle in the film version of *Only Women*, co-directed by Lizzie Borden
and Cecil B. DeMille, in which Stone plays himself and is duly disemboweled
in the film/theory remake of the beginning of Michel Foucault's *Discipline and
Punish*.) Having claimed truth and the world for all times and all places, the
Stone tablets are thus writ by this Moses impersonator:

> 1. Thou shalt not write about women except in relation to men and
> children. [The wife/mother plea suppresses the very reality of women's
> lives, forgetting both women's relationships with other women and the

exhausting fact that most women always have at least two full-time jobs – taking care of children and men.] Women are not a distinct caste, and their history is a story of complex interactions; 2. Thou shalt strive not to distort the evidence and the conclusions to support modern feminist ideology ... 4. Thou shalt not confuse prescriptive norms with social reality ... 9. Thou shalt be clear about what constitutes real change in the experience and treatment of women.[6]

Because Lawrence Stone is male and thus omnipotent, he, like his godly predecessors, knows 'what constitutes real change' in the experience of women or 'thou'.

This catalogue of imperative 'shalts' is an intellectual aberration – a paranoid delusion of divine intervention into feminist scholarship and history. I 'start with terror' when I imagine the collective, knowing laughter of educated readers at his chastisement of women writers and feminism. For 'Prince Stone', women (not just feminists) have broken the bonds of propriety and chastity by entering priestly male domains of 'history'; he martials his defensive attack on women under the disguise or banners of research. Like the prince's cloak, scholarship and prestigious chairs (a veritable star system of academia reminiscent of the Hollywood studio era, replete with gossip and credits, is operative in this magazine) provide various screens, briefly concealing, like the prince's invisible presence, the argument.

American Film joins *The New York Review of Books* in mockery through the terrain of 'with-it' popular culture in a breezy piece by Raymond Durgnat on Grace Jones – an essay and a female subject made strangely 'respectable' (as if Jones were not) by dropping sundry names, e.g., Visconti, Renoir and Vertov, in a swaggering display of his superior knowledge of and desire for her 'phallic-narcissistic swagger and strut'. (This lurid psychoanalysis suggests Lee Marvin's black leathered Liberty Valance in John Ford's film and describes Durgnat's argument and style.) After glorifying Jones and her traversals of boundaries, Durgnat suddenly turns on feminism, on women as the objects of his contempt, the real reason for his essay; he smugly writes with scorn:

> Jones disturbs the Brand X forms of feminism. She's too frivolous for its schoolmarms, too sexual for its puritans, too strong for its sensitive plants, too competitive for its pacifists, too capitalist for its radicals, too effective for its neurotics, too hetero for its separatists, too responsibly independent to put the blame on pop for everything (war, the weather, old age).[7]

Durgnat's dismissive compendium, modeled on Linnaeus rather than the Bible, reiterates the nauseating typologies used to assault feminism and employs biological arguments used to contain women, e.g., *frivolous, sensitive, pacifists, puritans, schoolmarms* and, of course, *neurotic* and *dependent*. It is not insignificant that *American Film* would publish, without notation, words of undisguised racism and sexism, setting women in opposition under the cover of praising a black woman – the imperialist tactic of divide and conquer, the King's move against the sisters, a gambit of subjection rather than subjectivity.

However, these all-knowing enunciators protest too much; perhaps they are afraid of something, including the assertive, stylish representations of Grace Jones. Perhaps women, white and of colour, are upping the ante, redirecting the terms of vision and spectacle in stories and theories which dance on opposite shores without the fatal end of patriarchy. In vastly different ways, Condit and other feminist artists

> play with our curiosity and finally refuse to submit to our gaze. *They turn being looked at into an aggressive act* [my emphasis] ... they are playing with the only power at their disposal – the power to discomfit, the power, that is, to pose ... to pose a threat ... They must exceed definitions of the proper and the permissible ... And there is pleasure in transgression.[8]

(As a qualification or addition to this acute remark by Dick Hebdige, women also have language 'at their disposal' – for some, a troubling incursion into grammars of power as women interrupt the masculine ecology of speech *and* dispose of, or trash, kingly discourses – which Condit does in the garbage sequence which concludes *Possibly in Michigan*.) Along lines similar to Hebdige, Mary Russo writes about masquerade:

> To put on femininity with a vengeance suggests the power of taking it off.[9]

Condit does 'pose a threat' by putting on femininity with a visual and narrative vengeance; her disconcerting irony and sweetly gruesome stories also 'put-on' and undo societal prescriptions and taboos regarding women's options to subjugation by violence of the gaze, letting us see and hear what often remains hidden, behaving with impropriety.

As Teresa de Lauretis suggests: 'It may well be, however, that the story has to be told differently. Take Oedipus, for instance'.[10] Feminist film and video are telling stories differently *and* looking at 'difference' differently – the latter, a key to feminist influences on current debates on post-modernism, particularly the issues focused on notions of 'the other'. As I argued in *Post-modern TV*, women are posited as the schizophrenic subject of postmodern culture, just as television is its latent object – the embodiment of every emblematic feature. Yet rarely are either subject or object acknowledged other than for feminism as 'other' – as 'great divide' or bipolarity (containing, in order of historical fashion, vestiges of Lacan's endless division of the subject in language, the split between 'I' of enunciation and 'I' of enounced, the separation of the inner world of the 'self' from the outside world of reality and facticity which can be mastered and owned, the division of subject from object, men from women, women from women, word from image, and soul from body).[11] I want briefly to elaborate on this strange situation of feminism's acclaimed marginality and unstated centrality through a selective reading of an important essay, 'The "Primitive" Unconscious of Modern Art', by a leading figure in the debate, Hal Foster.

Among complex, political issues, he explicates *bricolage*:

> Myth is a one-way appropriation, and act of power; *bricolage* is a process of textual play, of loss and gain: whereas myth abstracts and pretends to the natural, bricolage cuts us, makes concrete, delights in the artificial.

(Condit's work literally 'cuts up' and 'delights in the artificial'.) Up to this point, drawing on Lévi-Strauss and Roland Barthes, Foster's definition of the 'primitive style' is uncannily similar to feminist art and argument – against biology which for women emerges as the 'eternal', the goddess/whore myth. Foster provocatively asserts that 'The rupture of the primitive, managed by the moderns, becomes our postmodern event'; he concludes by invoking feminists for whom 'there are other ways to narrate this history'.[12] Thus, by extension and in/direct elision, feminism becomes the repressed, managed rupture of postmodernism – posited, like 'primitivism' earlier, *outside* the debate as the estranged, unknowable other, along with other races and cultures. In post-modern discourses, 'woman' is not fascinating as she was to modernism; 'feminism' is perhaps because, in this dazedly silent 1986, it is the only political, theoretically lively game in town.

However, if feminism is going to be invoked as a desirable dialogue or a discourse of salvation, it is time to realise that at least white, intellectual, middle-class feminism is not 'other' in the sense of being outside a shared history and politics of class and race; white women are 'o/Other' for psycho-analysis' male subjects and analysts for whom 'woman' *is* the problem; 'she' is a paradoxical dilemma which grants male identity and exists as an inscrutable mystery, in both myths serving as the object of male desire/fear rather than as a subject. Indeed, an exceedingly primitive unconscious is posited by the modernists, Freud and Lacan. Within this European, historical account of male sexuality/subjectivity, yes, 'woman' is other and lacking, truly a problem – with an essay by Freud 'On Femininity' but no comparable piece 'on masculinity'. But for political and fashionable US writers on postmodernism? The blind yet concerned visage of Oedipus, now miserable at Colonos, again misreads women or feminism which is alluded to rather than translated and which servilely works, without recognition, as both source of the argument and/or the condemnation of postmodern culture.

As we concluded our introduction to *Revision*, the task for feminists involved 're-vising the old apprehension of sexual difference and making it possible to multiply differences, to move away from homogeneity ...'[13] a notion picked up then amplified by Teresa de Lauretis to include 'differences among women' and 'differences within women': 'differences which are not purely sexual or merely racial, economic or (sub)cultural, but all of these together and often enough in conflict with one another'.[14] These delineations of heterogeneity, together *and* in conflict, of historical women are resolutely against the notions of 'purely' and 'merely' usually applied to eternal 'woman' and veer from princely mastery through colonisation, bipolarity, hierarchy and otherness.

Several strategies of 'heterogeneity' are apparent in recent feminist cinema and video: 1) the emphasis on enunciation and address to women *as subjects* (including multiple voices in personal dialogues and the use of private speech), a reciprocity between author, text, and audience involving collective/contradictory identifications and shared 'situations'; 2) the telling of 'stories' rather than 'novels' of grand master narratives as Walter Benjamin distinguished these two forms; 3) the inextricable bricolage of personal and theoretical knowledge; 4) the performance of parody or the telling of jokes, with irony and wit as women's allies rather than enemies; no wonder women in the audience laugh with such bursts of mutual delight; neither tale nor laughter is at their expense; 5) an implicit or explicit critique and refashioning of theories of subjectivity constructed by vision; and 6) a transgression of the boundaries between private and public spaces and experiences, entering with intimacy the 'public sphere' and unsettling these metaphorical and real spaces of power through confinement by looking and talking back. I will scatter these intersecting issues throughout the discussion of Condit's sassy video work.

Beneath the Skin (1981) and *Possibly in Michigan* (1983) are unnerving and funny retellings of Oedipus as tabloid sensationalism. Imagine Freud's essay on 'The "Uncanny"' as either a feminist fairytale or as a murderous scandal, excerpted in *The National Inquirer* and *Art Forum*, illustrated by photographs of masquerade women or mutilated corpses, and accompanied by bold headlines of first person quotations. This lucid critique/lurid exposé would return – collapsing criticism's bipolarity of art versus popular culture, fiction opposed to fact, simulation against the real, 'canny' against the 'uncanny' – as a performance staged by Cindy Sherman with voices by Lily Tomlin. Scholarly explications via 'theoretical' postmodernism would be published in *October* while personal stories of the artists would appear in *People*; clips from the piece would be shown on CBS on Sunday morning in the sacred 'art' slot near the end of the programme. Condit, Sherman, Tomlin, and Annette Michelson would intimately/polemically chat/assert on *The Phil Donahue Show* before a female audience of non-feminists. Or, as real life would have it, it would be shown on *The 700 Club*, with its own soundtrack, dubbed over by a gay poof. We would be held in a disconcerting uncertainty concerning origins, originals, mastery, truth, art, popular culture and 'the real' (all of which are complex processes, dispersed discourses which, like mass culture, most criticism posits as monoliths or 'things' which are locatable, almost tangible) – currently labeled 'pastiche' and 'schizophrenia' ('the transformation of reality into images, the fragmentation of time into a series of perpetual presents') as the emblematic condition of the postmodern object and its confused subject.[15] Or, as Barthes argued earlier,

> Taken aslant by language, the world is written through and through; signs, endlessly deferring their foundations ... infinitely citing one another, nowhere come to a halt ...[16]

Or in another interpretation of this crazy return, we would be as ambivalently delighted and unwarily off-centred as we are by watching Condit's videotapes. Their status as hyperreal – the mesmerising, fibrillating images of masquerade and the grotesque – is undercut by the irony of the smiling voice speaking of violence and death with the amazed, homey incredulity of backyard gossip or doubly displaced by innocent, sing-song exchanges and girlish operettas.

Beneath the Skin (Cecelia Condit, 1981)

Grisly scandal collides with female adolescence, just as sound intercepts image, derailing spectators and interpretation alike; the real violence in women's lives coincides with fairytales and princesses. Teresa de Lauretis concluded *Alice Doesn't* with a marvellous, riddling question: 'It is the signifier who plays and wins before Alice does, even when she's aware of it. But to what end, if Alice doesn't?'[17] Cecelia doesn't and Condit's work unravels the sentence's paradox while imaging blackly ironic, startling 'endings' to de Lauretis' question.

Condit's tapes unequivocally position us in the princess' place, Sleeping Beauty's swoon, that nightmare of Anne Sexton's poem in which the awakened princess 'married the prince':

and all went well
except for the fear –
the fear of sleep.

Briar Rose
was an insomniac . . .

I must not sleep
for while asleep I'm ninety
and think I'm dying.
Death rattles in my throat[18]

Unlike Freud and Sexton, Condit has no interest in either marriages to princes
or thieves' viewpoints, however fascinated she is, as they are, by sleep and
dream, violence and death. Her strategy – however 'unconscious' – is a
combination of Freud and Sexton, rewriting the 'uncanny' as a fairytale (a form
which Freud absolutely and repeatedly denied was an instance of 'uncanny'
experiences) and taking Sexton's feminist revisions to different, less lonely and
suicidal ends. Condit's translucent, artificial, video bodies are interrupted by
recreations and documentary footage of epileptic seizures and still photographs of mummies' heads; the 'classical' body is disrupted by the 'grotesque'
body; the private, controlled, sleeping beauty is transformed into the public,
uncontrollable epileptic or the decaying body of a murderous scandal; all are
instances of violent spectacle, exquisite corpses. No longer effaced or held in
private spaces by 'proper' discourse and decorous words, these are 'undisciplined', speaking bodies – on the frontier between the modern body and the
carnival body before the 17th century incarceration in asylums, prisons, and
homes, before the ascendancy of the word over the carnal, guilty flesh and
other great divides of power – adolescent rather than grown-up bodies which
suggest that another interpretation of masquerade as a possibility for feminism
rather than a disguise, lure, or mark of envious lack is necessary.

Via Bakhtin's work on carnival and Rabelais, Mary Russo writes in
'Female Grotesques: Carnival and Theory':

> The grotesque body is the open, protruding, extended, secreting body,
> the body of becoming, process, and change. The grotesque body is
> opposed to the classical body, which is monumental, static, closed, and
> sleek . . .

Condit's work alternates and merges the 'classical' body with the grotesque
body – the latter the erupting body on public display. Russo writes of historical, female performers: 'They used their bodies in public, in extravagant
ways that could have only provoked wonder and ambivalence in the female
viewer . . .'[19] This image of the body and the ambivalent spectator is applicable
to the 'style' of Condit's work:

> a body in the act of becoming. It is never finished, never completed; it
> is continually built, created, and builds and creates another body . . . a
> double body in which one link joins the other, in which the life of one
> body is born from the death of a preceding, older one . . . the body can
> merge with various natural phenomena . . .[20]

The carnival body is an indivisible body without inner/outer, self/other polarities in which the exterior is inauthentic, a cover-up; a body of doubled surfaces rather than inner recesses which are analysed, explained. Video is well suited to this transforming, seamless emergence of one surface from another, a fluid editing/processing capacity which Condit utilises with skill.

'[T]his hyperbolic style, this "overacting" can be read as double representations . . .'[21] 'Double representation' (both Bakhtin's 'double body' and the 'double-directed discourse' of parody) – extended to include the critique of the schizophrenic subject and the intersection of sound and image tracks – aptly describes Condit's tapes which also demonstrate a tactic suggested by Luce Irigaray and endorsed by Russo:

> to play with mimesis is thus, for a woman, to try to recover the place of her exploitation by discourse, without allowing herself simply to be reduced to it. It means to resubmit herself . . . to ideas . . . that are elaborated in/by masculine logic, but so as to make 'visible' what was supposed to remain invisible.[22]

(In certain ways, this reads like a summary of Foucault's and perhaps Bakhtin's projects which, however, were mainly about and for men.) Among the seemingly contradictory yet comparable exploitations to which Condit 'resubmits' are masquerade and epilepsy which she restages as extravagant, hyperbolic, spectacle, challenging the divisions of vision and the body while escaping the confines of 'discourse'.

Beneath the Skin (1981) opens with Condit's conversationally intimate, incredulous voice narrating: 'Let me tell you what a nightmare that *that* was. Most of the time it just feels like the news extravaganza that it was.'[23] Benjamin argued that storytellers speak of the 'circumstances' they have directly learned or 'simply pass it off as their own experience'.[24] Eliding story with the teller (raising issues of authorship), Condit's rehearsed, naive voice scales Midwest verbal registers of astonishment, stressing and elongating words like 'body', and relates a lurid, first person account of her boyfriend's murder of his previous lover whom he dismembered, 'mummified, decapitated, and wrapped in plastic' and stored in his apartment during his affair with her, the storyteller 'I'. The film is about 'this guy I had been seeing for the last four years, the police just found a body in his apartment . . .' The passions of the body become rumours, gossip, and scandal; perhaps they are real, or not: 'I'd never know if he killed her or not . . . a helleva way to continue a relationship . . .' The audience is caught off guard by off-handed comments and laughs – *The Star* as standup comedy *and* everyday life. The details of decapitation and odorous decay on the ironic sound track – 'But one of the funniest things about it . . . it came out that her head was missing' – parallel rapidly edited images of the fragmented female body which decomposes in video like the corpse in the story rots. The tape goes 'beneath the skin' by traversing the 'inside/outside' of the body (a sack, a container) to reveal skeletons, aging, death; beneath the surfaces to uncover horror or the 'unconscious'; beneath the romance of relationships – of the lyrics of Frank Sinatra dreamily singing 'I've got you … under my skin' – to reveal beatings and murder. Perhaps these are separate but equal terrains; or they are equivalent planes of representation; or, perhaps, this is not a modern body at all which can be present only through the distance of representation but rather an archaic, violent, unrepressed body. Recurring closeups of red lips and white teeth are juxtaposed with the verbal description of the corpse's dental records. ('But the most important of all human features for the grotesque is the mouth. It dominates all else. The grotesque face is actually reduced to the gaping mouth … a bodily abyss': Bakhtin.[25]) Life and death, the pin-up and the coroner's report, the fetish and the fact, the beautiful and the grotesque, and the word and the image are of equal value.

The collision, or (in) vertical montage, of a lurid tabloid story akin to *Rear Window*, *Psycho* and *Frenzy* of murder, dismemberment, and investigation (including Hitchcock's perversely comic 'eating' scenes) with images of young, masquerading girls and glimpses of death, illness, and age, resembles a gyrating Moebius strip in which sound and image tracks never meet but are indissolubly connected by us in the process of enunciation – a reciprocity between author, text, and audience. As Linda Hutcheon writes in her recent book, *A Theory of Parody*, parody, like Bakhtin's medieval carnival, 'exists in the self-conscious borderline between art and life, making little formal distinction between actor and spectator, between author and co-creating reader'.[26] For her, parody 'enlists the audience in contradiction' and activates 'collective participation'.[27] Depending on one's gendered experiences, the collective contradictions elicited by Condit's disarming, eye-catching work are more extreme, less appetizing, hard to swallow and even harder to digest for some viewers than others.

Her distinctive style involves an intricate montage which spirals and loops back, intersecting the lurid narration. Studio footage alternates with processed location shots; found black and white footage is mixed by/with video in an uncanny enunciation, placing the enounced of murder in a precarious irony. Visual delicacy, like the images of the sweet young woman, disguises *and* underscores the sensational story – is this real, is this possible, is this a fable, is this serious – or not? This exemplifies contradiction – of response, of the structure of irony, of women's lives, crossing the 'self-conscious borderline between art and life'. This emphasis on process and experience in a reciprocity between speaker/listener is also central to Benjamin's valorisation of the story as opposed to the novel which

> neither comes from oral tradition nor goes into it. This distinguishes it from storytelling in particular. The storyteller takes what [she] tells from experience – [her] own or that reported by others. And [she] in turn makes it the experience of those who are listening to [her] tale. The novelist has isolated himself.[28]

In this, the storyteller ('The first true storyteller is, and will continue to be, the teller of fairy tales'[29]) resembles the chronicler (rather than the contemporary historian) who is interested in interpretation rather than explanation, the terrain of the novel's narrative which has been divorced from 'the realm of living speech'. Thus, the listener has a stake not only in hearing but in remembering the story – a shared experience, a process. 'A [woman] listening to a story is in the company of the storyteller; even a [woman] reading [watching] one shares this companionship.'[30] It is this realm of interpretation via 'living speech' forged in shared experience which is intriguing for feminism and what distinguishes the work of Condit – a telling as much as a watching.

The initial and recurring visual image is an overhead 'glamour' close-up of a young woman's face – sleeping, artificially made-up and lit. This shot is overlaid with another female face, a visual trace outlining a divided, schizophrenic subject – a complex dialogue imbricated in much feminist work.

> Call them femininity and feminism, the one is made representable by the critical work of the other; the one is kept at a distance, constructed, 'framed', to be sure, and yet 'respected', 'loved', 'given space' by the other.[31]

(In this writing, women are 'other' with/for each other rather than another, a man, and thus a very different story.) The teller begins to identify with the murdered woman: 'I always thought that she was epileptic and I, diabetic, and I identified with her.' (Because Condit is epileptic, the status of 'I' is complicated, biographically elided with 'she'.) As the tape returns to the opening shot, the dreamer/teller, self/other, voice over/'other woman', the dead and the living merge, taking up the question of the real and fiction, the possible and the impossible, in a double denial that, like de Lauretis' Alice riddle, reaffirms women and the story's reality:

> But it was never real, it was just a bizarre story . . . but I had this dream that it was so real. I dreamed that it was me, not her, that he killed two years ago.
> It is characteristic that not only a man's knowledge or wisdom, but above all his real life – and this is the stuff that stories are made of – first assumes transmissable form at the moment of his death . . . Death is the sanction of everything that the storyteller can tell. He has borrowed his authority from death.[32]

(Benjamin and Bakhtin analyse the 'modern' concealment of death with arguments remarkably similar, again, to Foucault's theses.) Like the 'he' of Benjamin's remarks, Condit takes her authority from death and goes public as few women storytellers do, speaking about violence through the forbidden terrains of femininity, with sacrilegious moments of gallows' humour. This rewriting of Freudian bedtime stories as sensationalism concludes with 'And that's another story'. Like Scheherazade, Condit continues the tale two years later, this time radically revising Freud's interpretations and conclusions with a sweet tasting vengeance and without his proper cover of 'scientific discourse' which explains and contains the hysterical, spectacular body.

Possibly in Michigan (1983) is a feminist musical in which the couple doesn't, continuing the deathly, stifling scenario of *Beneath the Skin* which foreshadowed the musical style of multiple voices in a chanting, childlike operetta, 'gee i jo': 'Talk to us about Barbie and Ken, Barbie and Men, Ken and Men . . . Never ends.' Both tapes reverse the classical and modern text's hetero-sexual inevitability of Barbie and Ken, marriage or murder – both·resolutions or 'endings' functioning as containments of the male fear of castration posed by the 'lacking' spectacle of the female body. On the contrary, Condit gleefully realises Freud's imaginary, anxious scenario; cannibalism, an extreme exten-sion of dismemberment, castration and other Freudian metaphors and/or narrative, is the 'happy' ending.

Unlike the mainly singular storyteller of the first tape, three styles of voice alternate in this gruesomely enchanting fairytale of female adolescence: the acapella chorus; the sing-song dialogue/conversation between the two girl/women 'stars'; and the voice-over of Condit speaking about her characters, Sharon, Janice, and Arthur, in the conspiratorial, editorial voice no longer an 'I' but dispersed throughout the telling. This postmodern 'once upon a time' opens in a shopping mall of diffused pastels where two young women are pursued by surreal men wearing suits and grotesque animal heads. ('The head, ears and nose also acquire a grotesque character when they adopt the animal form . . . the eyes have no part in these comic images; they express an individ-ual . . . not essential to the grotesque': Bakhtin.[33]) The opening lyrics of the chorus cheerily prophesy: 'I bite at the hand that feeds me, slap at the face that eats me. Some kind of animal, cannibal . . . Animal? Cannibal?' Music sweetens the scenario which equates men with animals as the frog/prince is made literal and visible. While the mundane of shopping malls and everyday life is trans-formed into fantasy, the second use of the voice, a sing-song dialogue, exem-plifies Condit's disarming wit: 'He has the head and it's the size of a wolf.' A deep, echoing, male voice says: 'The better to eat you with, my dear . . . You have two choices . . . I will cut your arms and legs off and eat them, one by one, slowly.' The female chorus intones 'Why?' He: 'For Love.' Chorus: 'Why?' He: 'For Love.' Chorus: 'But love shouldn't cost an arm and a leg.'

As Sharon, the dreamer/actant, rides down the escalator, the third style of voice, Condit's voice, discusses women and violence, the complex concern beneath the veneer of fairytales, of her work, and of women's 'private' lives: 'Sharon attracted violent men. She had a way of making the violence seem as if it was their idea. Her friend, Janice, was cut from the same mold.' This frank, disconcerting analysis reiterates a line from *Beneath the Skin*: 'I realize that if I courted violence more, I might get myself seriously hurt.' In that tape she laughs, reminding me of the opening laugh of Sally Potter's 1979 film, *Thriller*, a laugh which occurs in blackness before the white of the first image, a laugh in concert with an aria of death. As Herbert Blau writes:

... that seeming remembrance of/in laughter which is a mnemonic stoppage of breath. It is the mystery of the interruption which preserves something tragic in comedy, since it seems a synopsis of death ... Which is to say that meaning stops for that moment, as if in homage to more than meaning ...

Violence is always more or less than meaning; Condit's art and laughter are 'synopses of death', stopped, as if gasping, by laughter; 'when laughter comes the meaning is deadly, or there's just no meaning at all'.[34]

The posing, giggling girls/women are from *Beneath the Skin*, including the raven-haired, sleeping/decaying beauty surrounded by red roses. Unlike the earlier tape, this story's violence exists more on the image track with sound as an ironic chorus or commentator:

Arthur longed for that sexual scent that smelled like home ... he had used so many masks to disguise himself that he had forgotten who he was. He imagined himself a frog transformed into a Prince Charming. He felt the moment he kissed her, he would become the man she wanted him to be.

Possibly in Michigan (Cecelia Condit, 1983)

This frog/prince inversion of Jacques Lacan's female masquerade as carnival follows the imaginary woman, Sharon, enters her home, kisses, then beats her – a startling intrusion of domestic life, brute reality amidst the glossed colours of fantasy. Janice, her friend, races to Sharon's house and shoots Arthur. These gossamer girls, together again, cook, eat and toss Arthur's remains into the garbage. Hacking the body into stew meat is a comic parody, a shared act of intimacy, and a grotesque equation of the body with food. This grisly meal concludes with the innocent, satisfied 'girls', presumably naked, made up, smoking cigarettes and coughing in a delightfully perverse, soft-focus rendering of adolescent friendship and misbehaviour. The tape concludes with the 'real' garbage man and truck picking up the garbage or prince, accompanied by 'natural' sound as the credits roll in this 'reality'.

This sensational remake of Freud which fragments and fetishises the female body while dismantling Oedipal narratives does indeed have conflicting effects on audiences, inverting Freud's analysis of the uncanny: an experience, a frightening effect which hinges on two figures – loss of the eyes and dismemberment – and which involves a discrepancy between the 'incredible' and the 'possible'.[35] (It is important to 'remember' that this essay depicts the dismembered, spectacular body – that 'animistic' body of yore which is not fully contained by Freud's discourse, dependent as his argument is on uncertainty and its repression.) Epilepsy and the beautiful female automaton creates 'doubts whether an apparently animate being is really alive; or conversely, whether a lifeless object might not be in fact animate'. This notion of the 'double' becomes, for Freud and Condit, 'a harbinger of death'.[36] Condit's beautiful faces decay, dissolving into eyeless skulls; her narratives detail the dismemberment which Freud feared and analysed:

> the substitutive relation between the eye and the male organ which is seen to exist in dreams and myths and phantasies . . . the threat of being castrated is what first gives the idea of losing other organs its intense colouring.[37]

Cannibalism, not only the losing but the devouring of 'other organs', is an 'intense colouring' of Freud's book. *Possibly in Michigan* is a serious and amusing challenge to the 'relation between the eye and the male organ', a personal, historical and recent equation certainly not 'substitutive' in women's 'dreams and myths and fantasies'.

The fear of/defense against castration is also elicited by what Freud labels 'the Medusa effect', a tactic which produces the very image which is feared for protection – yet another Freudian trope literalised in *Possibly in Michigan* in a shot of the masked man picking up a rock revealing a skull crawling with snakes which he throws through Sharon's window; it lands on her bed. The 'Medusa effect' is reiterated in a close-up of worms/snakes crawling over a photograph of Sharon. These special effects 'serve actually as a mitigation of the horror, for they replace the penis, the absence of which is the cause of the horror'. Freud seriously goes on to say: 'This is a confirmation of the technical rule according to which a multiplication of penis symbols signifies castration.'[38] (No wonder Helen Cixous' Medusa is laughing! This reads as if Freud were writing directions for a Milton & Bradley board game, or better, a television game show. I can hear the referee's admonition: 'You lose ten points on a technical rule: no multiplication of penis symbols.')

Condit's Medusa scene, like the images of epilepsy and the auto-mated doll-like women, takes Freud at his word; however, her 'Medusa effect' portends violence to women and rape rather than or before castration. Because of this, she breaks Freud's crucial rule by not symbolising disavowal but joyously 'performing' dismemberment, turning the imaginary scenario of the Oedipus complex into the conclusion of cannibalism and female friendship – uniting women in an ending and relationship that classical texts have avoided and contained. It's as if the two women of *Beneath the Skin*, like Mimi and Musetta of Puccini's *La Bohème*, then Potter's *Thriller*, joined forces and refused their murder by seemingly but perversely playing by then inverting or rewrit-ing the rules and kicking Oedipus out of the narrative. As Benjamin suggests: 'The wisest thing – so the fairytale taught mankind . . . is to meet the forces of the mythological world with cunning and high spirits.' The mythological world of Freud is met by Sharon, Janice, and Cecelia, a creative trio, 'with high spirits and cunning', living 'happily ever after' so that Scheherazade, speaking to/with women, will continue this trilogy in a promised third tape concerning an old woman, another fairytale figure which Condit will undoubtedly imagine in her off-centre way.

> In every case the storyteller is a [woman] who has counsel for [her] readers. But if today 'having counsel' is beginning to have an old-fashioned ring, this is because the communicability of experience is decreasing . . . After all, counsel is less an answer to a question than a proposal concerning the continuation of a story which is just unfolding.[39]

Unlike all the recent declarations of the death of feminism because completed, old-hat, a failure, or a mistake, the public, artistic formulation of female subjects, desires, pleasures and peculiarities continues to 'unfold' fifty years after Benjamin's words; the 'communicability' of women's private experiences is going massively, transgressively public. Cecilia Condit, just an 'old-fashioned girl' but what a wickedly clever one, is giving us counsel, making outrageous proposals, with laughter from the audience signaling possibilities. After all, without his cloak of invisibility, the prince doesn't stand a chance.

> *Could you imagine a world of women only?*
> the interviewer asked. *Can you imagine*
>
> *a world where women are absent?* (He believed
> he was joking.) Yet I have to imagine
>
> at one and the same moment, both. Because
> I live in both. *Can you imagine,*
>
> the interviewer asked, *a world of men?*
> (He thought he was joking.) *If so, then,*
>
> *a world where men are absent?*
> *(Adrienne Rich)*[40]

NOTES

1 Walter Benjamin, 'The storyteller: reflections on the works of Nikolai Leskov' (New York: Schocken, 1969), p. 92.

2 Sigmund Freud, 'The "uncanny"', in *The Standard Edition of the Complete Psychological Works of Sigmund Freud (SE)*, vol. XVII, (London: The Hogarth Press, 1964), p. 252.

3 The Brothers Grimm, *Grimm's Fairy Tales* (New York: Grosset & Dunlap, 1945), pp. 1–6.

4 Anne Sexton, 'The Twelve Dancing Princesses', from *Transformations*, 1971, collected in *The Complete Poems* (Boston: Houghton Mifflin Co., 1981), p. 281.

5 I am referring to several recent essays, for example, Hal Foster, '(Post)Modern polemics', in *Recodings: art, spectacle, cultural politics* (Port Townsend, WA: Bay Press, 1985); Andreas Huyssen, 'Mapping the postmodern', in *After the Great Divide: modernism, mass culture, postmodernism* (Bloomington: Indiana University Press, 1986); Craig Owens, 'The discourse of Others: feminists and postmodernism', in Hal Foster (ed.), *The Anti-Aesthetic* (Port Townsend, WA: Bay Press, 1983); UK edition: *Postmodern Culture* (London: Pluto Press, 1985). All three writers testify to the importance of feminism to debates on postmodernism.

6 Lawrence Stone, 'Only women', *The New York Review of Books*, vol. 32, no. 6, 11 April 1985, p. 21.

7 Raymond Durgnat, 'Amazing Grace', *American Film*, vol. 11, no. 4, January-February 1986, p. 35.

8 Dick Hebdige, 'Posing ... threats, striking . . . poses: youth, surveillance, and display', *Sub-stance*, nos. 37/8, 1983, pp. 85, 86. I have collapsed remarks from several paragraphs in this very interesting essay concerning youth sub-cultures – a topic which overlaps to a vague degree Condit's concern with adolescence or moments of passage.

9 Mary Russo, 'Female grotesques: carnival and theory', in Teresa de Lauretis (ed.), *Feminist Studies/Critical Studies* (Bloomington: Indiana University Press, 1986).

10 Teresa de Lauretis, *Alice Doesn't* (Bloomington: Indiana University Press, 1984), p. 156. This quotation is taken from a centrally valuable chapter, 'Desire in narrative' (pp. 103–157), which I highly recommend.

11 My essay 'Postmodern TV: Wegman & Smith' (*Afterimage* [US], December 1985) detailed a model of postmodernism as it related to video and feminism. This essay is a section of Part II, a continuation of that first essay, and discusses the female subjects and feminist films and video of postmodernism. The complete essay analyses films by Sally Potter, Yvonne Rainer, and Valie Export.

12 Hal Foster, 'The "primitive" unconscious of modern art', *October*, no. 34, Fall 1985, pp. 64, 65, 69. This last reference is comparable to other marginal allusions to feminism – 'For feminists, for "minorities", for "tribal peoples" ...' Taxonomy is not innocent, no matter how qualified by quotations.

13 Mary Ann Doane, Patricia Mellencamp, Linda Williams (eds.), 'Feminist film criticism: an introduction', *Re-Vision: essays in feminist film criticism* (Los Angeles: The American Film Institute; Frederick, Maryland: University Publications of America, 1984), p. 15.

14 Teresa de Lauretis, 'Aesthetic and feminist criticism: rethinking women's cinema', *New German Critique*, no. 34, Winter 1985, pp. 164, 168.

15 Fredric Jameson, 'Postmodernism and consumer society', in Foster (ed.), *The Anti-Aesthetic*, p. 125.

16 Roland Barthes, 'Change the object itself: mythology today', in *Image-Music-Text* (London: Fontana, 1977), pp. 167/8. This short, five-page essay is an update of Barthes's earlier work on mythology – cited by Foster.

17 Lauretis, *Alice Doesn't*, p. 186. The end of the book, like the classical Hollywood film, circles back to the beginning: 'In the heart of Looking-Glass country, between her fifth and sixth moves across the chessboard, Alice comes to the centre of the labyrinth of language'. (p. 1)

18 Anne Sexton, 'Briar Rose (Sleeping Beauty)', p. 293.

19 Russo, 'Female grotesques'.

20 Mikhail Bakhtin, *Rabelais and his World* (Bloomington: Indiana University Press, 1984), pp. 317/8.

21 Russo, 'Female grotesques'.

22 Quoted in Russo, 'Female grotesques'.

23 I have transcribed the videotapes and hope the quotations are accurate.

24 Benjamin, 'The Storyteller', p. 92.

25 Bakhtin, *Rabelais and his World*, p. 317.

26 Linda Hutcheon, *A Theory of Parody* (New York & London: Methuen, 1985), p. 72. Her chapter 'The paradox of parody', pp. 69–83, discusses Bakhtin's writings, taking issue with his negative regard toward modern parody, what she calls 'his rejection of the contemporary'. Thus Hutcheon argues that, 'We should look to what the theories suggest, rather than what the practice denies . . .'. (p. 71)

27 Hutcheon, *A Theory of Parody*, pp. 92, 99.

28 Benjamin, 'The Storyteller', p. 87.

29 Ibid., p. 102.

30 Ibid., p. 100.

31 De Lauretis, 'Aesthetic and feminist theory', p. 160.

32 Benjamin, 'The Storyteller', p. 94.

33 Bakhtin, *Rabelais and his World*, p. 316.

34 Herbert Blau, 'Comedy since the Absurd', *Modern Drama*, vol. 25, no. 4, December 1982, pp. 555, 556.

35 Freud, 'The "uncanny"', p. 250.

36 Ibid., p. 235.

37 Ibid., p. 231.

38 Freud, 'Medusa's head', *SE*, vol. XVIII, 1964, p. 273.

39 Benjamin, 'The Storyteller', p. 86.

40 Adrienne Rich, 'Natural Resources', *The Dream of a Common Language* (New York: W. W. Norton, 1978), p. 61.

Select Bibliography

Afterimage, no. 13: *Animating the Fantastic;* 1987.

Bakhtin, M., *Rabelais and his World,* Bloomington: Indiana University Press, 1984.

Barrowclough, S., *Not A Love Story, Screen,* vol. 25, no. 5, 1982.

Barthes, R., *S/Z,* London: Jonathan Cape, 1975.

———— *Image, Music, Text,* London: Fontana, 1977.

Bataille, G., *Death and Sensuality: a study of eroticism and the taboo,* New York: Walker and Co., 1962.

Bellour, R., 'Les Oiseaux: analyse d'une séquence', *Cahiers du Cinéma,* no. 219, October 1969.

———— 'The Obvious and the Code', *Screen,* vol. 15, no. 4, Winter 1974/5.

———— 'The Unattainable Text', *Screen,* vol. 16, no. 3, Autumn 1975.

———— 'Le Blocage symbolique', *Communications,* no. 23, Paris: Éditions de Seuil, 1975.

———— 'Hitchcock the Enunciator', *Camera Obscura,* no. 2, Fall 1977.

———— *Le Livre des Autres,* Paris: 10/18, UEG, 1978.

———— 'Psychosis, Neurosis, Perversion', *Camera Obscura,* nos. 3/4, 1979.

———— 'Symboliques', in *Le Cinéma Américain I,* Paris: Flammarion, 1979.

Benjamin, W., *Illuminations,* New York: Schocken, 1969.

Bergstrom, J., 'Enunciation and Sexual Difference', *Camera Obscura,* nos. 3/4, Summer 1979.

———— 'Alternation, Segmentation, Hypnosis: interview with Raymond Bellour', *Camera Obscura,* nos. 3/4, Summer 1979.

Bhabha, H.K., 'The Commitment to Theory', *New Formations,* no. 5, Summer 1988.

Blau, H., 'Comedy since the Absurd', *Modern Drama,* vol. 25, no. 4, December 1982.

Bloom, H., *Agon,* Oxford: Oxford University Press, 1982.

Bordwell, D., *The Films of Carl-Theodor Dreyer,* Berkeley: University of California Press, 1981.

Bovenschen, S., 'Is There a Feminine Aesthetic?', *New German Critique,* no. 10, 1977.

Breton, A., *What is Surrealism? Selected Writings,* ed. Franklin Rosemont, London: Pluto Press, 1978.

Brooke-Rose, C., *A Rhetoric of the Unreal: studies in narrative and structure, especially of the fantastic* (Cambridge: Cambridge University Press, 1981).

Brooks, P., *The Melodramatic Imagination,* New York: Columbia University Press, 1985.

Burgin, V., 'Diderot, Barthes, Vertigo', in V. Burgin, J. Donald and C. Kaplan, eds., *Formations of Fantasy,* London: Methuen, 1986.

Burgin, V., J. Donald and C. Kaplan, eds., *Formations of Fantasy,* London: Methuen, 1986.

Burke, E., *A Philosophical Enquiry into the Origins of our Ideas of the Sublime and the Beautiful* [1757], ed. J. T. Boulton, London: Routledge & Kegan Paul, 1958.

Campbell, J., *The Masks of God: primitive mythology,* New York: Penguin, 1969.

Carroll, D., 'Rephrasing the Political with Kant and Lyotard: from aesthetic to political judgements', *Diacritics,* Fall 1984.

———— 'Narrative, Heterogeneity, and the Question of the Political: Bakhtin and Lyotard', in M. Krieger, ed., *The Aims of Representation: subject/text/history,* New York: Columbia University Press, 1987.

Cixous, H., 'Fiction and its Phantoms: a reading of Freud's "*Das Unheimliche*" ("The 'uncanny' ")', *New Literary History*, vol. 7, Spring 1976.

Cook, M., 'Tips for Time Travel', in *Philosophers Look at Science Fiction*, Chicago: Nelson-Hall, 1982.

Copjec, J., '*India Song/Son nom de Venise dans Calcutta désert*: the compulsion to repeat', *October*, no. 17, Summer 1981.

Cowie, E., 'Fantasia', *m/f*, no. 9, 1984.

Creed, B., 'A Journey Through *Blue Velvet*', *New Formations*, no. 6, Winter 1988/9.

Crowther, P., 'The Kantian Sublime, the Avant-Garde, and the Postmodern: a critique of Lyotard', *New Formations*, no. 7, Spring 1989.

De Lauretis, T., *Alice Doesn't: feminism, semiotics, cinema*, Bloomington: Indiana University Press, 1984.

————— 'Aesthetic and Feminist Theory: rethinking women's cinema', *New German Critique*, no. 34, Winter 1985.

Dervin, D., 'Primal Conditions and Conventions: the genres of comedy and science fiction', *Film/Psychology Review*, Winter-Spring 1980.

Dickstein, M., 'The Aesthetics of Fright', *American Film*, no. 5, 1980.

Doane, M. A., 'Misrecognition and Identity', *Cine-Tracts*, no. 11, 1980.

————— 'The "Woman's Film" ', in M. A. Doane, P. Mellencamp and L. Williams, eds., *Re-Vision: Essays in feminist film criticism*, Los Angeles: American Film Institute/Frederick, Maryland: University Publications of America, 1984.

Doane, M. A., P. Mellencamp and L. Williams, eds., *Re-Vision: Essays in feminist film criticism*, Los Angeles: American Film Institute/Frederick, Maryland: University Publications of America, 1984.

Duras, M., *The Ravishing of Lol V. Stein*, New York: Grove Press, 1966.

————— *India Song*, New York: Grove Press, 1976.

Drew, W., ed., *David Cronenberg: BFI Dossier 21*, London: BFI, 1984.

Eisler, R., *Man into Wolf; an anthropological interpretation of sadism, masochism and lycanthropy*, London: Routledge and Kegan Paul, 1951.

Eisner, L., *The Haunted Screen*, London: Secker and Warburg, 1973 (first published Paris 1952; revised and reissued 1965).

Fletcher, J., 'Poetry, Gender and Primal Fantasies', in V. Burgin, J. Donald and C. Kaplan, eds., *Formations of Fantasy*, London: Methuen, 1986.

Foster, H. *Recodings: art, spectacle, cultural politics*, Port Townsend, Washington: Bay Press, 1985.

Freud, S., *The Standard Edition of the Complete Psychological Works of Sigmund Freud (SE)*, ed. and trans. J. Strachey, London: Hogarth Press, 1953–66; *The Pelican Freud Library (PFL)*, Harmondsworth: Penguin, 1973–.

————— [1908] 'On the Sexual Theories of Children', *PFL* vol. 7: *On Sexuality*.

————— [1913] 'Totem and Taboo', *PFL* vol. 13: *The Origin of Religion*.

————— [1915] 'A Case of Paranoia Running Counter to the Psychoanalytic Theory of the Disease', *SE* XIV.

————— [1916–17 (1915–17)] *Introductory Lectures on Psychoanalysis*, *SE* XV-XVI; *PFL* I.

————— [1918 (1914)] 'From the History of an Infantile Neurosis', *PFL* vol. 9: *Case Histories II*.

————— [1919] 'A Child is Being Beaten', *SE* XVII.

————— [1919] 'The "uncanny" ', *SE* XVII; *PFL* vol. 14: *Art and Literature*.

————— [1964] 'Medusa's Head', *SE* XVIII.

————— [1925] 'Negation', *PFL* vol. 11: *On Metapsychology*.

————— [1927] 'Fetishism', *SE* XXI; *PFL* vol. 7: *On Sexuality*.

————— [1931] 'Female Sexuality', *PFL* vol. 7: *On Sexuality*.

————— [1939 (1936–39)] 'Moses and Monotheism', *SE* XXIII.

————— [1940 (1938)] *An Outline of Psycho-Analysis*, *SE* XXIII.

Gallop, J., *Feminism and Psychoanalysis: the daughter's seduction*, London: Macmillan, 1983.

Harraway, D., 'A Manifesto for Cyborgs: science, technology, and socialist feminism in the

1980s', *Socialist Review*, no. 80, 1985.

Heath, S., 'Film and System, Terms of Analysis', *Screen*, vol. 16, no. 1 and no. 2, Spring and Summer 1975.

———— 'Difference', *Screen*, vol. 19, no. 3, Autumn 1978.

Hebdige, D., 'Posing . . . Threats, Striking . . . Poses: youth surveillance and display', *Substance*, nos. 37–38, 1983.

Horwitz, M. M., '*The Birds*: a mother's love', *Wide Angle*, vol. 5, no. 1, 1982.

Hugnet, G., *Fantastic Art, Dada, Surrealism*, ed. A. H. Barr Jr., New York: Museum of Modern Art, 1968.

Hume, K., *Fantasy and Mimesis: responses to reality in Western literature*, London: Methuen, 1984.

Hutcheon, L., *A Theory of Parody*, London: Methuen, 1985.

Huyssen, A., 'The Vamp and the Machine: Fritz Lang's *Metropolis*', *New German Critique*, nos. 24/5, 1981–2 (reprinted in Huyssen, *After the Great Divide: modernism, mass culture, postmodernism*, Bloomington: Indiana University Press, 1986).

Irigaray, L., *This Sex Which Is Not One*, Ithaca: Cornell University Press, 1985.

Jackson, R., *Fantasy: the literature of subversion*, London: Methuen, 1981.

Jameson, F., *Fables of Aggression: Wyndham Lewis, the modernist as fascist*, Berkeley: University of California Press, 1979.

———— 'Reification and Utopia in Mass Culture', *Social Text*, no. 1, 1979.

———— *The Political Unconscious: narrative as a socially symbolic act*, London: Methuen, 1981.

———— 'Progress Versus Utopia; or Can we imagine the future?', *Science Fiction Studies*, no. 9, 1982.

———— 'Postmodernism and Consumer Society', in H. Foster, ed., *The Anti-Aesthetic*, Port Townsend, Washington: Bay Press 1983.

———— 'Postmodernism or the Cultural Logic of Late Capitalism', *New Left Review*, no. 146, July–August, 1984.

Kaplan, C., '*The Thorn Birds*: fiction, fantasy, femininity', in V. Burgin, J. Donald and C. Kaplan, eds., *Formations of Fantasy*, London: Methuen, 1986.

Kavanaugh, J. H., ' "Son of a Bitch": feminism, humanism and science in *Alien*', *October*, no. 13, Summer 1980.

Kelly, M., 'Woman-Desire-Image', *Desire*, London: Institute of Contemporary Arts, 1984.

Klein, M., *The Writings of Melanie Klein*, vols. I–IV, London: Hogarth Press, 1975.

Kracauer, S., *From Caligari to Hitler: a psychological history of the German film*, Princeton: Princeton University Press, 1947.

Krichbaum, J. and R. A. Zondergeld, *Dictionary of Fantastic Art*, London: Barron's, 1985.

Kris, E., *Psychoanalytic Explanations in Art*, New York: Schocken, 1971.

Kristeva, J., *Powers of Horror: an essay on abjection*, New York: Columbia University Press, 1982.

Lacan, J., 'Some Reflections on the Ego', *International Journal of Psychoanalysis*, vol. 24, 1953.

———— *Écrits: a selection*, New York: Norton, 1977.

———— *The Four Fundamental Concepts of Psychoanalysis*, London: Hogarth Press, 1977.

Laplanche, J. and J.-B. Pontalis, 'Fantasy and the Origins of Sexuality', in V. Burgin, J. Donald and C. Kaplan, eds., *Formations of Fantasy*, London: Methuen, 1986 (first published in *Les Temps modernes*, no. 215, 1964; translation first published in *International Journal of Psychoanalysis*, vol. 49, 1968).

———— *The Language of Psychoanalysis*, London: Hogarth Press, 1973.

Lapsley, R. and Westlake, M., *Film Theory: an introduction*, Manchester: Manchester University Press, 1988.

Lash, S., 'Postmodernity and Desire', *Theory and Society*, no. 14, 1985.

Lem, S., 'The Time-Travel Story and Related Matters of SF Structuring', *Science Fiction Studies*, no. 1, 1974.

———— 'Cosmology and Science Fiction', *Science Fiction Studies*, no. 4, 1977.

Lévi-Strauss, C., *Myth and Meaning*, London: Routledge and Kegan Paul, 1978.

Lewis, D., 'The Paradoxes of Time Travel', in F. D. Miller and N. D. Smith, *Thought Probes*, New Jersey: Prentice Hall, 1981.

Lukacher, N., *Primal Scenes: literature, philosophy, psychoanalysis*, Ithaca: Cornell University Press, 1986.

Lyon, E., *'Woman of the Ganges', Camera Obscura*, no. 2, Fall 1977.

Lyotard, J.-F., *The Postmodern Condition: a report on knowledge*, Manchester: Manchester University Press, 1984.

Lyotard, J.-F. and Thébaud, J-L., *Just Gaming*, Manchester: Manchester University Press, 1988.

Mannoni, O., *Clefs pour l'imaginaire, ou, l'Autre scène*, Paris: Le Seuil, 1969.

Marcus, S., *The Other Victorians: A study of sexuality and pornography in mid-nineteenth-century England*, New York, 1964.

Mellencamp, P., 'Postmodern TV: Wegman & Smith', *Afterimage* (US), December 1985.

Mercer, C., 'That's Entertainment: the resilience of popular forms', T. Bennett, C. Mercer and J. Woollacott, eds., *Popular Culture and Social Relations*, Milton Keynes: Open University Press, 1986.

———— 'Entertainment, or the Policing of Virtue', *New Formations*, no. 4, Spring 1988.

Metz, C., *Language and Cinema*, The Hague: Mouton, 1974.

———— *Psychoanalysis and Cinema: the imaginary signifier*, London: Macmillan, 1982.

Mitchell, J., *Psychoanalysis and Feminism*, Harmondsworth: Penguin, 1974.

Modleski, T., '"Never to be thirty-six years old": *Rebecca* as female Oedipal drama', *Wide Angle*, vol. 5, no. 1, 1982.

———— 'The Terror of Pleasure: the contemporary horror film and postmodern theory', in T. Modleski, ed., *Studies in Entertainment: Critical approaches to mass culture*, Bloomington: University of Indiana Press, 1986.

Moretti, F., 'Dialectic of Fear', in *Signs Taken for Wonders*, London: Verso, 1983.

Morris, D., 'Gothic Sublimity', *New Literary History*, vol. XVI, no. 2, Winter 1985.

Morris, M., 'Postmodernity and Lyotard's sublime', *Art & Text*, no. 16, Summer 1984/5.

Mulvey, L., 'Visual Pleasure and Narrative Cinema', *Screen*, vol. 16, no. 3, Autumn 1975.

———— 'Afterthoughts on "Visual pleasure and narrative cinema" inspired by *Duel in the Sun*', *Framework*, nos. 15–16–17, 1981.

———— 'Impending Time', in *Mary Kelly: Interim (Part 1)*, catalogue, Edinburgh, Fruitmarket Gallery/Cambridge, Kettle's Yard/London, Riverside Studios, 1986.

———— 'Changes: thoughts on myth, narrative and historical experience', *History Workshop Journal*, no. 23, Spring 1987.

Nash, M., '*Vampyr* and the Fantastic', *Screen*, vol. 17, no. 3, Autumn 1976.

———— *Dreyer*, London: British Film Institute, 1977.

Neale, S., *Genre* London, British Film Institute, 1980.

———— '*Halloween*: suspense, aggression, and the look', *Framework*, no. 14, 1981.

———— 'Sexual Difference in Cinema', *Sexual Difference – Oxford Literary Review*, vol. 8, 1986.

———— 'Melodrama and Tears', *Screen*, vol. 27, no. 6, 1986.

O'Pray, M., 'On Adrian Stokes and Film Aesthetics', *Screen*, vol. 21, no. 4, Winter 1980/1.

———— 'Modernism, Phantasy and Avant-Garde Film', *Undercut*, nos. 3–4, March 1982.

———— 'Primitive Phantasy in Cronenberg's Films', in Wayne Drew, ed., *David Cronenberg*: BFI Dossier 21, London: British Film Institute, 1984.

Owens, C., 'The Discourse of Others: feminists and postmodernism', in H. Foster, ed., *The Anti-Aesthetic*, Port Townsend, Washington: Bay Press, 1983.

Penley, C., 'Feminism, Film Theory and the Bachelor Machines', *m/f*, no. 10, 1985.

Pirie, D., *A Heritage of Horror: the English Gothic cinema 1946–1972*, London: Gordon Fraser 1973.

Prawer, S. S., *Caligari's Children: the film as tale as terror*, Oxford: Oxford University Press, 1980.

Praz, M., *The Romantic Agony* [1933], London: Oxford University Press, 1970.

Rodowick, D. N., 'The Difficulty of Difference', *Wide Angle*, vol. 5, no. 1, 1982.

Rogin, M., *Ronald Reagan the Movie, and Other Episodes of Political Demonology*, Berkeley: University of California Press, 1987.

Rose, J., 'Paranoia and the Film System', *Screen*, vol. 17, no. 4, Winter 1976–77.

———— 'The Imaginary', in C. MacCabe, ed., *The Talking Cure*, London: Macmillan, 1981.

———— 'Introduction', in J. Mitchell and J. Rose, eds., *Feminine Sexuality*, London: Macmillan, 1982.

———— 'Femininity and its Discontents', in *Sexuality in the Field of Vision*, London: Verso, 1986.

———— 'Margaret Thatcher and Ruth Ellis', *New Formations*, no. 6, Winter 1988/9.

Rose, M., *Alien Encounters: anatomy of science fiction*, Cambridge, Mass.: Harvard University Press, 1981.

Rosolato, G., *Essais sur le symbolique*, Paris: Gallimard, 1969.

Rothman, W., *Hitchcock: The murderous gaze*, Cambridge, Mass., 1982.

Russo, M., 'Female Grotesques: carnival and theory', in T. de Lauretis, ed., *Feminist Studies/ Critical Studies*, Bloomington, Indiana: University Press, 1986.

Schoell, W., *Stay Out of the Shower*, New York, 1985.

Silverman, K., 'Masochism and subjectivity', *Framework*, no. 12, 1979.

———— *The Subject of Semiotics*, New York, 1983.

———— 'Fragments of a Fashionable Discourse', in T. Modleski, ed., *Studies in Entertainment: Critical approaches to mass culture*, Bloomington: University of Indiana Press, 1986.

Soble, A., *Pornography: Marxism, feminism and the future of sexuality*, New Haven, 1986.

Spoto, D., *The Dark Side of Genius: The life of Alfred Hitchcock*, New York 1983.

Stern, L., 'Point of View: the blind spot', *Film Reader* no. 4, 1979.

Stokes, A., *The Critical Writings of Adrian Stokes*, vol. III, ed. L. Gowing, London: Thames & Hudson, 1978.

Stone, J., 'The Horrors of Power: a critique of "Kristeva"', in F. Barker, P. Hulme, M. Iversen, D. Loxley, eds., *The Politics of Theory*, Colchester: University of Essex, 1983.

Theweleit, K., *Male Fantasies*, vol. 1, Cambridge: Polity Press, 1987.

Todorov, T., *The Fantastic: a structural approach to a literary genre*, trans. R. Howard, Ithaca: Cornell University Press, 1973.

Twitchell, J. B., *Dreadful Pleasures: An anatomy of modern horror*, New York, 1985.

Vale, V. and A. Juno, *Incredibly Strange Films: Re/Search*, no. 10, San Francisco, 1986.

Weston, J. L., *From Ritual to Romance: an account of the Holy Grail from ancient ritual to Christian symbol*, Cambridge: Cambridge University Press, 1920.

White, D. L., 'The Poetics of Horror', *Cinema Journal*, no. 10, 1971.

Willemen, P., 'The Fugitive Subject', in *Raoul Walsh*, Edinburgh Film Festival, 1974.

———— 'The Third Cinema Question: notes and reflections', *Framework*, no. 34, 1987.

Williams, L., 'When the Woman Looks', in M. A. Doane, P. Mellencamp and L. Williams, eds., *Re-Vision*, American Film Institute Monograph Series vol. 3, Frederick, Maryland: University Publications of America, 1984.

Wollen, P., 'Hybrid Plots in *Psycho*', *Framework*, no. 13, 1980.

Wood, R., 'An Introduction to the American Horror Film', in Bill Nichols, ed., *Movies and Methods, vol. II*, Berkeley: University of California Press, 1985.

———— *Hollywood from Vietnam to Reagan*, New York: Columbia University Press, 1986.

Wright, E., *Psychoanalytic Criticism: theory in practice*, London: Methuen, 1984.

INDEX OF NAMES

Duras, Marguerite, 147–9, 165, 169, 171
Durgnat, Raymond, 271
Dworkin, Andrea, 111

Effenberger, Vratislav, 255
Eggeling, Viking, 231
Eisner, Lotte, 19, 23, 25, 37
Eliade, Mircea, 47, 57
Elsaesser, Thomas, 19, 23–38, 228, 238
Eluard, Paul, 254
Ernst, Max, 253
Ewers, Hans Heinz, 32

Fanon, Frantz, 248
Fischinger, Oskar, 231
Fisher, Terence, 55
Fliess, Wilhelm, 44, 150, 233
Ford, John, 271
Foster, Hal, 273
Foucault, Michel, 226, 242–3, 266, 270, 277, 279
Frakes, Randall, 199
Francis, Freddie, 51, 54–5
Franju, Georges, 254
Freud, Sigmund, 20, 39–59 *passim*, 93, 95, 114, 120–1, 136–44 *passim*, 149–51, 186–8, 202–4, 233, 236, 238, 240–2, 256–7, 260, 269, 273–4, 276, 282–3
Friedrich, Caspar David, 244
Fuseli, Henry, 244

Gabriel, Teshome, 228
Gardearzabel, Gustavo Alvarez, 228
Gerrold, David, 201
de Ghelderode, Michel, 260
Gidal, Peter, 4, 231
Godard, Jean-Luc, 4
Goethe, J.W. von, 27
Gombrich, E.H., 256
Gramsci, Antonio, 247–8
Greenacre, P., 42
Greenaway, Peter, 254
Greig, Donald, 137, 142, 175–95

Habermas, Jürgen, 244
Heath, Stephen, 176
Hegel, G.W.F., 241
Heinlein, Robert, 201
Herz, Juraj, 254
Herzog, Werner, 24
Hitchcock, Alfred, 50, 91, 95–6, 110–11, 113, 118, 123, 125, 137, 142–4, 176–92 *passim*
Hitler, Adolf, 24
Hoffman, Dustin, 122
Hoffman, E.T.A., 24, 26, 28, 31, 238, 260
Holland, Agnuszka, 228
Hooper, Tobe, 92, 96, 242

Hooper, Dennis, 97
Hume, Kathryn, 18
Hutcheon, Linda, 278

Irigaray, Luce, 277

Jackson, Rosemary, 7, 18, 256
James, Henry, 18
Jameson, Fredric, 3, 197, 228–30, 231, 236–7
Jentsch, E., 121
Jones, Grace, 271–2
Joyce, James, 244
Juno, Andrea, 127

Kafka, Franz, 253, 255, 260, 263
Kalandra, Zaris, 254
Kant, Immanuel, 240, 241, 245
Kaplan, E. Ann, 112
Karloff, Boris, 47
Kavanaugh, James H., 214–15
Kayser, Wolfgang, 256–7, 260
Keen, Jeff, 254
Kelly, Mary, 85
Kermode, Frank, 207
Khan, Masud R., 40–2, 57
Klein, Melanie, 264–5
Kleist, Heinrich von, 240
Klossowoski, Pierre, 243
Kracauer, Siegfried, 19, 23–5, 29, 38
Kral, Petr, 263
Kris, Ernst, 256–7
Kristeva, Julia, 5, 20, 64–73, 76–83 *passim*, 233, 242–3
Kuntzel, Thierry, 210
Kyrou, Ado, 233

Lacan, Jacques, 6, 77–8, 80, 82, 139, 142, 166, 168, 171, 181, 210, 272–3, 281
Lang, Fritz, 32, 177
Laplanche, J., 6, 138–41, 149, 185, 192
Lapsley, Robert, 6
Lee, Christopher, 47
Le Fanu, Sheridan, 12
Leigh, Janet, 104
Lem, Stanislaw, 197
Lenz, Reinhold, 27
Lévi-Strauss, Claude, 77, 78, 139, 181, 182, 273
Lissitsky, El (Lasar Markovich), 244
Lovecraft, H.P., 41
Lugosi, Bela, 47
Lukács, Georg, 45
Lye, Len, 231
Lynch, David, 231, 254
Lyon, Elisabeth, 137, 147–73
Lyotard, Jean-Francois, 230, 231, 242, 243–8

Todorov, Tzvetan, 7, 11–13, 18–20, 237–8, 240, 242, 248
Tomlin, Lily, 274
Trnka, Jiri, 254, 259
Twitchell, James, B., 94
Tyrlova, Hermina, 259

Vale, V., 127

Walpole, Horace, 241
Walsh, Raoul, 141
Weaver, Sigourney, 86

Wegener, Paul, 32
Wells, H.G., 200
Westlake, Michael, 6
Wiene, Robert, 32
Willemen, Paul, 141
Williams, Linda, 114
Wisher, Bill, 199
Wittgenstein, Ludwig, 233
Wollen, Peter, 227
Wood, Robin, 19, 92, 95, 126, 176, 236–8, 247
Wyler, William, 182

INDEX OF FILM AND VIDEO TITLES

L'Age d'Or (France, Luis Buñuel, 1930), 262
Alien (US, Ridley Scott, 1979), 72–87, 91, 95, 109, 114, 198, 213–16, 221
Aliens (US, James Cameron, 1986), 91, 109, 114, 119, 205–6
All of Me (US, Carl Reiner, 1984), 122
Altered States (US, Ken Russell, 1981), 73
American Graffiti (US, George Lucas, 1973), 228
An American Werewolf in London (US, John Landis, 1981), 91
The Amitrville Horror (US, Stuart Rosenberg, 1979), 102
Amy! (UK, Laura Mulvey/Peter Wollen, 1980), 227
Android (US, Aaron Lipstadt, 1982), 204
The Annihilators (US TV pilot, 1986), 197
Attack of the 50-Foot Woman (US, Nathan Hertz, 1958), 100

Backstairs [*Hintertreppe*] (Germany, Leopold Jessner, assisted by Paul Leni, 1922), 29
Back to the Future (US, Robert Zemeckis, 1985), 200–202
Behind the Green Door (US, Mitchell Brothers, 1972), 122
Beneath the Skin (US, Cecelia Condit, 1981), 269, 272, 277–81
The Birds (US, Alfred Hitchcock, 1963), 68, 85, 102, 103, 111, 113, 115, 177–8, 185
Blade Runner (US, Ridley Scott, 1982), 91, 198, 200, 204, 213–14, 216–21
Blood Feast (US, Herschell Gordon Lewis, 1963), 127 (n. 1)
Bloodsucking Freaks [aka *The Incredible Torture Show*] (US, Joel M. Reed, 1978), 68
Blow-Out (US, Brian De Palma, 1981), 106
Blue Velvet (US, David Lynch, 1986), 142, 231